Sa-Moon Kang

Divine War in the Old Testament and in the Ancient Near East

Sa-Moon Kang

Divine War in the Old Testament and in the Ancient Near East

Walter de Gruyter · Berlin · New York
1989

Beiheft zur Zeitschrift für die alttestamentliche Wissenschaft

Herausgegeben von Otto Kaiser

177

Printed on acid free paper
(ageing resistent — pH 7, neutral)

Library of Congress Cataloging-in-Publication Data

Kang, Sa-Moon, 1942–
Divine war in the Old Testament and in the ancient Near East / Sa-Moon Kang.
p. cm. — (Beiheft zur Zeitschrift für die alttestamentliche Wissenschaft)
Bibliography: p.
Includes indexes.
ISBN 0-89925-278-8 (U.S.)
1. War — Biblical teaching. 2. Bible. O.T. — Criticism, interpretation, etc. 3. Military art and science — Israel — History. 4. Military art and science — Middle East — History. 5. Military art and science — Egypt — History. I. Title. II. Series: Beihefte zur Zeitschrift für die alttestamentliche Wissenschaft.
BS1199.W2K36 1989
221.8'355—dc19 88-27332
CIP

CIP-Titelaufnahme der Deutschen Bibliothek

Kang, Sa-Moon:
Divine war in the Old Testament and in the ancient Near East / Sa-Moon Kang. — Berlin ; New York : de Gruyter, 1989
(Beiheft zur Zeitschrift für die alttestamentliche Wissenschaft ; 177)
Zugl.: Jerusalem, Univ., Diss., 1984
ISBN 3-11-011156-X
NE: Zeitschrift für die alttestamentliche Wissenschaft / Beiheft

ISSN: 0934-2575

Satz und Druck: Arthur Collignon GmbH, Berlin 30
Bindearbeiten: Lüderitz & Bauer, Berlin 61

Dedicated to my beloved
mother and late father

Preface

This is a revised version of my doctoral dissertation which was carried out under the supervision of professors Menahem Haran and Moshe Weinfeld at the Hebrew University of Jerusalem in 1984.

During the preparation I received much help from a number of scholars. I am particularly grateful to professor Haran for his encouragement and concern shown from the beginning of my study to the accomplishment of the dissertation. Professor Weinfeld offered valuable and critical suggestions. Professor Raphael Kutscher at the Tel Aviv University and professor Marcel Sigrist at the École Biblique of Jerusalem read all the Mesopotamian sources and made many helpful comments and suggestions for improvement. Professor Irene Shirun-Grumach at the Hebrew University of Jerusalem also kindly read the entire Egyptian sources and saved me from many mistakes in the hieroglyphic readings. Dr. Galina Kellermann at the Hebrew University of Jerusalem also read the Hittite materials and made many helpful comments.

During my stay in Jerusalem I received financial aid from the Ecumenical Institute for Advanced Theological Studies (Tantur) and the Hebrew University of Jerusalem. I sincerely acknowledge my appreciation to the late Father Lane Kilburn and the rectors of Tantur; professors Walter Wegner, Walter Harrelson, the late George MacRae, David Burrell, Donald Nicholl, and D. Patinkin the rector of the Hebrew University. I would also like to express my appreciation to the editor of the BZAW series, Professor Otto Kaiser who has taken efforts to publish my revised dissertation in the above series. I am also greatly indebted to the members of Walter de Gruyter & Co. for their efforts and patience in the printing and production of the book.

I wish to express my gratitude to my colleagues, Mr. Chulsoo Cho and professor Sarah Koh who read the first draft and made it in good style. Finally I owe a great debt to my wife who typed the manuscript and encourged me in all stages of the work, and my daughter who was always patient with my studies.

Seoul, July 1987 — Sa-Moon Kang

Contents

PART TWO
                    YHWH WAR IN THE OLD TESTAMENT

Abbreviations

AASOR	Annual of the American Schools of Oriental Research
AB	The Anchor Bible
ADAIK	Abhandlungen des Deutschen Archäologischen Instituts Kairo
AfO	Archiv für Orientforschung
AHw	W. von Soden, Akkadisches Handwörterbuch
AnOr	Analecta Orientalia
AO	Der Alte Orient, Leipzig
AOAT	Alter Orient und Altes Testament, Neukirchen-Vluyn
ASAE	Annales du Service des Antiquités d'Egypte
ASTI	Annual of the Swedish Theological Institute in Jerusalem, Leiden
ATANT	Abhandlungen zur Theologie des Alten und Neuen Testaments, Zürich
BAR	The Biblical Archaeologist Reader
BASOR	Bulletin of the American Schools of Oriental Research
BBB	Bonner Biblische Beiträge
BDB	Brown-Driver-Briggs, A Hebrew and English Lexicon of the Old Testament
Bibl	Biblica, Rome
BIES	Bulletin of the Israel Exploration Society
BiOr	Bibliotheca Orientalis, Leiden
BJPES	Bulletin of the Jewish Palestine Exploration Society — Yedioth
BWANT	Beiträge zur Wissenschaft vom Alten und Neuen Testament, Stuttgart
BZ	Biblische Zeitschrift, Paderborn
BZAW	Beihefte zur Zeitschrift für die Alttestamentliche Wissenschaft, Berlin
CAD	The Assyrian Dictionary of the Oriental Institute of the University of Chicago, 1956ff.
CBQ	Catholic Biblical Quarterly
CT	Cuneiform Texts from Babylonian Tablets, etc. in the British Museum, London, 1896 ff.
CTM	Concordia Theological Monthly, St. Louis
Diss.	Dissertation
EA	Tell el-Amarna Tablets

Ed.	Edited
EJ	Encyclopaedia Judaica
ET	English Translation
ETR	Etudes Théologiques et Religieuses
HAT	Handbuch zum Alten Testament
HDR	Harvard Dissertation in Religion
HSS	Harvard Semitic Series
HTR	Harvard Theological Review
HUCA	Hebrew Union College Annual, Cincinnati
IB	The Interpreter's Bible, ed. G. A. Buttrick, 1951–57
ICC	The International Critical Commentary
IDBS	The Interpreter's Dictionary of the Bible with Supplementary Volume
IEJ	Israel Exploration Journal, Jerusalem
JAOS	Journal of the American Oriental Society
JBL	Journal of Biblical Literature
JCS	Journal of Cuneiform Studies, New Haven
JEA	Journal of Egyptian Archaeology, London
JJS	Journal of Jewish Studies, London
JNES	Journal of Near Eastern Studies, Chicago
JQR	Jewish Quarterly Review
JTS	Journal of Theological Studies, Oxford
KAT	Kommentar zum Alten Testament, ed. E. Sellin, continued by J. Herrmann
KBo	Keilschriftteste aus Boghazköy
KF	Kleinasiatische Forschungen
KS	Kleine Schriften (A. Alt, 1953–59; O. Eissfeldt, 1962 ff.)
MDIK	Mitteilungen des Deutschen Archäologischen Instituts in Kairo, Wiesbaden
MDOG	Mitteilungen der Deutschen Orient-Gesellschaft, Berlin
MVÄG	Mitteilungen der Vorderasiatisch-Ägyptischen Gesellschaft (Berlin), Leipzig
NCB	A New Concordance of the Bible I–III, ed. A. Even-Shoshan, Jerusalem, 1977–80, Hebrew
NF	Neue Folge
OBO	Orbis Bibicus et Orientalis
OLZ	Orientalistische Literaturzeitung (Leipzig), Berlin
OTL	The Old Testament Library
OTS	Oudtestamentische Studien, Leiden
OuTWP	De Ou Testamentiese Werkgemeenskap in Suid-Afrika, Pretoria
PBS	Publications of the Babylonian Section of the University Museum Philadelphia
PEQ	Palestine Exploration Quarterly, London

RA	Revue d'Assyriologie et d'Archéologie Orientale, Paris
RB	Revue Biblique, Paris
RHA	Revue Hittite et Asianique, Paris
SBL	Society of Biblical Literature, Dissertation Series
SBT	Studies in Biblical Theology
StBoT	Studien zu den Bogazköy-Texten
StOr	Studia Orientalia, Helsinki
ST	Studia Theologica, Lund, Aarhus
STZ	Sonderbände zur Theologische Zeitschrift
TDOT	Theological Dictionary of the Old Testament
THAT	Theologisches Handwörterbuch zum Alten Testament, ed. by E. Jenni and C. Westermann, Munich, 1971
TLZ	Theologische Literaturzeitung, Leipzig, Berlin
Tr.	Translated
TZ	Theologische Zeitschrift, Basel
UAVA	Untersuchungen zur Assyriologie und Vorderasiatischen Archäologie
UET	Ur Excavations, Texts, London, 1928 ff.
UF	Ugarit-Forschungen
VT	Vetus Testamentum, Leiden
VTS	Vetus Testamentum, Supplements
WHJP	The World History of the Jewish People, volumes II–III, ed. by B. Mazar, Tel Aviv, 1970–71; volumes IV–V, ed. by A. Malamat, 1979
WMANT	Wissenschaftliche Monographien zum Alten und Neuen Testament, Neukirchen
WO	Die Welt des Orients, Göttingen
YNER	Yale Near Eastern Researches
ZA	Zeitschrift für Assyriologie (Leipzig), Berlin
ZÄS	Zeitschrift für Ägyptische Sprache und Altertumskunde (Leipzig), Berlin
ZAW	Zeitschrift für die Alttestamentliche Wissenschaft (Gießen), Berlin
ZWT	Zeitschrift für Wissenschaftliche Theologie

Introduction

The purpose of this study is to investigate the motifs of divine war in the ancient Near East and in this light to research the motifs of YHWH war in the Old Testament. There are three issues concerning the problem of YHWH war. The first issue is the distinction between holy war and YHWH war. The main argument concerning YHWH war has been focused under the name of "holy war" by F. Schwally, M. Weber, J. Pedersen and especially G. von Rad.[1] Von Rad defines war in the ancient Israel as a sacral cultic institution undertaken by the confederation of the twelve tribes in the period of the Judges.[2] It was a reaction to an Amphictyonic event which occurred at Schechem on the occasion of the entry of the house of Joseph, which introduced the worship of YHWH to the tribes already existing in the land. His identification of holy war with the confederation of the twelve tribes was based on the Amphictyonic hypothesis of Alt-Noth by which the confederation of the twelve tribes in the worship of God YHWH had already existed in the period prior to the formation of a state.[3] Here YHWH is not a tribal God but "the God of

---

[1] F. Schwally, *Semitische Kriegsaltertümer* I: Der heilige Krieg im alten Israel (Leipzig 1901); M. Weber, *Ancient Judaism*, tr. and ed. by H. H. Gerth and D. Martindale (NY 1921–1952), 90–139; J. Pedersen, *Israel* 3–4: Its Life and Culture (London/Copenhagen 1934, 1947), 1–32. G. von Rad, *Der heilige Krieg im alten Israel* (Zürich 1951), – *Krieg*.

[2] *Krieg*, 17.

[3] A. Alt, "The Formation of the Israelite State in Palestine," *Essays on Old Testament History and Religion*, tr. by R. A. Wilson (Oxford 1966), 279 ff (– *EOTHR*); M. Noth, *Das System der zwölf Stämme Israels*, BWANT 4/1 (Stuttgart 1930, Darmstadt 1966). His hypothesis has been severely criticized by the following scholars: H. M. Orlinsky, "The Tribal System of Israel and Related Groups in the Period of the Judges," *Oriens Antiquis* 1 (1962), 11–20; B. D. Rathjin, "Philistine and Hebrew Amphictyonies," *JNES* 24 (1965), 100–104; G. Fohrer, 'Altes Testament – "Amphiktyonie und Bund?"' *ThLZ* 91 (1966), 801–16, 893–904; G. W. Anderson, *Israel*: Amphictyony, ʿAM, KAHAL, ʿEDAH, Essays in honor of H. G. MAY (Nashville/NY 1970), 135–51; R. de Vaux, "La Thèse de l'Amphictyonie Israélite," *HTR* 64 (1971), 415–36; R. Smend, "Zur Frage der altisraelitischen Amphiktyonie," *EvT* 31 (1971), 623–30; A. D. J. Mayes, *Israel in the Period of the Judges*, STB 29 (London 1974); M. C. Astour, "Amphictyony," *IDBS* (1976), 23–25; C. H. J. de Gues, *The Tribes of Israel* (Amsterdam 1976); O. Bächli, *Amphiktyonie im Alten Testament*: Forschungsgeschichtliche Studie zur Hypothese vom M. Noth, STZ 6 (Basel 1977); H. Seebass, "Erwägungen zum altisraelitischen System der zwölf Stämme," ZAW 90 (1978), 196–219.

Israel".[4] For von Rad the Amphictyonic event was not a political-mlitary act that was undertaken in religious dimensions.[5] In this context its sacral cultic background is the basic element for the understanding of holy war that had not existed in the historical realities. This idea of holy war is divorced from the historical reality of YHWH war, which happened as the actual battle. Thus the holy war theory is a post-battle interpretation built on a tradition of YHWH war experienced on the battlefield. In the strict sense the holy war is not YHWH war which was conducted and experienced by the ancient Israelites on the historical battlefield. Those scholars who describe the wars in ancient Israel as holy war, hold that their exclusive emphasis was the result of late theological reflection. Von Rad's view of holy war, as the Amphictyonic reaction, has already been severely criticized by a number of scholars and gradually a consensus seems to be emerging that the wars of ancient Israel should not be called "holy war", but YHWH war.[6] The expression "holy war" is not derived from the Old Testament context. The Biblical writers referred to YHWH wars in Num 21:14; I Sam 18:17; 25:28. YHWH war is not "Glaubenskrieg" as is *Jiḥad* of the Moslems, meaning a fight to spread their faith, but instead it is a war for the Israelites' existence as a people.[7]

The second issue is the distinction between the mythical and historical realities of YHWH war. Although many scholars such as R. Smend (1963), S. Talmon (1963), F. Stolz (1972), P. Weimar (1976), M. Lind (1980) and A. de Pury (1981)[8] call the wars in ancient Israel "YHWH war", instead of "holy war" which parellels with ἱερός πόλεμος of the Greeks, they have not distinguished the historical realities of YHWH war. YHWH war is not a sacral event but a historical reality in battle with religious dimensions. Smend has claimed that YHWH war was not the sacred cultic event of the tribal confederation, but first appeared at the event which the Rachel tribes experienced at the Reed Sea.[9] Thus the Rachel tribes appear as the

---

4 *Krieg*, 83.

5 *Ibid.*, 25–26.

6 R. Smend, *Yahweh War and Tribal Confederation*: Reflections upon Israel's Earliest History, tr. by M. G. Rogers (Nashville/NY 1970), – *Yahweh War*; F. Stolz, *Jahwes und Israels Kriege*, ATANT 60 (Zürich 1972), – *Kriege*; M. Weippert, "Heiliger Krieg in Israel und Assyrien," ZAW 84 (1972), 460–93 (– "Heiliger Krieg"); G. H. Jones, "Holy War or YHWH War?" *VT* 25 (1975), 642–58; P. C. Craigie, *The Problem of War in the Old Testament* (Michigan 1981), 48 ff.

7 R. de Vaux, *Ancient Israel*; Social Institutions I, ET (NY/Toronto 1965), 262.

8 S. Talmon, "YHWH War," *Encyclopedia Biblica* 4 (1963), 1064–65 (Hebrew); P. Weimar, "Die Jahwekriegserzählungen in Ex 14, Jos 10, Richter 4 and I Sam 7," *Bibl* 57 (1976), 38–73 (– "Jahwekrieg"); M. C. Lind, *Yahweh is a Warrior*: The Theology of Warfare in Ancient Israel (Pennsylvania/Ontario 1980); A. de Pury, "La Guerre Sainte Israélite: Réalité Historique ou Fiction Litéraire?" *ETR* 56 (1981), 5–38.

9 YHWH war, 110 ff.

original and true representatives of the war of YHWH. It is difficult not to see in the emigrants from Egypt the elements of the Rachel tribes and the first bearers of the tradition of the experience of YHWH war.[10] Moses was the first leader of YHWH war in an act of YHWH war. Smend does not, however, describe with complete conviction Moses during the Exodus and at Sinai, because far too little is known, not only about the Amphictyony but also about Moses.[11] Lind like Smend sees YHWH war in the Exodus event which was conducted solely by YHWH without the help of man.[12] But Talmon has pointed out that YHWH war was YHWH's help for his people in historical battles, not a mythical battle between God and gods.[13] Although YHWH war was widely known to us from the beginning of the period of the Canaan conquest, this interpretation was rooted in other battles such as David's battles. Stolz tried to find the reality of YHWH war in the early period of Israel. He maintains that the later levels of the texts concerning YHWH war were edited by Deuteronomistic writers, whereas the elements of YHWH's intervention which were known to Deuternomists belong to the earlier level of tradition with the motif of the coming of YHWH's spirit to a particular individual as in the case of Gideon and Jephtah.[14] He proposed a simple theory: more compact and profane sources are earlier, more complex and religious sources are later.[15] That many of the old narratives about YHWH war show little sign of understanding of the war as holy, supports this principle above. Most texts as to YHWH war belong to Deuteronomic (Dtn) and Deuteronomistic (Dtr) literatures. For the Deuteronomists the motif of YHWH war was a "Schema" of their life of faith and history of religion. But this motif was not the creation of Dtn or Dtr, but one of the early traditions of Old Testament religion. Thus the understanding of YHWH war is a consideration of Israel's earliest history, just as Smend put the origin of YHWH war in the Exodus event. This consideration did not come from cultic practice but from the concrete historical experience through the wars in Palestine. Smend concludes that the YHWH war was the special YHWHistic experience,[16] and that this YHWHistic experience continued for generations in all the provinces of the tribes or the people of Israel.[17] The confession of faith that YHWH, as the divine warrior, gave victory to them became the base for the formation of the concept of

---

[10] *Ibid.*, 113.
[11] *Ibid.*, 135.
[12] *Yahweh is a Warrior*, 47–64.
[13] See n. 8.
[14] *Kriege*, 127.
[15] *Ibid.*, 79–80.
[16] *Ibid.*, 12.
[17] *Ibid.*, 198.

YHWH war in the period of the conquest before the Davidic Kingdon. For it is improbable that YHWH was first known in the time of David in both North and South.[18] Stolz has presumed that holy war was finished with the time of Saul.[19] Weimar has pointed out that, although the stories of YHWH war in Ex 14, Josh 10, Judg 4 and I Sam 7 were already known as the Northern tradition before the time of the pre-monarchic, they were composed in the Jerusalem court of David. The five common elements of these stories that he found are:[20] a) the action of Israel plus the reaction of the enemy, b) the reaction of Israel (fear), c) the oracle of encouragement, d) Israel's victory through YHWH's intervention, e) the complete destruction of the enemy. But it is hard to see that the last element was the motif of YHWH war undertaken on the battlefield in the time of David. A. de Pury tried to balance the first issue, holy war in the literature or cultic action, and the second issue, YHWH war in historical battle. He, like Weimar, believes that the motif of YHWH war was the reaction to royal power and its reflexion of politic and strategy.[21] The motif of YHWH war was transformed as the day of YHWH by the 8th century prophets and later as the day of the cosmic intervention of YHWH in the cultic context of the post-exilic period. The motifs of YHWH war in the monarchic period were canonized as a schematization of holy war by Dtr.[22] The evidence supporting the second issue is limited mainly to the use of internal Biblical sources, while that of the third issue must be seen chiefly in the light of external Biblical materials.

The third issue is the possible connection between YHWH war in the Old Testament and divine war in the ancient Near East. A. E. Glock (1968), M. Weippert (1972), P. D. Miller (1973), T. W. Mann (1977) and P. C. Craigie (1981)[23] have discussed the motifs of YHWH war as being the same as the divine war in the ancient Near Eastern context. But they have not dealt with this in the overall context of the Near East. The limited materials do not provide an inclusive and universalistic idea for the understanding of YHWH war. Glock has discussed warfare in Mari and early Israel, chiefly based on the Mari archives. This comparative study suggested several common motifs on both sides: divine consultation

---

[18] *Ibid.*, 199.

[19] *Ibid.*, 201–2.

[20] "Jahwekrieg", 72.

[21] "La Guerre Sainte Israélite," 36.

[22] *Ibid.*, 37.

[23] A. E. Glock, *Warfare in Mari and Early Israel* (Unpublished Ph. D. Diss. of University of Michigan 1968), – *Warfare*; P. D. Miller, *The Divine Warrior in Early Israel*, HSM 5 (Cambr. Mass. 1973), – *Divine Warrior*; T. W. Mann, *Divine Presence and Guidance in Israelite Traditions*: The Typology of Exaltation (Baltimore/London 1977), – *Divine Presence*, also see n. 6.

and omens, enlistment, and compensation. He mentions warfare in early Israel as an expression of the rulership of YHWH which is not holy in the cultic sense.[24] He employs the Mari sources as a control for the historical interpretation of early Israel. But there is a time gap of close to half a millennium to connect both sides. For example, there were no chariots in early Israel. That this fact is in continuity with Mari is hard to accept. Weippert has discussed the issues of holy war in Israel and Assyrian contexts in a critical observation of von Rad's concept of holy war in Israel. Weippert has asserted that the concept of holy war mentioned by von Rad has not a special institution of Israel which could no conducted only by YHWH, God of Israel, but a general phenomenon of divine war in the ancient Near East. The two motifs of holy war that Weippert presumes are biblical,[25] the call to battle by means of the ram's horn, and the consecration of weapons, are commonly attested to in the ancient Near East. Weippert describes the general phenomenon of divine war as follows:[26]

> Die Götter ziehen dem Heer voran, die assyrischen Truppen sind die des Reichsgottes Assur, der Krieg ist der Krieg der Götter, die Feinde sind ihre Feinde, Mutlosigkeit and Gottesschrecken überkommen die Feinde schon for dem eigentlichen Kampf, in der Schlacht kämpfen vor allem die Götter, während die Menschen ihnen zu Hilfe kommen.

He has shown then that these elements of divine war in the New Assyrian contexts were adopted through the experience of the destruction of the northern kingdom of Israel (721 BC) by Deuteronomists.[27] If it is true, are there no elements of YHWH war during early tradition of ancient Israel before the Deuteronomic literature? The study of Craigie, like Weippert, is also limited to the Assyrian divine war in the first millenium BC.[28] Miller has discussed divine warfare in the Syro-Palestine context, chiefly Ugaritic. In the Ugaritic context war was a mythical divine war between god and god(s). The results of this study showed that warfare in early Israel was cosmic holy war.[29] The research of the mythical war in Ugarit does not provide any influence on the level of YHWH war on the historical battlefield. For YHWH as the divine warrior was the production of the Davidic empire, not the Canaanite pantheon. Mann, who supports the third issue, deals with the motifs of divine presence and guidance in Mesopotamia and Syro-Palestine. He points out that the motif of the divine vanguard in battle, as a basic element of divine presence, appears

---

[24] *Warfare*, 3.
[25] "Heiliger Krieg", 485.
[26] *Ibid.*, 484.
[27] *Ibid.*, 490.
[28] *The Problem of War in the Old Testament*, 117–22.
[29] *Divine Warrior*, 64 ff.

commonly in the ancient Near Eastern and Old Testament contexts.[30] In the ancient Near Eastern texts this vanguard motif which portrayed the god as being involved in historical battle, is described as the intervention of the god(s) on behalf of his (their) royal devotees in war. But this vanguard motif was a very popular motif in the ancient Near East. Thus the whole picture of this motif in the ancient Near East may provide greater clarity for the motif of YHWH war.

Recently, however, M. Weinfeld has discussed the eight divine war elements which have literary parallels in ancient Israel and in the whole ancient Near East, and even in ancient Greece.[31] These eight elements are: a) shooting stars to the enemy's horses and chariots, b) the pillar of fire and cloud which throw the enemy into panic, c) the light which drives the enemy into confusion, d) god's fire consuming the enemy, e) Stones from heaven thrown upon the enemy, f) thunder as the voice of god which makes heaven and earth tremble, g) the cloud which hides the people from the sight of the enemy, h) holding back the moving of the heavenly bodies such as sun and moon to get a final victory of war. This method of research overcomes the weaknesses of the previous research by exploring the whole picture of divine war in the different contexts of the ancient Near East. In the same line of research divine wars in the ancient Near East are discussed in Part One to shed light on YHWH war in the Old Testament which is discussed in Part Two.

The method employed is a comprehensive exegetical approach with study of the relevant texts. The fact that the texts are scattered throughout all three sections of the Old Testament and in the ancient Near Eastern writings warns one against any simplistic approach to the texts. An attempt is made to let them speak for themselves and thus avoid the danger of hearing what we wish to hear. All the available evidence, both internal and external, is taken into account and its help is sought to expound the texts.

Following the introduction, Part One examines a number of major ancient Near Eastern texts in order to compare the structure of divine war in general with that of YHWH war in particular. The purpose here is to examine the form and function of the various literary contexts found in the period between the third millennium and the first half of the first millennnium BC. These include: inscription, epic, hymnic, annalistic and ritual texts as well as graphic source in which the motifs of divine war

[30] Mann, *Divine Presence*, 27 ff.

[31] M. Weinfeld, "They fought from heaven," *Eretz Israel* 14 (1978), 23–30 (Hebrew); *id.*, "Divine war in Ancient Israel and the Ancient Near East," *Research in the Bible and the Ancient Near East*, Festschrift of the Seventy years of S. E. Loewenstamm (1978), 171–81 (Hebrew).

are found. These materials include Mesopotamian, Anatolian, Syro-Palestine and Egyptian.

Part Two attempts to apply conclusions from the ancient Near Eastern materials to the Old Testament, and especially to those stories which report the Reed Sea event, the conquest of the land, and the rise of the Davidic monarchy. The purpose here is not only to demonstrate the significant correspondence between the form and function of the motifs of divine war in the ancient Near Eastern texts and in the Old Testament, but also to deal with the special ways in which the Old Testament reflects Israel's particular historical and religious experiences. This section covers the motifs of YHWH war up to the time of the Davidic kingdom.

Part One
Divine War in the Ancient Near East

Chapter I
Divine War in Mesopotamia

1. THE CONTEXT OF DIVINE WAR

First of all, what was the ancient Mesopotamian context? T. Jacobsen has pointed out that all the Mesopotamian materials available show that the fourth millennium BC and the ages before it had been a moderately peaceful epoch in which gods are described as the power of fertility and plenty, as providers.[1] Wars and raids were not unknown; but they were not constant and they did not dominiate existence.[2] A Sumerian epic-tale, Enmerkar and the Lord of Aratta, depicts a golden age without war, even though there were some conflicts. This peaceful situation appears in the epic (lines 136–46):[3]

> Once upon a time there was no snake, there was no scorpion, there was no hyena, there was no lion, there was neither dog nor wolf, there was neither fright nor goose flesh, man had no rival.
>
> At that time, the mountain-lands' (of) Shubar-Hamazi (East),and the different-tongued: Sumer (South), the great "mountain" of the *me* of magnificence, Uri (North), "mountain" possessing all that is befitting, mountain-land (of) Mardu (West), resting in security, the whole universe, the people who are taken care of (by the god), addressed Enlil in one tongue.

This period is considered as Enlil's epoch[4] as the Early Dynastic god lists indicate that Enlil appears at the head of the Sumerian pantheon.[5] The

---

[1] T. Jacobsen, *The Treasures of Darkness*: A History of Mesopotamian Religion (New Haven/ London 1976), 25 ff (— *Treasures*).

[2] *Ibid.*, 77 ff.

[3] S. Cohen, *Enmerkar and the Lord of Aratta* (University Microfilms, Ann Arbor, Michigan 1973), 118–19 (— *ELA*). W. W. Hallo and W. K. Simpson count the Early Dynastic I as the golden age, ca. 2900–2700 BC (*The Ancient Near East*: A History, NY 1971, 34 ff, — *ANE*).

[4] H. Radau, *Sumerian Hymns and Prayers to God Nin-ib (Ninurta) from the Temple Library of Nippur*, 29/1 (Philadelphia 1911), 12 (— *Sumerian Hymns and Prayers*).

[5] W. G. Lambert, "The Historical Development of the Mesopotamian Pantheon: A Study in Sophisticatd Polytheism," *Unity and Diversity*: Essays in the History, Literature, and Religion of the Ancient Near East, ed. by H. Goedicke and J. J. M. Roberts (Baltimore/ London 1975), 195 (— *Unity and Diversity*).

Sumerian epics such as Lugalbanda do not deal with the motif of divine intervention in the historical battle.

However, with the beginning of the third millennium BC, sudden death by the sword in wars or raids by bandits joined famine as equally fearsome threats. This appears to have become the order of the day. No one was safe.[6] There were always threats of wars, as suggested in a cynical proverb in Mesopotamian wisdom: " You went and plundered enemy territory, the enemy came and plundered your territory."[7] Since that period, men could look for protection only to the institution of security which was originally temporary office. At the same time, with the new anxiety a new savior-figure came into being, the ruler exalted above men, fearsome as a warrior, awesome in the power at his command.[8] At the same time the role and function of the gods within their own local temples and towns were developed step by step to include broader duties. Most major gods began to hold office and have roles to play on the national political scene. According to Jacobsen, Mesopotamian kingship originated with leadership in war. When attack threatened, a young noble was chosen *pro tem* to lead the community in battle and was granted supreme powers during the emergency. When the gods came to be seen as rulers it was natural that they should be expected to provide protection against outside foes.[9] A seal of the Uruk period shows a historical battlefield. A bearded figure, surely the king, stands, spear in hand, upon the battlefield, where some of his fellows are still dealing with the enemy. Most of these are lying at their mercy with hands tied behind them. It is clear that a definite victory and actual historical event is commemorated on this seal.[10] This is confirmed by the records of a palace of Early Dynastic III date found in Fara, the ancient Shuruppak. In the records there are accounts of the repairs by the craftsmen, on war chariots coming and going from battle, and lists of troops upon their offices (670 men) going to battle.[11] It is also supported by the fact that in the archaic Ur texts of the periods of Jemet Nasr and Fara, ur-sag (warrior in Sumerian) appears with ten different kinds of personal names such as ur-sag-ág, ur-sag-banda or ur-sag-lam.[12] Moreover, the term, ur-sag was combined with the sign of divine

---

[6] See n. 2.

[7] C. G. Starr, *Early Man*: Prehistory and the Civilization of the Ancient Near East (London/ Toronto 1973), 84.

[8] Jacobsen, *Treasures*, 79.

[9] *Ibid.*, 83.

[10] H. Frankfort, *Cylinder Seals* (London 1939, 1965), 23.

[11] T. Jacobsen, *Toward the Image of Tammuz and Other Essays on Mesopotamian History and Culture*, HSS 21, ed. by W. L. Moran (Cambr. Massa. 1970), 148 (— *Tammuz*).

[12] E. Burrows, *Ur Excavations, Text* II: Archaic Texts (London 1935), 38, the numbers of proper names, 738—47 (— *UET* II).

determinative (𒀭) with which the following divine name is broken such as ur-sag ^{d} ... (plate 360 ii).[13] A good example is ur-sag ^{d}Utu[14] and ur-sag ^{d}Nanna.[15] It was the period in which the gods, who were powers in nature, had become powers in history. Consequently gods became rulers with the provider metaphor of the fourth millennium. The major function of gods in this period was protection and defense against enemies. The divine image as ruler, responsible for defense against external enemies and for prosperity and order internally, sharpened in the later period.[16]

2. THE CONCEPT OF DIVINE WAR

1

In the course of the transformation of the divine image war began to be recognized as a divine command (inim dingir = *am/wat ilī*). In the cone inscription of Entemena (ca. 2404–2375), when Ush, the ruler of Umma invaded the boundary of Lagash, Ningirsu made war against Umma by the command of Enlil as follows (Ent 28 col i 22–27):[17]

> ^{d}Nin-gír-su ur-sag ^{d}En-líl-lá-ke$_4$ inim si-sá-ni-ta Umma^{ki} - da dam-ḫa-ra e-da-ak
>
> Ningirsu, the warrior of Enlil, made war against Umma by his righteous command.

The above passages show that the war was carried out by the command Enlil, the father of the gods. In the case of Entemena the command of Enlil was a punishment to Ush, the violator of the boundary treaty which was set up by the divine witness. In the Mari sources the same idea appears: "by the command of Dagan and Itūr-mēr, my lord, I (king) turned their (enemies') cities into a mound and a ruin."[18] Hammarabi, the Old Babylonian king, expressed the same idea: "upon the command of Anu and Enlil he destroyed the walls of Mari and Malgūm."[19] In the inscription of Nebuchadnezzar I, his attack of Elam was considered as the command by

---

[13] *Ibid.*, pl 42, no. 360 ii.

[14] *Ibid.*, 38, no. 747.

[15] *Ibid.*, 38, No. 745.

[16] Jacobsen, *Tammuz*, 18.

[17] E. Sollberger, *Corpus des Inscriptions Royales Presargoniques de Lagaš* (Geneva 1956), 37 (– *CIRPL*); E. Sollberger and J. R. Kupper, *Inscriptions Royales Sumériennes et Akkadiennes* (Paris 1971), 71 (– *IRSA*).

[18] *Warfare*, 24, n. 20.

[19] *Ibid.*, n. 23.

Marduk, the divine warrior (col I 12–13).[20] According to this statement his war against Elam was not his own desire but a divine mission. In these descriptions of the victors, warfare was the divine command to remedy a wrong.[21] The duty of Kings was to carry out the divine commission. In a later period the formula, "by the command of god(s) (*ina dīn/amāt/qibīt/siqir DN* or *ilī*) the kings carried out the campaigns," became a conventional usage in the war descriptions of the royal inscriptions.

2

Another aspect of war is that war was considered as a lawsuit. The Mesopotamian kings appealed to their divine warrior to judge their cases of war. Warfare in Mari documents of the 18th century was regarded as a judgment of the gods for violation of treaty. The treaty document itself is a "tablet of the life of the gods (*ṭuppu nīš ilānī*)."[22] The reference is to swear an oath before the gods. A breach of treaty was to invoke to wrath the deities who witnessed the ratification of the treaty. In the epic of Tukulti-Ninurta he appealed to Shamash as follows (col III 13′–15′, 19′–20′):[23]

13′. [in]a na[nm]urtinima ša qable/i dēn bērini lū mui[rx]
14′. ni[l]qi ūmuma šâtu kīma kīni ša ḫābile/i išallal [xxx]
15′. [ul] [i]ššakan salīmu balu mitḫuṣe/i ka [l xxx]
19′. u[m]ma kuldamma ina taqrubti ša zikarē arkat ahāmiš i nip[rus]
20′. ina isin tamḫari šâtu ētiq māmīti ai ela pagaršu lid[du]

When we meet in battle, let the ... judge/win the case between us.
we ⌜shall⌝ meet on this day, in the manner of a just man (who) takes [the spoil] of an evildoer.
Peace will not be made without conflict, all ⌜f...⌝
So come to me on the battlefield of the servants, (and) let us settle the case together
In this festival of battle, may the oath-breaker not rise up, (but) let them throw down his corpse.

This appeal to god is based on the fact that oaths and treaties were normally ratified before a sanctuary or symbol(s) of the attending gods. Here Shamash was called the judge (col II 37′). The judgment of the god Shamash as the judge was to punish Kashtiliash, king of the Kassites who coveted the battle, the breaker of the oath. The war as lawsuit was also a

---

[20] L. W. King, *Babylonian Boundary-Stones and Memorial Tablets in British Museum* (London 1912), 31 (– *BBS*).

[21] A. E. Glock, "Early Israel as the Kingdom of Yahweh," *CTM* 41 (1970), 597.

[22] Glock, *Warfare*, 46.

[23] P. Machinist, *The Epic of Tukulti-Ninurta I*: A Study in Middle Assyrian Literature (Unpublished Ph. D. Diss. of Yale University 1978), 90–91 (– *TN Epic*).

remedy for violation of a treaty through the divine judgment. In this epic both Tukulti-Ninurta and Kashtiliash recognize that victory or defeat depended upon divine judgment.

3

Here we can see that god gave not only his command to make war or to judge it as lawsuit, but also himself intervened in battle. In the cone inscription of Entemena, when the ruler of Umma invaded the border of Lagash, Ningirsu, the divine warrior, intervened to fight against Umma, the divine intervention of Ningirsu is described as follows (Ent 28 col i 28–31):[24]

> inim-^{d}En-líl-lá-ta sa-šuš-gal bí-šuš SAḪAR.DU$_6$.TAG$_4$-bi edin-na ki-ba ni-uš-uš
>
> By the command of Enlil (Ningirsu) threw great throw-net (over Umma). He heaped up their burial-mounds upon the ground of the field.

This intervention of Ningirsu in the battle already appeared in the stele of the Vultures. Even though the parallel part to the above quotation is a reconstruction by Jacobsen, the intervention motif of Ningirsu was well depicted as follows (col VII 15–25):[25]

> [On that day Ningirsu threw the great throw-net over Umma, stabbed it with the sword, smote it with weapons. On its corpses,] 3600, be they stabbed with the sword, [he heaped up their burial-mounds.]

This intervention motif is clearly seen in the fragments of the stele of the Vultures which were found in Tello (*ANEPS*, nos. 298–301). Two fragments from the obverse side of the stele are the enemies Eannatum caught in a net. The large human figure, nude above the waist, wears a long chin-beard, arranged in five locks curled at the ends and massive hair which is contained in a chignon resting upon the shoulder. The figure has been interpreted as representing the god Ningirsu or Eannatum. In the right hand is held a mace with which he smites the nude figures, with shaved faces and heads, contained in a net. The net is surmounted by the symbol of Ningirsu a lion-headed eagle which grasps with its talons the backs of two lions. Another fragment (no. 301) depicts the vultures carrying away the corpses of the enemy. The vultures carry away from

---

[24] Sollberger, *CIRPL*, 37; *IRSA*, 71. The use of net as a tool to catch the enemies again appears in *Enuma Eliš*. In single combat of Marduk and Tiamat Marduk made a net (*sapāru*) to enfold Tiamat (Tab IV:41) and spread it out to enfold her (line 95). After Tiamat was slain, her helpers, the gods, were thrown into net, and they found themselves ensnared (line 112).

[25] T. Jacobsen, "The Stele of the Vultures Col I–X," *S. N. Kramer Anniversary Volume AOAT* 25, ed. by K. Bergerhaf, et al. (Neukirchen-Vluyn 1976), 258–59.

the battlefield with their beaks and claws the heads and an arm of the slain. In the fragment (no. 300) Eannatum is leading his soldiers over bodies of enemy dead (above) and troops led by Eannatum in his chariot (below). The soldiers wear tight-fitting helmets and are heavily armed with shields, spears, maces, and axes. They march over a road made of the bodies of enemies laid feet to feet and head to head. The leader wears a more elaborate helmet, with ears and a burn represented, and is clothed in a flounced skirt and a skin thrown over his left shoulder. In the lower register the troops are shown marching in close formation and carrying spears and axes. Again they are led by Eannatum who rides in a chariot. His left hand holds an outstretched spear and his right grasps a sickle-sword. At the front of the chariot is a quiver and an axe. Moreover, Utu, the divine warrior, as well as Ningirsu, participated in the battle to support Eannatum. Jacobsen may venture to restore tentatively (col VIII 6–23):[26]

> On that day Utu rose for Eannatum at his right, and tied a diadem(?) on his forehead. At the sign of Ningirsu Eannatum was ferociously skirmishing with Umma in... the beloved field and acreage of Ningirsu.

However, the actual battle of Eannatum against Umma is described as follows (col IX 2 – X 4):[27]

> Against Eannatum a man shot an arrow and he grew weak from the arrow. He broke it off, but could not continue fighting in the front rank (lit. "before them"). The man burst into a triumphal song... Eannatum like an evil rainstorm blew... into Umma...

Col VII 30 – VIII 3 shows that the real victory was brought by the revolt inside Umma:[28]

> [nam-lú-u_x uru-na] šu e-na-zi šàg_4-Umma^{ki} -ka ì-gaz
>
> [and in his city the populace] raised hand against him and he was killed inside Umma.

A fortunate revolt in Umma – presumably due to internal dissensions – would be outside the control of Eannatum and so would naturally be attributed to a supernatural intervention by Ningirsu. This revolt inside the enemy was understood as a way of divine intervention.

In the Šu-Sin inscription of two divine wariors, Inanna and Enlil intervened to destroy the enemies of Šu-Sin of Ur (ca. 2037–2029). The text says (col II 1–13):[29]

> in order to destroy the memory of its famous blackheaded people, in order to subdue its great far-reaching mountain ranges, Inanna (and) Enlil came in to the help of Šu-Sin, the mighty king, the king of Ur, the king of the four quarters.

---

[26] *Ibid.*

[27] *Ibid.*

[28] *Ibid.*

[29] M. Civil, "Šu-Sin's Historical Inscriptions: Collection B," *JCS* 21 (1967), 29.

In the Mari letters the idea of divine intervention in the military events is found in the following formulas:[30]

a) You (Dagan) walked at the side of Ilā-kabkabū.
   Ilā-kabkabū destroyed his fortress (*ARMT* I 3:15).
b) Since the deity has destroyed the enemy... (*ARMT* II 24:9).
c) The god marches with my lord at the side of his troops (*id.*, 50:12′).
d) The protecting deity of my lord has led me,
   and the expedition of my lord is safe (*id.*, 130:26).
e) May the god Šamaš smash the weapon(s) of that enemy (*ARMT* III 15:7–8).

In the Assyrian royal inscriptions the idea of divine intervention was expressed as the divine help and support. We find a formula in the inscription of Adad-narari I (1307–1275) as follows:[31]

> With the strong weapons of the god Ashur, my lord; with the support of the gods An, Enlil, and Ea, Sin, Shamash, Adad, Ishtar, and Nergal, most powerful among the gods, the awesome gods, my lords; I captured by conquest the city Taidu, his great royal city, ...

His son, Shalmaneser I showed a similar attitude: with the support of Ashur and the great gods, my lords, that city I captured, destroyed, and sowed *Kudimmus* over it.[32] With the support of the god Ashur and the great gods, his lords, and has no rival, capturer of enemy districts above and below, the lord at whose feet the god Ashur and the great gods have subdued all rulers and princes.[33] In the Tukulti-Ninurta inscriptions we also find a similar description of the divine support in battle three times. It is striking that the same motif also occurs in his epic against Kashtiliash which we will discuss below. We read text 5 (col II 48 – (III) 65a):[34]

48. ina tukulti ša ^{d}Aššur
49. ^{d}Enlil u ^{d}Šamaš ilānī rabûtī
50. bēlīya ina riṣuti
51. ša ^{d}Ištar bēlat šamê irṣiti
52. ina panī ummaniya
53. illiku itti
54. kaštilašu šar $^{(māt)}$karduniaš
55. ana epiš tuqmati
56. asniq abiktu
57. ummanatešu aškun
58. muqtablišu ušemqit
59. ina qirib tamḫari šâtu

---

[30] Glock, *Warfare*, 23–24, 29–30.

[31] A. K. Grayson, *Assyrian Royal Inscriptions* I (Wiesbaden 1972), no. 393 (– *ARI*).

[32] *Ibid.*, no. 528.

[33] *Ibid.*, no. 526.

[34] E. Weidner, *Die Inschriften Tukulti-Ninurtas I. und seiner Nachfolger*, AfO Beiheft 12 (Graz 1959), 12, 27.

60. kaštilašu šar kašši
61. qāti ikšud kišād bēlutišu
62. kīma galtappi ina šēpīya
63. akbus šallusu
64. u kamusu ana maḫar dAššur
65. bēlīya

With the support of the gods Ashur, Enlil and Shamash, the great gods, my lords, (and) with the aid of the goddess Ishtar, mistress of heaven (and) earth, (who) marches at the fore of my army, I approached Kashtiliash, king of Karduniash, to do battle, I brought about the defeat of his army (and) felled his warrior. In the midst of that battle I captured Kashtiliash, king of the Kassites, (and) trod with my feet upon his lordly neck as though it were a footstool. Bound I brought him as a captive into the presence of Ashur, my lord.

In the inscriptions of Tiglath-pileser I he confirmed his victory with the help of Ashur: "with the help of Ashur, my lord, I gathered my chariots and my troops. I looked not behind me. Mount Kashiari, a difficult region, I traversed. With their twenty thousand warriors and their five kings I fought in the land of Kutmuhi and I defeated them".[35] Especially this motif, as Mann has pointed out,[36] is concentrated in the inscriptions of Sargon II, Sennacherib and Ashurbanipal. Sargon II confessed his victory with the help of Ashur, Nabu and Marduk, his favorite gods: "with the help of Ashur, Nabu, (and) Marduk, I crossed the Euphrates with my mighty hosts and turned my face toward the city of Dur-Ladinnu,..."[37] Sennacherib also stated that he led his third campaign in victory against Syro-Palestine; siege of Jerusalem, with the help of the god Ashur:[38]

(Trusting) in the aid of Ashur, my lord, I fought with them and brought about their defeat. The Egyptian charioteers and princes, together with the charioteers of the Ethiopian king, my hands took alive in the midst of battle.

After Sennacherib prayed for victory over the mighty foe, "the great gods, Ashur, Sin, Shamash, Marduk, Nabu, Nergal, Ishtar, of Nineveh, Ishtar of Arbela, the gods in whom I trust, they came to my aid".[39] Esarhaddon had a similar concept of the divine help for the victory over the enemies.[40]

With the help of Ashur, Shamash, Nabu and Marduk, the gods, his allies, he walks aright and attains to his desires, — all who were not obedient to him, the princes who did not submit to him, like a reed of the brake, he has snapped and trodden them under his feet.

---

[35] D. D. Luckenbill, *Ancient Records of Assyria and Babylonia* I (NY 1926, 1968), no. 221 (– *ARAB*).

[36] Mann, *Divine Presence*, 62.

[37] *ARAB* II, no. 35.

[38] *Ibid.*, no. 240.

[39] *Ibid.*, no. 253.

[40] *Ibid.*, no. 575.

In the inscription of Ashurbanipal the same idea appears, when Gyges of Lydia conquered his own enemies "by the help of Ashur and Ishtar, the gods, my lords."[41] This concept of divine help simply shows that the king conquered his enemies with divine aid. Thus it is seen that this expression tends to emerge during particular historical situations – renaissance of imperial supremacy – of Assyrian imperial might.[42] It is significant that the fullfilment of the concept of divine war in the Mesopotamian context is to be found mainly during the reign of the last four powerful kings of the Assyrian empire – Sargon II, Sennacherib, Esarhaddon and Ashurbanipal.

4

The result of intervention of the divine warriors was the decisive defeat of the enemy. What was the reason for this defeat? What did the victims think about defeat? According to the epic of the Tukulti-Ninurta, the reason why Marduk and his fellow gods were angry and left Kassite was the oath-breaking by Kashtiliash. Tukulti-Ninurta claims before Shamash that he kept the oath of Shamash but Kashtiliash broke the divine oath as follows (col II A 13′–24′):[43]

13′. "O Šamaš, lord ⌜...⌝, I kept your oath, (and) I feared your greatness.
14′. He who is not ⌜...⌝ transgressed before your ⌜...⌝, (but) I safeguarded your judgment.
15′. When our fathers made an agreement before your divinity,
16′. (And) established an oath between them, they invoked your greatness.
17′. You are the hero, who since times past were the judge of our fathers, not changing (verdicts),
18′. And you are the god who now watches over our loyalty setting (things) right.
19′. Why, then, since times past has the king of the Kassites contravened your plan (and) your judgment?
20′. He has not fear[ed] your oath, has transgressed your command, has schemed falsehood.
21′. He has committed crimes against you, O Šamaš: be my judge.
22′. Bu[t as for him who] perpetrated no wrong against the king of the Kassites, a[ct favorably toward him.]
23′. [By] your great [command] grant. ⌜...⌝ victory to the one who keeps the oath.
24′. [For him who does not obey] your command, destroy h[is] people in the defeat of battle."

All the gods as well as Marduk decided to punish Kashtiliash, the breaker of oath and left their sanctuaries. It is interesting to find the abandonment motif as follows (col I B 38′–46′):[44]

---

[41] *Ibid.*, no. 784 (p. 298).

[42] Mann, *Divine Presence*, 65.

[43] Machinist, *TN Epic*, 77–79.

[44] *Ibid.*, 65.

38′. Marduk abandoned his august sanctuary, the city [ ]
39′. He cursed the city of his love, Kar- [ ]
40′. Sin left Ur, [his] cult center [ ]
41′. With Sippar and Larsa, Š[amaš became wroth]
42′. Ea [abandoned] Eridu, the house of wisdom [ ]
43′. Ištaran became angry w[ith]
44′. Anunitu no longer approaches Agade [ ]
45′. The mistress [of] Uruk gave up [her city]
46′. The gods were extremely angry and [ ]

In the above descriptions the victor was to justify why he could conquer the Babylonia of Kashtiliash II. In his view divine abandonment is clearly due to the wrongdoing of Kashtiliash and his dynasty.[45] This motif of wrong and divine abandonment goes back at least to the late third millennium. In the curse of Agade the tutelary goddess Inanna left her shrine in Akkad and turned her weapons against her own city, because of the desecration of the shrine of Enlil by Naram-Sin.[46]

She who had lived there, left the city,
Like a maiden forsaking her chamber,
Holy Inanna forsook the shrine Agade,
Like a warrior hastening to (his) weapon,
She went forth against the city in battle (and) combat,
She attacked as if it were a foe.

In the sources of Nebuchadnezzar I the reason why Marduk left Elam was the same breaking of an oath by the Elamites. The Elamites did not revere Marduk, but instead blasphemed. They became haughty, trusted in themselves, forgot Marduk, and finally broke their oath. The term, wicked Elam (*ṣenu elamu*) appears often in several texts. Thus the devastation wrought on Elam was a just punishment for Elam's breaking of an oath. The reason why Marduk left Babylon was also similar in Enmeduanki and related matters, Babylon's own sins which provoked Marduk to anger, led him to command the gods to desert the land. As a result, the people were incited to sin, became godless, and evil multiplied. So the Elamites invaded, destroyed the cult centers; and removed the gods ...:[47] "Good departed and evil was regular. The lord became angry and got furious, he gave the command and the gods of the land abandoned it (...) its peoples were incited to commit crime." According to another text, however, this evil took place by Marduk's plan: "the Elamite enemy has tended his evil work, and Marduk instigated evil against Babylon (*nakru elamû urriḫ lemnētu*

[45] *Ibid.*, 154.

[46] J. B. Pritchard (ed), *Ancient Near Eastern Texts Relating to the Old Testament*, 3rd ed. with Supplement (Princeton 1969), 648 (— *ANETS*).

[47] W. C. Lambert, "Enmeduranki and Related Matters," *JCS* 21 (1969), 128–30.

u bēl ana bābili ušakpidu lemuttu)."[48] If so, can it be said that the sin of Babylon was also the will and plan of Marduk? This question is more problematic. According to the statement above, the cause of the destruction of Babylonia was the plan of the gods. Babylonia has no freedom of choice, but must follow the divine decree, the given destinies. Thus there is no reason why Marduk should intervene in the Babylonian conflict with Elam.

5

However, the appearance of the abandonment motif in a composition of victims seems to be unknown in Mesopotamia before the epic of Tukulti-Ninurta, though later it is well documented, particularly as a tradition of the New Assyrian kings.[49] In the Sumerian lamentation over Ur, and over Sumer and Ur which were composed by the disaster victims, the composers do not recognize any human sin as the cause of the divine act to destroy.[50] They tried to explain to their fellow citizens how their cities suffered political collapse at the end of the Ur III period. Destruction is due, rather, to the decision of the heads of the pantheon, An and especially Enlil. Moreover, in the prophetic text of Marduk the Elamite conquest of Babylon and plunder of Marduk's statue was not an event of defeat by Elam but was his simple business journey for Elam.[51] In his prophetic text Marduk talks about his three times of journeys which mean the past history of Babylonia down to the time just prior to Nebuchadnezzar's Elamite campaign, and the emphasis is on the earlier move of Marduk's statue: Hittite (I 13–38), Assyria I 3'–17'), and Elam (I 18' – II 18). Roberts mentions that Muršiliš' capture and removal of Marduk's statue was the first business journey ordered by Marduk himself to establish trade connections between Babylon and Hatti (I 13–19).:[52]

13. DUG_4.GA(*aqbi*) *a-na* KUR(*māt*) *ḫat-ti* DU-*ik*(*allik*)
14. *ḫat-ti-i áš-al*
15. GIŠ.GU.ZA(*kussi*) ^{d}*A-nu-ti-ia*$_5$
16. *i-na lib-bi-šá ad-di*
17. 24 MU.AN.NA.MEŠ(*šanāti*) *i-na-lib-bi-šá* TUŠ(*ašbākū*)*-ma*
18. [K]ASKAL.MEŠ(*ḫarrānāt*) DUMU.MEŠ(*mārī*) KÁ.DINGIR.RA(*bābili*)^{ki}
19. *i-na-lib-bi-šá* GIN-*in*(*ukīn*)

---

[48] J. J. M. Roberts, "Nebuchadnezzar I's Elamite Crisis in Theological Perspective," *Essays on the Ancient Near East in Memory of J. J. Finkelstein*, CAAS 19, ed. by M. de J. Ellis (Hamden 1972), 186, n. 37 (– "NEC").

[49] Machinist, *TN Epic*, 154, n. 22.

[50] *Ibid.*, 153.

[51] R. Borger, "Gott Marduk und Gott-König Sulgi als Propheten: Zwei Prophetische Texts," *BiOr* 28 (1971), 3 ff (– "Propheten").

[52] Roberts, "NEC", 184 ff.

I myself gave the command. I went to the land of Hatti. I questioned Hatti. The throne of my Anuship I set up within it. I dwelt within it for 24 years, and I established within it the caravan trade of the Babylonians.

The second journey to Assyria was Tukulti-Ninurta's removal of the Marduk statue following his victory over Kashtiliash, as seen in the epic of Tukulti-Ninurta. Here the reason for his journey is obscured by a break. He left willingly for Babylon and visited Assyria. But now he completed his stay there and came back home (I 12′–15′a):[53]

12′. [xxx] DIR(*umallī*?]-*ma* KUR(*māt*) *aš-šur* ŠUD$_x$-*ub*(*akrub*)
13′. [xxx] NAM.MEŠ(*šīmāti*) NÍG.BA(*aqīs*)-*su*
14′. [xxx]ŠE(?) BA *an-na* GI.NA(*kīna*) SUM(*addin*)-*šu*
15′. [*aḫ-ḫi-s*]*a* ...

I fulfilled [my days(?)] and I blessed the land of Assyria. [...]
I bestowed destinies to her [...] and
I gave firm promise (?) to her:
I turn to home.

The third trip to Elam – the Elamite conquest of Babylon and plunder of Marduk's statue – was also Marduk's own idea. He does not refer to the event as a defeat. He himself gave command for his departure from Babylon (I 21′–23′):[54]

21′. [*an-na*]-*ku* DUG$_4$4.GA(*aqbi*)
22′. *a-na* KUR(*māt*) ELAM.MA(*elamti*)^{ki} DU(*allik*)-*ma*
23′. DU.MEŠ(*allikū*) DINGIR.MEŠ(*ilū*) DÙ.A.BI(*kalâma*) *a-na-ku-ma* DUH$_4$.GA (*aqbi*)

I myself gave the command.
I went to the land of Elam, and all the gods went with me
I alone gave the command.

Here it is seen that the victims tried to explain these disasters as a free divine journey, not as punishment for wrong. The reason why Marduk returned to Babylon was just a fulfillment of his days and years outside Babylon by his own will.[55] This was a temporary departure from his normal friendly relations with his city, not part of a movement that led to a goal not hitherto reached. For all the aspects of human affairs belong to the sphere of gods. A key word of this understanding is "to be destined to be." Everything in the universe was laid down by divine decree. Man's duty was to conform to these decrees. Everything should remain immovable. But things did in fact change, and destinies also changed by divine control and intervention in history. The reasons for the control of the

---

[53] *Ibid.*, 184.

[54] *Ibid.*

[55] *Ibid.*, 187, n. 58; cf., W. G. Lambert, "Review Article to History and the Gods by Albrektson," *Or* 39 (1970), 170–177.

given destinies could vary from case to case, but with humans it was normally a failure to conform to the divine decrees. As far as the cuneiform texts tell us, divine intervention does not concern itself with a movement in history. Lastly we will see Lambert's opinion above divine control of history. He states:[56]

> The intervention could be entirely whimsical, but if purposeful it was intended to maintain the norms or destinies, The important thing is that in the Mesopotamian view the events of history did not lead on from one point to another. Rather, everything was established in the beginning and ideally should have stayed that very way. History on this view is like the vibrations of a taut string when plucked — in due course the string ceases to vibrate and returns to the state it was in at the beginning.

Thus the above evidence shows that the victory or defeat in battle depends upon the divine decision and intervention, though the victims did not recognize their defeat as their wrongdoing in the early period. In this sense, the wars were the wars of gods, and the gods were the gods of war. It is natural that gods are called divine warriors.

3. DIVINE WARRIORS

From the pre-Sargonic period as we have seen above, the gods began to intervene in wars. From this period and onwards the active gods in war had become warriors like Ninurta (Ningirsu). People began to believe that the god is a warrior (dingir ur-sag)[57] or my warrior is my god (*qurādi ilī*).[58] Ninurta already had a warrior title, ur-sag in the stele inscription of Eannatum (col IV 5). The warriorship (nam-ur-sag) of the gods was fully expressed in the Sargonic period. Most of the divine warriors in the Sumero-Akkadian pantheon appeared in this period and beyond. From this period there were around fifty divine warriors in the Sumero-Akkadian pantheon.[59] The major warriors among them are: Ninurta, Nergal, Zababa, Sin, Shamash, Adad, Ishtar and so on.[60] It is the general view that the concept of divine warrior was a reflex of thought

[56] W. G. Lambert, "Destiny and Divine Intervention in Babylon and Israel," *The Witness of Tradition*, OudtestStu 17 (Leiden 1972), 71.

[57] J. J. M. Roberts, *The Earliest Semitic Pantheon*; A Study of the Semitic Deities Attested in Mesopotamia Before Ur III (Baltimore/London 1972), 127 (— *Semitic Pantheon*).

[58] *Ibid.*, 129. The terms, *qarrādu* and *ālilu* are used as the epithet of god, king, soldier and others (W. von Soden, *Akkadisches Handwörterbuch* II, Wiesbaden 1958—1972, 905, — *AHw*; *The Assyrian Dictionary of the Oriental Institute of the University of Chicago*, A/1, 348, — *CAD*).

[59] W. Heimpel, "Held", *Reallexikon der Assyriologie* 4, ed. by D. O. Edzard (1972—1975), 289—90.

[60] K. Tallqvist, *Akkadische Götterepitheta*, StOr 7 (Helsinki 1938), 297—98 (— *AGE*).

that the king was warrior (*šarrum qarrādum*).[61] The king was also a charismatic leader who had supreme force and prestige in war. It is supported by the term, lugal-ur-sag which already appeared in the first historic period as a personal name.[62] The king was called a warrior of warriors (*qarrād qarrādī*).[63] Here we will deal with only the chief divine warriors of each empire in the Mesopotamian context: Ninurta in the pre-Sargonic period, Innana/Ishtar of Akkad, Marduk of Babylonia, and Ashur of the New Assyrian kingdom.

1) Ninurta (Ningirsu), a pre-Sargonic Divine Warrior

1

Ninurta/Ningirsu as the Erscheinungsform of Ninurta is the farmer's version of the god of thunder and rainstorms of the spring like Enlil.[64] Ninurta is a divine warrior who was first to have the warrior title, ur-sag-^{d}En-líl-lá in the pre-Sargonic period. The rains and the general humidity in the air in spring make the ground soft enough to be broken by the plow, so Ninurta is also god of the plough. His name may in fact contain an old cultural loan word for that instrument (urta) and may mean "lord plough". This fertility aspect of Ninurta is his initial function in nature. At the turn of the third millennium, however, a new concept was shaped by the political developments. The epithets "ruler and king", were applied to the gods. They became powers in human affairs, in history.[65] Under the conditions of that time, Ninurta, who was a power in nature, became a power in human affairs, in history. Thus his ruler image was that of a divine warrior who was responsible for defense against external enemies, not simply a provider. His new image as a divine warrior was strikingly depicted in the hymn of Ninurta's journey to Nippur (lines 204—208), completely different from his image in the Tammuz materials:[66]

204. en kur gul-gul gaba-ri nu-tuk-a
205. mè maḫ-bé súr-bi du_7-du_7
206. ur-sag gal á-x[ ] è - a
207. kal-ga a-ma-ru-^{d}En-líl-lá
208. ^{d}Ninurta dumu maḫ ékur-ra

---

[61] *Sumerian Hymns and Prayers*, 3.

[62] *UET* II, 34, no. 484 of personal name; *AHw*, 905.

[63] Hammurabi was called a warrior of warriors (A. Sjöberg, "Ein Selbstpreis des Königs Hammurabi von Babylon," *ZA* NF 20, 1961, 151, line 11I.

[64] Jacobsen, *Tammuz*, 32.

[65] Jacobsen, *Treasures*, 43.

[66] J. C. Cooper, *The Return of Ninurta to Nippur*: An-gim dím-ma, AnOr 52 (Rome 1978), 100—101 (— *Angim*); Jacobsen, *Tammuz*, 328.

The lord, who destroys the 'mountains', who has no rival,
Who butts angrily in that magnificent battle,
Great warrior, who goes forth in his might,
Strong one, Deluge of Enlil,
Ninurta, magnificent scion of Ekur.

In a later hymn he is described as the only warrior of heaven (ur-sag-aš-an-na-ke$_4$).[67] It is supported by the fact that in the literary materials in the third and second millennia, his military role predominated. With this sociopolitical phenomenon, the nonhuman forms of gods had been transformed into the human forms. His earliest name was *Imdugud*, which means "rain-cloud", and his earliest form was that of the thundercloud, envisaged as an enormous blackbird floating on outstretched wings, roaring its thunder cry from a lion's head.[68] A curious survival of this nonhuman form of the god is preserved in the Lugalbanda epic in which the hero meets the god in his bird shape. Anzu, lion-beaded eagle says himself: "you (Lugalbanda) are man, so I will decide your destiny, let you have not enemy in the mountain" (lines 108–109).[69] A plaque from Tello confirms this nonhuman form of Ninurta, an eagle with spread wings, seizing with its claws the back of two lions, with their heads upward to bite the eagle's wings – the emblem of Lagash. He was also expressed in other nonhuman forms such as a bull, ram or lion. In *Angim* he was a horned wild bull, a wild ram and a stag, the great bull of mountains (lines 26–27), the lion who received the fearsome *me* in Abzu, or as a storm who swept the rebellious lands like a deluge. In Lugale he butts like a storm and hurls the eight winds against the rebellious lands (line 77). But later the nonhuman form of Ninurta as an eagle headed scepter appears on the boundary stone of Nebuchadnezzar I at the end of the second millennium.[70] With the growing tendency toward anthropomorphism the old nonhuman forms were gradually disassociated from the god as merely his emblem, symbol of the god. Thus when the god went to war with the army, it was in the emblem that he was encountered. In *Angim* his three emblems appear before and after him in battle (lines 65–68):[71]

65. Udanne, the all-seeing god, and
66. Lugalanbadra, the beared lord (?), go before him, and
67. The awesome one of the "mountain", Lugalkurdub,
68. The [ ] of lord Ninurta, follows behind him.

---

[67] A. Falkenstein, *Sumerische Götterlieder* I (Heidelberg 1959), 94 (– *SGL* I).

[68] Jacobsen, *Treasures*, 128.

[69] C. Wilcke, *Das Lugalbandaepos* (Wiesbaden 1969), 102–103.

[70] J. B. Pritchard, *The Ancient Near East in Pictures Relating to the Old Testament*, 2nd ed. with Supplement (Princeton 1969), no. 519 (– *ANEPS*).

[71] Cooper, *Angim*, 64–67.

On a cylinder seal of the middle of the third millennium Ninurta appears as a god in human form with a bow, and is accompanied by a lion. On a plaque from Tello Ninurta appears in the human form clothed in a long skirt and wearing a headdress of two plumes or palms.[72] In the Dyala region as early as the second Early Dynastic period representations on seals show the bird god growing a human lower body. Later when Gudea saw his lord Ningirsu in a dream, the god appeared with *Imdugud's* wings, and his lower parts ended in flood. Even in Assyrian times in the first millennium, a relief of Ashurnasirpal's that graced Ninurta's temple in Nimrud shows the god in human form, but still winged. Significantly he is throwing thunderbolts at his own older form, winged bird-lion.[73]

Accompanying the humanization of the outer form of Ningirsu, the thunderstorm god, was the socialization of his inner form. In the thunder the ancients not only heard the roar of the lion or the bellow of the bull, but also at times the rumble of the war chariot, while the lightening became the flash of arrows in the sun. Thus Ningirsu rode on his war chariot and drove it across the skies, rain pouring out of his mouth. In *Angim* he makes earth and heaven tremble: "You step, heaven and earth tremble, when you raise your arm, a shadow is cast" (lines 84–85). The human form of the god as victorious charioteer became a war leader, a king. At this time kingship was only just emerging. In this sense Eannatum's kingship was given by Ningirsu: "Ningirsu in great joy gave him the kingship of Lagash" (col V 13–18).[74] In *Angim* the martial aspect of Ninurta which was endowed by Enlil, An, Inanna and Enki, is well described by himself (lines 162–67):[75]

162. I am the exceedingly mighty lion-headed one of Enlil, whom he engendered in his strength,
163. The storm under the heavens, shackle of the gods,
164. I am the (one) whom An, in his great might has chosen,
165. I am the mace that destroys the 'mountains', fit for kingship on high,
166. I am the strong arm in battle, inspired by Inanna,
167. I am the warrior, destined with Enki to be suited for the fearsome *me's*

Ninurta was perfect warrior (ur-sag šu-du$_7$-a),[76] the sovereign who swept on like the deluge, fierce warrior of Enlil (ur-sag-ḫuš-^{d}En-líl-lá),[77] or the warrior of the gods (ur-sag-dingir-re-e-ne).[78] Another hymn tells of his warriorship as king and lord (lines 3–10):[79]

---

[72] *ANEPS*, no. 598.

[73] Jacobsen, *Treasures*, 128.

[74] Jacobsen, *AOAT* 25 (1976), 256–57.

[75] Cooper, *Angim*, 86–89.

[76] *Ibid.*, line 80.

[77] *Ibid.*, line 72.

[78] *Ibid.*, line 8–9.

[79] *ANETS*, 577.

3. (my king) who like Erra has perfected heroship, Dragon with the "hands" of a lion, the claws of an eagle,
4. Lord Ninurta who like Erra has perfected heroship, Dragon with the "hands" of a lion, the claws of an eagle,
5. My king who vanquishes the houses of the rebellious lands, great lord of Enlil, You, with power you are endowed.
6. Lord Ninurta who vanquishes the houses of the rebellious lands, great lord of Enlil, You, with power you are endowed.
7. My king, when your heart was seized (by anger), You spat venom like a snake,
8. Lord Ninurta, when your heart was seized (by anger), You spat venom like a snake,
9. My king, toothed (pickaxe) that uproots the evil land, arrow that breaks up the rebellious land,
10. Lord Ninurta, toothed (pickaxe) that uproots the evil land, arrow that breaks up the rebellious land,

In addition, he is depicted as the first warrior of his father in *STVC* 35 (lines 73–75):[80]

73. en ^{d}Nin-urta-ke$_4$ pa$_4$ -š eš-a-a-na
74. ur-sag na-nam ur-sag na-nam ur-sag kur nu-è
75. ur-sag-me-en ^{d}Nin-urta na-nam ur-sag kur nu-è

The lord Ninurta, the first one of his father,
is the warrior, is the warrior, the warrior
who let the mount land not escape.
The warrior is Ninurta, the warrior
who let the mount land not escape.

Moreover, his warlike aspect which fills foreign peoples with terror is well depicted in the Gudea cylinder (A 9:20–10:5):[81]

I, Ningirsu, who hold back the wild water,
the great hero Enlil,
the lord who has no opponent:
my house, my Eninnu, the lord of foreign lands...,
my weapons, Sharur subjugate all enemy lands,
my tremble appearance the land of ths enemy cannot endure,
my outstretched arm no one withstands,
(10) my dear father, in (his) great love, king, storm Enlil,
whose wild appearance does not rise from the land of the enemy,
Ningirsu, hero of Enlil,
gave me for a name.

---

80 Falkenstein, *SGL* I, 110.

81 A. Falkenstein, *Sumerische und Akkadische Hymnen und Gebete* (Zürich/Stuttgart 1953), 147 (– *SAHG*).

2

A weapon is the basic tool of a warrior. In *Angim* Ninurta has many kinds of the valorous weapons (lines 129–52): *šarur* on his right, *šargaz* on his left, Udzuninnu fifty-toothed storm, *agasilig*-ax like dragon, seven-bladed cutlass, *alluḫappu*-net like a cow of battle, *šuškal*-net, the seven-fanged great serpent, heavenly dagger, fifty-headed mace which swept on like the deluge of battle and that consumes the rebellious lands like fire, the *mir*-snake like a deluge bow, and so on. These kinds of weapons of Ninurta are also found in the Gudea Cylinder (B 13): 21–14:9):[82]

> The seven-headed mace, terrible weapon of battle,
> The weapon which the two regions cannot bear, club of battle
> The mace, the weapon, the lion-headed ...
> Unopposable in the "mountains",
> The "tongue-knife", nine emblems, the valorous arm,
> His bow that sounds like a mess-forest,
> His furious arrow, that streaks like lightening in battle,
> His quiver, lions whose tongues lash out at a terrifying serpent,
> The arm(s)of battle, so that the royal *me's* would be fulfilled –

His *šarur* is the flood-storm weapon for the battle against which none can protect. The epithat of *šarur* in the Gudea Cylinder B 7:24 is "mi-tum-an-na," heavenly mace, or the deluge of battle (8:2). Gudea made it to subjugate the mountain in battle (7:19). The *šargaz* is also the seven-headed mace which destroys the enemies. *šarur* and *šargaz* are the most important weapons of Ninurta which are found at the head of the list of Ninurta's weapons in *CT* 25, 14:17 ff. Two weapons among the deified weapons of Ninurta seem to have achieved independent stature in the pantheon of the first millennium theologians.[83] Ninurta's *šuškallu*-net is mentioned in the New Assyrian recension of Lugale 1:13: "warrior, whose *šuškallu*-net overturns the enemy" (*qarrādu ša šuškallašu ajābu isaḫḫapu*). The fifty-headed mace (šita mi-tum middu ^{giš}tukul sag-ninnu) is found in various texts.[84]

We also find the same characters of Ninurta as an eternal warrior who destroys the enemies of Šusin of Ur (2037–2029) in a hymn (lines 1–4):[85]

> 1. ur-sag-ul gal-le-eš nir gaba-gál zà-pirig ul sa_7 -ga
> 2. ^{d}Nin-urta x mar-uru_5 ug-gal šen-šen-na ru-ru-gú
> 3. á-gál un-erím x-ra-su urú gul-lu á-dam saḫar-re-eš gi_4
> 4. ^{d}Nin-urta am-gal gu_4-si-AŠ bàd-gal šu ...

---

[82] *Ibid.*, 176–177; Cooper, *Angim*, 160.

[83] Cooper, *Angim*, 122.

[84] *Ibid.*, 130.

[85] A. Sjöberg, "Hymns to Ninurta with Prayers for Šūsîn of Ur and Būrsîn of Isin," *Kramer Anniversary Volume*, *AOAT* 25 (1976), 412–13.

Eternal warrior, greatly respected, with a broad chest, with the strength of a lion, beautifully created,
Ninurta, ..., devastating flood, great lion, stepping into the battle,
The strong one who ... the enemy, a destroying flood, turning crowded places into dust,
Ninurta, the great wild ox, "unicorn", ... a great wall.

In the prayers of Amarsin of Isin (1895—1874) Ninurta is depicted as the heroic warrior (lines 142—146):[86]

142. [ur-sag] á-zi-da-^{d}En-líl-lá kur ki-bal gul-gul
143. $^{[d]}$Nin-urta á-zi-da-^{d}En-líl-lá kur ki-oal gul-gul
144. lugal zi-ga-ni a-ma-ru na-me sag nu-sum-mu
145. ^{d}Nin-urta u_4 -súr-mè-a erim-e-gìri-KIN-di
146. nam-ur-sag da-da-ra-šè du_{11}-ga šul gaba-ri nu-tuk-a

[The heroic warrior], 'the right arm' of Enlil, who destroys the enemy land,
Ninurta, 'the right arm' of Enlil, who destroys the enemy land,
The king, whose rising (is) the flood against which no one ran rush,
Ninurta, the furious storm (?) of battle, who tramples upon the enemy,
He is girded for warriorship, a man without rival,

Assurbanipal states: "Ninurta, the supreme god, you are the warrior."[87] In the so-called Harem inscription of Sargon II, Ninurta, the lord of power, from whom is his strength: "to Sargon, the king of Assyria, ... grant him unrivaled might, manly strength, send forth his arms and let him smite his foes."[88]

3

From the early period Ninurta was identified with Zababa, a divine warrior of Kish, because of his heavenly body, an eagle. For Zababa is explained as ^{mul}ID-ḪU (*našru*).[89] But in *An-Anum* Zababa belongs to one of the members of the Ninurta family with Uraš. In a later period Ninurta (^{d}Utu-u_{18}-lu)[90] is also identified with Nergal (^{d}Utu ḫé-gál),[91] Adad (^{d}Utu-gal-gal),[92] Marduk (^{d}Amar-utu)[93] and Nabu (^{d}Gu-utu),[94] be-

[86] *Ibid.*, 420—21.

[87] *SAHG*, 315.

[88] *ARAB* II, no. 126.

[89] A. Jeremias, *Handbuch der altorientalischen Geisteskultur* (Berlin/Leipzig 1929), 378 (— *Geisteskultur*).

[90] *Ibid.*, 191; R. Borger, *Assyrisch-Babylonische Zeichenliste*, AOAT 33 (Neukirchen-Vluyn 1978), no. 381 (— *ABZ*).

[91] A. Deimal, *Pantheon Babylonian*: Nomina Deorum (Romae 1914), 192.

[92] Tallqvist, *AGE*, 476.

[93] Jeremias, *Geisteskultur*, 191.

[94] *Ibid.*

cause of their common element of sun (𒀭) like Shamash. Especially Ninurta (^{d}Maš)[95] and Nergal (^{d}Maš Maš) as the childlren of Enlil are related in the common element, the first one (𒈦). Yet in *An-Anum* they have their own family group in Tablet V and VI respectively.[96] Ninurta and Adad, or Ninurta and Nergal as a pair of divine warriors appear in the divine names of the Assyrian inscriptions.

Ninutra is a son of Enlil and Ninlil. His wife is Bau/Gula or Ninkarra. His well-known emblem is the lion-headed eagle, *imdugud*. In the astronomical context Ninurta is described as the lord of summer or of the southpole. He is called the navel of earth or the holder of ligament of the womb of heaven and earth.[97] His numnber is 50 like his father Enlil's number, which corresponds with 50 epithets of Marduk or 50 temples of Gudea.[98] So in a later tradition he became Marduk of the pickaxe.[99] A hymn shows this monotheistic tendency in the later Babylono-Assyrian pantheon like that of Marduk:[100]

> Lord, your anger is the (raging) floodstorm;
> you are the highest warrior of the gods,
> O lord, your face is the sun god, your hair, Aya,
> your eyes, O lord, are Enlil and Ninlil.
> The pupils of your eyes are Gula and Bēlit-ilī
> the irises of your eyes are the twins, Sīn and Shamash,
> the lashes of your eyes are the rays of the sun god that ...
> The appearance of your mouth, O lord, is Ishtar of the stars
> Anu and Antum are your lips, your command...
> your tongue (?) is Pabilsag of the above...
> The roof of your mouth, O lord, is the vault of heaven and earth, your divine abode,
> your teeth are the seven gods who lay low the evil ones.
> The sphere of your cheek, lord, is the rise of the shining star
> both your ears are Ea and Damkina,
> the spokesman of wiseman...
> your head is Adad,
> the heaven and earth what the foremen built
> your forehead is Shala,
> the beloved husband, who the heart rejoices
> your neck is Marduk,
> the judge of heaven and earth.

---

95 Borger, *ABZ*, no. 74.

96 H. Zimmern, *Zur Herstellung der grossen babylonischen Götterliste An-(ilu) Anum*, VSGW 63/4 (1911), 119 ff.

97 Jeremias, *Geisteskultur*, 189.

98 *Ibid.*, 269.

99 *Cuneiform Texts from Babylonian Tablets in British Museum*, part 24 (London 1908), 50, obv 47406, 3 (*^{d}Marduk ša al-li*), — *CT*.

100 Jacobsen, *Treasures*, 235; *SAHG*, no. 10.

The identification with the parts of Ninurta's body and all the gods is a correspondence of function between the parts of Ninurta's body and the deities identified with phenomena of the cosmos. Here one can see the unitary aspect of Ninurta as the great warrior of the world, who includes in himself each aspect of the great gods in the Sumero-Akkadian pantheon. The unity is of a different kind: a unity of essence, as it were, a recognition of sameness of will and power in the bewildering variety of divine personalities. He was the exalted warrior of the world (*qarrādu šaqu ša māti*).[101] He was the honoured one, lord, great warrior (ulim-ma-umman ur-sag-gal), because of his unrivalled warriorship. Thus the evidence above suggests that the warrior image of Ninurta began to appear from the middle of the third millennium BC. Since that time the tradition of his divine warriorship was transmitted to the Neo-Babylonian period. In the later period Ninurta with Marduk and Ashur became a triad of divine warriors in the Mesopotamian religion.

2) Inanna/Ishtar, the Sargonic Divine Warrioress

1

Inanna had already appeared in the pre-Sargonic period. Yet she did not show her warlike aspect. With the rising of the Sargonic empire she was exalted as a divine warrior. Despite the complex traditions, in the Sargonic period, Inanna of Uruk or Kullab, who was known as the daughter of Nanna, the sister of Utu with Ishkur had the title "*qarrādu*" (*eš*$_4$-*dar-ur-sag*).[102] In the process of humanization, the rain god Innana like Ninurta tended to be envisaged as a warrior riding her chariots into battle. In Enmerkar and the lord of Aratta, Inanna, the queen of all the land, is described as the heroine fit for battle, as the heroine of the battle ground, who makes the troops dance, the dance of Inanna (nin ur-sag mè-a túm-ma ^{d}Inanna ur-sag mè-saḫar-ra ka sag KI.E.NE ^{d}Inanna di-dam).[103] The battle was the dance of Inanna to the Sumerian. She appears in a hymn as the strong and terrible one who strikes down all opposition. As a result all the lands are hers. She prides herself on her power as goddess of war in a *balbale* song:[104]

> My father gave me the heavens,
> gave me the earth,
> I am the lady of heaven,

---

101 S. Langdon, *Sumerian and Babylonian Psalms* (Paris 1909), 227 (— SBP).

102 Roberts, *Semitic Pantheon*, 30; L. P. P. Dhorme, *La Religion Assyro-Babylonienne* (Paris 1910), 85.

103 Cohen, *ELA*, lines 288—90.

104 *SAHG*, 67—68, no. 7; Jacobsen, *Treasures*, 138.

Is there one god who can vie with me?
Enili gave me heaven,
gave me earth,
Kingship he gave me,
queenship he gave me,
waging of battle he gave me,
the attack he gave me,
the floodstorm he gave me,
the hurricane he gave me!
The heavens he set as a crown on my head,
the earth he set as sandals on my feet,
a holy robe he wrapped around my body,
a holy sceptre he placed in my hand.
... I am a warrior.

The warlike aspect of Inanna as goddess of rain and thunderstorm is very close in character to her brother Ishkur and to Ninurta mentioned above.

Later Inanna was adopted as the divine warrior of his own city, Akkad, by Sargon. During Sargon's early campaigns Enlil, the chief deity of the Sumerian pantheon, had mainly helped Sargon, according to inscriptions. Enlil judged Sargon's case with Lugalzaggesi captured. Sargon brought him in fetters to the gate of Enlil; Enlil gave Sargon no opponents; Enlil gave him the territory from the upper sea to the lower sea and so on.[105] Despite the great support of Enlil, the god list which represents the political entities shows the following order of gods: Inanna, An and Enlil. Inanna was the god of Sargon's own city; An was the city-god of Uruk; Enlil was the city-god of Nippur who had authority over all of Babylonia. This is the historical order in which Sargon gained authority over the political entities for which they stand; first Akkad, then Uruk by the victory over Lugalzaggesi, and lastly all of Babylonia.[106] Inanna as a warrior played an important role in Sargon's political development. We find the warlike character of Inanna in nin-mè šár-ra, the exaltation of Inanna. We read (lines 26—31):[107]

26. igi-mè-ta
nìma-ra-ta-si-ig
27. nin-mu á-ní-za
KA.KA ì-durud$_x$(KÚ)-e
28. u$_4$ - du$_7$ -du$_7$ - gim
ì-du$_7$ -du$_7$ -dè

[105] H. Hirsch, "Die Inschriften der Könige von Agade," *AfO* 20 (1963), 65:8 (— "Inschriften").

[106] Jacobsen, *Tammuz*, 420.

[107] W. W. Hallo and J. J. A. van Dijk, *The Exaltation of Inanna*, YNER 3 (New Haven/London 1968), 16—19 (— *Inanna*).

of the code of Hammurabi he describes Inanna's warlike characteristics in the first person as follows:[119]

> May Inanna, the lady of battle and conflict, who bares my weapons, my gracious protecting genius, the admirer of my reign, curse his rule with her great fury in her wrathful heart! May she turn his good into evil; may she shatter his weapons on the field of battle conflict; may she create confusion (and) revolt for him! May she strike down his warriors, (and) water the earth with their blood! May she throw up a heap of his warrior's bodies on the plain; may she show his warriors no mercy! As for himself, may she deliver him into the hand of his enemies, and may they carry him away in bonds to a land hostile to him!

Tiglath-pileser I (1114–1076) describes his goddess Ishtar "foremost among the gods, mistress of tumult who adorns battles".[120] In his building inscription Sargon II (725–706) praises his war goddess Ishtar who helps him in his war: "In the fight and battle may she go to his help (*ina šašmu u tahazu lillik riṣušu*; II:15)."[121] Esarhaddon (680–669), son of Sennacherib, describes Ishtar as his divine guide in battle: "the goddess of battle and warfare, who goes by the side of the king, her favorite one, the terrible one of his enemies (*ilat qabli u tahazi alikat idi šarri migiriša muraššibat garīšu*)".[122] To Ishtar, the lady, surpassing great ruler of heaven and earth, the powerful warrior-(queen) of the gods; Ishtar of Uruk, the noble princess, who receives heaven's decree(s).[123] In a hymn she herself proudly tells of her warlike aspects:[124]

> When I stand in the front (line) of battle
> I am the leader of all the lands,
> when I stand at the opening of the battle,
> I am the quiver ready to hand,
> when I stand in the midst of the battle,
> I am the heart of the battle,
> the arm of the warriors,
> when I begin moving at the end of the battle,
> I am an evilly rising flood,
> when I follow in the wake of the battle,
> I am the woman (exhorting the stragglers):
> "Get going! Close (with the enemy)!"

Inanna also pronounces herself, "I am the warrior," "supreme who shouts a war-cry in the midst of the mountain," "an exalted net spread out in the

---

[119] *ANETS*, 179–80.

[120] Grayson, *ARI* II, no. 8.

[121] A. T. Clay, *Babylonian Texts*: Miscellaneous Inscriptions in Yale Babylonian Collection, I (New Haven 1925), 54 (– *BT* I).

[122] *Ibid.*, 58–59.

[123] Luckenbill, *ARAB* II, no. 730.

[124] Jacobsen, *Treasures*, 137.

field of storm-wind or fire flaming," or "warrior without champion."[125] In a hymn to Ishtar we read (K 257, obv 59–70):[126]

> I am supreme. The hand of him who vies with me shall not stand with my hand.
> My mighty pace fills the earth.
> I am supreme. The foot of him who vies with me shall not stand with my foot.
> Who is there before me? Who is there behind me?
> From the lifting up of mine eyes who can escape?
> From the rush of my onslaught who can flee?

This warriorship as one of some 100 *mes* was given to her by Enki.[127] Besides the evidence above, she was called "*bēlē tahazi* with Adad," "*bēlit qabli u tahazi*," "*bēlit ummani*," "*qarritti ilāni* or *ilāti*," and so on.[128]

In the cylinder seals Ishtar is depicted as a war goddess standing or seated on a crouching lion. Over her shoulders there are two quivers with arrows; in her right hand she holds the staff composed of a mace and two feline heads; in her left hand the curved sword.[129] Identified by an inscription on the face of this stele is the figure of Ishtar of Arbela standing on a lion. She is armed with a sword and a quiver. Her headdress consists of a high conical crown, the top being decorated by vertical incisions and a star-disc.[130] Her emblem is the eight-pointed star. The emblem of the star-disc appears on the top of two steles of Hammurabi from Susa.[131] The two star emblems on top of the stele of Naram-Sin must be that of Ishtar, his patron warrior.[132] On the stele inscription of Nebuchadnezzar I the first symbol of the upper register is Inanna/Ishtar, the eight-pointed star inscribed on a disc, with the triad gods, Sin and Shamash.[133] Thus the eight-pointed star, the emblem of Ishtar became a triad god with Sin and Shamash in the Mesopotamian pantheon as a symbol of protection. We find this triad-divine emblem in the curved stones.[134] Ishtar's spouses were the great gods, An, Enlil, Nergal, Ninurta, as well as Tammuz. The warlike Innana/Ishtar thus can go back as far as the time of Sargon.[135] Her warriorship was deeply rooted in the history of Mesopotamian religion since the later part of the third millennium and beyond, even in the Hittite context.

---

125 J. D. Prince, "The Hymn to Belit," *JAOS* 24 (1903), obv line 17, 42–44, rev 7.

126 *Ibid.*, 110–114.

127 G. Farber-Flügge, *Der Mythos Inanna und Enki unter besonderer Berücksichtigung*, StPoh 10 (Rome 1973), Tab I 3:2, II 5:53.

128 Tallqvist, *AGE*, 337.

129 *ANEPS*, nos. 525–26, 704; Jeremias, *Geisteskultur*, fig 173 a–c.

130 *ANEPS*, nos. 522–24.

131 *Ibid.*, nos. 514–15.

132 *Ibid*, no. 309.

133 *Ibid.*, No. 519.

134 *Ibid.*, nos. 422, 444, 447, 453, 518–20, 837.

135 Cf., Prince, *JAOS* 24, 108.

3) Marduk, the Divine Warrior of Babylonia

1

Actually Marduk was known as a minor god as early as the third millennium. He is identified with the Sumerian god of thundershowers, Asalluhe.[136] In the Weidner Chronicle, Marduk, the son of the temple of Apsû, looked with joy upon him (Sargon) and gave to him sovereignty over the four quarters. However, (because of) the wrong he (Sargon) had done, he (Marduk) became hostile towards him (Sargon).[137] In the chronicle of Early Kings, because of the wrong he (Sargon) had done, the great lord Marduk became angry and wiped out his people by famine (*ana ikkib ipušu bēlu rabû* ᵈ*Marduk igugma ina ḫušaḫḫu nišēšu igmur*).[138] Then on the several seals of the Sargonic period the figure of Marduk appears as the son of Ea. He was already worshiped in that period. In the cylinder seal of the Sargonic period, Marduk like Aššur is depicted as a divine warrior with solar qualities, the sun-god. He is characterised by rays issuing from his shoulders, by a saw with which, as supreme judge, he cuts decisions and by his stance with one foot upon a mountain.[139]

However, later Marduk was accepted as the national god of Babylon as Ashur, the national god of Assyria in the Assyrian royal pantheon only during the middle Babylonian period and especially during the reign of Nebuchadnezzar I (post-Kassite period), not during the reign of Hammurabi.[140] In the prologue of *the code of Hammurabi* Marduk was appointed at this time only as the "*illilūt kiššat nišī*," "the governor over the people," which had formerly rested on Enlil by Anu and was made great among the Igigi-gods (*in igigi ušarbi'ūšu*) by them.[141] Lambert has pointed out that it was over the people, not over the gods, that Marduk was given authority, and Anu and Enlil made him great among (*in*) the Igigi-gods, not over (*eli*) the Igigi-gods.[142] At that time Marduk became one of the great gods, not the head of the Babylonian pantheon. But in the epilogue of his law code Hammurabi states that Marduk gave him his ability which has no equal and commissioned him to guide people aright, while Inanna and Zababa gave him his mighty weapon. He rooted out the enemy above

---

136 Jacobsen, *Tammuz*, 25; W. Sommerfeld, *Der Aufstieg Marduks*, AOAT 213 (Neukirchen-Vluyn 1982), 7 ff.

137 A. K. Grayson, *Assyrian and Babylonian Chronicles* (NY 1975), 148–49 (– *ABC*).

138 *Ibid.*, 154.

139 *ANEPS*, no. 685.

140 W. G. Lambert, "The Reign of Nebuchadnezzar I: A Turning Point in the History of Ancient Mesopotamian Religion," *The Seed of Wisdom*: Essays in Honour of T. J. Meek, ed. by W. S. McCullough (Toronto 1964), 3 ff – "Nebuchadnezzar").

141 Col. 1:11–15.

142 Lambert, "Nebuchadnezzar", 6.

and below. He made an end of war (24:22–32). However, Marduk became the leading divine warrior in the campaign of Nebuchadnezzar I against Elam, and was exalted as the chief deity and national god of the Babylonian pantheon. In his stele-inscription Nebuchadnezzar I shows that Marduk sent him forth against Elam.[143] This passage clearly suggests that Marduk, the divine warrior (^{d}Marduk ur-sag) supported Nebuchadnezzar I in destroying the Elamites. The first evidence for his change of title and status occurs in the stele-inscription under discussion (col I 13): "the king of the gods, Marduk (*šar ilānī ^{d}Marduk*)." Since that time Marduk's kingship over the gods is commonly attested in literary and non-literary materials.[144] It is reasonable that the military triumph of Nebuchadnezzar I over Elam, especially the celebrated return of the statue of Marduk from Elam to Babylon, was an opportunity to celebrate "Marduk, king of gods who destroyed Tiamat, the traditional enemy against Babylon," or "Marduk permanent lord of the gods of heaven and earth." Jacobsen states that if Tiamat represents the Sealand like Yam of the Baal myth, the battle between Marduk and Tiamat reflects the political tension between Babylon and the Sealand in the early half of the second millennium.[145] Somewhat later than Hammurabi, Ulamburiash of Babylon conquered the Sealand (*māt-tam-ti*) after Ea-gamil, the king of the Sealand, fled to Elam.[146] Jacobsen goes on to suggest that the battle drama, altogether a new type of religious drama instead of the earlier fertility drama, began to dominate from the end of the second millennium.[147]Although in some cases rooted in older fertility dramas, this new form comes to be the preferred vehicle for a new political drama celebrating and reaffirming the birth of the nation as a divine achievement that was from the beginning, in mythical time.[148] It would be natural that the final stage of the exaltation of Marduk draws near to the time of reunification of the Babylonian world under Nebuchadnezzar I at the end of the second millennium.[149] The exaltation of their divine warriors by the historical heroes already had appeared in the exaltation of Inanna by Sargon and her daughter, Enḫeduanna, and that of Ninurta/Ashur by Tukulti Ninurta I. It was a theological device of heroes to exalt their divine warriors, to remember the founding or renaissance of their empires as a divine achievement and help. In this sense it is understandable that Nebuchadnezzar I exalted Marduk as his divine helper in the Babylonian reunification.

---

143 King, *BBS*, 31 col 1:12.

144 Lambert, "Nebuchadnezzar", 6, no. 9.

145 Jacobsen, "Religious Drama in Ancient Mesopotamia," *Unity and Diversity*, 76.

146 Grayson, *ABC*, 156.

147 *Unity and Diversity*, 72 ff.

148 Jacobsen, *Unity and Diversity*, 76.

149 Mann, *Divine Presence*, 50.

2

Marduk's weapons are a mace and dagger.[150] Marduk is the fire which is lighted. In the Babylonian seal Marduk shows his triangular symbol. In the Babylonian steles the warlike aspect of Marduk is depicted as a spear point (*marru*) on a shrine beside which is a horned dragon.[151] In another stele Marduk holds a curved sword in his right hand, while he holds the rod and ring in his left.[152] In *Enuma Eliš* (Tab IV 35–58, 92–102) the terrifying picture of Marduk as divine warrior is surrounded by weapons such as arrows, bows and quivers in front and behind. Most of them are the expressions of storm phenomena and personifications of warfare like Inanna in the exaltation of Inanna. From the end of the second millennium Marduk became supreme god over all the gods until Nabu, his son rose to be his equal by the time of the late Babylonian empire. Thus in later time the functions of the major deities in the pantheon are focused on the function of Marduk like Ninurta. The list (*CT* 24:50. K 47406 obv) is:[153]

Uraš (is)	Marduk of planting.
Lugalidda (is)	Marduk of the abyss.
Ninurta (is)	Marduk of the pickaxe.
Nergal (is)	Marduk of battle.
Zababa (is)	Marduk of warfare.
Enlil (is)	Marduk of lordship and consultations
Nabû (is)	Marduk of accounting.
Sîn (is)	Marduk who lights up the night.
Šamaš (is)	Marduk of justice.
Adad (is)	Marduk of rain.
Tišpak (is)	Marduk of troops.
Great Anu (is)	Marduk of …
Šuqumuna (is)	Marduk of the container.
[(is)]	Marduk of everything.

A remarkable number of major gods are here identified with aspects of Marduk, with functions of his that correspond to their own characteristic natures, functions, and powers — to say that Marduk in his role of helper in battle to the kings of Babylon is Ninurta is to say that his reaction and his martial prowess are the same as those of Ninurta.

---

150 Frankfort, *Cylinder Seals*, PLXVIII h–j.

151 *ANEPS*, nos. 453–54, the first from the left in the first register; 519–21, the first from the left in the third register; 533: "Göttersymbole und Attribute," *Reallexikon der Assyriologie* 3, 486.

152 *ANEPS*, no. 523.

153 Lambert, *Unity and Diversity*, 197–98.

4) Aššur, the Divine Warrior of Assyria

1

Aššur is the city-god of Aššur. From Shamshi-Adad I (ca. 1815–1782) onward there appeared to have been strong tendencies to identify him with the Sumerian Enlil, and not only titles of Enlil but deities associated with him and cult places of his in Nippur are duplicated in Aššur in Assyria. Later under Sargon II, there were tendencies to identify Aššur with Anshar, the father of An in the creation myth. Under Sennacherib the primeval achievements of Marduk were transferred to Aššur as it had been done in the political struggle with Babylonia. In this sense the image of Aššur seems to lack all real distinctiveness. Aššur supported the Assyrian arms against enemies, and later received detailed written reports from Sargon II and Sennacherib about their campaigns. Besides Aššur the old divine warriors, Ishtar, Ninurta, Nergal and Adad, appeared in the same war fields. As a consequence Aššur as the national god of Assyria began to be recognized as a divine warrior from the time of Shalmaneser I (1274–1245) onward. In his inscription the god Aššur is described as a valiant warrior:[154]

> Aššur, valiant hero, capable in battles, crusher of enemies, the one who makes resound the noise of battle with his enemies, whose aggressive battle flashes like a flame and whose weapons attack like a merciless death-trap, ...

In the epic of Tukulti-Ninutra Aššur appears as the first vanguard god of the gods who participted in battle: "Aššur in the vanguard went to attack; the fire of defeat burned upon the enemy (col V A 33')."[155] In the letter of Sargon II his warlike character is well depicted (lines 118 ff): "Aššur is the mighty warrior (*qarrādu*), whose strong rage subdues the rulers of the world in fearfulness."[156]

Moreover, the kings in the royal inscriptions were the fighters against the enemies of the god Aššur and the enemies of Assyria were those of the god Aššur.[157] The troop of the king is recognized as the troop of the god Aššur. The weapon with which the king got victory was given from the god Aššur. So the war was the war of the god Aššur as the war of Israel was the war of Yahweh. The war is carried out by the command of Aššur (*ina zikir ^{d}Aššur*), or by that of Aššur and Ishtar or other gods.[158] Thus the victory given was the victory of the god Aššur. The booty of war was his property.

---

[154] *ARI* I, no. 526.

[155] Machinist, *TN Epic*, 118–19.

[156] Tallqvist, *Der Assyrische Gott*, *StOr* 3/4 (1932), 100 (– *Assyrische Gott*).

[157] Tallqvist, *Assyrische Gott*, 94.

[158] *Ibid.*, n. 8.

In the Assyrian historical inscriptions the god Aššur is described as a divine warrior. Especially in the letter to Aššur recounting the event of the eighth campaign of Sargon II, Sargon called Aššur, "father of gods, the great lord, hail, all hail!"[159] In addition, the name of Aššur was added to that of the early divine warriors like Dagan-Aššur, Ninurta-Aššur, Aššur-Ishtar or Adad-Aššur and so on.[160] Aššur has not only the epithet of Marduk but also the great warrior like Yahweh, man of war (Ex 15:3).

2

His strong weapon was a capturing net and snare; this is seen in oath formulas. The *šuškallu*-net already was the well-known weapon of Ninurta as the symbol of the unavoidable divine punishment from the pre-Sargonic period. Another net *saparu* was used by Marduk over Tiamat.[161] The weapons of the god Aššur are found in the attack of Esarhaddon against Egypt.[162]

8. atmuḫ rittūya qaštu dannatu mulull[u gešru]
9. ša ᵈAššur šar ilānī umallû qā[tūya]
10. kīma arī nadri peta agappa meḫret [ummanīya]
11. abubaniš allak šiltaḫi ᵈAššur la p[adu]
12. ezziš šamriš ittaṣi[xxx]
13. ᵈSarur ᵈSargaz illaku ma[ḫarīya]

I grasped in my hand the mighty bow, the powerful dart
which Aššur, king of the gods, had put into my grasp.
Like a raging eagle, with wings outspread, in front of (my troops)
like a flood I advanced. The unsparing lance of Aššur,
fiercely, violently was let loose [...].
Shar-ur and Shar-gaz went before me.

Aššur was called *bēl taḫazi* like Nergal, or *abūbu izzu* (fearful tornade) like Ninurta, Nergal, Enlil or Ishtar, or *ūmu nanduru* (evil demon), or the god of your fathers.[163] Thus Ashurbanipal praises Aššur as the hightest national god who is identified with national political aspirations in a hymn:[164]

Mighty lord of the gods,	all knowing one;
Powerful national lord of the gods,	determiner of fates;
Aššur mighty lord,	all knowing one;
Powerful national lord of the gods,	determiner of fates;

---

159 *ARAB* II, No. 140.

160 Tallqvist, *Assyrische Gott*, 97, n. 4.

161 *Enuma Eliš*, 4:41.

162 Mann, *Divine Presence*, 249.

163 Tallqvist, *AGE*, 266 ff; Jacobsen, *Treasures*, 159.

164 C. G. Cumming, *The Assyrian and Hebrew Hymns of Praise*, CUOS 12 (NY 1934, 1966), 81.

Aššur almighty one, lord of the gods, lord of the lands;
His greatness (I will praise), his sublimity proclaim;

Thus we can see that the new divine warrior who started as a city-god finally became a national god of the Assyrian empire in the process of the political development, and in the Assyrian pantheon Aššur appears as the chief national warrior with other traditional divine warriors: the national warrior and traditional warriors.

4. WAR CONDUCT

We wonder how the divine war were conducted by the kings in Mesopotamia. We may consider the three stages of conduct of the divine wars: before battle, battle, and post-battle.

1) Before Battle

The first task before battle was the divine consultation. There was a profound conviction that no military action could succeed unless its plan had the prior approval of the gods. Thus no military expedition set forth without a series of favorable omen signs. The diviners were required to determine whether the gods were favorably or unfavorably disposed toward the impending military action. The diviners employed several techniques for the divine consultation. These techniques were observations of natural phenomena such as astronomical features, birds, extispicy performed on animals, and dreams, as well as an oracle or casting lots. Diviners not only determined the moment of departure but accompanied military expeditions to insure favorable participation of the gods in warfare. In Mari there is an example of a military expedition marching out from Babylon under the leadership of *bārûm*-priests or diviners as follows (*ARMT* II 22:23–31):[165]

Ilušu-naṣir, the *bārûm*-priest, a servant of my lord "leads" the forces of my lord
A Babylonian *bārûm*-priest goes
with the Babylonian forces.
These 600 troops are (now)
in Šabazim. The *bārûm*-priests are gathering
omens. When an omen appears favorable
150 soldiers
go out and 150 return.

[165] Glock, *Warfare*, 130.

Here it may be that the diviner determines *when* a military action has the support of the gods. The diviner determines *when* the troops go out and come in. Both the number of men involved and their mission are outside the province of the diviner (*ARMT* II 39:68–70).[166]

1

Next, we will see the liver omen which was a popular method to discern the divine will before battle. It was to sacrifice a sheep and to inspect its liver by *bārûm*-priests. The detailed inspection of a liver is written as the omen formula of protasis and apodosis: *šumma šīli...nadi* 'if a hole lies (on...)', or *šumma* (some part of the liver) *pališma šutebru* 'if... is perforated and (the hole) goes (all the way) through', the 'condition' is illustrated on the model, with an apodosis written as a 'caption' to it.[167] Here we find a sample of an unfavorable omen:[168]

šumma ina ašid (SUḪUŠ) *ṣēr* (EDIN) *imitti* (15) *ubāni* (ŠU.SI)
šīlu (U) *nadi* (ŠUB-*di*) *nakru ana mātiya* (KUR.MU)
iḫ-ḫab-ba-tam-ma ne bi x ERIM MU *i dak* x x [ ]
KUR-za LAL

If in the base of the right side of the finger there is a hole: the enemy will make a razzia against my country...

One hears frequently the request of the omen reports. The reports were either very favorable (*ma-di-iš ša-al-ma*), favorable (*ša-al-ma*), unfavorable (*ú-ul ša-al-ma*), very unfavorable (*ma-di-iš la-ap-ta*). It was thus not simply a "yes" or "no" answer from the diviner.[169] The people believed that these kinds of omens were answered by the god Adad, the lord of omen (*bēl bīri*).

2

Moreover, the divine oracle which supports the victory was given to the kings or the diviners in a formula, "god delivers (literally, to fill out) X (enemy) into the hand of Y (*ilu X ana qāt Y mullûm*)." In a Mari letter we find the god Dagan who gives to Zimrilim his oracle of victory over the kings of the Yaminites. Dagan says to the governor in a dream: "why are the messengers of Zimrilim not in constant attendance upon me, and why does he not lay his full report before me? Had this been done, I

[166] *Ibid.*, 131.
[167] B. Landsberger and H. Tadmor, "Fragments of Clay Liver Models from Hazor," *IEJ* 14 (1964), 202.
[168] I. Starr, "Omen Texts Concerning Holes in the Liver," *AfO* 26 (1978–1979), 47.
[169] Glock, *Warfare*, 132.

would long ago have delivered the kings of the Benyaminites into the power of Zimrilim (*šarrānnī ša binīyamina ana qāt Zimrilim umtallišunuti*)".[170] The same phrase occurs often like the biblical idiom, "נתן ביד", in several places: "I (Dagan) will d[eli]ver into the power of Zimrilim the house of the seven conferedates and all their possessions."[171] "I (Dagan) shall deliver your enemies into your hand."[172] In the epilogue of the code of Hammurabi "Inanna, the lady of battle and conflict, delivers the man who did not heed my words which I wrote on my stele into the hand of his enemies."[173] The formula is also found in the Amarna letters. Tushratta, king of Mitanni, writes to Amenophis III of Egypt (Tab 17, II:32 ff):[174]

> kī nakrūtu ana mātiya ittalka ^{d}Tešub bēlī ana qātīya iddinšuma u addukšu
>
> When the enemies came to [my] country, Teshub, my lord, gave them (lit., him) into my hand and I beat them.

The same mode of expression is used in a building inscription by Nebuchadnezzar II (col III 2:18 ff):[175]

> nišim rapšatim ša ^{d}Marduk bēlī umāllû qātūya ana babilam$^{(ki)}$ ukanniš
>
> The numerous peoples, which Marduk, my lord, had delivered into my hand, I brought under Babylon's dominion.

Thus the delivery formula is a very common usage in Mesopotamia which expresses the idea that god gave to someone a gift such as land, kingship as well as victory. The reason why the gods gave the favorable oracles to the kings does not appear in the documents. But all those who obtained the divine oracle claimed that they were the beloved and favorite of their divine warriors. There are two formulas to indictate the divine favor. Thus the beloved of the god(s), ki-ág divine name (*narām* DN), and the favorite of the god(s), še-ga divine name (*migir* DN), were frequently given to the kings who obtained the divine oracles. These formulas were given as the epithets of the kings who were beneficiary of a special favored relationship to the gods. The *narām* DN is widely attested, and in the Old Babylonian period almost assumes the qualities of a title, being passed on

---

170 *ANETS*, 623, 630–31; G. Dossin, "Une Révelation du Dieu Dagan à Terqa," *RA* 42 (1948), 131. Sometimes the oracle answer was given like that: "the (oracula) word was very favorable to my lord, or not favorable (*ARMT* X 4:7, 11), or do not go on an expedition. Stay in Mari" (*ibid.*, X 50:24–25).

171 *ANETS*, 625; *ARMT* XIII, 23:14–15.

172 *ANETS*, 630; *ARMT* X, 7:21–22.

173 *ANETS*, 179.

174 S. A. B. Mercer (ed.), *The Tell El-Amarna Tablets* I (Toronto 1939), 64–65.

175 *Ibid.*

from king to king and dynasty to dynasty, and rarely missing even from the shortest inscriptions.[176] It seems that to be the favored and chosen of the heart of the gods were conditions to receive a divine oracle and help.

2) Battle

According to the divine oracle, the kings conducted their campaigns. In an Old Babylonian royal inscription Hammurabi acted by the will of the gods, not by his own will. He states:[177]

> I, Hammurabi, acted (by) the great command of An and Enlil, (by) the omen of Utu and Ishkur, by the supreme power of Marduk, by the splendour of Zababa and Inanna who walk at my right side...

The divine warriors not only gave the oracles but also they themselves participated in the campaigns of the kings. In a genuine building inscription of Naram-Sin, an Old Babylonian copy of a unique piece of Old Akkadian literature in which Erra, another name of Nergal went out with Naram-Sin (lines 33–36):[178]

> 22. Ilum erra u narām-^{d}sîn
> 34. puḫriš illiku rušu u šu
> 35. tattakpiš mātam qabalšu
> 36. itnallak ištašu qurādum erra

> The god Erra and Naram-Sin
> Went together, his companion and he.
> His battle overwhelmed(?) the land
> As the warrior Erra went with him.

In the epic of Naram-Sin we also find the divine participation in his campaign (col II 2–6 obv):[179]

> Naram-Sin marched on his way,
> the gods of the land marched with him,
> in front Nergal(?) marched,
> behind Zababa (protected) with two horns,
> the emblems of Annunit and Silaba ... pair by pair.

It is interesting that not only the gods of the lands but also Nergal and Zababa, the powerful divine warriors participated in the campaign of Naram-Sin. Moreover, the emblems of Annunit and Silaba, the two visible signs of divine warriors emphasize the divine participation in his campaign. Especially here Nergal was lord of battle and combat, lord of war and

---

[176] W. W. Hallo, *Early Mesopotamian Royal Titles*: A Philological and Historical Analysis (1957), 137.

[177] *IRSA*, IVC6i.

[178] W. G. Lambert, "Studies in Nergal," *BiOr* 30 (1973), 361.

[179] H. G. Güterbock, "NS Epos," 46–47; Borger, *ABZ*, 449.

king of war (*bēl qab-li u ta-ḫa-ẓi bēl tam-ḫa-ri šar tam-ḫa-ri*).[180] In the course of the divine battle the capture of the statues of the victims' gods was the last stage of battle to confirm the defeat.[181].

In addition, the climax of the divine intervention was the collective attack of the major divine warriors. It is found in the epic of Tukulti-Ninurta (col V A 33′–40′):[182]

33′. Aššur in the vanguard went to the attack; the fire of defeat burned upon the enemy.
34′. Enlil... in the midst of the foe, (and) sends flaming arrows smoking.
35′. Anu pressed the unpitying mace upon the wicked.
36′. The heavenly light Sin imposed upon them the paralyzing weapon of battle.
37′. Adad, the hero, let a wind (and) flood pour down over their fighting.
38′. Šamaš, lord of judgment, dimmed the eyes of the armies of the land of Sumer and Akkad.
39′. Heroic Ninurta, first of the gods, smashed their weapons.
40′. And Ištar beat (with) her skipping rope, driving their warriors insane.

Behind the gods, his helpers, Tukulti-Ninurta in the vanguard of the army, began the battle. He shot an arrow; (and) with the weapon of Aššur, which can crush a fierce attack, he felled a corpse. The warriors of Aššur declared: "To the fight!" (and) went to meet death. Thus Tukulti-Ninurta obtained the victory. It was a good example of the divine war in Mesopotamia.

3) Post-Battle

The final stage of divine war is to treat the spoils which were taken from the enemy. It is natural that the spoils belong to the gods, for a war is the war of gods. So the spoils were dedicated to the divine warriors. In his inscription Rimush (2278–2270) dedicated the booty which he took from Elam to the moon god, Sin.[183] He also gave Enlil tribute from the booty of Elam.[184] Similar contents appear in the inscription of Ititi: "Ititi, supreme judge, the son of Ininlaba, dedicated (this object) from the booty of Gasur to the goddess Inanna."[185] In the inscription of Nebuchadnezzar II he dedicated to Marduk and Nabu the booty:[186] "I had them brought into Esagila and Ezida before Marduk the great lord of the gods and

---

[180] E. von Weiher, *Der Babylonische Gott Nergal*, AOAT 11 (Neukirchen-Vluyn 1971), 73.
[181] Machinist, *TN Epic*, 151.
[182] *Ibid.*, 118–121.
[183] *UET* I, no. 10.
[184] Roberts, *Semitic Pantheon*, 148.
[185] Grayson, *ARI* I, 2.
[186] L. Legrain, *Royal Inscriptions and Fragments from Nippur and Babylon*, PBS 15 (Philadelphia 1926), 38.

before Nabu his dutiful son who loves my royalty." The booty includes then all things of the enemy: "his gods, his goddess, his property, his people, great and small, I (Ashurbanipal) carried off to Assyria" (no. 808).[187] Ashurbanipal treated similarly the booty which he took (no. 814):[188]

> The people and spoil of Elam, which at the command of Aššur, Sin, Shamash, Adad, ... I had carried off, the choicest I presented unto my gods.

The booty was distributed to the king and military personnel, as well as to the gods. In letters of Mari a king complains to his capitains who did not bring his share as well as the divine portion (*ARMT* II 13:24–35):[189]

24. šipṭam kīam addin ummami
25. qaduma isiqti bēlīya
26. [zitt]i la tadinanim
27. asak ^{d}Dagan u ^{d}Iturm[e]r
28. asak šamši-^{d}Addu u yasmaḫ-^{d}A[ddu]
29. GAL.MAR.TU DUB.SAR.MAR.TU GAL.KUD u labuttê
30. ikul ša šallat rēdêm iṭeru
31. ana pīya u GAL.KUD niš šarrim aškunma
32. šallat rēdêm ul iṭer
33. warki šepṭiya UD 10 KAM ul waṣī
34. tuppum ša aḫika ikšudam ummami
35. asakki ikul ina wardī ša šallat rēdêm ikima

and thus did I proclaim my ordinance as follows:
"You have not given me my (share),
as well as my lord's portion (of the booty).
The *asakku* of the god Dagan and the god Itūr-Mer,
the *asakku* of Shamshi-Adad and Yasmaḫ-Adad
the "colonel", the military scribe the "major" and the "captain"
have eaten, who have deprived a soldier of his booty.
In my mouth and (in that) of the "major" I placed an oath by the king
that the booty of a soldier should not be taken.
After my ordinance the tenth day had not yet passed
(when) a letter from your father came (saying) as follows:
"He of (my) servants who steals the booty of a soldier has eaten my *asakku*."

In line 35 taking booty parallels eating the *asakku* of the god/king to whom it belongs. The breaking of the oath and the command of a god is treated as the eating of *asakku* (taboo) or the violation of a holy or banned

---

187 *ARAB* II, 308.

188 *Ibid.*, 311.

189 F. Thureau-Dangin, "ASAKKU", *RA* 38 (1941), 42–43; A. Malamat, "The Ban in Mari and in the Bible," *Biblical Essays* 1966 – Proceedings of the 9th Meeting of Die Ou Testam. Werkgemeenskap in Suid Afrika, 44–45.

objects.[190] After a millennium the tradition of *asak šarrim*, a taboo existing outside the sphere of the gods in contrast to that of *asak ilim* was also found in the Assyrian royal inscriptions. In the records of the sixth campaign of Sennacherib we can find this (no. 322):[191]

> From the booty of the lands which (I had conquered), 30,500 bows, 30,500 arrows, I selected from among them, and added to my royal equipment. From the great spoil of enemy-(captives), I apportioned (men) like sheep to all of my camp, to my governors, and to the people of my (large) cities.

This evidence suggests that the booty was distributed to the several kinds of men only, not to the god. Therefore all the evidence above shows that the booty was dedicated to the gods and was distributed to men.

Another action was to erect a monument or boundary stone to remember the victory of the battle and the praise of the divine warriors. Entemena built a boundary stone (na-rú), after the victory over Umma. In the works of Esarhaddon (680–669) he says: "I had (also) made (this) stele (bearing) my name-inscription and had written thereupon the praise of the valor of my lord Aššur, my own mighty deeds – when I was marching (against the enemy) upon the trustworthy oracles of my lord Aššur – as well as my triumphal personal achievement, and I erected it, for all days to come (so that) it was to be seen by the entire country of the enemy."[192]

There are some descriptions which show a purification ritual after battle such as washing the body or weapons used. In the inscription of Yahdum-Lim, after he conquered the Mediterranean area, he performed a purification ritual: "He marched to the shore of the Sea, an unrivaled feat, and offered sacrifices to the Ocean as (befitting) his high royal rank while his troops washed themselves in the Ocean."[193] This idea of a purification ritual is one of the important motifs of the divine war in the ancient Near East.

---

190 Malamat, *ibid.*, 41.

191 *ARAB* II, 147.

192 *ANETS*, 293.

193 *Ibid.*, 556.

Chapter II
Divine War in Anatolia

1. THE CONTEXT OF DIVINE WAR

In this chapter we will deal with the divine war motif in the Hittite context which was formed by the Hattians in the second millennium BC in Anatolia. It is shown by the Hattian throne names of the Hittite rulers from Ḫattušiliš I to Šuppiluliuma II such as Ḫattušiliš, Muršiliš and Hantili, all exhibiting the Hattic sufformative *-il*, to which a Nesite theme vowel *i* has been added. The stem of these names was probably a toponym (Ḫattušiliš: *Ḫattuš* + *-il*). But the Hattians were completely assimilated into the culture of the foreign immigrants who arrived about 2000 BC in the central plateau of Asia Minor. The immigrants rose to hegemony over the plateau urban centers about 1700 BC. This new group adopted the phrase, "men of Hatti (*LÚ*$^{me\check{s}\ uru}$*Ḫatti*)" to identify themselves and their capital on the site of the old Hattian city of Ḫattuš from Neša. Since that time the term Hittite became common as a designation of the new Anatolian power of the Old and New kingdom (1700–1200 BC).[1] The Old kingdom was a state, while the New kingdom was a strong empire which had many vassals during the 14th–13th century BC.[2] The reason that the New kingdom achieved the supremacy over the enemy was probably due to the use of a new war machine, the light horse-drawn chariot, and to the diplomatic arrangement with minor buffer states.[3] The horse chariot was not a Hittite invention but was developed in a Hurrian milieu about the middle of the second millennium and its use rapidly spread through the Middle East. The superiority of the Hittites in chariot warfare lay not in their possession of this weapon (all their enemies had it too) but their variation of the basic pattern to suit their own purposes. The ultimate problem in chariot design is to reconcile speed and manoeuvrability with fire power and security. Thus a charioteer has a triple function; he had simultaneously to control his chariot, fight an offensive

---

[1] Among the ethnic groups under the name Hittite, two (the Neo-Hittites and the Hittites in the OT times) are distinguished from the second millennium Anatolian kingdom (H. A. Hoffner, *Peoples of Old Testament Times*, ed. by D. J. Wiseman, 1973, 197–200.

[2] O. R. Gurney, *The Hittites* (1952, 1962), 21–38.

[3] J. G. Macqueen, *The Hittites and their Contemporaries in Asia Minor* (1975), 96.

battle, and defend himself.[4] The diplomatic activities are shown in the various political documents and treaties with the Hittite vassals.[5] In this situation we wonder how the Hittitians understood their wars.

2. THE CONCEPT OF DIVINE WAR

1

How was divine war understood in the Anatolian context? It is observed that in the period of the Hittite kingdom the concept of divine war is clearly to be seen as a lawsuit (DI). Several times Muršiliš II and Ḫattušiliš III proclaim an imminent war as a lawsuit that ought to be decided by the Hittite gods, especially by the weather-god of Hatti, who is entreated to act as arbiter.[6] When Muršiliš II had decided to subject anew the Arzawa land which had defected, he put before the rebellious Arzawa king a formal request to submit to his overlord. When it was rejected, he declared (*KBo* III 4 obv. II 13—14):[7]

13. kinunawa eḫu nūwa zaḫḫiyauwaštati
14. nūwannaš dU BĒLĪYA DINA[M] ḫannāu

Let us fight then! May the Storm god my lord decide our lawsuit.

The same idea is attested in the autobiography of Ḫattušiliš III. Ḫattušiliš asked for his patron goddess Ishtar and the Storm god to judge their conflicts (III 71—72):[8]

71. eḫu nūwannaš dIŠTAR uruŠamuḫa dU uruNerikkaya
72. ḫanneššar ḫannanzi

Now, let Ishtar of Samuha and the Storm-god of Nerik decide our lawsuit.

When Ḫattušiliš was in conflict with Urhi-Teshub, his nephew, he asked for the judgment of the goddess Ishtar. The text (*KBo* IV 29 II 1—12) reads as follows:[9]

1. nūwaza zig LUGAL.GAL ammugmawaza LUGAL.TUR
2. nūwannaš eku ANA dU ENYA

---

[4] *Ibid.*, 98.

[5] E. F. Weidner, *Politische Dokumente aus Kleinasian*, BoSt 8/9 (1923, 1970). There are ten treaties between the Hittites and their Neighbours (— *PD*).

[6] V. Korošec, "The Warfare of Hittites from the Legal Point of View," *Iraq* 25 (1963), 164; A. Goetze, "Warfare in Asia Minor," *Iraq* 25, 126.

[7] A. Goetze, *Die Annalen des Muršiliš*, MVÄG 38 (1933, 1967), 46 (— *AM*).

[8] A. Goetze, *Ḫattušiliš*, MVÄG 29 (1925, 1967), 28—31; E. H. Sturtevant and G. Bechtel, *A Hittite Chrestomathy* (1935, 1952), 76—77 (— *Chrestomathy*); H. Otten, *Die Apologie Ḫattušiliš III*, StBoT 24 (Wiesbaden 1981), 22—23.

[9] Goetze, *Ḫattušiliš*, 48—49.

3. U ANA ^{d}IŠTAR ^{uru}Šamuḫa GAŠANYA DI-ešni
4. tiyaweni nūwaza man zig DI-ešnaza
5. šaraziš nūwa tug šarazziyaḫḫandu
6. manmawaza ammugma DI-ešnaza
7. šarazziš nūwa ammug
8. šarazziḫḫandu
9. nu ANA ^{d}IŠTAR ^{uru}Šamuḫu GAŠANYA Šu-an
10. šara eppun numu ^{d}IŠTAR ^{uru}Šamuḫa GAŠANYA
11. warriššišta nu šarazzi
12. katterraya anda maruwa[i]t

You (Urhi-Teshub) are the great king, but I am a small king. Let us go to judge before my lord, the Sun-god (^{d}U) and my lady, Ishtar of Samuha. If you prevail in the lawsuit, they will hold you. But if I rather prevail in the lawsuit, they will hold me. I raised my hand to my lady, Ishtar of Samuha and Ishtar came to me to help and she separated between the victor and defeated.

In the ritual ceremony before the battle of Muršiliš II against Kashkean, the gods of the enemy as well as the gods of the Hittites are summoned to judge this lawsuit (*KUB* IV 1). The intercessional god Zithariyas is bringing his case before all of the Hittite gods, the Sun-goddess of Arinna, the Storm-god, the patron god (^{d}LAMA) and all the gods. He appeals his case to them: "take your own case to heart, pass judgment on your own case in passing judgment on the case of Zithariyas, bolt out the Kashkean country, O gods (I 31–35)."[10] Goetze explains that the controversy which had arisen between the two parties was considered as a legal case. A lawsuit between two ordinary individuals may turn out to be too difficult for the highest court to judge so that it must be turned over to the gods to decide by ordeal. In the same way a lawsuit pending between two kings, neither one of whom concedes himself to be in the wrong, must be brought before the gods who will decide by the ordeal of war. This explains at the same time why the combattants watch out for miraculous happenings like the falling of a meteor, the collapse of a wall, etc. They may presage the stand which the gods will take.[11]

2

However, divine war is really defined by the motif of divine intervention in the historical battles. This motif was mainly concentrated in the time of the New kingdom. In the New kingdom the kings were primarily not only the military leaders of the nation but also the prominent religious men.[12] One of the oldest Hittite texts, the Anitta inscription

---

[10] *ANETS*, 354.

[11] Goetze, *Iraq* 25, 126–27.

[12] Gurney, *The Hittites*, 215.

already gives us the idea of divine intervention in battle. The text (obv 10–12) says:[13]

10. [nu ^{m}pi]tḫanaš attašmaš appan šaniya uitti
[ḫ]ullanzan hullanun ^{d}UTU-az utne
12. [kuit k]uitpat arāiš nuš ḫumandušp[at h]u[llanu]n

10. But after my father Pithana I struck down a revolt in the same year. Whenever
12. any land rebeled, I struck them all down with [help from] Šiu.

Since that time the expression "to fight with the help of god" (*ḫulla*-DINGIR) became an old formula for the annalistic writing in the New kingdom period. In the inscription of Ḫattušiliš I of 17th century we can find a similar idea of the divine help in battle. The text known as the "Acts", or "Annals" of Ḫattušiliš I exists in both Akkadian (*KBo* X 1 consists of a single one-column tablet, Akk) and Hittite (*KBo* X 2 version, the best preserved copy of a two-column tablet, Hitt).[14] The ductus of both *KBo* X 1 and X 2 shows them to be new Hittite copies of the 13th century BC.[15] This text shows us the divine war motif where the sun god helped Ḫattušiliš I in battle. The text (Akk obv 13–15 – Hitt I 27–32) says:[16]

Akkadian	Hittite
13. LUGAL.GAL Tabarna narām ^{d}UTU ana šūnišu iškunšu	27. LUGAL.GAL Tabarnaš NARĀM ^{d}UTU ^{uru}Arinna
	28. numuzakan an[da ginuwaššaš ha]l[i]š[t]a(?)
14. u qāsusu iṣbatma ina panišu irṭub alakam ana šerti ^{uru}Nenašša	29. numu kešš[arta DIB-ta/ IṢBAT ? n[ašmu ME-ya piran
	30. ḫuwaiš nu INA ^{uru}Ninašša ME-ya pāun
15. ittalak ina panišu iptatu	31. numu maḫḫan LÚ^{meš} ^{uru}Ninašša menaḫḫanda
	32. auir nu [KÁ.GAL.ḪI.A] EGIR-pa ḫeššir

[13] E. Neu, *Der Anitta-Text*, StBoT 18 (1974), 10–11. But Gurney sees that the deeds of Anitta were legendary and were later worked into the form of an apocryphal royal inscription (*ibid.*, 20).

[14] H. Otten, "Keilschrifttext, Ḫattušiliš I's Annal," *MDOG* 91 (1958), 73–84; A. Goetze, "Critical Reviews of *Keilischrifttexte aus Boghazköi* X (1960) by H. G. Güterbock and H. Otten," *JCS* 16 (1962), 24–30; F. Imparati and C. Saporetti, *Studi Classici e Orientali* 14 (1965), 40–85; H. C. Melchert, "The Acts of Ḫattušiliš I," *JNES* 37 (1978), 1–22.

[15] Melchert, *op. cit.*, 3.

[16] Imparati and Saporetti, *SCO* 14, 46, 77; Melchert, *ibid.*, 8.

13. The great king, Tabarna, beloved of the Sun-goddess, him she (goddess) put on her (lit. his) lap.
14. And she held his hand and went before him into the battle against Nenassa,
15. They (the enemies) opened up (the gates)[17] before him.

27. The great king, Tabarna, beloved of the Sun-goddess of Arinna.
28. Then the goddess herself [ ] me [to me].
29. and [she took] my hands and turn before me into the battle,
30. and I went into the battle against the city of Nenassa
31. and when the men of the city of Nenassa saw me,
32. they opened [the gates of the city].

Unfortunately the Hittite equivalent (I 28–29) of the first part (Akk obv 13–14) is lacunas. Akk obv 13 can be seen as a nominal sentence in the third person such as Akk obv 28, where the nominal sentence is certain. In Hitt I 27 Tabarna is also nominative form. In Akk obv 13 the possessive -*ŠU* (his), instead of -*ŠA* (her) is a mistake of a scribe for it would require agreement between the possessive and that which is possessed.[18] ^{uru}Arinna after ^{d}UTU in Hitt I 27 is added as a late sign.[19] The Akkadian permits restoration of the sense of Hitt I 28–29, but the precise wording is uncertain. Goetze restores the phrase "*genuwaš ḫallaššiya* – place on the knees", Hitt I 28, based on the song of Ullikumi (*KUB* XVII 7 + III 11–12).[20] Melchert suggests that the traces in Hitt I 29 point to *kešš*(*arta*) versus the *ŠU*(*it*/*az*) of KUB XXIII 31 obv 7 and that the traces before the following -*mu* look more like [*n*]*a-as* than simply *nu*-.[21] He follows the suggestions of DIB-*ta* of H. Kümmel and of *IṢBAT* of H. Hoffner, yet even it will hardly fit the space. The subject of *IṢBAT* should be third person feminine which is identified with the goddess of Arinna, in contrast to the object form -*ŠU*. In Hitt II 8 ^{d}*UTU* ^{uru}*Arinna* is consistently identified with ^{d}UTU. In any case the subject must be a solar deity. The formula "go into battle before" (*INA PANI- irṭup alākam*) is an expression of habitual action which equates to a unique Hittite formula "*piran ḫuwaiš*" in Hitt I 30.[22] From that time "*piran ḫuwā(i)*" became a very

[17] *KÁ.GAL.ḪI.A* may be inserted as object of *iptatu* = *ḫe-eššir* after H II 7, even both texts omit it (Melchert, *ibid.*, 9).

[18] Goetze, *JCS* 16, 25.

[19] Neu, *Anitta-Text*, 127–31. The female Sun-goddess of Arinna is thus far not attested in a text in old ductus. In this view the omission of ^{uru}*Arinna* and the masculine pronominal reference of A obv 13 may not be errors, but rather reflections of Hittite origin where all cases of ^{d}*UTU* referred to the male Sun-god (the Indo-European ^{d}*Šiuš*). In the later copies of H, most references to solar deity were corrected to ^{d}*UTU* ^{uru}*Arinna* (Melchert, *op. cit.*, 12, n. 25).

[20] Goetze, *JCS* 16, 25.

[21] *Op. cit.*, 8–9.

[22] von Soden, *AHw* II (M–S), 963; Melchert, *ibid.*, 9; Otten, *MDOG* 91, 79, n. 17.

common formula which expresses divine guidance in battle in the annalistic writing style.[23] At least this section shows us the fact that the goddess helped the king Ḫattušiliš I in his campaign against Nenassa. Here the Sun deity held Ḫattušiliš I's hand to defend him whereas in Akk obv 29–30 (Hitt II 8–9) "he held the hand of the enemy – Alaḫḫa which was hostile to me (Ḫattušiliš) to attack (^{d}UTU *qa[ss]u iṣṣabat* ^{uru}*Alaḫḫa ikkir-ma*)." The gods who intervened in battle were called the divine warriors in the Hittite pantheon.

In the Hittite context war was also recognized as a divine command. Mawattališ went down to the lower city by the command of his patron deity (*A-MA-AT* DINGIR^{lim}-*ŠÚ*) and took the gods of Hatti and carried them down in to the lower city (Hatt VI 75–76).[24] It seems that this idea was an influence of the Mesopotamian divine war.

3. DIVINE WARRIORS

1) Teshub

The major divine warrior in the Hittite pantheon was Teshub, the Storm-god of Hatti, sometimes called the Storm-god of Heaven (^{d}U ^{uru}Ḫatti/*nepisas* ^{d}IŠKUR).[25] He was a god of battle, like his consort, the Sun-goddess of Arinna, and was closely identified with the military fortunes of the nation.[26] He already was the supreme deity in the inscription of Anitta, but is not identified with the Sun-god (^{d}UTU). In the imperial period he was identified with the Hurrian Teshub, the Storm-god, as the Sun-goddess of Arinna to Hebat. The Storm-god Ishkur, in Akkadian Adad, is interchanged in the ideogram ^{d}U in the old and late Hittite texts.[27] He alone may represent the Hittite nation in diplomatic dealing with foreign powers. In the treaty between Šuppiluliuma, king of Hatti and Mattiwaza, king of Mitanni, the Storm-god played the main role with the Sun-god, Šamaš and other gods.[28] The Storm-god is called lord of Hatti (*bēl* ^{uru}*Ḫatti*), lord of curse (*bēl maḫîri*), and lord of help (*bēl reṣṣuti*).[29]

---

[23] Goetze, *AM*, 287,

[24] Sturtevant, *Chrestomathy*, 68–69.

[25] Neu, *Anitta-Text*, obv 57 (pp. 116–31). Anitta built three temples for three gods: Ḫalmašuit, the Storm-god, and *Šiu*. Both *Šiu* and the Storm-god in the ritual text were called king's mother and father (*KUB* XXXV 165, 21 ff) or the Sun-goddess of Arinna and the Storm-god of Hatti in the late texts.

[26] Gurney, *The Hittites*, 142.

[27] Neu, *Anitta-Text*, 116.

[28] Weidner, *PD*, no. I rev 36 ff (pp. 28 ff); no. II rev 8 ff (pp. 48 ff).

[29] *Ibid.*, no. I rev 40–41 (pp. 28–29).

In the treaty between Ḫattušiliš III and Ramses II in Egypt, in order to establish good relationships between the two countries, the Storm-god with the Sun-god (^{d}UTU) was represented as the divine protector.[30] The Storm-god is attested to as a god of many different places such as the Storm-god of Halab, the Storm-god of Nerik, and that of Šamuha and so on.[31] He is clothes in a kilt, decorated by bands of spiral and diagonal designs, held by a girdle, through which is thrust a short sword with a curved point. In the right hand he has a battle-axe with four prongs. On the front of the helmet are horns (*ANEPS* no. 38).[32] On the sculpture of the main gallery, Yazilikaya, we find a warlike picture of Teshub like a general who is leading the armies holding the sickle-sword.[33] In a stele found in Zinjirli Teshub is depicted as a divine warrior who holds a fork-shaped weapon in his left hand and a battle-axe (broken) in his right hand and a sword in his girdle.[34] In a relief at Boghazköy, Teshub holds a battle-axe with four prongs in his right hand.[35] On Hittite monuments, the Storm-god Tesshub is presented mostly as a warrior armed with a club, or mounting a war chariot.[36] In an Amarna letter which Tušratta, the king of Mittani, sent to the pharaoh Amennophis III, Teshub is described as a divine warrior who gave the enemy into my (the king of Mittani) hand.[37]. It is interesting that Teshub, the Storm-god, corresponds with that of Akkadian, Adad, and that of Syro-Palestinian, Baal as a divine warrior.

2) The Sun-Goddess of Arinna

The consort of Teshub, the Sun-goddess of Arinna was also recognized as a war goddess who supported the kings in battle or in time of national danger. Muršiliš II described that: "the Sun-goddess, my lady smote these hostile countries for me."[38] Another goddess, Ishtar who is visualized as a winged figure standing on a lion, was also recognized as a

---

30 *Ibid.*, no. VIII obv 11, 24 (pp. 114 ff); cf. *ANETS*, 202, ns. 4–5. In the Egyptian version of the Sun-god (*^{d}UTU*) became Re, the Sun-god of Egypt and the Storm-god (*^{d}Tešub*) do Seth, Egyptian Storm-god (S. Langdon and A. H. Gardiner, "The Treaty of Alliance between Ḫattušiliš king of Hittite, and the Pharaoh Ramses II of Egypt," *JEA* 6, 1920, 187).

31 Weidner, *PD*, no. I rev 42 ff (pp. 28–29).

32 Cf., *ANEPS.*, nos. 36, 178, 490.

33 Gurney, *The Hittites*, 144.

34 *Ibid.*, pl. no. 28.

35 *ANEPS*, no. 36.

36 U. Oldenburg, *The Conflict Between El and Baal in Canaanite Religion* (Leiden 1969), 64, n. 2 (— *Conflict*).

37 See no. 174 of chapter I. Cf., B. Albrektson, *History and the Gods*, CB I (Lund 1967), 39.

38 Gurney, *The Hittites*, 176.

war goddess by Ḫattušiliš III. She was a goddess who gave a weapon (gišKU) to him in the battle (*KBo* VI 29 I 12).[39] In his apology Ḫattušiliš III tells us how Ishtar enabled him always to prevail against enemies. She continued to aid him whenever he was faced with crises. When he had a conflict with his nephew about the throne, he tells of Ishtar's supports.[40] Because my lady Ishtar had previously promised me the throne, so now she visited my wife in a dream (saying): 'I am helping thy husband, and all Hattusas will turn to the side of thy husband.' Ishtar was called the lord of battle (*bēlit qablu*).[41] Besides Teshub and his consort or Ishtar, there were the minor divine warriors such as Wurunkatte (*KUB* XXVIII 6 rev 1, 3) or Wasizzil who was called UR.MAḪ which is identified with Hattic *ták-ki-ḫal* and with Sumerian UR.SAG.[42]

4. WAR CONDUCT

1) Before Battle

1

The first action before battle as seen in the Mesopotamian context is to seek the divine will with regard to the war which will be fought: divine consultation. It is expected to avoid defeat or remove any conditions offensive to the gods. It was carried out through the divination activity: to seek the oracle/omen by the diviners or priests. This is a very popular phenomenon in the ancient Near East. In the Hittite context the divine intention was sought through an oracle (*ariyašeššar*)/omen (IZKIM), or dream (*tešḫa*) by the diviners. Muršiliš II asked for the divine will in three ways in his prayers: "Either let it (divine will) be established by an omen, or let me see it in a dream or let a prophet declare it ([*nuwarat naššu* SISA]-*tarunašmawa* [*ra*]*tzakan* [*tešḫit uwallu našmawarat* lúDINGIRlim-ni]nzama me-mau)".[43] The same method of divination is attested in the story of the oracle inquiring of Saul in I Sam 28:6.

In connection with the war three types of the oracle were used to seek the divine will: KIN (lottery)-, MUŠEN (augury)- and KUŠ-oracles

[39] Goetze, *Ḫattušiliš*, 46–47.

[40] *Ibid.*, 30–33.

[41] Tallqvist, *AGE*, 337.

[42] E. Laroche, "Hattic Deities and their Epithets," *JCS* 1 (1947), 209.

[43] A. Goetze, "Die Pestgebete des Muršiliš," *KF* 1/2 (1929), 206–9. ET is *ANETS*, 394–95.

(extispicy).[44] KIN (*anniyat*) oracle is a technique to obtain the divine intention by lot. This method was not clearly known, but its origin was in central Anatolia. It was carried out by ^{sal}ŠU-GI (the old woman) from the Old kingdom. ^{sal}ŠU-GI conducted the KUŠ oracle as well as the KIN oracle in the period of the New kingdom.[45] Among the 500 KIN oracles we know, we find an example in which Muršiliš II requested knowledge of the divine will for a campaign in the territory of Kashkean, after he had destroyed some places. Muršiliš II requested nine oracles during the three days' campaign against Sunnupassi and Pittalahsi. Among them three (nos. 2, 6, 7) were favorable, while two (nos. 3, 5) were unfavorable. Unfortunately the last parts of the rest are lacunas. The text (*KUB* XXII 25 obv 19–24, 32–35) is:[46]

19. nu INA ^{uru}Nerik andan pāizzi nu URU-an uetezzi parāmazakan
20. ^{uru}Nerikkaz arḫa ariyami man kurur$^{\text{ḫi.a}}$ ḫudak RA-mi
21. manza EZEN wuruliyaš ḫudak DU-mi nu DINGIR^{lum} arḫa udaḫḫi
22. manmaza DINGIR^{lum} KI.MIN nu KIN SIG$_5$-ru pankušza ZAG-tar innarawatarra daš
23. nat LUGAL-i SUM-an INA UD 2^{kam} ^{d}MAḪ DU-^{iš} aššu ^{d}ZABABA-ya daš nat ANA LÚ^{meš} ^{uru}Ḫatti SUM-an
24. INA UD 3^{kam} DINGIR^{meš} DU-ir ME KASKAL-ya dair nukan EGIR-pa ^{giš}DAG-ti SIG$_5$

19. go into Nerik and build the city. But concerning Nerik I will
20. seek, moreover, an oracle, whether I should first strike the enemies
21. or first perform the purullii-feast and bring home the deity-
22. But if the deity is likewise, the lot-oracle should be favorable. All took correctness and strength
23. and gave them to the king. On the second day the goddess Ḫannahanna rose up. She took salvation and Zababa, and gave (them) to the people of Ḫatti.
24. On the third day the gods rose up and took a battle and a campaign. Again to the throne-*favorable.*

- -

32. ... ^{uru}Nerikkazmazakan arḫa ariyami
33. man kur[ur$^{\text{ḫi.a}}$ ḫu]dak RA-mi manza EZEN wuruliyaš ḫudak DÙ-mi
34. [manmaza DINGIR^{lum} KI.MIN] nu KIN SIG$_5$-ru LUGAL-ušza EGIR-p[a] arḫa waštul
35. ... da]s nan ANA LÚ^{meš} ^{uru}Ḫatti paiš NU.SIG$_5$

32. ... but concerning Nerik I will seek an oracle

---

[44] A. Goetze, *Kleinasian* (München 1957), 148–50; A. Kammenhuber, *Orakelpraxis, Träume und Vorzeichenschau bei den Hethitern* (Heidelberg 1976), 9–13 (– *Orakelpraxis*). Kammenhuber adds one more oracle, *MUŠEN-ḪURRI* oracle. The oracle sources: *KBo* IX 150.12 ff; XVI 53, 97; XVIII 146.1 ff (?); XXII 264 vv. I 1 ff, 14 ff; *KUB* V 1:17 + II 9 ff (see A. Ünal, *Ein Orakeltext über die Intrigen am hethitischen Hof*, 1978, 15).

[45] Kammenhuber, *Orakelpraxis.* 120.

[46] von Schuler, *Die Kaškäer*, UAVA NF 3 (1965), 176–79.

33. whether I should first strike the enemies or first perform the purullii-feast
34. [If the deity is likewise,] the lot-oracle should be favorable, but the king has outrage from behind,...
35. ...ta]ken and given them to the people of Hatti-unfavorable

The above texts show that in the favorable case (obv 19–24) the divine warriors stand with the king and army, while in the unfavorable case (obv 32–35) there is something wrong with the king, as with king Saul. Ḫattušiliš III used the KIN oracle technique for the campaign against Taptena and Hursama (*KUB* V 1 obv II 53 ff).[47]

2

The second type of divine consultation is the MUŠEN oracle which had begun to be used from the time of Muršiliš II. It was to know the divine will from the observation by the diviner of a bird flying; first, its going and coming (*pait* and *uit*), and next, its up and down pattern or meeting with other birds (lúIGI.MUŠEN or MUŠEN.DU) used in the period of the New kingdom. Sometimes it was on the fighting of two birds.[48]. *KUB* XVIII 5 II 1–11 shows a sample technique of the MUŠEN oracle.[49]

1. našta alliyaš EGIR ÍD EGIR-an [katta]
2. TUŠ-uš uit našzakan gišḫaraui eša[t)
3. nan kuitman ušgauen damaišman
4. alliyaš araḫza IṢBAT naškan EGIR Í[D]
5. EGIR-an šara aššuwaz uit nammaš pāriyawan
6. TAR-uan uit ÍD-maškan pāriyan UL araš
7. gišḫarauimaššan kuiš alliyaš ešta
8. naškan arḫa araiš našza gulzašsa
9. appa uit naškan EGIR ÍD EGIR-an šara
10. aššuwaz uit naškan ÍD-an pāriyan uit
11. nammaš páriyawan pāit

1. Behind the river an *alliya*-bird flew again
2. TUŠ-uš [downwards] and sat on a poplar tree.
3. While we were watching him, he grasped another
4. *alliya*-bird somewhere. Behind the river
5. he came upwards again with the advantage. Further,
6. he went on the other side TAR-u-an. But he did not reach the river opposite.
7. The *alliya*-bird, who was on the poplar tree,
8. flew away. (To?) *gulzaš*
9. he came back. Behind the river

---

[47] A. Ünal, *Ḫattušiliš III* I (1974), 60–61.

[48] Goetze, *Kleinasien*, 148.

[49] A. Ünal, "Zum Status der Augures bei den Hethitern," *RHA* 31 (1973), 46–47.

10. he came behind upwards with the advantage.
    Then he came opposite to the river.
11. Further he went, opposite.

Moreover, determination of an important event was interpreted with technical terms such as before and behind (*piran* – *appan*), up and down (*šara* – *katta*), this side and the other side (TAR – GUN), by the special diviners. Muršiliš II twice requested bird oracles in his 19th year campaign against Taggašta, and marched to battle at night, according to the result of the oracle. We read it (*KBo* V 8 I 17 ff):[50]

17. ...numu MUŠEN aran ḫarta
18. maḫḫanma istantanun ŠA LÚ^{meš} ^{uru}Taggaštama kuieš
19. ERIN^{meš} NARARIE anda warriššanteš ešir
20. nat arḫa parašeššir šenaḫḫaiamu namma piran
21. natta tiškir maḫḫanma ŠA KUR ^{uru}Taggašta ERIN^{meš}NARARIE
22. arḫa parašeššir ammukma IŠTU MUŠEN tarnattat namma
23. nu INA KUR ^{uru}Taggašta pāun numu ištamaššan kuit
24. ḫarkir nušmaškan namma UD.KAM-az ŠU.DIM$_4$-it EGIR-panda
25. UL pāun nu MI-az iyaḫḫat

17. an oracle-bird rose up.
18. But when I paused, – what to auxilaries
19. of Taggašta was, hurried here to help,
20. that dispensed, laid itself thus before me
21. not in ambush. But as soon as the auxilaries of the land of Taggašta
22. had dispensed, the option was again given to me from the (oracle-) bird to move on,
23. and I moved to the land of Taggašta. And because they had experienced from me
24. I moved therefore on that day in an open attack behind them
25. not this way, I marched at night.

Since the time of Muršiliš II the bird oracle was used very often for military campaigns. 184 bird oracles are known to us.[51]

3

The third type of oracle is the KUŠ (SU/TE) oracle which is to seek the divine will through the examination of the entrails of sacrificed animals. This was a very popular Mesopotamian omen style that we mentioned in the previous chapter.[52] The extispicy (literally, the observation of all the exta) is the later label rather than hepatoscopy which utilized the liver with the gall bladder. The late label – extispicy – represents a characteristic Mesopotamian development. The Hittite extispicy probably had

[50] Goetze, *AM*, 148–49.
[51] Kammenhuber, *Orakelpraxis*, 10.
[52] A. L. Oppenheim, *Ancient Mesopotamia* (1964, 1977), 213 ff.

been influenced by the Hurrian divination. In the Hittite context the liver inspection (*IŠTU* uzuNIG.GIG) first was used for the prince Kantuzzili, a brother of Šuppiluliuma I, by lúAZU (Akk *bārû*) of the Sun-god.[53] lúAZU, the earlier *bārû* rather than lúḪAL, was summoned to sacrifice a sheep and inspect its liver to determine whether the gods were favorably or unfavorably disposed toward the matter in question.[54] The MUŠEN-Ḫurri oracle which is a variation of the KUŠ oracle in the Hittite context was carried out by lúḪAL in the special magic ritual (SISKUR), through the examination of the bird's entrails. This Hurrian influenced oracle had frequently been used by Ḫattušiliš III.[55] The communication technique is devised for the deity to convey messages upon request through the medium of the body of an animal which was to be slaughtered for this purpose. The expert (*bārû*), first addresses the oracle gods, the Sun-god and the Storm-god (Šamaš and Adad in Mesopotamia), with prayers and benedictions, requesting them to "write" their message upon the entrails of the sacrificial animal. He then investigates, in traditional sequence, the animal's organs, such as the windpipe, the lungs, the liver, the gall bladder, and the coils in which the intestines are arranged, looking for deviations from the normal state, shape, and coloring. Predictions are based on atrophy, hypertrophy, displacement, special markings, and other abnormal features of the organs. An exact description was made possible by an elaborate and complicated technical terminology which referred to their normal as well as to their abnormal features with scientific accuracy.[56] At the same time two or three of the above types were used together to know clearly the divine will for the military campaign. *KBo* II 6 – *KUB* XVIII 51 is a mixture of the three above of KIN, MUŠEN and KUŠ oracles. Muršiliš II shows the use of the two combined oracles in his campaign against Kannuwara in 9th year. Muršiliš in the first person asks his field general Nuwanza to seek an oracle and the result is as follows:[57]

29. Will [it] not be determined [for you with bird] and with flesh-signs?
30. [Because] Nuwanza the great of wines, sent to me a message
31. [and wrote to me: will you not ask] the bird-message and the fortune-teller priest for me
32. [and will it] not be determined [for me with bird – and with] flesh-signs?

Among the other divination methods such as moon or stars, the oil omen is an interesting one to define the divine will for a campaign. This formula consists of protasis and apodosis like the *šumma izbu* form in

---

[53] Kammenhuber, *Orakelpraxis*, 16.
[54] *Ibid.*, 110–11.
[55] *Ibid.*, 28.
[56] Oppenheim, *Ancient Mesopotamia*, 212.
[57] Goetze, *AM*, 116 (*KBo* IV 4 II 29–30).

Mesopotamia.[58] When the diviner poured oil into a bowl of water which he held in his lap, it was done to establish the will of the deity about the campaign. The movements of the oil in the water, in relation to the surface or to the rim of the cup could portend for campaign's victory or defeat. The answer is given two ways: victory or defeat. The text (*KUB* XXXVII 198 rev 12—15) shows us as follows:[59]

12. [.........^{meš} *2 i-na imitti* 1 *i-n*]*a šumēli izziz*^{iz} *ummānī*^{i} *re-ṣi iraššī*^{ši} *manzāz ìl amēli a-na damiqti*^{ti}
13. [.........]^{meš} *2 i-na šumēli* 1 *i-na imitti izziz*^{iz} *ummān* ^{lú}*nakri re-ṣi iraššī*^{ši} *manzāz ìl amēli a-na lemutti*^{ti}
14. [.........] 2 *i-na imitti* 1 *i-na šumēli izzizū*^{meš}*-ma ša imitti ibbalkitū*^{meš} *kišitti*^{ti} *qāti-ja marṣu imât*^{at}
15. [.........^{meš}*2 i-na šumē*]*li* 1 *i-na imitti izzizū*^{meš}*-ma ša šumēli ibbalkitū*^{meš} *kišitti*^{ti} *qāt* ^{lú}*nakri marṣu iballuṭ*

12. [.........two right, one] left remaining :: my army is preserved by a helper; the place of the protective god concerning good.
13. [.........].. two left, one right remaining :: the army of the enemy is preserved by a helper; the place of the protective god concerning evil.
14. [.........] two right, one left remaining and then it crosses over to the right side :: my hand spoil; the sick will die.
15. [......... two lef]t, one right remaining and then it crosses over to the left side :: the hand spoil of my enemy; the sick will recover.

The idea of hand spoil (*kišitti qāti*) in lines 14—15 is also attested in the Egyptian and the Biblical contexts.

4

Another technique of the divine consultation was divine revelation by means of a dream. When the enemy Armadatt and others, especially his brother Muwatalli, brought malice against Ḫattušiliš III, the divine warrior, Ishtar appeared in Ḫattušiliš' dream and said to him (I 37—38):[60] "Shall I abandon you to a (hostile) deity? Fear not (*DINGIR*^{lim}*-ni-wa-at-ta am-mu-uk tar-na-aḫ-ḫi nu-wa li-e na-aḫ-ti*)." Ishtar also appeared in the dream of Ḫattušiliš' wife and encouraged her (IV 9—15):[61]

9. ...ANA ^{lú}MU.DI.KA-wa ammug
10. piran ḫuiyami nūwazakan ^{uru}KUBABBAR-aš ḫumanza
11. IŠ.TU ŠA ^{lú}MU.DI.KA neiari šallanununwaran
12. kuit ammug nūwaran ḫuwappi DI-ešni ḫuwappi

[58] Cf., E. Leichty, *The Omen Series Šumma Izbu*, Texts from Cuneiform Sources 4 (1970).
[59] G. Pettinato, *Die Ölwahrsagung bei den Babyloniern* I, Studi Semitici 21 (1966), 95—99.
[60] Sturtevant, *Chrestomathy*, 66—67; Goetze, *Ḫattušiliš*, 10—11; Otten, *StBoT* 24, 6—7.
[61] Sturtevant, *Chrestomathy*, 78—79; Goetze, *Ḫattušiliš*, 30—31; Otten, *StBoT* 24, 24—25.

13. DINGIR^{lim}-ni UL para UL kuwapikki tarnaḫḫun
14. kinunaiawaran karapmi nūwaran ANA ^{d}UTU ^{uru}PU-na
15. AŠ.SUM ^{lú}SANGA.UTTIM tittanumi...

I shall march before your husband. And all Hattusas shall be led with your husband. Since I thought highly of him, I did not — no, not ever — abandon him to the hostile trial, the hostile deity. Now also I will exalt him, and make him priest of the Sun-goddess of Arinna. Do you also make me, Ishtar, (your) patron deity?

Up to now, other divination techniques for military campaigns are not known to us. Through the oracle/omen or dream, thus, the Hittites believed that the divine intention for their campaigns was given to them, favorable or unfavorable. In a favorable case fighting against the enemy means to follow the god's will and to participate in the war in which the god himself fights against the enemy. The soldiers need a solemn attitude toward the gods who stand beside the soldiers.

This attitude is expressed in the ritual activities to reaffirm the divine will and to purify the body and soul of the soldiers. The soldier's mind is strengthened through a ritual activity before battle. The necessary ritual was the purification ritual. Not only the king himself, but also the army had to be ritually clean. The army had to march through a gate erected from sticks of wood and between two halves of a sacrificed prisioner. One believed that the contamination which had made the army unfit to conquer the army could not pass such an obstacle and thus was left behind.[62] *KUB* IV 1 shows a ritual undertaken before battle at the boundary of the enemy by Šuppiluliuma I when he conducted a military campaign against Kashkean. First they sacrificed one sheep to all the gods and one sheep to Zithariyas, the intercessional god. They request his intercession to all the gods of Zithariyas, then they speak as follows (I 11—16):[63]

See! Zithariya is appealing to all the gods. The sanctuaries which had long been assigned to Zithariyas' worship, the countries which have fallen into turmoil, in all of them they would celebrate great festivals for him. But now the Kashkears have taken them. The Kashkears have begun war.

Then they appeal to all the gods about the plundering that Kashkean did: "The sanctuaries have been taken away by Kashkean not from Zithariyas alone, they have been taken away from all your gods, all of you; from the Sun-goddess of Arinna, from the Storm-god of Nerik, from the Storm-god and so on." Thus they are expecting a judgment to be passed on their lawsuit by their gods who are entreated to act as arbiters. The priest brings a sacrifice to the Hittite gods, the Storm-god of the army and the warrior-god (Wurunkatte). They give them to drink as much as they think fitting. They return to the army and go to battle in this condition.

---

[62] Goetze, *Iraq* 25, 129.

[63] von Schuler, *Die Kaškäer*, 168; *ANETS*, 354.

5

The last stage of the preparatory ritual activity was the soldier's oath. The soldiers swear to fight with their heart and soul for the king and for the gods in the ceremony. It is an oath before the gods. It anyone breaks these oaths, he betrays the king of the Hatti land, and turns his eyes in hostile fashion upon the Hatti land; certain punishment should be given to him just as the gods of the oath bound the hands and feet of the army of the Arzawa country (the enemy) and made them unable to move. Here is a sample text (*KBo* VI 34 II 19–30).[64]

> He places malt (and) malt loaf in their hands, they crush them and he speaks as follows: "Just as they grind this malt loaf between mill stones, mix it with water, bake it and break it up — whoever breaks these oaths and does evil to the king (and) the queen, the princes (and) to the Hatti land, let these oaths seize him! Let them grind their bones in the same way! Let him soak in the same way! Let him be broken up in the same way! Let a cruel fate be his lot!" The men declare: "So be it!"

Besides the standing army, according to the size and importance of the campaign or battle, the army could be mustered, and the vassals, under the treaties they had concluded, also had to furnish their levies. In this way, quite sizable armies could be mustered. When the Hittite-Egyptian war took place, one has calculated that the Hittites gathered about 30,000 men from all over their empire and concentrated them in Northern Syria. We hear that king Kargamish in preparation for his operation marched contingents through the Tsurus to join his brother. These marches covered long distances, but this seems to have been nothing unusual.[65]

6

In connection with the motif of war preparation it may be suggested that the leadership of the kings as war commanders was endowed by the divine warriors. The kings as war commanders were predestinated by gods from before birth in the Mesopotamian and Egyptian contexts. But in the Hittite context this idea is not attested. We find only the idea of post-destination which is guaranteed by divine warriors after birth. In his apology Ḫattušiliš III tells us of his endowment by Ishtar. Ishtar took his hand and guided him by her divine power (*para ḫandandatar*). Ḫattušiliš wrote in the first person (I 5) as follows:[66]

> ŠA ^{d}IŠTAR para ḫandandatar memaḫḫi
> I tell Ishtar's divine power; let humankind hear it.

---

[64] N. Oettinger, *The Militarischen Eide*, *StBoT* 22, ET by Goetze (1976), 10; *ANETS*, 353.

[65] Goetze, *Iraq* 25, 127; *id.*, *Kleinasien*, 125.

[66] Sturtevant, *Chrestomathy*, 64–65; Goetze, *Ḫattušiliš*, 7–8, 52 ff; Otten, *StBoT* 24, 4–5.

Muršiliš II testified that in the battle the Storm-god showed his divine power to him (*nuẓa* ^dU NIR.GÁL ENYA *para ḫandandātar tekkuššanut*).[67] The meaning and connotations of *para ḫandandātar* (short form, *ḫandātar*) have been the focus of many lexical studies rivalling the attention given to the Sumerian ME. It means divine power usually displayed as an outpouring of grace to strengthen, deliver, or encourage its recipient. Goetze defines it as "schicksalbestimmende Kraft der Götter or göttliches Walten."[68] It comprises a fundamental quality of deities which distinguishes them from humans,[69] as the war leaders in the Bible were led by the spirit of Yahweh. Thus the above passage shows us that human war commanders were led by the divine power in battle.

An accompanying element with the leadership of the war commander is divine favor. All the war leaders always get the favor of their patron deities. In the Mesopotamian context this element was very common. Later it was given to kings as a royal title. In the Egyptian context kings tell about the divine favor given to them: "I (Ahmose) let you know what favors came to me".[70] In the Hittite context the divine favor was the same as with others. The king, Šuppiluliuma as a warrior of the land of Hittite was one who got the favor of the Storm-god (*narām*, Akk).[71] After Muršiliš gave his son, Ḫattušiliš III to Ishtar's service, his fortune began to change. He saw *lulu* at her hand. This non-Hittite word is explained by Friedrich as good, prosperity, or Gedeihen.[72] Ḫattušiliš wrote, "I got the divine favor of Ishtar." At the same time when he obtained divine favor and his brother's favor, the people envied him. The text (I 28−32):[73]

28. ...numu ^dIŠTAR GAŠANYA kuit
29. kaniššan ḫarta ŠEŠYA-iamu ^mNIR.GÁL-iš
30. aššu ḫarta numukan GIM-an UN^{meš}-annanza
31. ŠA ^dIŠTAR GAŠANYA kaniššuwar ŠA ŠEŠYA-ia
32. aššulan auir numu aršanir

Now because My Lady Ishtar had favored me and my brother Muwattallis was well disposed toward me, when people saw My Lady Ishtar's favor toward me and my brother's kindness, they envied me.

Here the word for divine favor, *kaniššuwar* is parallel to the word for human kindness, *aššul* (SILIM-ul). Yet sometimes the parallelism of the two words is interchanged. *Aššul* is used for divine favor (ŠÁ DINGIR^{lim}

---

[67] Goetze, *AM*, *KBo* III 4, II 16 (p. 46, 305).

[68] Goetze, *Ḫattušiliš*, 53.

[69] H. Wolf, *The Apology of Ḫattušiliš Compared with the Analogy of* ... (1967), 34 (− *The Apology of Ḫattušiliš*).

[70] M. Lichtheim, *Ancient Egyptian Literature* II (1976), 12 (− *AEL*).

[71] Weidner, *PD*, no. I obv 1 (pp. 2−3).

[72] Goetze, *Ḫattušiliš*, obv I 20 (pp. 8−9, 60).

[73] Goetze, *Ḫattušiliš*, 8−9; Sturtevant, *Chrestomathy*, 66−67; Otten, *StBoT* 24, 6−7.

aššulm, III 55) or for divine and human favor (ŠÁ ^{d}IŠTAR Ú ŠÁ ŠEŠYA-ia aššul, II 75). *Kaniššuwar* is used for human favor (ŠÁ ABĪYA-iamu Ú ŠÁ ŠEŠYA kaniššuwar pēsta, *KUB* VI 29 I 12–13).[74] These words, para ḫandandatar, kanniššuwar or aššul are expressions to indicate a certain divine quality which gods gave to human war commanders. When the divine spirit and favor leave them, they lose their quality as war leaders and are defeated by the enemy.

2) Battle

1

According to the favorable divine signs and confidence, a campaign beings. Whenever the armies marched to the land of the enemy, Ishtar or other divine warriors marched with the armies to supply the necessary vigour and led them in safety. In the acts of Ḫattušiliš I the Sun-goddess of Arinna marched before him (Hitt I 29 = Akk obv 14).[75] Here the Hittite phrase, "[*n*]*a-aš-mu MÈ-ya piran ḫuwāiš* she/god went before me in my battle)," is parallel to the Akkadian, "*ina pani-šu irṭup alākam.*" In the Hittite version *mu*, the object of *piran* is changed into the Akkadian -*ŠU* (his). This vanguard motif is attested in the treaty between Mattiwaza, king of Mitanni and Šuppiluliuma I, king of Hittite (1350 BC). Šuppiluliuma told Mittiwaza as follows:[76]

ù ilânî^{pl} šá šarri rabî šar mat [^{al}H]a-at-ti it-tal-ku a-na pa- ni-ni

Then the gods of the great king, the king of the land of Hatti, went before us.

Here Šuppiluliuma promises to Mattiwaza, a vassal king who begs for help from the threat of the enemy, that the gods of the Hittites as well as he and his vassals, will help Mattiwaza, and sends him off, newly equipped for battle and accompanied by another royal vassal. The expression, *piran ḫuwāi-*, to go before (in battle), is a typical Hittite formula to indicate divine help. The formula is the favorite expression of Muršiliš II in his writings such as the annals and the acts of his father, Šuppiluliuma. Whenever his grandfather (Tudhaliya III), his father, and he encountered a fierce enemy, the Hittite gods (*piran ḫuwair* (went before) them.

In the deeds of Šuppiluliuma first Muršiliš II remembers the divine help given to his grandfather in the battle.[77]

---

[74] See Goetze, *Ḫattušiliš*, 64.

[75] Otten, *MDOG* 91, 79, n. 17.

[76] Weidner, *PD*, no. II obv 41 (p. 45).

[77] H. G. Güterbock, "The Deeds of Šuppiluliuma as Told by His Son, Muršiliš II," *JCS* 10 (1956); *BoTU* 35 XIX 10 E i 13–14 = *VAT* 7443 (p. 65); *BoTU* 34 D iv 34–39 (p. 66); F 26′–27′ (p. 67); *BoTU* 34 F iv 7′–10′ (p. 75); F iii 17′, 43′–46′ (p. 67); *BoTU* 44 + 46 i 2′–3′ (p. 108); *BoTU* 44 ii 19′–21′ (p. 111) and passim.

nu ANA ABI ABIYA DINGIR^{meš} piran ḫuwair nu
pair [ANA] KUR ^{uru}Maššа ^{uru}Kammalaya ḫarnik[ta]

The gods helped my grandfather, (so that) he went (and) destroyed the land of Mašša and Kammala.

The motif of the divine help in battle is well attested in the annalistic texts of Muršiliš.[78]

.........numu ^{d}UTU ^{uru}Arinna [GAŠANYA] ^{d}U NIR.GÁL ENYA ^{d}Meizzulaš DINGIR^{meš} ḫumanteš piran ḫuwair

And the Sun-goddess of Arinna, [my lady], the proud Weather-god, my lord, Mezzulas (and) all the gods stand by me.

Ḫattušiliš III shows the same formula to express Ishtar's guidance and help in the battle: "Then my lady Ishtar helped me and I defeated him (numu ^{d}IŠTAR GAŠANYA piran ḫuwaiš nan ḫullianum nu ŠU-an udaḫḫun)".[79]

Another formula to express divine help is *kattan tiya-* (stand by) or *appan* (EGIR-*an*) *tiya-* (stand behind.)[80] Muršiliš described how and when his father met the enemy, the gods stood by his father's side (*BoTU* 34 I 7′–9′).[81]

7′. ... nušši DINGIR^{meš} kattan tier [^{d}UTU ^{uru}TUL-na]
8′. ^{d}U ^{uru}Ḫatti ^{d}U KI.KAL.BAD ^{d}IŠTAR LÍL nu ^{l}[^{ú}KÚR]
9′. pangarit BA.BAD $^{lú.meš}$SU.DIB-anna me[kkin IṢBAT]

And the gods stood by him: [the Sun-goddess of Arinna], the Storm-god of Hatti, the Storm-god of the army, and Ishtar of the battlefield, [so that] the en[emy] died in multitudes.

In his annals Muršiliš shows the same formula of divine help (*KBo* III 4 I 25–26):[82]

nūwamu ^{d}UTU ^{uru}Arinna GAŠANYA kattan tiya nūwamukan uni araḫzenaš KUR.KUR ^{lú}KÚR piran kuenni

The Sun-goddess of Arinna, my lady came down to me and destroyed the surrounding enemy lands before me.

In connection with a god's help an interesting thing is the help of DINGIR^{meš} ABĪYA, my father's gods. In the Deeds of Šuppiluliuma

[78] Goetze, *AM*, *KBo* III 4, I 38–39 (p. 23), II 4 (p. 44), II 26 (p. 51), II 39 (p. 57) and passim.

[79] Sturtevant, *Chrestomathy*, II 24–25 (p. 71); Goetze, *Ḫattušiliš*, 16–17.

[80] *Ibid.*, IV 16 (*nu-mu ^{d}IŠTAR GAŠAN-YA EGIR-an ti-ya-at*).

[81] Güterbock, *JCS* 10, 63.

[82] Goetze, *AM*, 22–23.

Muršiliš II asserted that "the gods of my father helped the lords." The text (*BoTU* 41) is as follows (A I 26–27):[83]

ANA BĒLU^{meš} DINGIR^{meš} ABĪYA piran ḫuwair

2

Another positive formula to indicate divine help is "god gives X into my hand (*X DINGIR ŠU-i dāi-*)." In the proclamation of Telipinus the phrase is found (I 20–21):[84]

manapa LUGAL-uš ^{uru}Lawazzantiya uwanun Laḫḫas[mu
^{lú}KÚR] ešta nu ^{uru}Lawazzantiyan waggariyat nan
[DINGIR^{meš}] kiššarimi dair

When at that time I, the king, came to Lawazzantiya, Lahhas was hostile to me, and incited Lawazzantiyas to rebellion. And the gods delivered it into my hand.

Ḫattušiliš III uses the same formula to express the idea of divine help in his apology: a combination of the delivery formula and total destruction:[85]

^{lú}KÚR^{mes}-mukan $^{\text{lú.meš}}$aršanatalluš ^{d}IŠTAR GAŠANYA
ŠU-i daiš našza kattan arḫa ziennaḫḫun

Envious enemies My Lady Ishtar put into my hand;
and I destroyed them utterly.

The phrase to express divine intervention and help in battle is very commonly attested in all the ancient Near Eastern context, as well as in the Bible. Thus the above evidence shows that the Hittite kings asserted that they had the victory over their enemies with the help of their personal and later national divine warriors.

Then how did the Hittite divine warrior help the kings and army in battle? The evidence shows that the methods of divine intervention were miracles through nature and history. Muršiliš II reported in the annals of the first ten years of his reign that his army camp saw the thunder-bolt of the strong Weather-god and that this thunder-bolt destroyed the land of the cities of Arzawa and Apasa (*KBo* III 4 II 15–19):[86]

15. maḫḫanma iyaḫḫat nu GIM-an INA $^{\text{ḫur.sag}}$Lawaša arḫun
16. nuza ^{d}U NIR.GÁL ENYA para ḫandandātar tekkuššanut
17. nu ^{giš}kalmišanan šiyat nu ^{giš}kalmišanan ammel KARAŠ$^{\text{ḫi.a}}$-YA
18. uškit KUR ^{uru}Arzawayan uškit nu ^{giš}kalmišanas pait
19. nu KUR ^{uru}Arzawa GUL-aḫta ŠA ^{i}Uḫḫa-LÚ-ya ^{uru}Apašan URU-an GUL-aḫta

[83] Güterbock, *JCS* 10, 90–93. Cf., A II 3, 34.
[84] Sturtevant, *Chrestomathy*, 188–89.
[85] I 59, III 45.
[86] Goetze, *AM*, 46–47.

15. But as I marched, as I reached there to the mountain of Lagaša,
16. there the proud Weather-god, my lord, showed his divine power,
17. and he attached a thunderbolt there. And my army saw the thunderbolt,
18 the land of Arzawa also saw it, and the thunderbolt went forth there,
19. and struck the land of Arzawa, it also struck the Lhhaluis city of Apasa;

In his annal of the 27th year, Muršiliš tells how the gods seized the people of Kalasma who broke their oath, and that brother betrayed brother, friend betrayed friend, and one killed the other (*KBo* II 5 IV 12–18).[87] Muršiliš in the first person singular also tells of a miracle while pursuing Sunupassaer (*KUB* XIV 20 11–22):[88] "The proud Weather-god, my lord, stood beside me. It rained all night so that the enemy could not see the campfire of the troops. But as soon as the weather became clear in the early evening, the proud Weather-god suddenly raised the storm and brought it and it went before my troops, making them invisible to the enemy. So I arrived at the land of Malazzia and burnt and destroyed it utterly." Under this divine intervention the Hittites customarily attacked the enemy at night. The night attack is a stratagem of the divine war which had been undertaken in the Mesopotamian and Egyptian contexts. Here a brief account of a stratagem of night attack comes from the annals of Muršiliš II (*KBo* V 8 III rev 18–30):[89]

> So I turned my face in the opposite direction towards Pittaparas. But when night fell, I turned about and advanced against Pitaggatallis. I marched the whole night through, and daybreak found me on the outskirts of Sapidduwa. And as soon as the sun rose I advanced to battle against him; and those 9,000 men whom Pitaggatallis had brought with him joined battle with me, and I fought with them. And the gods stood by me, the proud Storm-god, my lord, the Sun-goddess of Arinna, my lady, the Hattian Weather-god, the Hattian KAL, the Weather-god of field camp, Ishtar of field and Jarris stands by me, I destroyed the enemy.

Then what kinds of weapons did the Hittites use in their campaigns? The main forces of the campaigns which were undertaken mainly in summer, not winter, were the foot-soldiers and the light horse-drawn chariots. Anitta speaks of 1,400 men and 40 chariots. The effectiveness of chariotry depended on its swiftness and manoeuvrability, in part also on its weight. It was operated with a crew of three: besides the chariot warrior who did the fighting, there was a separate chariot driver and a third man whose function was to cover him with a shield from hostile missiles. The chariot driver is called *kusi*, – a Hurrian word, – the third man probably *šananu*, which is likely to be Hurrian in origin too. Since the bow formed part of the chariot's standard equipment the charge of the chariot was

---

[87] *Ibid.*, 192–93.

[88] *Ibid.*, 194–95. Cf., M. C. Lind, "Paradigm of Holy War in the Old Testament," *Biblical Research* 16 (1971), 21.

[89] Gurney, *The Hittites*, 109.

preceded by a swarm of arrows.[90] The foot-soldier continued to play his part in defending and attacking. The dress in which he appears on Anatolian sculptures is probably his battle dress. The weapons used in the campaigns were given by the gods. Ḫattušiliš III tells us that he received a weapon from Ishtar of Šamuha (*KBo* VI 29 I 11–12):[91] "numu ^{d}IŠTAR ^{uru}Šamuḫa GAŠANYA ^{giš}KU pešta (Ishtar of Šamuha, my lady gave me the wooden weapon)."

3

The final action in battle is to destroy the enemies and their cities. An interesting idea is the total destruction of the conquered cities. The whole point of this idea is that the site of the defeated city is to become sacred to the gods and inaccessible to men. Anitta, the great king tells us: "My god Šiu and throne goddess Halmasuit handed the enemy over (to me), in the night and I (Anitta) took them with power and I sowed the weeds on their place *(ZÀ.AḪ.LI-an a-ni ẹ[-nu-un])*".[92] The following context in Anitta 49–51 makes it clear that the purpose of the act is to make the site sacred in the double sense of this word: "sacred" to the gods, but "accursed" (off limits) to men. In Anitta 20 ff it is stated explicitly that a city is handed over to the Storm-god and that no one is to settle there again, as in the case of Jericho (Josh 6:21–27).[93] In his acts Ḫattušiliš I continually emphasizes the same idea, the destruction of the conquered cities. The city of Ulluma was razed to the ground as in the Anitta text. We see the evidence in Hitt I 36–37 = Akk obv 17:[94]

Hitt 36. nu KUR$^{\text{[u]ru}}$Ulman ḫarninkun nuššikan pidišši
37. [$^{\text{gi]š}}$SAR šunniyanun
Akk 17. ^{uru}Ullumma uḫalliqšuma ini qaqqarišu Ú.ḪUL ida arraššu

I destroyed utterly the land of Ulma and he (Akk) sowed weeds in its ground.

In Akk obv 17 it is better to emend *Ú.UL* as Ú.ḪUL (vile grass) rather than the negative sense. For in Hitt I 37 ^{giš}SAR can be related with Ú in A obv 17.[95] It was dedicated as pasture to the bulls drawing the Storm-god's chariot. A solemn curse was inflicted upon anybody who resettled such towns and thereby withdrew them from the god's use. But it is a curious fact that Ḫattusa itself had been subject to such treatment by

[90] Goetze, *Iraq* 25, 125.
[91] Goetze, *Ḫattušiliš*, 46–47.
[92] Rev 46–48 (p. 12–13).
[93] Melchert, *JNES* 37, 10.
[94] Imparati and Saporetti, *SCO* 14, 46, 78.
[95] Melchert, *JNES* 37, 10.

Anitta of Kuššar; nevertheless, it had been rebuilt and in fact became the capital of the prosperous Hittite empire.[96]

Moreover, the city of Haššuwa was completely plundered (Akk obv 35 ff).[97] So Ḫattušiliš I heaped dust upon it (Haššuwa). The same phrase is also attested in Hitt II 51–52: "I heaped dust upon them (*tiyanun nu-šamas SAḪAR.HI.A-is*)."[98] The climax of Ḫattušiliš' total destruction is embodied in his order that the king of Ḫaḫḫu be yoked to a cart (LUGAL ŠA uruḫaḫḫ i ANA gišMAR.GID.DA tūri[yanun]).[99] This predatory attitude toward an enemy was loyalty to the gods who gave the order to attack an enemy and was also consecration to them. But the idea of total destruction, as Gurney observed, is not attested in the Assyrian annals. There is complete absence of that lust for torture and cruelty which characterizes the annals of the Assyrian kings in their victories.[100] Muršiliš II like Ḫattušiliš I consecrated the territory of the conquered city of Timnuhala to the Weather-god, so that no man should dwell there any more. The text (*KUB* XIX 37 = 2 *BoTU* 60) tells us:[101]

15. [nammamu] uruTimmuḫalaš kuit kappilalliš ešta
16. [nammaš] arpuwan AŠRU nukan uruTimmuḫalan
17. [ANA d]U ENYA šippandaḫḫun nan šuppiyaḫḫun
18. [nušš]i ZAGmeš-uš teḫḫun nanzan DUMU AMILUTI
19. [U]L kuiški ešari

15. Because [further] Timmuḫala was hateful to me,
16. [further, it is] an adversely situated place, I dedicatd Timmuḫala
17. [to the] Weather-god, my lord, and declared it to be sacrosanct.
18. [And I] established borders around it, and within them no man will
19. dwell.

In his autobiography Ḫattušiliš III characterizes the cruelty of warfare in his time by saying in a land ravaged by war it was not possible to sow corn during the next ten years. The text (II 15) reads as follows:[102] "*[ku-id-ma ŠÁ MĀT].TIM iš-tap-pa-an e-eš-ta nu-uš-ma-áš I.NA MU X KAM SE NUMUN(?) Ú.UL an-ni-eš-ki-ir* ([But in the districts] that had been cut off they did not plant seed for ten years)." Total destruction, however, was not consistent. Ḫattušiliš I did not destroy utterly in all his campaign. When he marched to the town of Saḫuitta, he did not destroy [it]. But he devastated its territory (Akk obv 2–3).

96 Goetze, *Iraq* 25, 129.

97 Korošec, *Iraq* 25, 160.

98 The ending *-iš* is either a mistake for *uš* or a late nominative plural used as an accusative (Melchert, *JNES* 37, 20).

99 H III 41–42.

100 Gurney, *The Hittites*, 115.

101 Goetze, *AM*, 168–169; Korošec, *Iraq* 25, 165, n. 62.

102 Goetze, *Ḫattušiliš*, 16–17; Sturtevant, *Chrestomathy*, 68–69.

3) Post-Battle

The kings who won the victory first brought lots of booty, consisting of cattle, sheep and other objects made of silver or gold, to the king's palace in Hattuša. When Ḫattušiliš I speaks of the booty he brought, he begins with the remark that "silver and gold (found there) had neither beginning nor end (Akk obv I 37) or that his house was full with the treasures (Akk obv I 9)."[103] But only the divine statues were spared and removed either to the temple of the Sun-goddess of Arinna, or to the temple of the Weather-god of Hatti, or some other temples. There are records that the victors, after victory, brought the divine statues which were found in the defeated countries and put them in the temples of the victor's gods.

In connection with the carrying of the divine statue, Anitta brought back his god's statue which was captured by the enemy just like the returning of the Ark in the Bible: "I, Anitta, the great king brought back the statue of our god, Šiu from Zalpuwa to Nesa (Akk obv 41–42)."[104] The carrying of the divine statues in the Mesopotamian context was understood as a divine journey from one place to another as well as a defeat. But in the Hittite context the carrying of the divine statue from the defeated country can be understood as a defeat of the gods of the conquered lands by the gods of the victorious country.

After the victory, the victors used to build a stele (ŠU) or monument to remember their victory and the praise of the divine warriors. After the battle Ḫattušiliš III asserts: "*ŠU-an wedaḫḫun*, I built a stele" (II 25, 44). The use of ŠU (Hitt *keššar*) as a victory stele or monument is more problematical. In Ugaritic and Hebrew יד can have this meaning. In I Sam 15:12 and II Sam 18:18 the יד is used as a victory stele/Zeichen. Yet, in Sumarian and Akkadian, neither ŠU nor *qātu* carries this meaning.[105] This attitude was a thanksgiving expression to their patron deities who gave the victory. This gratitude to the gods was continued to invigorate the historical battle which took place in the vicinity. But in the course of time the historical fact of the battle tended to be forgotten and it then came to be explained as the commemoration of some historic encounter. Here the perpetuation of the historical battle was transformed into the mythical elements beyond historicity in the cult. It means a ritual combat beyond historicity in order to perpetuate the victory in a historical battle. One

---

103 A obv 4–5 (from city of Zabbar), 10–12 (city of Arzawa) and passim. Cf., Korošec, *Iraq* 25, 160, n. 16.

104 Neu, *Anitta-Text*, 12–13.

105 Wolf, *The Apology of Ḫattušiliš*, 52–53.

finds a Hittite ritual combat as a good example (*KUB* XVII 35 III 9–16):[106]

9. They divide the (group of) young men into halves, and they name them.
10. One half they call "men of Ḫatti,"
11. and the other half they call "men of Maša."
12. The "men of Ḫatti" have bronze weapons, but the "men of Maša"
13. have reed weapons. And they fight.
14. And the "Men of Ḫatti" win, and a prisoner they take,
15. and to the god they devote him. And the god they pick up,
16. and into the temple they carry him home. On the postament they put (him) down.

Likewise, in a battle drama the idea of the divine war has been preserved in the mind of the people from generation to generation.

[106] C. W. Carter, *Hittite Cult-Inventories* (Unpublished Ph. D. Diss., The University of Chicago 1962), 143.

Chapter III
Divine War in Syro-Palestine

1. THE CONTEXT OF DIVINE WAR

In this land there was no strong empire that exercised the divine war throughout the whole history except the Davidic kingdom. We suppose that the Hyksos had at one time formed a strong kingdom in this land, but we know little about them. In this context the main sources are the Ugaritic materials. The principal Ugaritic sources are mythological, though not entirely so.[1] The sources we see are historical sources in which god(s) is said to participate on the battlefield. At the same time, to be relevant, the war should be a war between man and man in which god destroys the enemy; the enemy should be historical, not a war between god and god(s). Many scholars believe that the Krt epic has at least a historical core or background, but this is not without doubt.[2] In this epic it is clear that the god El, father of the gods and head of the Ugaritic pantheon, helped the king Krt to regain his kingship through El's definite support. After the destruction of Krt's family and kingdom, El came to Krt in a dream and gave him instructions about a military campaign to get a wife: ritual activities, muster of armies, gathering of supplies and way of march. These motifs of a military campaign have much in common with what we have discussed in the previous chapters.

The same text shows that at sunrise on the fifth day Krt went to the border of Udam, tarried at the city and encamped at the town (*grnn ʿrm šrm pdrm*).[3] But before the attack of Krt, Pabil, the king of Udam, sent a message to Krt through his messengers and asked Krt to take a peace-

---

[1] Besides *Krt* and *Aqhat* epics among Ugaritic sources there are some religious (C. H. Gordon, *The Ugaritic Textbook*, AnOr 38, Rome 1965, *UT* 1, 2, 5, 9, 17, 19, 107), diplomatic (*UT* 118) and Administrative texts (*UT* 108, 110, 301, 307, 324, 400), as well as epistles (*UT* 18, 26, 32, 54, 89, 95, 101, 117) and inventories (*UT* 12, 92).

[2] Albright, Ginsberg, Gray and Beyerlin have admitted a historical nucleus behind the *Krt* epic and the existence of a dynasty, in all probability the dynasty of Ugarit. But how much may be fact and how much fiction can hardly be determined in the present state of knowledge; neither the name of *Krt* nor that of king Pabil occurs in any historical texts (J. C. L. Gibson, *Canaanite Myths and Legends* by G. R. Driver, OTS 3, Edinburgh 1978, 23 – CML).

[3] Gibson, *CML*, 14:212–13.

offering and not to besiege Udam (14:249–261). Thus it is thought that the proposed battle between Krt and Pabil was not in fact actualized, and there are no further references to El's intervention beyond the dream. Because the battle did not occur, there is no evidence to determine whether the motif of divine intervention was used in a way similar to the Mesopotamian sources. Thus it is considered that the Krt campaign was completed through diplomatic channels and that Krt finally took Huray, the first-born of Pabil, as his wife without an actual battle.

In the Aqht epic there is also not attested the motif of divine war in which a god helps Aqht in the historical battle. The epic deals only with the conflict between Anat and Aqht.[4] On this point, we have to remember one thing in particular, namely, the relationship between myth and epic. Myth and epic are not clearly distinguished but both are correlative. In epic, a historical fact is shaped by inherited mythic patterns and language, so that an epic has a vertical dimension in addition to its horizontal-historical dimension. In this sense, one must be aware of the possible mythological use of history as well as of the historical use of myth.[5] In this process, the historical narrative becomes a myth in the technical meaning of a ritual text, but this inevitably means that its historical character is diluted.[6] So on this ground one can use the mythical texts of Ugarit, such as the Anat and Baal cycle (AB), as supplementary sources for our discussion.

That the AB cycle is mythological does not mean that Baal or Anat had never been participants in the human conflict or in the historical war. The new Ugaritic text RS 24, 266 shows the possible intervention of Baal in the historical conflict: "If a strong one attacks your gate, a warrior your walls, raise your eyes to Baal (praying), O Baal, please drive away the strong one from our gate, the warrior from our walls... and Baal will hear your prayer. He will drive away the strong one from your gate, the warrior from your walls."[7] Moreover, it is interesting that in the Egyptian sources Baal under the name of Seth was involved in the historical wars. We should not overlook the fact that the Canaanite religion and culture were

---

[4] Gordon has at various times described *Aqht* as an 'epic', in 1941 (*The Living Past*, NY 1941, 154), a 'saga', in 1943 (*The Loves and Wars of Baal and Anat*, NY 1943, 33–34), or a 'legend', in 1965 (*UT* 290), while Ginsberg has called it a 'tale' or an 'epic' (*ANETS*, 149), and 'myth' in 1945 ("The North Canaanite Myth of Anat and Aqhat," *BASOR* 97, 1945, 3–10), see C. Conray, "Hebrew Epic: Historical Note and Critical Reflections," *Biblica* 61 (1980), 23, ns. 91–94.

[5] J. J. M. Roberts, "Myths versus History," *CBQ* 38 (1976), 13.

[6] B. Albrektson, *History and the Gods*, CB 1 (1967), 117.

[7] J. C. de Moor, A Review Article of "*Divine Warrior in Early Israel*", by P. D. Miller, *UF* 7, 610.

under the continuous influence of Mesopotamia.[8] If Mesopotamian people believed that their gods led them on their historical battlefields, it is to be supposed that the Ugaritic people also believed that their gods led them on their historical battlefields. Moreover, this supposition is supported by the fact, that the Ugaritic and Akkadian literary traditions have a common origin. Recently Y. Avishur has suggested that the word-pairs common to Ugaritic and Akkadian show the Ugaritic borrowing from Akkadian.[9] In the case of the pairs common to three languages, Akkadian, Ugaritic and Hebrew, half (8) of the pairs may be natural or chance happenings, while the other half demand a genetic relationship and a common literary heritage.[10] This common literary heritage supports the view that the Ugaritic culture may be thought of as an extension of the Mesopotamian tradition.

The Ugaritic sources which we have up to now, however, give little help for our understanding of how Israel utilized the motif of divine war within the narration of a historical event. It is assumed that the motif of divine war is not the vindication of the weak, but the political propaganda of the strong, that is, the victor, as the Egyptian literature shows.[11] It is thus considered that the motif of divine war was the main focus of the heroic literature which was created in the heroic age, the formative period of the nascent national existence.[12] However, it seems that the Ugaritic kingdom had never been a strong state like the Akkadian kingdom of Sargon. Ugarit was a vassal state of the Hittite kingdom. It seems that nearly 300 Amarna letters which were sent by the Canaanite rulers in the Syro-Palestine area show that they were weak rulers as vassals of the Egyptian Pharaoh and wanted his help to protect themselves from enemies such as the ʾApiru (SA.GAZ) around the middle of the second millennium. Therefore it is seen that there was no strong kingdom that conducted the divine war until the Davidic kingdom was established on the soil of Syro-Palestine. The available sources for the historical divine war are the Moabite,[13] the Zakir,[14] and the Karatepe[15] inscriptions, and some of the Amarna letters[16] (nos. 17, 147). But these sources are later materials than

---

[8] *Ibid.*, 608.

[9] Y. Avishur, *Pairs of Words in Biblical Literature and Their Parallels in Semitic Literature of the Ancient Near East* (Unpublished Ph. D. Diss. 1974), 428–29 (Hebrew).

[10] *Ibid.*, 454–64.

[11] R. J. Williams, "Literature as a Medium of Political Propaganda in Ancient Egypt," *The Seed of Wisdom*, T. J. Meek Festschrift, 14–30.

[12] C. E. Amerding, *The Heroic Ages of Greece and Israel*: A Literary and Historical Comparison (University Microfilms, Ann Arbor, Michigan 1968), 260.

[13] J. C. L. Gibson, *Textbook of Syrian Semitic Inscriptions* I (Oxford 1971), 71–82 (– *TSSI*).

[14] *TSSI* II (1975), 6–16.

[15] *Ibid.*

[16] Mercer, *TA*, Nos. 17, 147.

those of the Davidic period, except the Amarna letters. In *EA* 147:13–15 Baal is only depicted as the Storm-god like Hadad: "... who utters his (battle) cry in the heaven, like Hadad so that the whole land shakes at his cry."[17] These common descriptions are attributed to the image of a Storm-god such as Ninurta, Teshub and Adad. In the rest of the late source we will see how the war was understood and conducted.

2. THE CONCEPT OF DIVINE WAR

In this context the concept of war was the same as in other Near Eastern contexts. In the Moabite Stone, Mesha, king of Moab, describes how he conducted his wars by the command of Chemosh, the divine warrior. Chemosh said to Mesha: go, take Nebo against Israel (line 14), or go down, fight against Hauronan (line 32). So Mesha went and fought against them and obtained the victory. In the Karatepe inscription Azitawada, king of the Adanites, describes how, according to the will of Baal and of the gods, he added horse to horse and shield to shield and army to army (ABC lines 7–8). These descriptions show that the war and armament were conducted by the command of gods. In this sense the god is the commander of the war while the king is the carrier of the divine command.

3. DIVINE WARRIORS

1) Chemosh

Chemosh in Moab like YHWH in Israel was considered as the divine warrior. He was the national god of the Moabites (Num 21:29; I K 11:7,33 etc.).[18] In the Ebla tablets, Chemosh is found as the theophoric component of proper names such as *kmsʾm or kmsʾl.*[19] In Akkadian documents, the name appears as *^{d}ka-am-mus* or as the theophoric component of proper names such as *ka-mu-su-na-ad-bi.*[20] As we mentioned above, Chemosh participated in the historical battle between Moab and Israel to help Mesha. In the case of Jahaz, Chemosh himself drove the king of Israel out before Mesha:[21] "When the king of Israel had fortified Jahaz, and occupied it,

---

[17] F. M. Cross, *Canaanite Myth and Hebrew Epic* (Cambr. Massa. 1973), 151 (– *CMHE*).

[18] Gibson, *TSSI* I, 71–82; A. H. van Zyl, *The Moabites*, POS 3 (Pretoria 1960), 180–83, 196 ff.

[19] von H.-P. Müller, "Religionsgeschichtliche Beobachtungen zu den Texten von Ebla," *ZDPV* 90/1 (1980), 10–11.

[20] B. Oded, "Chemosh", *EnJu* 5, c. 390.

[21] J. Liver, "The War of Mesha, King of Moab," *PEQ* 99 (1967), 15 ff.

Chemosh drove the king of Israel out before Mesha (lines 18–19)." Thus Mesha attributed his victories over Israel to his divine warrior Chemosh, dedicating a *bāmāh* to him at Dibon. Mesha also prescribed for him the Israelite city of Nebo and part of the spoils of the war. That Chemosh was a warrior is supported by the Greek name of the site Areopolis (Rabbath Moab), since Areo is the name of the Greek god of war (Jerome, Pl 23, col 909).[22] The passage in which Jephthah argues with the king of Ammon, "Do you not hold what Chemosh your god gives you to possess?" (Judg 11:24), alludes to Chemosh as a divine warrior. It means the Israelites regarded the god of the enemy as the subduer who throws down enemies.[23] Chemosh may be identified with Nergal, a divine warrior in Mesopotamia as in ^{d}*ka-am-mus* ^{d}*Nergal* (*CT* 24 36:66). Support for the identification may be found in the list of gods at Ugarit in which the name *kmṯ* appears next to the god *ṯṯ*, whose name suggests earth.[24] The compound Ashtar-Chemosh in line 17 may refer to the goddess Ishtar, the Akkadian divine warrior who is considered Chemosh's mate.

2) Baal and Others

It is interesting that, though Baal, Anat and Reshep do not appear in the literary sources which describe the historical battles, the three gods are depicted as divine warriors in the other Near Eastern materials outside Syro-Palestine. First, Baal is the proper name of the Storm-god as well as an appellative in Syro-Palestine. Originally he was a foreign Storm-god identified with Adad/Hadad who is one of the divine warriors of the Amorites. The earliest direct proofs of the title Baal being applied to Hadad in Syro-Palestine, date from the mid-eighteenth century BC, when the famous Adad of Aleppo was referred to as ^{d}*IM be-el Ha-la-ab*^{ki} (Adad, lord of Aleppo).[25] Baal, like Adad holding in each hand a double three-pronged fork, representing lightning, and a bow,[26] was a divine warrior. He brandishes a club in his right hand, and holds in his left hand a lance with point resting on the ground and the upper part extending upward in the form of a tree or stylized lightning. He wears a pointed cap, from which emerge two horns.[27] This representation is to be identified as F. M.

---

[22] *Op. cit.*, c. 390.

[23] Van Zyl. *The Moabites*, 181.

[24] Oded, *op. cit.*, c. 390; *UT*, glossary, 1035a.

[25] P. J. van Zijl, *Baal*, AOAT 10 (1972), 351.

[26] *ANEPS*, no. 501.

[27] *Ibid.*, no. 490.

Cross shows,[28] with the description of the victorious warrior Baal in the mythical text of Ugarit as follows:

šbʿt brqm [yr]	Seven lightning bolts [he (Baal) casts],
ṯmnt ʾiṣr rʿt	Eight magazines of thunder,
ʿṣ brq y[mn]	[He brandishes] a spear (tree) of lightning.

In the same way Baal is also identified with Teshub, the Storm-god warrior in the Hittite pantheon, holding a three-pronged fork in his left hand and a battle-axe in his right hand. Baal is depicted as a divine warrior in the inscriptions of Ramses II like Seth: "He (Ramses) seized his weapon of war; he girded his coat of mail; he was like Baal in his hour."[29] "No man is he who is among us; it is Seth great of strength, Baal in person."[30] "I (Ramses) was after them like Baal in his moment of power, I slew them without pause."[31] In the records of Syro-Palestine of Ramses III, he is portrayed as Baal: "He appears like Baal on the battlefield, or as a great power like Baal in the foreign land, or as killer of the enemies like Baal in the moment of his raging" and so on.[32]

Anat is depicted as a divine warrior in the very same way. On an Egyptian stone stele, Anat is clearly portrayed as a divine warrior. She is represented as sitting on a throne, holding a shield and spear in her left hand, wielding a battle-axe in her right hand.[33] On the lower part of another stele (Louvre C 86), Anat holds a shield and a lance in her right hand, and brandishes a club or axe with her upraised left hand.[34] Ramses III calls Anat and Ashart his shield.[35] This evidence is a striking parallel with the war-like description of Anat in the mythological texts at Ugarit. We read of Anat as a destroyer (*ʾnt hbly*):[36]

mḫšt mdd ỉlm ảr(š) ṣmt ʿgl ỉ ʿtk
mḫšt klbt ỉlm ỉšt klt bt ỉl žbb

I did destroy Arash the darling of the gods,
I did silence Atik the calf of El,

---

[28] *CMHE*, 148, no. 5; *Ugaritica* V no. 3:3b–4. Fisher and Knutson translate *ʿṣ brq* as "tree of lightning" and the symbol of Baal's spear which corresponds to the picture of Baal in Egypt (*ANETS*, 249) as the cedar tree (An Enthronement Ritual at Ugarit, *JNES* 28, 1969,. 157–59). J. C. de Moor, "Studies in the New Alphabetic Texts from Ras Shamre," *UF* I (1969), 180.

[29] Lichtheim, *AEL* II, 64.

[30] *Ibid.*, 67.

[31] *Ibid.*, 69.

[32] R. Stadelmann, *Syrisch-Palestinensische Gottheiten in Ägypten* (Leiden 1967), 40.

[33] W. Beyerlin (ed), *Near Eastern Religious Texts Relating to the Old Testament*, tr. by J. Bowden (Philadelphia 1978), 194 (– *NEROT*).

[34] *ANEPS*, no. 473.

[35] *ANETS*, 250.

[36] Gibson, *CML*, 3 D 40–43.

I did destroy Ishat the bitch of the gods,
I did make an end of Zabib the daughter of El.

In Ugarit both Baal and Anat are called *mhr bʿl mhr ʾnt* (*CTA* 22 A 7, B 8), while Baal alone is called *aliyan qrdm* (*CTA* 3 iii 11).[37]

Lastly, Reshep is considered a warrior outside Syro-Palestine. He is Amorite in origin. About fifty Egyptian stelas, ostraca, papyri, amulets and scarabs pertain directly to Reshep, about half of them (25) portray the warlike aspect of Reshep who holds a lance or mace-axe in one hand, and a shield or spear in the other, and brandishes a fenestrated axe over his head.[38] He wears a quiver-full of arrows in some cases (E 22, 39, 46). In the Egyptian context, Reshep is identified with Montu, a war god, while in the Mesopotamian context, he is identified with Nergal, a war god. He was a warrior title *ršp ṣbi* (*UT* 2004:15), and is called *bʿl ḥẓ* (the lord of arrows) in *UT* 1000:3.

These three warriors above were not limited as any particular national state gods, and were not attested in any historical battles. Rather, they seem to be the mythic-historic warriors who were known even to other cultures.

4. WAR CONDUCT

In Syro-Palestine the war conduct cannot be systematically described, because of the lack of materials. Yet we find an inquiring of the divine oracle by Zakir, king of Hamat. When Zakir was seiged by an alliance of seventeen kings, probably Bar-hadad, king of Damascus with his Northern Syrian vassals, Zakir lifted up his hand to the lord of heaven, and the lord of heaven answered him through seers and messengers in the first person as follows:[39] "Fear not, because it was I who made you king, [and I shall stand] with you, and I shall deliver you from all these kings who have forced a seige upon you." In his inscription Zakir described how he was delivered by the intervention of Baal Shamayn. Presumably, the liberation of the city had been achieved by the intervention of the Assyrian king Adad-nirari III (810–783 BC). This probably took place in 796 BC, since in this year there was an Assyrian expedition as far as in Northern Syria.[40]

---

[37] Gibson, *CML*, p. 49. The *m* of the word, *qrdm* must be seen as the enclitic *m*, because of the parallelism. Cassuto translates this phrase as "the mightiest warrior" (*The Goddess Anath*, tr. by I. Abrahams, Jerusalem 1971, 59), not "the mightiest of warriors" as the constructive (Gibson, *ibid.*).

[38] W. J. Fulco, *The Canaanite God Rešep*, AO 8 (New Haven 1976), 2–22.

[39] Gibson, *TSSI* II, no. 5, A 13–15; B 23–27.

[40] *NEROT*, 230.

We suppose that the Syro-Palestinian people also exercised other methods of divination for military activities but these are not well known to us.

In the Moabite stone, Mesha describes how, according to the command of Chemosh, he went out at night and fought against them from dawn until midday. The night attack is a military strategy of the divine war. In the Hittite context the same method is attested. But the decisive action was the divine intervention. When Zakir was besieged by enemies, the god put all these kings to flight who had set up a siege wall (line 15). In the Mesha stone Chemosh drove the enemy before Mesha (line 19). As in other Near Eastern contexts the victory was given by the gods. Mesha brought the ram of YHWH and dragged it before Chemosh (line 18). In line 12 Mesha brought Uriel, their David and dragged him before Chemosh in Karyoth (cf., I Sam 15:8,33). At the same time Mesha killed all the people and consecrated them and the city to his divine warrior Chemosh. This idea of ban is attested only here and in the Bible (see below). The war custom to build a stele after victory was a usual activity. Zakir set up a stele before the god Ilu-wer (lines 13—14). Mesha made the high place (*bāmāh*) for Chemosh in Qarhor, and built it as a sign of victory, for the god had saved him from all the kings and let him realize his desire on all his enemies (line 4).

5. ḤEREM

1

In the Syro-Palestinian context an important motif relating to divine war is *ḥerem*, "ban". Ban denotes the status of being prohibited from common use or contact either because of proscription as an abomination to god or because of consecration to god.[41] For what is distinctive in the concept of ban is the absolute prohibition of the banned objects. Anyone touching the ban thus himself becomes a devoted object and as such must be put to death, as in the story of Achan (Josh 7:16—26). The second sense agrees with the meaning of ban in the Moabite stone. Here ban means consecrated to the deity: Mesha consecrated his conquests to his divine warrior, Chemosh (lines 11—18).[42] In the Bible a field (Lev 27:21), or the first fruits (Num 18:14) or any other object could be dedicated to the Lord as ban; and such things were set aside for use by the priests (Lev 27:28; Ezek 44:29).

---

[41] M. Greenberg, "Ḥerem", *EnJu* 8, c. 344.

[42] Gibson, *TSSI* I, pp. 71—83; Liver, *PEQ* 99, 25.

The idea of ban is not attested in the ancient Near Eastern context except in the Moabite stone and in the Bible.[43] However, recently Malamat has suggested the presence of the motif of ban at eighteenth century Mari. He argues that the notion of ban is found in the expression to eat "*asakkum*" of a god or king. The violation of ban which marks certain spoils of war for the sanctuary treasury or for sacrificial offering to the deity, is summed up in the expression "to eat *asakkum*."[44] The use of the term *asakku* at Mari denotes the property belonging exclusively to divinity or royalty. But in the later sources such as the Nabataean or the early Roman such an idea of ban is found.[45]

In the Moabite stone of the ninth century (850 BC) the motif of ban is well attested. Mesha, king of Moab took Nebo, a town of Israel and then made ban as follows:[46]

16. זה ואהרג כל[ה] שבעת אלפן ג[ב]רן וגרן וגברת ו[גר]
17. ת ורחמת כי לעשתר כמש החרמתה ואקח משם א[ת (?)]
18. לי יהוה ואסחב הם לפני כמש ...

I (Mesha) slew all in it (Nebo), seven thousand men and women, both natives and alien, and female slaves; for I devoted it to Ashtar-Chemosh. I took thence the [ram] of Yahweh and dragged them before Chemosh (lines 16—18).

In the case of Ataroth we find similar passages:[47]

11. ... ואהרג את כל הע(ם (?)]
12. הקר רית לכמש ולמאב ואשב משם את אראל דודה וא(ס]
13. הבר לפני כמש בקרית

And I slew all the inhabitants of the town, as a sacrificial offering (ryt) for Chemosh and Moab. I brought back from there the lion figure of defeater and dragged it before Chemosh at Karyoth (lines 11—13).

The above evidence shows the utter destruction of the people extending only as far as in the Ai model, in which the cattle and other spoils were allowed to be taken but not the people (Josh 8:1—29). The words, **העם** and ... **כלה**, in lines 11 and 16 indicate that it does not include the animals or other spoils. Moreover, the spoils such as the lion figure of defeater or the ram of Yahweh were dragged before Chemosh to be kept as treasure in the sanctuary, as in the Jericho model in which only the metal objects:

---

[43] C. H. W. Brekelmans, *De Ḥerem in het Oude Testament* (Nijmegen 1959), 128—45. He has discussed the possible indications of Ḥerem in the Hittite, Egyptian, and Mesopotamian contexts, and in other late Roman, Celtic, Gallic and German contexts. But the answer is negative except for the Moabite stone. At Mari the idea of Ḥerem was not known, even though the similar words, *asakka akalu*, are attested (— *Ḥerem*).

[44] "The Ban in Mari and in the Bible," 41.

[45] Greenberg, "Ḥerem", c. 348; Gibson, *TSSI* I, 81.

[46] Gibson, *TSSI* I, 75—76.

[47] *Ibid.*

gold, silver, copper and iron, were allowed to be deposited in the sanctuary of Yahweh (Josh 6:1–27). The obscure word, ryt in line 11 may be rendered "a sacrificial object of devotion" as a response to god who had given the victory.[48] Thus the slaughter of the Israelites was to be regarded as an offering of Mesha's devotion to his divine warrior, Chemosh. In this respect, it is probably understood that the concept of ban means a faithful devotion to Mesha's own god, Chemosh, rather than the extermination of the Israelites. For the people of the other towns he conquered such as Medaba or Jahaz were not destroyed. Thus in this context ban is a devotional consecration to god.

In this sense it may be said that the notion of ban may be compared with that of qodesh 'holiness'. The manner in which ban (anathema) and qodesh (holiness) function as polar concepts, their objects depending entirely on one's religious perspective, is aptly put by Snaith.[49] All of those taken were devoted to Chemosh, because until their capture they had belonged to YHWH. What was qodesh to YHWH was ban to Chemosh. Contrariwise, what was qodesh to Chemosh was ban to YHWH. One god's qodesh was another god's ban. The devotees of one god, therefore, destroyed all they could capture of the other god's property, whether it was animate or inanimate. In this connection it is natural to regard the enemy as ban and his destruction as an act of devotion to god. The enemy of the Israelistes is ban, then the Israelite, too, might become ban.[50] The enemy is the devotee of his god, then the Israelites, too, might become the devotees of their god. Thus the devotee of one god is the destoyer of another god. The battle is god's battle, the enemy is god's enemy such as in the biblical context. Chemosh himself drove the king of Israel out before Mesha (line 19). In the Bible Deuteronomistic laws speak of the native of Israel's land as ban; other cases are very rare; none occurs in the wars of the period of the Judges or from the reign of David on. But even the limited ban of Deuteronomy does not seem to have been an early concept. For the laws prior to Deuteronomy do not mention such a ban.[51]

---

[48] The exact meaning of the word *ryt* is still uncertain. Gibson, following G. A. Cooke, renders it "spectacle" from the stem *ryt*. Gibson cites possible renderings (G. Ryckmans, *Ex Oriente Lux* 14, 1955–56, 81), such as "an object of satisfaction for," or "a sacrifice to appease." For the word *ryt* in the Minean inscription from northern Arabia is identified as a sacrificial offering which is offered to the gods 'Aṯtar and Wadd (*ibid.*, 79, n. 12; Liver, *PEQ* 99, 24, n. 33); Brekelmans, *Ḥerem*, 29–32.

[49] N. Snaith, *The Distinctive Ideas of the Old Testament* (London 1944), 33 (— *Distinctive Ideas*).

[50] J. Pedersen, *Israel*: Its Life and Culture, II–IV (London/Copenhagen 1947), 272; Greenberg, "Ḥerem", c. 347.

[51] Greenberg, "Ḥerem", c. 347; M. Weinfeld, "The Conquest of Canaan Land and the Native Ḥerem," *Beth Mikra* 12 (1967), 123–24. Weinfeld suggests that the original Ḥerem upon the inhabitants of Canaan was a simple religious decree (124).

2

Recently N. Gottwald has suggested an insight into the socioeconomic value of ban.[52] Criteria that applied to people captured also applied to goods captured, with necessary modification-socioeconomic selectivity. The animal booty was treated in two ways, with socioeconomic purpose: horses were destroyed because they belonged to an alien war technology and could not be profitably used by their captors, whereas oxen were kept because they nourished the free peasant cultivating and fertilizing his fields, carrying loads, and providing occasional meat. The same criterion was applied to the treatment of metals under the ban, according to their metalic value. In ancient Canaan metalic work represented a kind of key to cultural superiority. For the metals were monopolized by the central authorities. In the story of the conquest of Jericho the exemption of certain metals from the destruction is found as an example. Thus the practice of ban may be seen to be an important feature in the conduct of divine war.

However, the relationship of ban to defense war as holy war, which von Rad asserts, is still problematic. For the practice of ban is not applied to the defense war context. If the theory of defense war as holy war is correct, why ban was not practised in the period of the Judges?[53] In the Judges period the ban is already passé, mentioned only in the introduction (Judg 1:17) and conclusion (21:11).[54] Ban, frequent in Joshua but uncharacteristic of the Judges period, was originally the result of an *ad hoc* decree which was regarded as providing a proper rationale for those who participated in the battle.[55] The function of ban in the conquest period was not the purification of the faith of the Israelites. It is a later development of Deuteronomic theology during or after the time of the religious reformation of Josiah. It will be discussed in detail in the next part. As a whole, it is at least clear that in Mesha's mind ban belonged within a theological framework of the national god's punishment and salvation of his people which had been produced in the pattern of divine war.[56]

Finally, we may note the several features in which the Moabite stone parallels the biblical motifs, requiring only the substitution of Chemosh for YHWH and Moab for Israel, notwithstanding the different context:[57] a) Chemosh as the national god of Moab is a divine warrior, while YHWH as the national god of Israel is also a divine warrior. b) The defeat of

---

[52] N. Gottwald, *The Tribes of Yahweh*: A Sociology of the Religion of Liberated Israel, 1250–1050 BCE (NY 1979), 547–48.

[53] Brekelmans, *Ḥerem*, 188–89.

[54] R. G. Boling, *Judges*, AB 6A (NY 1975), 16.

[55] *Ibid.*, 58.

[56] N. Gottwald, "Holy War in Deuteronomy: Analysis and Critique," *Review and Expositor* 61 (1964), 301.

[57] *Loc cit.*

Mesha is caused by Chemosh's anger (line 5), while the victory of Israel occurs with YHWH's support. c) The victory of Mesha occurs with Chemosh's support (line 19), while the defeat of Israel is caused by YHWH's anger. d) Chemosh speaks to Mesha in exactly the same words (line 14, 32), as YHWH does to Saul or David (I Sam 23:34). e) The practice of ban occurs both on the Stone (line 17) and in the Bible (I Sam 15). f) The sanctuaries are situated at high places (*bāmôth*), and the worship of Chemosh is connected with one place in particular, qarho (line 3). g) The captives are spared to work on building projects (lines 25–26, II Sam 12:31). The Moab stone thus confirms that in the middle of the ninth century Mesha also knew the theological framework of divine war, as shown in the Bible.

Chapter IV
Divine War in Egypt

1. THE CONTEXT OF DIVINE WAR

In the previous three chapters we have dealt with the divine war motifs in the continental context of the ancient Near East: Mesopotamia, Anatolia and Syro-Palestine. We now need to study the last Near Eastern section, Egypt, in order to see the whole picture of the divine war in the ancient Near East and to compare it with the YHWH war in the Bible. By the time that the Israelites first emerged as a nation, the Egyptian civilization had reached its zenith and was already on its decline. The central position of Syro-Palestine between the great powers of Egypt and Mesopotamia rendered it vulnerable to the changing political fortunes and prey to the ambitions of its neighbouring states. It was inevitable that the Hebrews should inherit much from these older centres of culture.[1]

When did the divine war motif appear in the Egyptian context? During the earlier periods of Egyptian history there was no lack of warlike activity, but it was on a comparatively small scale; only under the New kingdom period do we meet with large scale campaigns organized on a national basis and in line with the imperialistic policy. It is generally said that from the beginning Egypt was a peaceful country and that the Egyptians never admired a military career, for the conditions under which they lived were not favorable to the development of a military nature. The main factor was the natural geographical one, the contrast between the desert and the sown land (Red and Black land). Only 3.5 percent of the modern state of Egypt is cultivatable and habitable. The remaining 96.5 percent is barren and uninhabitable desert. Today perhaps 99.5 percent of the population lives on the 3.5 percent of the land which will support a population.[2]

The main geographic factor was the physical isolation of the land of Egypt by desert. It was a natural defense against outsiders. Thus, because of the natural security from foreign invasion, in contrast to their contemporary neighbours — the Mesopotamians, the Anatolians or the Syro-

---

[1] R. J. Williams, "The Egyptians," *Peoples of OT Times*, ed. by D. J. Wiseman (Oxford 1973), 79.

[2] J. A. Wilson et al, *Before Philosophy* (Maryland 1946, 1963), 40.

Palestinians – the Egyptians were in a happy position of geographic isolation. It was necessary for them therefore to maintain a major and constant force against attack. Any potential threat could be seen at a considerable distance, and it was unlikely that anyone would penetrate Egypt with damaging force. This relative sense of security bred in the ancient Egyptian an essential optimism about his career in this world and the next.[3] Another natural factor was the Nile river. As Herodotus said, Egypt is the gift of the Nile,[4] the Nile provided the multiple richness, even though there were some challenges which arose out of the possibility of a low Nile. But in Toynbee's terms of an environmental challenge and a human response, these were problems to be met progressively. The Nile cuts north out of Africa, surmounts five rocky cataracts, and finally empties into the Mediterranean. These cataracts form Egypt's barriers against the Hamitic peoples to the south, just as effectively as the deserts and the sea restrained the Libyan (*ṯmḥw*) and Demitic peoples to the north, east, and west.[5]

Thus the ancient Egyptians began to feel that these environmental factors warranted a superior isolationism, which led to a distinction between "men", on the one hand, and Libyans or Nubians or Asiatics, on the other.[6] They thought that Egypt was a flat pancake of fertile black soil (—), whereas every foreign country consisted of corrugated ridges of red sand. The same hieroglyphic sign was used for 'foreign country' that was used for 'highland' or 'desert' (𓈉): a closely similar sign used for 'mountain' (𓈋), because the mountain ridges which fringed the Nile valley were also desert and foreign. The Egyptian pictorially grouped the foreigner with the beast of the desert and denied to the foreigner the blessings of fertility and uniformity.[7] At the same time they used to think that the land of Egypt which occupied the central place in the Libyan, Nubian and Asiatic countries, was the navel of the earth, just as the Israelites did: טבור הארץ (Judg 9:37).[8]

Nevertheless, we find the motif of divine war in the military conquest of Lower Egypt by the king of Upper Egypt, Narmer, for the formation of the united kingdom. In the upper right of the back side of the Narmer Palette (*ANETS* no. 296) it is seen that Horus, the sky god in the form of a falcon, had delivered the Northern captive from the papyrus land,

---

3 J. A. Wilson, *The Burden of Egypt* (Chicago 1951), 13; Q. Wright, *A Study of War* I (Chicago 1942), 149.

4 Wilson, *The Burden of Egypt*, 9 (Herodotus ii:5).

5 Wilson, *Before Philosophy*, 43.

6 *Ibid.*, 41.

7 *Ibid.*, 47.

8 S. Morenz, *Egyptian Religion*, ET by A. E. Keep (London 1973), 42 ff.

the Delta, to the king, Narmer.[9] O. Keel[10] and others[11] suggest that this was intended to convey the message that the falcon-god Horus has subdued the Northerners — who are designated by the head and the enlarged piece of land with the six water plants. The goddess, Hathor, a protective deity who appears as a pair of cows' heads with human faces on the top of both sides of the Narmer Palette, is also watching the warlike activities of Narmer. Moreover another factor for the divine war in this Palette is the four divine emblems which are marching to the battlefield by the four standard bearers on the top register of the front side of the Palette. The four divine emblems are the divine visible participation: two falcons (Horus), a wolf (Seth/Upwawet) and the royal placenta (Min).

In the stone relief from Sinai (Wadi Maghara), Cheops (Dyn. 4) destroys his enemy before the god Thot, lord of the foreign land.[12] In an iconographic of the temple of Pepy II (Dyn. 6) the divine participation appears in the scene of destruction of the enemies by the king as in the Narmer Palette.[13] It is clear that this motif of divine war had been preserved throughout the history of the Old and New kingdom (OK & NK) periods in the real battles, the royal cultic activities or drama.[14] Yet we do not find many graphic materials in addition to the literary.

Thus the major concern of the contemporary Egyptians was not war campaigns but abundant and eternal life. This is confirmed by the fact that the major literary compositions in the Old and Middle kingdom (MK) periods were didactic in nature: the instruction for Kagemni, that of Ptahhotep, or the autobiographies, and so on. In contrast, there are very few war descriptions in this period. For example the warlike spirit of the OK is not fully shown in the autobiography of Uni of Dyn. 6 (2300—2150 BC). The OK values were chiefly earthly success and wealth. That was the world order which the gods had given. Thus the OK became the strongest state among her neighbours. There were no great peoples in her neighbourhood to contend with, and no fertile lands within her reach to covet. When we compare the wars in the OK with those in later periods or with those of Assyria, the wars in the OK must be pronounced mere razzias, simple raids for loot or slaves, not in an imperialistic sense. As in

[9] Hallo and Simpson, *ANE*, 204—5.

[10] O. Keel, *Wirkmächtige Siegeszeichen im Alten Testament*, OBO 5 (Göttingen 1974), 55 ff (— *Siegeszeichen*).

[11] G. Steindorff and K. C. Seele, *When Egypt Ruled the East* (Chicago 1942, 1957), 117. But A. H. Gardiner sees the falcon-god Horus as the king Narmer (*Egypt of the Pharaohs*, London 1961, 1980, 404).

[12] Keel, *Siegeszeichen*, 55, pl 23.

[13] *Ibid.*, 56, pl 24.

[14] E. Hornung, *Geschichte als Fest*: Zwei Vorträge zum Geschichtsbild der Frühen Menschheit (Darmstadt 1966), 15 ff.

the OK, war in the MK continues to be little more than a series of loosely organized predatory expeditions, the records of which clearly display still little the warlike character of the Egyptian. As Egyptologists have observed, the ancient Egyptians were never experts in the art of war, even though they were great masters in making pyramids or temples.[15] They did not appear to have been as militaristic or truculent as the Assyrians or the Hittites, even though they conducted several expeditions to the East and the West, e. g. those unter Pepy II. In this period only the arrow and knife were used as war weapons, which every fighting man carried with him in great quantity.[16] The composite bow or light chariots with six spoked wheels were not used at that time, but only later in the NK period did the Egyptians adopt these from the Hittite weaponry.

From the First Intermediate period the old Egyptian feeling of security, isolation and special selection began to shake. Yet the decisive factor in the breaking of the feeling of security was the invasion of the Hyksos (*ḫ3swt*). In the beginning of the Second Intermediate period, the Hyksos, who are called the Asian conquerors, totally broke down the old Egyptian feeling of security, isolation and special election. The Hyksos invasion was a turning point in Egyptian history.[17] The prophet Neferti declared that the lack of police security permitted the Asiatic entry: "Foes have arisen in the east, and the Asiatics have come down into Egypt ... No protector will listen ... The wild beasts of the desert will drink at the rivers of Egypt and be at their ease on their banks for lack of someone to scare them away."[18] The focus of the contemporary Egyptian was the liberation from the Hyksos. From the liberation war of Kamose and Ahmose in the NK period onwards we find many literary and graphical sources of the divine war. We will concentrate on the motifs of divine war in the period of the NK: the concept of war, divine warrior and the war conduct.

2. THE CONCEPT OF DIVINE WAR

1

How was divine war understood in the Egyptian context? In the Carnarvon Tablet I, Kamose, the beloved of Amun-Re, says (1:4):[19] "my desire is to save Egypt (*ib.i r nḥm kmt*)." Therefore, according to the

---

[15] S. Curto, *The Military Art of the Ancient Egyptians*, ET by A. Coath (Turin 1971), 3 (— *The Military Art*).

[16] *Ibid.*, 5.

[17] D. B. Redford, "The Hyksos Invasion in History and Tradition," *Orientalia* 39 (1970), 1—51.

[18] Wilson, *The Burden of Egypt*, 111.

[19] A. H. Gardiner, "The Carnarvon Tablet I," *JEA* I (1916), 102.

command of Amun, he sailed down to Middle Egypt, just north of Hermopolis, in order to destroy a Hyksos vassal. He describes the situation in the first person singular (1:10):[20]

> ḫdi.n.i n nḫt.i r s3s3 ʿ3mw m wḏ Imn mty sḫrw
>
> I went north because I was strong (enough) to attack the Asiatics by the command of Amun, the just of counsels.

The complete victory soon came to Kamose. After the victory, there was a festival in Thebes. Women and men came to see him; every woman embraced her neighbour; nobody was weeping; and incense was burnt (?) to Amun in the place where it is said: "Receive good things as his hand gives the scimitar to the son of Amun, ... Kamose... (II 32–35)."[21] The above passages show that the wars against the Hyksos were carried out by the command of Amun (*wḏ Imn*) and that divine weapons were given to Kamose and as a consequence the victory was granted to him. In his annals, Thutmose III (1490–1436 BC) described his first campaign to the Asiatic countries as carried out by the command of Amun-Re the king of the gods (*Urk* IV 649:1):[22]

> mi wḏt n it.f. Imn-rʿ [ʿ3] nḫt iṯi.f
>
> According to the command of his father, mighty and victorious Amun-Re, that he conquer.

After the victory, Thutmose III tells his army that all the foreign lands are placed in this town by the command of Re (*ḫft wḏ Rʿ*) on this day (*Urk* IV 660:6). In the lists (a, c) of the Asiatic countries under the Egyptian Empire in the temple of Amun at Karnak, his victorious campaign was the result of the command of the god Amun:[23]

> m wḏyt.f tpt nt nḫt
> mi wḏt n it.f Imn sšm sw r w3wt nfrwt
>
> On his first victorious campaign, according to the command of his father Amun, who led him to the good ways.

Amunhotep II (1438–1412 BC), the son of Thutmose III, also shows us the same idea, i. e. his campaign was commanded by his god Amun:[24]

> wḏ.n.f iṯi.f t3 nb dmḏ nn nhy.f
>
> He (Amun) commanded him to conquer all lands without fail (lit. its few).

---

[20] *Ibid.*, 104; *ANETS*, 232.

[21] L. Habachi, *The Second Stela of Kamose and His Struggle against the Hyksos Ruler and His Capital*, ADAIK 8 (Glückstadt 1972), 42–43.

[22] K. Sethe, *Urkunden der 18 Dynastie* (Berlin 1927, 1961), 649:1 (— *Urk* IV); Lichtheim, *AEL* II, 30.

[23] *Urk* IV 780:8–9; *ANETS*, 242.

[24] W. Helck, *Urkunden der 18 Dynastie* 17 (Berlin 1955), 1278:4 (— *Urk* IV); Lichtheim, *AEL* II, 40.

In this sense to wage war is to carry out the divine command rather than a human command. To participate in battle is to follow the divine command. All the participants do their best to obey their divine command.

2

Moreover, war is not only the divine command, but also the prepared divine plan. Ramses II described his Kadesh battle as conducted by the plan of his divine warrior, Amun. Therefore, the king did his best for the battle, in order not to break the divine plan: [25]

> pḥ.n.i n3 ḥr sẖrw n r.k Imn bw sni.i p3y.k sẖr
>
> I arrived here according to the plan of your mind (lit. mouth), O Amun, I have not transgressed your plan!

In his inscribed monuments from Gebel Barkal, Thutmose III testifies that his victory was brought "by the plans of my father Amun-Re who commanded for me all foreign people (*m sẖrw it.i [Imn-Rʿ] wḏ n.i ḫ3styw nbw*)."[26] In *Medinet Habu* (MH) II pl 99 Ramses III leads two lines of captives, representatives of all his campaigns in the north of Egypt, to the Teban, Amun, Mut and Khonsu who stand in a shrine, and reports to them that he carried out all their plans in his expeditions (lines 13—15):[27]

> šm.i ḥr-gs tn w3t.k ii.n.i ḥr wḏ.k
> sẖrw.k nb ḥr ḫpr di.k ḥ3ḳ
>
> I went forth on the side of thy way; I have returned at thy command. All thy plans have come to completion as you have caused to plunder.

Thus in the Egyptian context the war was understood as the divine plan and command. To conduct war is to carry out the divine will. The Egyptian word, military campaign (*wḏyt*) corresponds with the word command (*wḏ*). The duty of the king is to carry out the divine commission. So the Egyptian religion never condemned war, because of its divine sanction.

This is contrasted with the modern conception of war by von Clausewitz, who defines war as "an act of violence intended to compel our opponent to fulfill our will."[28] How can we understand the contrast? In the royal inscriptions of the battle or Kadesh by Ramses II over Muwatalliš of Hittite (1296 BC), the Egyptian king asserts that he fought by the divine plan and command and obtained the victory by the divine help.

---

[25] K. A. Kitchen, *Ramesside Inscriptions* II (Oxford 1968), § 120 (— *RI*); Lichtheim, *AEL* II, 66.

[26] *Urk* IV 1237:32.

[27] *RI* V 86:13; W. F. Edgerton and J. A. Wilson, *Historical Records of Ramses III* (Chicago 1936), 104 (— *HRR*).

[28] C. von Clausewitz, *On War* (1832, 1968), 101.

But these descriptions do not reflect the exact historical scene. For from Egyptian sources, we know more about the Egyptian victory of the battle of Kadesh than we do about any others, due to the various sources which have been engraved on no less than three temple walls and also written on a papyrus, or in a proper bulletin which included comprehensive graphic descriptions engraved on temple walls. But the Hittite sources suggest that Egypt was defeated in the Kadesh battle (*KUB* XXI 17, 1:14–20).[29]

It is hard to decide to whom was really ascribed the victory of this battle. Goetze has pointed out that the Egyptian victory means that "das Heer des Ramses der drohenden Vernichtung entging und trotz starker Verluste den Rückweg antreten konnte."[30] It is also supported by the fact that the Kadesh battle inscription does not mention anything about the spoils which the pharaohs were accustomed to carry off with them after the victory. Ramses II was, in fact, successful on the tactical level but not on the strategic level, because the Egyptian aim to break through the enemy lines at Kadesh and to reconquer the last dominion of Thutmose III was thwarted. Thus, from the battle of Kadesh to the period of Ramses II, Amurr and Kinza were never part of Egyptian territory. On the historical level, however, the success could still be attributed to Ramses II, because in the peace that followed, the Hittite power declined rapidly, while the Egyptians remained strong and were able to exercise a subsequent and millenary civilising function. Therefore the description of Ramses II's victory is only partly illustrative of other contemporary battles.[31]

The concept of war as the divine lawsuit is attested in the mythical conflict between the gods Horus and Seth, in which Seth was judged guilty. But in the victory hymn over the Libyans by Merneptah, the Libyan chief was judged by the gods: the divine Ennead declared him guilty of his crimes.

3. DIVINE WARRIORS (ʿḥ3-nṯr)

Who were the gods who gave the plans and commands to the pharaohs? The initial point of the divine warrior comes from the understanding that the function of the king was the warrior (*ʿḥ3*) who subdued the enemy and the breaker of war.[32] In the Egyptian context the pharaohs were the divine incarnators. The warlike function of kings reflects the warlike function of gods. The divine warrior is reflected in the human warrior, the king. So the king's *hmhmt*, as a fighter who destroyed the

[29] A. Goetze, "Zur Schlacht von Qadeš," *OLZ* 11 (1929), 834–37.

[30] *Ibid.*, 837.

[31] Curto, *The Military Art*, 29.

[32] Hornung, *Geschichte als Fest*, 14.

enemy or one who breaks the new arrow (*ḥwj* or *dr*), makes all the enemy land tremble. In his poem concerning the Kadesh battle Ramses II was depicted as a crusher who destroyed all the lands through his fear (*nrw*) which was a unique weapon to overthrow the enemy. In *MH* II pl. 79:23 Ramses III was called the lord of terror or the lord of sword (*nb sfṯ*). In his victory hymn over the Libyans Merneptah was symbolized as the one who cast the terror of eternity (*ḥryt n nḥḥ*) in the hearts of the Libyans.

The soldiers do not protect the king but the king protects the soldiers. Kamose declared: "I never neglected (*b3g*) for my army (Karnak stele, line 25)."[33] Thutmose I was the fortress for his army (*Urk* IV 85:3). Amenophis II defended firmly his army (*ibid.*, 363:14). The army did not play a great role, especially in the royal cult or the battle drama. Only the king played the great role. Even though the king is depicted in the cult, the king is the first and only, without second, and all in all. There is no equal to him.[34] In this sense god was recognized as the warrior (*ʿḥ3wty*). Like the relationship between the army and the king, the king does not protect the god. The god fought against the enemy of the kings and gave the victory to them. Amun has called the lord of victory (*nb nḫt*). No one stands before these divine warriors. The following formulas express the incomparability of the divine warriors:[35] *nn wn mity.f* (There is no equal to him.), *nn ky ḥr ḫw.f* (There is none beside him.), *nn snnw.f* (There is no second to him.), or *nn nṯr m snt r.f* (There is no god like him).

Originally the god was bound to his district which belonged to him and in which he was worshipped. Thus, for example, the god of Memphis was Ptah and the lord of Thebes was Montu. The function of these local patron deities was usually limited to their concern for their city, and every god was, in a sense, a war god for his own region. They possessed no power beyond its limit. There were a few of them, however, who attained a more extensive sphere of influence as a result of the increase in importance of their native cities. When smaller groups amalgamated into larger cities and districts, the gods of the constituent groups amalgamated into the god of the most powerful unit in the group. If the age was warlike, one of the attributes of such a deity would be that of a war-god. But whenever the age and location were not warlike, the war attribute of the deity receded into the background. As a matter of fact, the Egyptians themselves like the Akkadians and Hittites did not develop great war-gods; those deities in their pantheon who retain their warlike attributes were Asiatic,

---

33 E. Hornung, "Zur geschichtlichen Rolle des Königs in der 18 Dynastie," *MDIK* 15 (1957), 127.

34 *Ibid.*

35 E. Otto, *Gott und Mensch* (Heidelberg 1964), 11–13; M. Görg, *Gott-König-Reden in Israel und Ägypten*, BWANT 5 (Stuttgart 1975), 101–4 (– *Gott-König*).

and were introduced during the Empire.[36] In spite of this situation Amun developed fully into the national god who intervened in national affairs during the NK period.

In the first united kingdom Horus was already recognized as a divine warrior on the Narmer Palette even though he did not have a warlike epithet. Thot, the local god, was understood by Cheops. Montu, Ramses II's patron god, was represented as the warrior who holds a bow, and "the opener of the way" is understood as the god who opened the way for troops through the enemies' land. Here we will deal with only two divine warriors in the NK period: Amun and Seth.

1) Amun-Re

Amun-Re is the combination of two gods: Amun and Re. Amun became a divine warrior in Dyn. 18 as a result of the victories of the Theban monarch. The warlike title of Amun was *ḳn*, a brave man (*Imn ḳn*).[37] He was originally a principal god of Hermopolis and was transferred from there to Karnak in Dyn. 11, so that he eventually was the local deity of Thebes, but later, when Thebes flourished, he became the national god of the NK as king of gods (*nswt nṯrw*) with the identification of Re. It is in Dyn. 6 that we find on a button the earliest cryptographic writing of Amun's name. It has been suggested that the name Min, the storm god, might have been an older form Amin and that this then would be similar enough to the name Amun to indicate that Min established himself at Thebes in the guise of Amun by the time of Dyn. 11.[38] For during the troubled times of the Second Intermediate period it was Amun of Thebes who became the divine champion of Egyptian independence; and during the Hyksos wars and the subsequent expansion of Egyptian power in Asia and Nubia, it was the favour of Amun more than any other single factor to which the kings piously attributed their victories in the field and their political and administrative successes at home. Furthermore, it was as the son of 'his father, Amun', that the pharaoh now claimed divine right to the throne.[39] At Karnak the subordination to 'Amun-Re, king of the gods', of the other prominent divinities of the Egyptian pantheon was emphasized by the construction of small temples to these deities within the precincts

---

[36] W. Helck, "Kriegsgott", *Lexikon der Ägyptologie* III/5, ed by W. Helck and W. Westendorf (Wiesbaden 1979), 788–89.

[37] *Urk* IV 34:2, 894:16, 895:2; R. O. Faulkner, *A Concise Dictionary of Middle Egyptian* (Oxford 1976), 279.

[38] G. A. Wainwright, "The Origin of Amūn," *JEA* 49 (1963), 22–23; K. Sethe, *Amun und die acht Urgötter von Hermopolis* (Berlin 1929), 22.

[39] W. C. Hayes, "Egypt: Internal Affairs from Thuthmosis I to the Death of Amenophis III," *CAH* II/1, 10a, 13.

of Amun's own vast shrine.[40] In the victory hymn of Thutmose III we can find the warlike character of Amun (line 5):[41]

3wi.i ʿwy.i ḏs.i nwḥ.i n.k st dm3.i iwntyw sty m ḏbʿ ẖ3
mḥtyw m ḥfn m sḳr-ʿnḫ di.i ḫr rḳw.k ḫr ṯbṯ.k

I stretched my own hands out and bound them for you,
I fettered Nubia's Bowmen by ten thousand thousands,
The northerners' hundred thousand captives.
I made your enemies succumb beneath your soles.

In the stele of Amunhotep III the warlike character of Amun, who gave all the foreign enemies from four directions to the king, is well depicted (lines 28–30):[42]

di.i ḥr i rsy bi3i.i n.k
di.i pẖr n.k wr Kš ẖst
ẖr inw.sn nb ḥr psḏw.sn

di.i ḥr.i r mḥty bi3i.i n.k
di.i iw.t(w) n.k ẖ3st pḥwy sṯt
ẖr inw.sn nb ḥr psḏw.sn
di.sn n.k ḏt.sn m msw.sn
sbi tw r di.t.k n.sn ṯ3w n ʿnḫ

di.i ḥr.i r imntt bi3i.i n.k
di.i iṯi.k Tḥnw nn whi.i.sn
ḳd mnnw pn ḥr rn n ḥm.i
pẖr.w gs sbty wr ḥr tkn.w r pt
grg m msw wr.w iwntyw t3-sty

di.i ḥr.i r wbn bi3i.i n.k
di.i iw.t(w) n.i ẖ3st nw Pwnt
ẖr ẖ3w nb nḏm nw ẖ3st.sn
r dbḥ ḥtpw im.f
ssn.t(w) ṯ3w n ddi.k

Turning my face to the south I did a wonder for you,
I made the chiefs of wretched Kush surround you,
Carrying all their tribute on their backs.

Turning my face to the north I did a wonder for you,
I made the countries of the ends of Asia come to you,
Carrying all their tribute on their backs.
They offer you their persons and their children,
Beseeching you to grant them breath of life.

Turning my face to the west I did a wonder for you,
I let you capture Tjehenu, they can't escape!

---

40 *Ibid.*, 14.
41 *Urk* IV 612:13–17; *AEL* II, 36.
42 *Urk* IV 1656–57; *AEL* II, 46–47.

Built is this fort and named after my majesty.
Enclosed by a great wall that reached heaven,
And settled with the princes' children of Nubia's Bowmen.

Turning my face to sunrise I did a wonder for you,
I made the lands of Punt come here to you,
With all the fragrant flowers of their lands,
To beg your peace and breathe the air you give.

At the height of the Theban power Amun formed the Theban triad with Mut and Khonsu. However, with the change of Egypt's foreign policy following the reign of Amunhotep II from one of military aggressions to one of relatively peaceful relations with the rest of the known world, Amun began to subordinate his role as a god of war and bringer of victory and to be absorbed into the fertility god more completely than ever before.[43] Moreover, in the period of Akhenaten the name of Amun was banned, and it was never permitted to remain immune. Whoever bore a name compounded with that of Amun was obligated to change it, and the king himself changed his name Amunhotep (Amun is satisfied) into Akhenaten (who is beneficial to Aten). Instead of Amun, Akhenaten began to worship the sun-god Re.

Re was the Sun-god of Heliopolis; from Dyn. 5 onward he became the national god of Heliopolis. Although one of the Hyksos rulers, Apopis, himself called the son of Re to indicate the official successor of pharaoh, it was Re who supported Kamose, who repelled Apopis. Even before the period of Akhenaten Re was one of the minor gods who controlled the Theban empire. But in the time of Akhenaten he was without equal and was entitled not only to universal, but even to the sole worship of his adherents. The other gods were nothing but different forms or manifestations of the sun-god himself. Like the position which Amun had won a century before, he had been elevated as king of the gods to be the chief divinity of the Egyptian world-empire.[44] Following Akhenaten, Dyn. 19 and 20 became the Ramesside period as influenced by the sun-god Re. Nevertheless, during Dyn. 19 and 20 the power of Amun was renewed by Ramses II and III. In the stele of Ramses II found at Beth-Shan, Amun-Re, who holds a scimitar in his right hand and a scepter of his left, says (lines 5–6):[45]

I am giving thee thy boundaries as far as thou desirest, to the frontiers of the supports of the sky. Accept for thyself a sword against all foreign countries, so that thou mayest cut off the heads of those who have rebelled against thee, thou being Horus (placed) over the Two Lands.

---

[43] Hayes, "Egypt", 14.

[44] Seele und Steindorff, *When Egypt Ruled the East*, 204.

[45] J. Černý, "Stela of Ramesses II from Beisan," *Eretz Israel* (1958), 76.

Amun-Re was called the killer of the foreigners (*sm3-ḫ3styw*),[46] ruler of all gods (*ḥk3 nṯrw nb*), lord of heaven (*nb pt*),[47] lord of gods (*nb nṯrw*),[48] or lord of scimitar (*nb ḫpš*).[49] Thus Amun-Re was, *par excellence*, the divine warrior of the new Egyptian empire in the second half of the second millennium BC.

2) Seth

Seth was a major war god of Dyn. 19 and 20. He was originally god of Ombos like Horus of Behdet or Ptah of Memphis. In the Heliopolitan Ennead he is son of Geb and Nut and brother of Osiris, whom he murders. He was the storm god. From early times he was known as the god of confusion. In *the Book of Dead* 39, in a spell to drive away Apopis, a demon, Seth is introduced as saying: "I am Seth who causes confusion and thunders in the horizon of the sky, whose heart is as (that of) the *nbḏ*."[50] From the early dynasty Seth was known as the lord of a foreign country, while Horus was lord of the home country.[51] For a short time he was even elevated to the dignity of god of state, beside Amun, Re and Ptah. But Seth's warriorship begins from the time of the Hyksos. During the Hyksos domination Seth was considered the god of the Hyksos. In the Egyptian state the Hyksos worshipped Seth (*Pap. Sallier* I 1:2—3):[52]

> Then king Apopis made him Seth as lord, and he did not serve any god who was in the palace of king Apopis. He appeared at the break of day to make the daily sacrifices of ... to Seth.

Ramses II confesses that he is the son of Seth who supported him. In his so-called peace treaty between Egypt and the Hittites at Karnak, Seth's warlike characteristic is described (line 20):[53]

> iw.i rḫ.kwi ḫrw n it.i Stḫ nḫt r t3 nb
> snḫt.n.f ḫpš.i r ḳ3 n pt 3t.i r wsḫ n t3

> I know the voice of my father Seth victorious to every land, since he has made my arm mighty to the height of heaven and my strength to the width of earth!

In the beginning of Dyn. 19 Seth was made the state god with Amun-Re by Sethos I. This is suggested by the fact that the army that set forth for

---

46 *Urk* IV 1228:1

47 W. Helck, *Die Ritualszenen auf der Umfassungsmauer Ramses II in Karnak* (Wiesbaden 1968), scenes 14, 56, 67.

48 *RI* V 47:27 (*MH* II pl 77:27).

49 *Ibid.*, 42:32 (MH I pl 46:32).

50 H. T. Velde, *Seth, God of Confusion* (Leiden 1977), 106 (— *Seth*).

51 *Ibid.*, 110 (Papyrus Sallier 4, IX:4).

52 *Ibid.*, 121.

53 M. C. Kuentz, "Stele du Marriage," *ASAE* 25 (1925), 208; *ANETS*, 257.

Palestine consisted of three divisions: that of Amun, of Re and of Seth, while it seems that in Dyn. 18 the army consisted only of the divisions of Amun, Re and Ptah, but not of Seth.[54] On the upper part of a stele found at Tell-Nebi Mendu, Sethos I is depicted as adoring Amun-Re, Seth, Montu and a goddess.[55] In the stele of the year 400 erected by Ramses II he praises Seth as follows:[56]

> 'Hail to thee, O Seth, Son of Nut, the great of Strength in the Barque of Millions,
> felling the enemy at the prow of the Barque of Re, great of battle cry ...!
> Mayest (thou) give me a good life time serving (thy) *ka*,
> while I remain in [thy favor] ...!

In the well-known Israel stele of Merneptah, Re had turned towards the Egyptians while Seth turned against the Libyans (c. 11):[57]

> ḫ3ʿ Stḫ ḥ3.f r p3y.sn wr fḫ n3y.sn wḥywt ẖr-s t-r r.f
>
> Seth turned his back upon their chief
> By his order their settlement was ruined

It is hard to imagine that during Dyn. 19 the exaltation of Seth is not Seth in his Asiatic form, but Seth of ancient Egyptian tradition.[58] For after Dyn. 20 Seth was pulled down because he was identified as a foreign god. After Ramses II, as long as Egypt had colonial interests in Syria and Palestine, this positive attitude towards Seth does not seem to have altered in essence. Seth is often mentioned on the monuments of Ramses III at Medinet Habu, as he was on the monuments of Ramses II. Thus the identification of Baal and Seth in the Egyptian context was made on the basis of a war god rather than a fertility god.[59]

But after Dyn. 20 Seth lost his warlike character and finally was treated as a demon by the Egyptians, because of the loss of authority over part of Asia, or due to a movement of nationalism as a reaction to the Assyrian invasions. It seems that no new temples were built for Seth after Dyn. 20. There is not even any evidence that the existing temples of Seth were restored. His name, which had appeared so often in the personal names of Dyn. 19 and 20 (about 53), disappears from those of the ensuing period.[60] H. T. Velde has pointed out that on the mythological level Seth is a disturber of the peace, on the cosmic level a thunder god, and on the geographical level a foreigner.[61] It may be suggested that on the political level Seth was considered as a divine warrior only during the NK period.

---

[54] Velde, *Seth*, 130.
[55] *Loc. cit.*
[56] *ANETS*, 253.
[57] *RI* IV 15:11 (Cairo).
[58] Velde, *Seth*, 122.
[59] *Ibid.*, 129.
[60] *Ibid.*, 139.
[61] *Ibid.*, 118.

4 WAR CONDUCT

1) Before Battle

As has been shown in the preceding section, war was understood as a divine plan and command. Thus the Egyptians on the battlefield did not appear to have propitiatory or oracular sites, such as was customary among other peoples like the Hittites. Yet there is a record in the Punt reliefs that the pharaoh Hatshepsut heard an oracle of Amun that the ways to Punt should be searched out, that the highways to the Myrrh-terraces should be penetrated: "I will lead the army on water and on land, to bring marvels, from god's land for this god, for the fashioner of her beauty."[62] In the Konosso inscription, Thutmose IV tells us that when he received a message reporting a revolt in Wawat, he went forth to the temple to consult the god and divine oracle was granted as follows:[63]

> Behold, his majesty, he himself petitioned in the presence of the ruler of the gods (Amun), that he might counsel him concerning the affair of his going — and learns concerning that which should happen to him; leading for him upon a goodly road to do that which his *ka* desired, as a father speaks to his son. He (Amun) produced his seed in him (the king).

We also see the god Amun, who appears in a dream and promises victory in the second campaign of Amunhotep II.

1

There are several litarary styles to express the divine oracle. The first formula is that god will put you over the head of an enemy. In *MH* II pl 101:6–9 we find the oracle of Amun:[64]

> sʿ3y.i nẖt.k di.i snḏ.k m ibw t3w H3nbw
> šʿt.k wrt m ʿt.sn iw ḥm.k sḳr .f st
> ʿwy.k dm3 m tp ẖrwy.k di.n.i tw m-ḥr tp.sn

> I magnify thy victories, and I set the fear of thee in the hearts of the lands of the Haunebut. Dread of thee is great in their limbs. Thy majesty is one who will smite them, while thy hands are clasped together upon the head of thy foes. I have set thee over their heads.

The second formula is that the god will put the enemy under one's feet. In the Libyan campaign Ramses III tells us that Amun-Re made the enemy prostrate under his feet. We read as follows (*MH* I pl 23:58):[65]

---

[62] *Urk* IV 342; J. H. Breasted, *Ancient Records of Egypt* II (Chicago 1906–7), § 285 (— *AR*).

[63] *AR* II § 827; Helck, *Übersetzung zu den Heften 17–22* (1961), 143–44 (— *Übersetzung*).

[64] *RI* V 92–93:6–9; *HRR*, 106. It also appears in *MH* I pls 13:4, 22:6, 23:57–58, 92:2. 120a–c.

[65] *RI* V 17:57–58.

Imn-rʿ it.i špssy ḥr ḥdb t3 nb ẖr rdwy.i
iw.i m nswt ḥr ẖrt.f r ḏt

Amun-Re, my august father, (makes) prostrate every land under my feet, while I am king upon (his) belongings forever.

In *MH* II pl 92:8 the enemies testify to Rameses III that "your father Amun has set us under your feet forever."

The third formula is that the god delivers the enemy into your grasp (*di.n.i x m 3mm.ḳ*). It is a common formula found in the ancient Near Eastern context. Merneptah used the formula in his victory hymn:[66]

imi sw m ḏrt Mr-n-Ptḥ ḥtp-ḥr-m3ʿt
di.f bši.f ʿm.f mi dpy

Give him into the hand of Mer-ne-Ptah Hotep-her-Mat,
that he may make him disgorge what he has swallowed, like a crocodile.

In the Ramses III inscription the same formula is attested: "He (Amun-Re) put the chief of the Meshweh into my hand (*MH* II pl 75:2)."

The last formula is that god will put the enemy under your feet and into your grasp. Amun-Re promises to Ramses III (*MH* II pl 99:4–6):[67]

di.n. [i] n.k ḳny nb nḫt nb ẖr ṯowy.k
wr nw t3 nb dmḏ m 3mm.k

I have given you all valor and all strength beneath your soles, and the chiefs of every land together in your grasp.

These oracles were conducted by the priest in the temple. The methods of divination by the priests are not as well known to us as those of Mesopotamian divination. After this divine oracle was given, the war leader receives a sword from the gods. Amun tells Ramses III, "take the sword, my son, receive you the sword, O mighty king (*MH* II pl 120 a–c)." We read that Amun had given his mighty sword to his son (*MH* I pl 17:16). The motif of receiving the divine weapon is also found in the Hittite and Mesopotamian context. At the same time the divine power, *ḳa*, like the Sumerian *me*, was granted to the pharoahs.

2

The next step is the withdrawal procession from the temple. Ramses III holding the sickle-sword and a bow, leaves the temple, after receiving his commission from Amun. The pharaoh is followed by the war-god, Montu and preceded by priests carrying four standards, those of Upwawet (the opener of the ways), of Khonsu, of Mut and of Amun.[68]

---

[66] *RI* IV 17:20; *ANETS*, 377b.
[67] *RI* V 85:4–6.
[68] Edgerton and Wilson, *HRR*, 5.

Another task is to recruit soldiers to supplement the standing army. It is usually assumed that there was no standing army during the OK, but apart from the feudal levies, there is clear evidence that the pharaohs of the MK maintained their own standing army.[69] There was also a commander of recruits (*imy-r ḥwnw nfrw*) as well as the commander of shock troops or general. During the new dispensation of the NK we meet, for the first time, a large standing army organized on a national basis and officered throughout with professional soldiers. We know that from the time of Ramses II the standing army existed on a permanent basis: the veterans when discharged even received a small holding.[70] The standing army was divided into two corps, one stationed in Upper Egypt and another in Lower Egypt. The service army consisted of chariotry and infantry. During the NK the chariot was widely used after it was brought to Egypt from Canaan (as its first appearance on Egyptian monuments and on Kassite office seals from the 16th century in Mesopotamia demonstrates).[71] The sickle sword we find as early as Dyn. 3 of Ur, but even earlier, during the second millennium, it was widely used in the entire Near East from Syria to Egypt, when it was adopted by the Egyptian army at the time of the NK, possibly together with the chariot.[72]

The infantry included two main classes of soldiers: trained soldiers (*mnf3t*/*mnfyt*) and troops of recruits (*ḥwnw nfrw*). The *mnf3t* was further distinguished into two groups: trained men and shock troops. Infantry were recruited from the tribes of Nubia, but these are not to be confused with the Medjay; for the latter term, the Nubian district of Medja, had by Dyn. 18 come to mean the armed police who patrolled the desert borders. But for the wars the local recruitment was no longer sufficient to fill up the cadres of the army. The army was divided into regiments, which consisted of 200 or 250 men under Ramses IV, and were commanded by a standardbearer in battle. The main body of the infantry was recruited by conscription carried out by the scribe of recruits (*sš nfrw*). Under Ramses III one man in ten was taken for service, temple employees being exempt. The soldiers conscripted were called *ʿnḫw nw mšʿ* (later *rmṯt ms*ʿ) in contrast to the voluntary military man (*wʿw*).[73] In the Kadesh battle, 20,000 infantrymen, consisting of the four divisions of Amun, Re, Ptah and Seth, took part against 10,000 charioteers, each chariot carrying three men, 3500 chariots and 8000 Hittite infantrymen. Curto suggests that during the NK the infantry was equipped with helmet, lance and shield, and sometimes with armour; while the brigade numbered 5000 men (1900

---

[69] R. O. Falkner, "Egyptian Military Organization," *JEA* 39 (1939), 37.

[70] Curto, *The Military Art*, 20.

[71] Y. Yadin, *The Art of Warfare in the Biblical Lands* (1963), 136 (— *Warfare*).

[72] *Ibid.*, 131.

[73] Faulkner, *JEA* 39, 45.

Egyptians and 3100 mercenaries).[74] These effective soldiers were distributed in 20 companies of 250 men; each company was divided into 5 platoons of 50 men. The decisive factor was the adopted chariot from the Hittites. The chariotry company numbered 50 elements, organized in 10 sections of 5 chariots each. Each chariot was ridden by two men, a fighting man who acted as a charioteer and a shield-bearer; the former was provided with full equipment, which was kept in the chariots' pockets: two javelins, bow and arrows for long-range combat, dagger, scimitar, mace and axe for close-range combat since the charioteers sometimes dismounted. Thus the chariotry company consisted of 100 men. To this it was added a specified number of light infantrymen equipped with javelin or bow, whose task was to defend the chariots. We have no information on the archers. The special shock troops functioned autonomously, and with all probability were composed of forces and a staff which varied from one time to the next according to the war plan. Finally, the most effective soldiers were the standard-bearers whose divisional standards consisted of a long spear with the god's effigy on top and trumpeters. The army carried with it a statute of the god whom the king worshipped in his position as chief priest.

2) Battle

1

Expeditions begin with a march towards the enemy. For example, in the year 22, during the fourth month of winter, the army of Thutmose III began to march from Egypt to Palestine. Each of the four divisions marched under the protection of a god, the patron of the town where the unit was quartered: Amun of Thebes, Re of Heliopolis, Ptah of Memphis, and Seth of Pi-Ramses in the Eastern Delta. Each division consisted of an infantry brigade, a chariotry company and archery-corps. The major general directly commanded the brigade and indirectly the chariotry and the archers.

The divine warrior preceded the king and army in their standard. When Ramses II marches towards the country of the enemy, Amun-Re says to him:[75] "Behold, I am in front of you, my son (*mk wi r-ḥ3t.k s3.i*)." The god Thoth says to him:[76] "Behold, I am behind you (*mk wi ḥ3.k*)." The divine guidance in front of (*r-ḥ3t*) or behind (*ḥ3*) the marching army was a popular idea in the ancient Near Eastern context. The gods go before the king, while the king goes before the army. In the Megiddo

[74] Curto, *The Military Art*, 16 ff.

[75] *RI* V 13:1–2 (*MH* I pl 17:1–2).

[76] *RI* V 10:1 (*MH* I pl 13:1).

battle Thutmose III says, "I shall not let my valiant army go before me from this place (line 53)." And he went before his army. The divine vanguard (*ḥ3t pr*) and rearguard (*pḥwy*) motifs were a very popular theme in the ancient Near East.

Here we find another motif of the divine presence during the way of the expedition: *Mitsein* idea.[77] In the crucial moment of the battle of Kadesh we see that Amun upholds Ramses III and exhorts him from behind (poem 126–27):[78] "I am with you, I, your father, my hand is in yours (*tw.i ḥnʿ.k ink it.k ḏrt.i m.k*)." The Pharaoh Merneptah of Dyn. 19 describes how and when he and his army went forth to overthrow the land of Libya, the hand of the god was with them; even Amun was with them as their shield.[79] The "*mitsein*" formula has also been used to indicate divine protection or blessing in the various contexts. In the Mesopotamian context *ittia ilu* or *ittia Nabu* was used as a formula to express the divine protection. This formula expresses a basic structure of the faith and thought of the ancient Near Eastern people in the second millennium BC.

Just before the beginning of battle the king, as the supreme commander in chief, gives the final encouragement. For example Thutmose III gave his final encouragement in the Megiddo battle (lines 83–84):[80]

> grg ṯn sspd ḫʿw.tn r-ntt iw tw r ṯḥn r ʿḥ3
> ḥnʿ ḫrwy pf ḫwy m dw3w ḥr-ntt tw tw...
> –
> mn ib mn ib rs rs
>
> Prepare yourselves! Make your weapons ready!
> For one will engage in combat with that wretched foe in the morning; for one...
> –
> Steadfast, Steadfast! Vigilant, Vigilant!

Ramses II raised his voice to shout to his army in the first person in the poem of the Kadesh battle (lines 169–73):[81]

> Steady, steady your hearts, my soldiers;
> Behold me victorious, me alone,
> For Anum is my helper, his hand is with me.
> How faint are your hearts, O my charioteers,
> None among you is worthy of trust!

The pharaoh used a similar phrase for his shield-bearer who feared the surrounding enemy in the midst of battle (line 215):[82] "Stand firm, steady

[77] Cf., Görg, *Gott-König*, 69; *id.*, "Ich bin mit Dir," *Theologie und Glaube* 70 (1980), 220–40.
[78] *RI* II 44:127.
[79] *AR* III § 581.
[80] *Urk* IV 656:2–5, 11–12; *AEL* II, 32.
[81] *AEL* II, 67.
[82] *Ibid.*, 68.

your heart, my shield-bearer." At the same time the gods were also ready to fight. In the war against the peoples of the sea we hear that the god himself was ready to fight for Ramses III against the enemy: "Now the heart of this god (Amun-Re), the lord of gods was prepared and ready to ensnare them (the Palestine confederates) like a bird."[83]

With the trumpet sounding the attack, the soldiers begin to fight with the enemy. We see scenes in which the bugler sounds a call to attack in *MH* I–II pls 17, 29, 62, 109, 118 and so on. The Thutmoside army and that of Ramses II, when in battle formation, consisted of first the light infantry, then the king and his guard, finally the divisions. The latter moved forward with the swarming archers in the van, behind them the infantry gathered in the middle, with the chariotry on the flanks to prevent them from being surrounded, and to be ready to come into action as soon as the enemy gave in, in order to pursue him and to turn his retreat into flight thereby taking the greatest possible advantage of that favourable situation. Under Ramses III we see that the infantry brigades were divided into three specialized corps: the lancers, the mercenaries with short lances and swords, and the veterans with heavy maces. These corps were drawn up in battle oder on three successive lines: the lancers acted as light infantry for the initial thrust, the mercenaries as heavy infantry in order to smash through the enemy lines, the mace-bearers as reserves.

2

With the beginning of the battle, the gods begin to intervene directly or indirectly through natural phenomenon such as storms or shooting stars. In the Megiddo battle we see the intervention of Amun and Seth for Thutmose III. Amun is protecting his person in the melee, with the strength of (Seth pervading) his limbs. In the poetical stele of Thutmose III, Amun-Re tells us that he came to let the pharaoh conquer the whole world (lines 13–15):[84]

I came to let you tread on Djahi's chiefs,
I spread them under your feet throughout their lands;
I let them see your majesty as lord of light,
so that you shone before them in my likeness.

I came to let you tread on those of Asia,
to smite the Asians' heads in Retjenu;
I let them see your majesty clad in your panoply,
when you displayed your weapons on your chariot.

I came to let you tread on eastern lands,
to crush the dwellers in the realm of god's land;

[83] *ANETS*, 262 (*MH* I pl 46:19).

[84] *AEL* II, 36–37.

I let them see your majesty as a shooting star,
that scatters fires as it sheds its flame.

In the midst of Kadesh Ramses II is along, there is none with him. His numerous troops have deserted him; not one of his chariotry looks for him and he keeps on shouting for them, but not one of them heeds his call. In this critical moment the pharaoh confesses that Amun saved him:[85]

I know Amun helps me more than a million troops,
More than a hundred thousand charioteers,
More than ten thousand brothers and sons
Who are united as one heart.
The labors of many people are nothing,
Amun is more helpful than they;

Here we will see another method of the divine intervention on the battlefield. In the report of the watchmen of the first Syrian campaign of Thutmose III we find the miracle of the shooting star which destroyed the enemies as follows (lines 34—35):[86]

[ist re-tp].w w3 r ii.t r ṯḥnt m grḥ r irt rsyt nt-ʿ
iw wn wnwty sp 2 ii.t sb3 m ii n rsy.sn n ḫpr mytt
wd.n.f r.s m ʿḳ3.f n ʿḥʿ wʿ im [sm3.n.i sn.w mi
ntyw n ḫpr mḥi ḥr snfw.sn ḫrw] m gbgbyt ist r.f
[nsrt] m s3w.sn m sḏt r ḥrw.sn n gm wʿ dt.f im.sn
n nw3.f r ḥ3 nn ḥtrw.sn ḫ3rw [m]...

[the guards] were about to meet in the night to make the regular change of the guards. It was the second hour that a star came from their South. The likeness never happened. It radiated against them in its straight place. No one stands there. [I killed them (the enemies), until they were not alive in their bloodshed floating] and cast down in a heap. [The royal serpent] was at their backs with fire to their faces. No one among them found his hand, none looked back, their horses were not there, which were scattered [in].

In the Marriage stele Ramses II reports that when he conducted the Syrian campaign in bad weather, Seth performed a wonder in which the rain and the cold weather were changed into summerlike days (*Aub Simbel* 1:36:39):[87]

"His majesty considered, and took counsel with his heart: How will it be with those whom I have sent out, who have gone on a mission to Syria, in these days of rain and snow which fall in winter. Then he made a great offering to his father Seth, and with it pronounced the following prayer: Heaven rests upon your hands; the earth is under your feet. What you command, takes place. [May you cause] the rain, the cold wind and the snow [to cease] until the marvel you design for me shall have reached

[85] *RI* II 41:118—19 (L_2); *AEL* II, 65 ff.
[86] *Urk* IV 1238—39; Helck, *Übersetzung*, 10.
[87] Velde, *Seth*, 133.

> me. Then his father Seth heard all that he had said. The sky became peaceful and summer-like days began."

In the Syrian campaign Amun-Re performed a miracle for Ramses III: "Amun-Re pursued them (the enemies), destroying them. Those who entered the mouths of the river were ensnared like birds in a net."[88] It was Amun-Re who overthrew for him the lands and crushed for him every land under his feet. In the second Libyan war in year 11 of Ramses III we see the dramatic intervention of the divine warrior, Sekhmet (*MH* II pl 80:29):[89]

> The great heat of Sekhmet mingled with their heart [the enemies'], so that their bones burned up in the midst of their bodies. The shooting star [was] terrible in pursuit of them.

The next method is that god himself stretches out his hand toward the enemy. This is an invisible sign of the divine intervention. In the poetical hymn of the victory of Thutmose III we hear that "I (Amun) myself have stretched out my two hands to destroy the enemy."[90] In the Libyan war of Ramses III we find a similar expression: "Montu is stretching out the mighty arm and sending his arrow to the spot to destroy the enemy."[91] The popular method of divine intervention was to place in the enemy a divine fear and thereby to confuse the enemy in the battle. Seth was called the god of confusion.

The Egyptian sources do not speak of tortures inflicted upon the prisoners, massacres of them, or destruction of the conquered towns. Nevertheless, Hittite and Israelite sources abound in incidents of this type.[92] Through the divine intervention victory is given to the king in battle. Here the victory is given only by the divine warrior without man's help. In the literary descriptions, although the soldiers fought against the enemy, only the fighting of the divine warriors for them is mentioned.

3) Post-Battle

The victory was credited to two gods: the king-god who led the army and the imperial god who gave his sanction to the wars. After the victory, the homecoming of the king and the soldiers was greeted by the gods and the people. We read the welcoming speech of Amun for Thutmose III upon his return from the battle of Megiddo in the poetical stele:[93]

---

88 *ANETS*, 263 ff.
89 *HRR*, 80.
90 *AEL* II, 36.
91 *MH* I pls 18:2, 22:21 and passim.
92 Curto, *The Military Art*, 21.
93 *AEL* II, 35–36.

You come to me in joy at seeing my beauty.
My son, my champion, Menkheperre, everliving!
I shine for love of you, my heart exults
At your good coming to my temple.
My hands have endowed your body with softness and life,
How pleasant to my breast is your grace!

At the same time th entire army rejoiced and gave praise to Amun for the victory he had given to his son on that day. They also lauded their king and extolled his victory. In the Amada stele we hear of Amunhotep II returning in joy to Egypt from the victory over the Nubians. Then six men of the enemy were hung on the face of the Wall of Thebes, to show the king's victories forever and ever in all the countries of the Negro land.[94] When Ramses II returned in peace to Egypt, the gods of his land hailed him and said: "Welcome, our beloved son, King *Usermare-sotpenre*, the Son of Re, Ramses, Beloved of Amun, given life!" The gods granted him millions of jubilees forever.[95]

When Amun-Re permitted a campaign against the Asiatics and lent his sword to the pharaoh, with the divine standard leading the way into battle, the god had to be repaid after the victory with an extensive share of the booty. The booty which the soldiers brought back from the enemy was given to the god. As time went on, Amun grew in wealth, with every victory adding to his resources. A document of Ramses III, in speaking of the temples of Egypt and their property, gives an extraordinary picture of the ecclesiastical wealth at the end of the NK. For example, after the victory over the Libyans in year 11, the pharaoh took more than forty thousand cattle. Two-thirds of these beasts were presented to Amun who had more than four hundred thousand large and small cattle. Together with the dedication of the booty, the captives of the king were carried off and given to the gods to become slaves in the temples. In *MH* II pl 78 Ramses II presents two columns of Libyan prisoners to Amun and Mut. The chief beneficiaries of the pharaoh's devoted generosity were Amun of Thebes, Re of Heliopolis and Ptah of Memphis, while other gods remained relatively poor. As a result of the booty the temple building for the gods had increased in the NK period. In the poetical stele the god Amun says to Thutmose III:[96]

You have built my temple as a work of eternity,
Made longer and wider than it had been,
With its great gateway "Menkheperre-feasts-Amun-Re,"
Your monuments surpass those of all former kings.

---

[94] *ANETS*, 247–48.
[95] *AEL* II, 71.
[96] *AEL* II, 38.

After the campaign of the Euphrates, Thutmose III erected a stele (*wḏ*): "my majesty set up my stele on the mountain of Naharain, carved on the rock (lit. mountain, *ḏw*) on the western side of the Euphrates."[97] He also ordered his scribe to record [the victories his father Amun had given him] in an inscription in the temple which his majesty had made for [his father, Amun, so as to record] each campaign...[98] Ramses II built several monuments for his divine warrior. He said: "I built great pylons for you (god), myself I erected their flagstaffs; I brought you obelisks from Yebu."[99]

The hand and phalli, as evidence of the slain among the spoil, were carried off to the king. Cutting off the hand is a popular war custom in the ancient Near East. In the Libyan campaign Merneptah carried off the phalli (6111) as a spoil.[100] Several times in the campaigns of Ramses III we see the carrying off of the phalli.[101] A similar custom appears in the story of Saul and David (I Sam 18:25–27). After David destroyed the Philistines, he brought 100 phalli to Saul. In the light of the above history of divine war in the ancient Near East we will examine the motifs of YHWH war in the Bible in the following part.

---

97 *Urk* IV 1232:13.

98 *ANETS*, 235.

99 *AEL* II, 65.

100 *AR* III § 587–88.

101 *MH* I Pls 22, 75.

Summary

In Part One the ancient Near Eastern historical sources indicate the following motifs of the divine war:

1. In the ancient Near Eastern context war was recognized as originating from divine command. Especially in the Egyptian context it was understood as the divine plan, for the divine consultation like an omen or oracle to seek the divine will before the war was not attested, except for a few cases, because the war was considered as the divine plan given by the divine warrior. Thus the duty of the king was to carry out the war as a divine mission.

The concept of war as a lawsuit chiefly appears in the Hittite and Mesopotamian historical sources, but not in the Egyptian historical sources. The Hittite and the Mesopotamian kings appealed their battle to their divine warriors like Ninurta or Teshub. This concept presupposes an international treaty relationship between the two nations. In this sense war is an ultimate remedy for wrong used as a divine judgment for violation of a treaty. God is a judge as well as a warrior.

The concept of war as the divine intervention in battle was well depicted in the literary and graphic sources from the end of the fourth millennium BC in Egypt (Narmer Palette) onwards, but mainly fluorished only in the periods of the New kingdom. The concept was half a millennium earlier than that of the Mesopotamian divine war. The Mesopotamian concept of war as the divine intervention in battle mainly appeared from the middle of the third millennium onwards, whenever the new empire was established throughout the whole history of Mesopotamia such as the Sargonic, the Old Babylonia and the Assyrian Empires. This motif was a universalistic idea that appeared whenever a new empire was established. In this sense the political-military entity was the expression of divine rulership.

2. The basic concept of the divine war is that god is a warrior who fights against the enemy. This concept was strongly attested in the Hittite and Mesopotamian context, but not in the Egyptian context. In the Mesopotamian context the god Ninurta (Ningirsu) was the first divine warrior who fought against Umma in the historical battle of Umma and Iagash. Ninurta was called a divine warrior (ur - sag). The other divine warriors began to appear with the establishment of each empire like Inanna/Ishtar of the Sargonic, Marduk of the Old Babylonian, and Aššur of the Assyrian Empire. They are related to particular historical kings as the god

Marduk was related to Hammurabi and Nebuchadnezzar I. Besides these major divine warriors there were about fifty divine warriors from the third millennium to the first millennium BC in the Mesopotamian context. The major divine warriors were rain-storm gods.

In the Egyptian context there were not as many divine warriors as those of Mesopotamia. Primarily the Egyptian divine warrior was only Amun-Re. The god Seth was originally the Asiatic divine warrior. In the Hittite context the chief divine warrior was Teshub and his wife the Sun-goddess of Arinna. In his annals, Muršiliš II always recorded that he gained the victory with help of his divine warrior.

3. The war starts with the divine consultation to seek the divine will through the accepted methods like omens, oracles or others by the priests. Whenever a military campaign was planned, the divine will was sought by the various divine consultation methods, and with a favorable divine answer the military action began. In the Mesopotamian context the liver-omen was a popular divine consultation method to discern the divine will before battle. This involved sacrificing a sheep and inspecting its liver by the bārum priest to discern either the divine favor or not. Another popular method was to obtain an oracle. The oracle formula, "god delivers the enemy into the hand of X", was a well known favorable oracle form. In the Hittite context there are three types of divine consultation: KIN (lottery), MUŠEN (augury), and KUŠ (extispicy). KIN is a technique used to obtain the divine will by lot. The answer is favorable or unfavorable. MUŠEN is used to know the divine will by the observation of a bird flying. KUŠ is used to seek the divine will through the examination of the entrails of the animal that was sacrificed. This technique is expressed in the formula of protasis and apodosis like the *šumma-izbu*. These methods were conducted by the priests. The motif of the divine consultation also appears even in the ancient Chinese context (c. 15 C BC).

4. The war begins after the discernment of divine favor. In the case of a favorable answer the divine warriors gave not only their oracles to make war, but they themselves also participated on the battlefield to destroy the enemies. This divine participation began with the divine march before the king and army. The visible symbols of divine participation in battle were the divine standards or statues which were widely used. These symbols' loss and subsequent return were often important signs of the religio-political events. Such objects were also used in the vanguard motif in the context of a cultic procession to ensure that divine participation in battle was not ephemeral.

The climax of divine war is the divine intervention in battle by miracles of natural phenomena such as flood or rain-storms, or historical events of revolt amongst the enemies, or as the terror of the divine warriors themselves.

The idea of total destruction is found clearly only in the Anatolian context. But it was not attested to in the neighbouring contexts before the first millennium BC. The initial point of this idea is that the defeated enemy becomes sacred to the divine warriors and inaccessible to men. This attitude was to ensure loyalty to the divine warriors who gave the order to attack the enemy. However, this was not true in every war, and is found only in the case of offensive war.

5. The victory is attributed to the divine warrior and the spoils also return to god(s). For the victory is ultimately divine victory. From beginning to end the divine war begins with god and ends with god. In this sense the war is divine war as in case of the war of Ninurta or the war of Aššur. The enemy is the enemy of the divine warriors. The victory is the victory of the divine warriors. Thus the ancient Near Eastern kings used to erect the steles or monuments, or to build temples to commemorate the victory of the divine warriors.

6. The ideology of the divine war was perpetuated in the cultic event in order to ensure the divine protection continuing in the day to day context. KUB XVIII 35 shows a good example of a battle drama which was intended to perpetuate the victory of the historical battle as superior. This reactualization was a post-battle event. This ritual battle is beyond the actual historicity of the battle, even though the battle was rooted in a historical battle. The interrelationship of the real battle event and the post-battle event, like that of the fact and interpretation, is intermingled and forms two poles in the formation of divine war. However, a reinterpretation never preceded the actual event.

Part Two
YHWH War in the Old Testament

In Part One the motifs of divine war in the four different contexts of the ancient Near East were examined: Mesopotamia, Anatolia, Syro-Palestine and Egypt. We delineated the motifs of divine war in the historical contexts, not mythical. We found that the motifs of divine war began to appear mainly in the rising period of each nation/empire. The Syro-Palestine sources indicated that the motifs of divine war in the historical contexts are not found before the period of the Davidic kingdom. The divine war in Ugarit, a vassal state of the Hittite kingdom, which had not practiced military-political power in the historical context, was a mythological divine war such as in the Baal myth. In Part Two the motifs of YHWH war in the historical battles of the Bible will be examined in the light of the divine war in the ancient Near Eastern context above. The decisive factor for dating the motifs of YHWH war is not the age of the Near Eastern motifs of divine war, but its motifs and function should be within the traditions of Israel, if the point of contact is not clear. It is necessary to examine the wars from the descriptions of the Sea event in Ex 15 to those of the major wars in the times of the Davidic kingdom, in order to define when the motifs of YHWH war in the historical battle appeared in the Bible.

In the war traditions of the Exodus-Conquest it is a question as to whether the biblical passages reflect the *post-battle* theological interpretation of YHWH war without historical reality or the expressions of the historical experience in which the early Israelites felt the help of YHWH on the battlefield. So it is necessary that the biblical materials, especially the Deuteronomistic sources, be examined. The motifs of YHWH war are parallel to those of divine war of the ancient Near East which are attested in the historical contexts. But they are distinguished from those of YHWH war in the exilic and post-exilic period in which there was a vacuum of military-political power, because there was no monarchy. Here the motifs of YHWH war go beyond the historical level having eschatological and apocalyptical dimensions.

Chapter V
Wars in the Traditions of Exodus-Conquest

1. THE SEA EVENT

Recently some scholars have proposed that the song of Miriam (Ex 15:21b) shows the motif of the war of YHWH.[1] Miriam praises:

Sing to YHWH,
For he is highly exalted,
Horse and driver
He has thrown into the sea.

This passage reflects that YHWH intervened to throw a historical enemy into the Sea, even though we cannot define who the enemy was without relating it to the Exodus traditions. R. Smend has proposed that the Reed Sea event was experienced and carried out by the Rachel tribes as the war of YHWH. According to him, the Rachel tribes appear in the arable land as the original and true representatives of the war of YHWH.[2] But he recognized that it is certainly a question of a deliverance from the peril of an enemy in which he (YHWH) threw the military power (horse and driver) into the Sea.[3] F. Stolz has supported the above idea of Smend and called the Exodus event "Anstoß zum bleibenden Bekenntnis von der Kriegsherrshaft Jahwes."[4] But Stolz also doubts that the actual battle took place, and sees that the defeat of the enemy was interpreted as a war of YHWH.[5] Most recently M. C. Lind has supported the same idea that the Exodus and wilderness period was the time of holy war "par excellence," more significant than either the period of the Judges (G. von Rad), or of the conquest of Canaan (P. D. Miller). The Exodus rather than the Conquest or the Judges provides the fundamental paradigm of holy war in the Old Testament on the basis of Ex 15:1–21.[6] Then, can we find the historical reality of the battle at the Sea? If not, is it a mythical reality?

---

[1] Smend. *Yahweh War*, 109 ff. M. Weippert sees that the song of Miriam reflects the idea of the war of YHWH, and that from the short song the later expanded victory songs were derived ("Heiliger Krieg," 460–61).

[2] *Yahweh War*, 113.

[3] *Ibid.*, 110.

[4] *Kriege*, 196–97.

[5] *Ibid.*, 196.

[6] *Yahweh is a Warrior*, 46–47.

The parallel poetic description to the song of Miriam (Ex 15:21b)[7] as the oldest source to the Sea event is also found in the first verse of the song of the Sea (Ex 15:1b).[8] Most scholars agree that the song of Miriam is not "short = early" but the earliest or the oldest song in the Old Testament, even though dating the song is impossible. Many scholars disagree about the date of the song, so there is no consensus of opinion about the song.[9] Here the three aspects of the Sea event will be examined: the Sea tradition, its relationship with the Exodus tradition and the mythological understanding of the Sea event.

---

7 The song of Miriam (Ex 15:21b) is parallel to Ex 15:1b the song of the Sea, except for the different verbal conjugations: In v. 21b the verbal form is a second person masculine plural imperative, but in v. 1b a first person singular cohortative. F. M. Cross considers both passages as an incipit or an initial word of the song of the Sea (J) and that of Miriam (E), *CMHE*, 123–24. But G. W. Coats points that v. 21b and v. 1b cannot be equated as doublets from two older sources, because a cohortative introduction for v. 21b is also found in the Septuagint and the Vulgate ("The Song of the Sea," *CBQ* 31. 1969, 8–9). Thus M. Noth properly observes a change in setting: v. 21b begins with a hymnic invitation to the assembled crowd, while v. 1b now becomes the intent of an individual to praise God, a feature which derives from the individual thanksgiving (M. Noth, *Exodus*, ET by J. S. Bowden, Philadelphia 1962, 123; Coats, *op. cit.*, 9).

8 A satisfactory name for the song has yet to be found. This song was called "a song of Moses" (P.Haupt, J. C. Rylaarsdam and others), or "a song of Miriam" (Cross and D. N. Freedman). Yet now most scholars call it "a song of the Sea" even Cross (*CMHE*, 112 ff) and Freedman ("Divine Names and Titles in Early Hebrew Poetry," *Magnalia Dei*: The Mighty Acts of God, G. E. Wright Festschrift, ed. by F. M. Cross et al, Garden City/NY 1976, 57–63, – "Divine Names and Titles"). The song has been characterized as a hymn (G. Fohrer), enthonement psalm (S. Mowinckel), litany (Muilenberg), victory psalm (Cross-Freedman), hymn and thanksgiving psalm (M. Noth) because it does not reflect any one genre in its form (B. S. Childs, *Exodus*, OTL, Philadelphia 1974, 243–44).

9 A. Bender "Das Lied Exodus 15," *ZAW* 23, 1903, 47) dated the song of the Sea c. 450 BC, on the basis of Aramaisms. P. Haupt ("Moses' Song of Triumph," *AJSL* 20/3, 1904, 153–54) dated the song even one century later c. 350, on the basis of the same content in Neh 9:11. Following them for the late dating: A. H. McNeile, *The Book of Exodus* (London), 88; H. Schmidt, "Das Meerlied, Ex 15:2–19," *ZAW* 49, NF 8 (1931), 59–66; J. Pedersen, "Passahfest and Passahlegende," *ZAW* 52 (1934), 161–75; G. Beer, *Exodus*, HAT 3 (Tübingen 1939), 79–84; Noth, *Exodus*, 120–26; A. Lauha, "Das Schilfmeermotiv im Alten Testament," *VTS* (Leiden 1963), 39; G. Fohrer, *Überlieferung und Geschichte des Exodus*: Eine Analyse von Ex 1–15, BZAW 91 (Berlin 1964), 110–15; Coates, *CBQ* 31, 4; A. Ohler, *Mythologische Elemente im Alten Testament* (Düsseldorf 1969), 73–80 (– *Mythologische Elemente*); O. Loretz, "Ugarit-Texte und Israelitische Religionsgeschichte: The Song of the Sea," *UF* 6 (1974), 245–47. However, since W. F. Albright, mainly, some of his students have argued the early date for the song of the Sea (13th–10th century BC). Albright dated the song the 13th century BC, on the basis of Ugaritic parallels (*From the Stone Age to Christianity*, NY 1957, 14); Cross and Freedman see that the song was composed in the 12th century, but the present form of the song is dated in the 10th century (*Studies in Ancient Yahwistic Poetry*, SBL dissertation 21, 1975, 45–68);

1

The first issue is the historical reality of the battle at the Sea. Do Ex 15:1b and 21b describe the historical battle at the Sea as the nucleus of the Exodus traditions or are they a later theological reflection? L. S. Hay has assumed that "one is able to reconstruct with reasonable certainty the actual event."[10] He sees v. 21b as the original, perhaps dating from a time very near the event it celebrates, from which the song of the Sea grew up.[11] According to him, the form of battle is somewhat removed from the historical event. But the fact that it later came to be understood as an example of holy war presupposes an earlier straightforward story of a military encounter between the Hebrews and their enemies.[12] As mentioned above, Smend has proposed that it was the Rachel tribes who had experienced the historical battle at the Sea. But the Israelite tribes who later become well known, as Noth has pointed out,[13] were essentially constituted only in the course of the occupation in Palestine, and hence did not even exist as *tribes* before then. Nevertheless, Noth has suggested that the fact of the saving of Israel through the destruction of an Egyptian force in the Sea forms the historical basis of the tradition.[14] However,

---

Cross, *CMHE*, 112–44: Freedman views the early date ("Divine Names and Titles," 59–60) on the basis of the divine name YHWH exclusively; D. A. Robertson, *Linguistic Evidence in Dating Early Hebrew Poetry* (Missoula, Montana 1972), 155 (– *Linguistic Evidence*). However, some scholars do not accept the early date for the song of the Sea (S. Mowinckel, "Psalm Criticism between 1900 and 1935: Ugarit and Psalm Exegesis," *VT* 5, 1955, 13–33). The decisive issue for dating a Hebrew poem is not the age of the original Canaanite formula, but its form and function within Israel's traditions (Childs, *Exodus*, 246). Those who place the song between the early and late dates, mainly suggest the period of the united or the early divided monarchy (P. C. Rylaarsdam, *Exodus, IB* I, 941); J. D. W. Watts, "The Song of the Sea – Ex XV," *VT* 7 (1957), 371–80; J. Muilenburg, "A Liturgy on the Triumphs of Yahweh, " *Studia Biblica et Semitica*, T. C. Vriezen Dedicata (1966), 238–50; S. E. Loewenstamm, *The Tradition of the Exodus in its Development* (Jerusalem 1972), 112–14 (– *The Tradition of the Exodus*), Hebrew; M. Weinfeld sees that the song of the Sea in all probability dates from Solomonic times, but whatever its date it is obvious that the expression מכון לשבתך here refers to the temple (*Deuteronomy and the Deuteronomic School*, Oxford 1972, 196). But J. Goldin points out that the same expression above is not as a place for god's abode, and the מקדש is the pre-Solominic central sanctuary (*The Song at the Sea*, New Haven/London 1971, 46, n. 53). He assumes that the song of the Sea was the workmamship of Anathothites or ex-Shilonites (*ibid.*, 57).

10 L. S. Hay, "What really Happened at the Sea of Reeds?" *JBL* 83 (1964), 401.

11 *Ibid.*

12 *Ibid.*, 402.

13 *A History of Pentateuchal Traditions*, ET by B. W. Anderson (NY 1972), 50 (– *Pentateuchal Traditions*).

14 *Exodus*, 120.

bearing the epic character even of the prose account of Ex 14 in mind, it would be in vain try to discover what really happened.[15] Because the materials we have are the traditions transmitted by the concern of faith. Thus whether or not Miriam sang a song at the time of the reported miracle is of course beyond our knowledge, simply because there is no way for the historian to know such a real fact. Of course, the place where the Sea miracle took place is certainly not provable with absolute certainty. We can only trace how the Israelites perceived the Sea event after they had settled in the literary form. Yet it does not mean that the Israelites who had come from Egypt did not have any kind of experience at the Sea. It only means that there is no evidence that they had experienced the historical intervention of YHWH in the battle at the Sea. Ex 15:21 does not show, as C. Westermann has suggested,[16] that a certain battle took place: only a simple mythopoetic description in which YHWH destroyed a certain enemy, a horse and chariotry. Moreover, none of the texts reporting the event at the Sea describe a military conflict between two armies.

Nevertheless, J. P. Hyatt believes the probability of a military encounter between the Israelites and Egyptians, though he admits that this is never stated in the narratives.[17] Lind asserts that the Sea event in Ex 13—14 was depicted as a battle:[18] Israel went up from Egypt "equipped for battle (13:18)." The verb "encamp and its cognate camp" are used by both the Israelites and Egyptians (13:20; 14:2,9,19,20). The word "fight" is used in 14:14. Discomfited (14:24) is a holy war term and clogging (14:25), used in reference to chariot wheels, may also refer to such discomfiture. But all the traditions agree that it is not a battle in the usual sense, for YHWH is the sole warrior who gives political salvation to his people by an act of nature, and J draws out an implication for faith.[19] Thus it is reasonable to say that the song of Miriam, like the women's eulogy of Saul and David,[20] is a simple expression of praise to YHWH without reference to the historical reality of the battle at the Sea, just as a later theological reflection which could have been experienced only a

---

[15] R. de Vaux, *The Early History of Israel*: To the Exodus and Covenant of Sinai, ET by D. Smith (London 1978), 384 (— *EHI*).

[16] *The Praise of God in the Psalms*, ET by K. R. Crim (Virginia 1965), 90.

[17] *Commentary on Exodus* (London 1971), 157.

[18] *Yahweh is a Warrior*, 54.

[19] *Ibid.*, 59.

[20] S. Gevirtz has suggested that the writing took place not only after the event in question but doubtless also long after the fall of the house of Saul and establishment of the house of David, and seeking causes to explain the rift that occurred between two, he has utilized this bit of folk poetry as evidence (*Patterns in the Early Poetry of Israel*, SAOC 32, Chicago 1973, 15—16).

cultic context.[21] Through the cultic act or memory the Sea event could have been actualized to be a contemporized event for a generation removed in time and space from the original Sea event. For the history of the Sea tradition cannot be confined to a time and space. Rather, in the Sea tradition the victory event demonstrates a distinct openness toward the future. It develops unique significance for each new generation, significance that can produce mutations in old details or create new details.[22] Later Israel, removed in time and space from the original event, yet still in time and space, found in her tradition a means of transforming her history into redemptive history. Because the quality of time was the same, the barrier of chronological separation was overcome.[23] In the process of the transformation of tradition, the Sea event had become a vehicle of the Exodus tradition.

2

The second issue is the understanding of the relationship between the Sea tradition and the Exodus tradition. Recently G. W. Coats has suggested that the expression that God led the people around by the way of the wilderness toward the Yam-Suf[24] (Ex 13:17a—E) shows that the Sea event had been completed and the wilderness period had begun. According to him, because of the murmuring motif (Ex 14:11—12),[25] the Yam-Suf event is a post-Exodus event which has its setting in the wilderness. So he believes that the development of the Yam-Suf tradition in both J and P, therefore, points to the position which this tradition holds, not as the nucleus of the Exodus theme, but as the beginning for the theme of Yahweh's aid to the people in the wilderness.[26]

However, this understanding is due to the confusion between the Sea and the Yam-Suf event: the Old Testament is inconsistent in its assigning the Sea event to the wilderness tradition. Moreover, the lack of consistency reflects not some accidental confusion, but rather a complex development of tradition. In different circles and in different times this Sea event was portrayed in different viewpoints and terms. B. S. Childs points out that

---

21 N. Lohfink, "Das Siegeslied am Schilfmeer," *Das Siegeslied am Schilfmeer*: Christliche Auseinandersetzungen mit dem Alten Testament (Frankfurt 1965), 102—28.

22 G. W. Coats, "History and Theology in the Sea Tradition," *ST* 29 (1975), 58.

23 B. S. Childs, *Memory and Tradition in Israel*, SBT 57 (London 1962), 85.

24 The English translation of Yam-Suf as Reed Sea cannot be retained, since reeds do not grow in either the gulfs of Suez or Akaba. Instead either Yam-Suf as a transliteration of the Hebrew or the Red Sea as an indication of the modern term which most nearly corresponds to it should be used (G. I. Davies, *The Way of Wilderness*, 1979, 74.

25 G. W. Coats, "The Reed Sea Motif," *VT* 17 (1967), 255.

26 *Ibid.*, 258.

in JE the Sea event is part of the wilderness tradition, but in P it rather functions as an integral part of the Exodus traditions.[27]

The Sea and the Yam-Suf could be distinguished as two different places in Ex 13:18 and the Priestly sources. In Num 33:8–11 (P) we see the two different seas: the Sea and Yam-Suf. "They (the Exodus peoples) passed through the midst of the Sea (הים) into the wilderness, ... and they moved from Elim and encamped by the Yam-Suf. And they moved from the Yam-Suf and encamped in the wilderness of Sin." Here the Sea through which the Exodus peoples passed and the Yam-Suf where they encamped are distinguished as two different places. In this context there is no mention of crossing the Yam-Suf and destroying the enemies. The crossing of the Sea is already a *past event*. Now the peoples who crossed the Sea are going toward the Yam-Suf. In the prose narrative in Ex 14 the Sea through which the children of Israel went on dry ground, is not called the Yam-Suf, just הים (Ex 14:22,29; 15:19). In Ex 14 the word "the Sea" occurs 18 times but the Yam-Suf does not occur even once.[28] Certainly the Yam-Suf of I K 9:26, which is considered as the Gulf of Akaba, is called τῆς ἐσχάτης θαλάσσης ἐν γῇ (the Sea at the end of the land) in the LXX. Yet in II Ch 8:27 it is called הים.

In the case of Josh 24:6–7 (E): "You (the Israelites) came to the Sea, and the Egyptians pursued after your fathers with chariots and with horsemen to the Yam-Suf, but (YHWH) brought the Sea upon them, and covered them." Here the Yam-Suf looks like a gloss in the previous mention of the Sea.[29] But the LXX gives "the Yam-Suf" in the first two places. Here the description of the disaster to the Egyptians omits the entry of the pursuers into the Sea and only states that it was by the Sea that they were destroyed, not the Yam-Suf.[30] By the time of Nehemiah the Sea tradition was completely distinguished from the Yam-Suf. Neh 9:9–11 shows us: "You (YHWH) heard their cry at the Yam-Suf... And you divided the Sea before them (the Israelites), so that they went through the midst of the Sea on the dry land, and you threw their pursuers into the deeps, like a stone into the mighty waters." The content of this verse looks like that of the story in Ex 14. Especially the last sentence of v. 11 is very close to Ex 15:5b. The Yam-Suf in Neh 9:9 appears as a place where YHWH heard the voice of the people in Egypt before the Exodus.

In the earlier sources[31] the Yam-Suf appears as a distant Sea scarcely known away to the east or the south, of which no man knew the boundary.

---

[27] Childs, *Exodus*, 222.

[28] Vv. 2 (2 times), 9, 16 (2), 21 (3), 22, 23, 26, 27 (3), 28, 29.

[29] G. A. Cooke, *The Book of Joshua* (Cambridge 1918), 216; Cross, *CMHE*, 133.

[30] J. A. Soggin, *Joshua*, OTL, ET by R. A. Wilson (London 1972), 234.

[31] Ex 10:19; 13:18; 15:22; Josh 24:6; Num 14:25; 21:4 (E); 33:10 (P); Dt 1:40; 2:1; Judg 11:6 (D).

It was the Sea at the end of the land (Jer 49:21). It was never the Sea of Reeds.[32] The P account never said the Israelites crossed the Yam-Suf. In fact, not until the story of the crossing of the Sea was interwoven with the great creation myth was it mentioned. Moreover, in the E account the Yam-Suf is remembered as a fleeing place of the Israelites. While in the P account the Yam-Suf is recorded as a stopping place during the journey of the Exodus peoples.[33] However, in the process of the transformation of the Sea tradition, the Sea began to identify with the Yam-Suf and so was related with destroying the enemy of the Exodus tradition. In the book of Deuteronomy the tradition of Israel's deliverance at the Yam-Suf plays not only a minor role, but appears only in Dt 11:4. The parenetic context of v. 4aβ states: "how He (YHWH) made the water of Yam-Suf overflow them (the Egyptians) as they pursued after you, and how the Lord destroyed them unto this day." This idea is integral to the homiletical concerns of the author who seeks to actualize the past in a challenge for present action.[34] As mentioned above, the Song of Miriam indicates only the destruction of the enemy at the Sea. In this sense the song corresponds to an early fragment of tradition preserved by J in Ex 14:27b. YHWH shook the Egyptians into the midst of the Sea. Moreover, Ex 15:4a adopts the verb ירה, instead of the verb רמה in vv. 1b and 21b, in order to express the same meaning: He (YHWH) hurled pharaoh and his army into the Sea. S. I. L. Norin has asserted that this adaptation of ירה is a sign of late Deuteronomic addition to the Yam-Suf (v. 4b).[35] Yet both verbs are used for the same meaning, but with different directions: רמה means to hurl down, ירה to throw up.[36] In the hymn of Ishtar we find the verb *ramû* in the description of her features: "She is glorious, beads are cast down over her head (*šar-ḫa-at i-rimu ra-mu-ú re-šu-uš-ša*)."[37] So the parallel of the verbs רמה and ירה is a poetic expression to match the sense, not a sign for a late addition.

But in this context there is no motif of the Israelites' crossing of the Sea. Even in J there is no account of the crossing of the Sea or of any movement for that matter by the Israelites.[38] The idea of a crossing of the Sea can only have been derived from the priestly version. J affirms YHWH's victory over the enemy without reference to the Israelites' escape.

---

[32] N. H. Snaith, "ים סוף: The Sea of Reeds: The Red Sea," *VT* 15 (1965), 398.

[33] M. Haran, *Ages and Institutions in the Bible* (TA 1972), 58–60 (Hebrew).

[34] B. S. Childs, "Deuteronomic Formulae of the Exodus Traditions," *W. Baumgartner Festschrift* (1967), 34.

[35] *Er Spaltete das Meer*: Die Auszugsüberlieferung in Psalmen und Kult des alten Israel, CBOT 9 (Lund 1977), 94.

[36] Goldin, *The Song at the Sea*, 101.

[37] F. Thureau-Dangin, "Un Hymne À Ištar," *ZA* 22 (1925), 172, line 11.

[38] Childs, *Exodus*, 221.

E also reflects the crossing of the Yam-Suf (Ex 13:18); 15:22),[39] but does not mention the reference to the destruction of the enemy. Some scholars contend that the motif of the crossing of the Sea did not influence that of the crossing of the Jordan (Josh 3—4). On the contrary, the description of the crossing of the river influenced that of the crossing of the Sea in Ex 14.[40] But it seems that the two crossings are independent in the early period, for the Jordan tradition does not mention any reference to the defeat of the enemy in the waters, while the Sea event does. R. de Vaux believes that the account of the crossing of the Jordan was transferred to the tradition of the Exodus, which originally consisted only of the miracle of the destruction of the Egyptian army in the Sea and did not contain the Israelites' crossing of the Sea.[41] From the post-exilic period onward the combination of the division and the crossing of the Yam-Suf and the destructiuon of the enemy appears in the thanksgiving to YHWH (Ps 136:13—15):

> To Him (YHWH) who divided the Yam-Suf in half,
> For His kindness is eternal
> And made Israel pass through the midst of it,
> For His kindness is eternal
> But shook off pharaoh and is host into the Yam-Suf.

In v. 13 the verb גזר is in contrast to the verb with the same meaning as the בקע in the P story (Ex 14:16,22). In addition, v. 15 parallels a sentence in the J story: YHWH shook off the Egyptians into the Sea. Only two things differ: The Egyptians changed into pharaoh and his hosts, and the Sea into the Yam-Suf respectively. The same tradition of the combination of the Yam-Suf, instead of the Sea and the Exodus tradition, was continually transmitted even in the second canonical writings.[42] Thus the above passages show that the Sea tradition had been transferred to the tradition of the Yam-Suf. However, the motif of the drowning of the Egyptians at the Sea, as S. E. Loewenstamm has asserted,[43] should be sought in the old motif of the Lord's victorious fight against the Sea. For the Sea tradition bears clear marks of the historicizing of a mythological tradition. Moreover, in the J account the rescue at the Sea follows the Exodus from Egypt, and the Sea event clearly belongs to the wilderness tradition.[44] But from the beginning the Sea event did not firmly belong to the tradition

---

[39] Haran, *op. cit.*, 58.

[40] De Vaux, *EHI* II, 604, n. 36.

[41] *Ibid.*

[42] Wisdom 10:18; 19:7; Judith 5:13; I Macca 4:9 (E. Hatch and H. A. Redpath, *A Concordance to the Septuagint* I, 1897, Graz, Austria 1975, 548b).

[43] *The Tradition of the Exodus*, 109 ff.

[44] Childs, *Exodus*, 222.

of the salvation of Israel from Egypt. Thus the older tradition only tells of the perishing of the Egyptians at or in the Sea, without postulating that the Israelites were in actual contact with the Sea at all.[45]

3

The third issue is that the Sea event is a mythopoetic theological understanding of the saving act of YHWH the Lord of history. The first idea in this understanding is the adoption of foreign myths. G. I. Davies assumes that the Miriam Song views YHWH's enemies as human (horse and chariot) and the Sea as the natural element which YHWH uses for their destruction. It contains no trace of Ugaritic mythology.[46] Loewenstamm observes that in the beginning there was only a myth of YHWH battling with another god, as in the case of the Baal myth. Only later in Israel's history the myth was historicized and the enemy became Egypt.[47] This understanding is based on the old oriental traditions describing the triumph of the god of heaven over the gods of the Sea and River: the Baal myth, Enuma Elish or Sun mythology. With the parallel to the emphasis of the influence of the Canaanite myth, O. Kaiser has suggested the influence of the Egyptian Sun mythology.[48] Recently W. Wifall proposed that the framework of the Yam-Suf tradition was not basically Canaanite but originated in Egypt, where it had been applied to the Sun-god and his daily submergence into and emergence from the lake and field of reeds or Shi-Hor. The Egyptian solar mythology and insignia were adapted in the Palestinian city states of the Egyptian empire during the 2nd millennium BC to the cults of the Canaanite gods, El and Baal. Israel was exposed to influences from both Egypt and Canaan during the 2nd millennium BC, and the cult of YHWH replaced that of El in the city-state of Jerusalem during Israel's monarchy.[49] In other words, it is seen that the ancient Near Eastern tradition concerning the victory of a god over his enemies, which was connected with the creation and the enthronement of the god, influenced the formation of the idea of YHWH's victory at the Sea in the whole range of YHWH's saving acts throughout history. Therefore it is observed that the Sea event, as saving history originally belonged to the cultic confession of YHWH as the God of history, and that it was only after centuries of development that its contents

---

[45] S. Herrmann, *Israel in Egypt*, SBT 27, ET by M. Kohl (London 1973), 59.

[46] A review article of "Er Spaltete das Meer," by S. I. L. Norin, *VT* 31 (1981), 112.

[47] Loewenstamm, *The Tradition of the Exodus*, 101–20.

[48] O. Kaiser, *Die Mythische Bedeutung des Meeres in Ägyptian, Ugarit und Israel*, BZAW 78 (Berlin 1959), 37; B. F. Batto, "The Reed Sea: Requiescat in Pace," *JBL* 102 (1983), 27–35.

[49] "The Sea of Reeds as Sheol," *ZAW* 92 (1980), 332.

were shaped into the great literary composition of the Pentateuch.[50] For the event at the Sea was so unique and extraordinary that it came to constitute the essence of the primary Israelite confession and was regarded as the real beginning of Israel's history and the fundamental act for Israel.[51]

However, in the Baal myth or Egyptian Sun mythology the enemy of the god is Yam, a Water-god, while in the Song of Miriam the enemy of YHWH is not the Sea but man and beasts such as horses and chariots. So YHWH does not fight against the Sea.[52] The Sea in Ex 15:1b,4,21b is not a weapon which YHWH used to destroy the enemy, but nature itself. A similar idea can be found in the extra-biblical sources in which god or men threw the enemy into the water or the Sea as punishment. In Maqlu III:101 we find the idea: "May (Sin) throw you (sorcerer) into the catastrophe by either water or fire (*ana miqit mê u ìšāti lid-di-ki-ma*)."[53] In the records of the fall of Nineveh (BM 21901) we find a similar idea: "they (the Babylonian king and soldiers) defeated them (enemies) completely and threw them into the River-Zaban (*ana nār GN it-ta-du-šú-nu-tú*)."[54] The same idea also appears in the non-battle contexts.[55] These descriptions are expressions which mean the complete destruction of the enemy. In contrast to the song of Miriam, in J, E and P the Sea was a weapon which YHWH used to defeat the enemy: "The water returned and covered the chariots and horsemen (14:28a); YHWH brought the Sea upon the Egyptian (Josh 24:7); the Sea covered the enemy (15:10)." In J and E YHWH does not bring the Sea directly, but through a strong east wind. During the night the Lord drove back the Sea with a strong east wind (14:21b). After YHWH causes a panic in the Egyptian army, the water flows back into its old bed; the Egyptians, fleeing toward it, are met and overwhelmed. In P through the miracle of Moses the Sea was used for the destruction of the enemy.

The concept of the redemption of Israel by YHWH received a peculiar enlargement when the elements of the creation myth, the struggle with chaos, were welded into it. This procedure was suggested by the common appearance of the catchword "Sea" both here and in the creation myth. The event took on primeval dimensions, and was transferred from its historical setting to the beginning of history; indeed it stood for Israel at the beginning of her whole existence. Therefore it was only a short step to Deutero-Isaiah's characteristic equation of creation and redemption.

---

50 H. Gottlieb, "Myth in the Psalms," in *Myths in the Old Testament*, ed. by B. Otzen, H. Gottlieb and K. Jappesen (London 1980), 71.

51 Noth, *Pentateuchal Traditions*, 50.

52 Ohler, *Mythologische Elemente*, 75.

53 *CAD* N/I–II, 73.

54 *Ibid.*, 73.

55 *Ibid.*; The Codex of Hammurabi 108:25; 133b:26; 143:12.

Because he understood creation as a saving event, he was also able to describe YHWH's saving act towards Israel as creation (Is 43:1, 44:24). The coincidence of creation and the historical saving event in Is 51:9 ff is unique.[56] These expressions were also changed into historical descriptions in the later period for those who wanted to know the historical aspects. The Deuteronomistic movement responded to this demand of the contemporary people.[57]

The second idea is the mythologization of history. Cross has recognized that mythic elements were present at the beginning of Israel's history when YHWHism emerged from its mythopoetic environment. The myths of creation and kingship became recrudescent with the intoduction of kingship and its ideology, especially in the Solomonic era with the institution of the dynastic temple.[58] Thus Cross believes that it was the tendency to mythologize historical episodes to reveal their transcendent meaning: The mythological battle of the Canaanite epic was used by Israel to express her historical war experience.[59] But our text implies that it is not a battle between YHWH and the Sea, but a battle between YHWH and the historical enemy of Israel. But who the historical enemy of Israel was cannot be defined. And it does not mean that the mythological expression of an historical event can always be identified with the historical experience. It is just a symbolic expression of Israel's redemption by YHWH alone. For the Israelites at the Sea did not play any role. Thus the Sea account in Ex 14–15 represents the tension between an actual historical event in the Egyptian delta during the 19th dynasty and a mythological framework which gives these events a transcendent meaning.[60]

The final idea is that the saving tradition comes from a legal conception. Von Rad has suggested that the idea of ransom for redemption no longer regards the saving event in its military aspect, but as a liberating legal act of YHWH.[61] It is supported by the concept of the word הוציא, which does not appear in the early prophets and is derived from a strict liberation from slavery in a legal context.[62] Actually the remembrance of a deed of YHWH in war is the primary and most certainly the oldest datum in the confession concerning the deliverance from Egypt. But the working up of the narrative afforded the possibility of expanding the event both in its technicalities and in its theological aspect. Noteworthy too is the increase in the miraculous element as the stories are handed on.

---

56 G. von Rad, *Old Testament Theology* I, 178.

57 Norin, *Er Spaltete das Meer*, 208.

58 *CMHE*, 135.

59 *Ibid.*, 144, 162–63; Mann, *Divine Presence*, 125–26.

60 Wifall, *ZAW* 92, 332.

61 von Rad, *Old Testament Theology* I, 175–78.

62 I. Wijngaads, "הוציה and העלה," *VT* 15 (1965), 92.

Here what took place is understood conceptually, in a way which is thought of as far more than a mere military event. What calls for chief mention here is the idea of the redemption from Egypt, which at a later time, that is, from Deuteronomy onwards, became the dominant theme.

Therefore, the battle at the Sea cannot be considered as an event of YHWH war in which YHWH intervened in the historical context. Rather, it is a theological understanding of the redemptive history which has developed in the history of tradition,[63] especially in the light of the victory of David by YHWH over the neighbouring enemies. The Sea event demonstrates the distinctive openness for future redemption by the absolute power of YHWH in view of the teleological scope.

2. THE WAR OVER THE AMALEKITES

Ex 17:8–16 (J)[64] informs us that the Israelites who were in the wilderness had a victory over the Amalekites who were a nomad tribe of the Sinai peninsular in the region of Kadesh (Gen 14:7) at Rephidim. Although Joshua and his selected people went to fight against the Amalekites, the victory depended only upon the action of Moses. Whenever Moses held up his hand, the Israelites prevailed; and whenever he lowered his hand, the Amalekites prevailed (v. 11). Some commentators see this action of the lifting up the hands as an impersonal magical effect.[65] In fact, in this context the hands are the instrument of power to determine the victory. But there is nothing improbable in seeing in the tradition a historical memory from the wilderness period. For it is not difficult to imagine that Israel fought the Amalekites at some desert oasis. Moreover, the vow of perpetual enmity to the Amalekites in Dt 25:17 ff or I Sam 15:30 reflects a humiliating defeat of Israel by the hands of Amalek in the early history of Israel. So Israel considered the destruction of the Amalekite as a national duty, until king Saul fulfilled it. V. 12 shows that in spite of the influence emanating from Moses, the battle against the Amalekites was so hard that it lasted a whole day before the Amalekites were defeated; because of this Moses had to have his raised hands supported by Aaron and Hur. At least, it may be said that the Amalekites were weakened by the Israelites after the formation of the united Monarchy. This theory is also supported by the phrase "חלש לפי חרב, to disable with the edge of the sword" (v. 13) which is a similar expression to "הכה לפי חרב, to smite

[63] S. Hermann, *Israel in Egypt*, SBT 27 (1973), 63–64.

[64] This text which consists of vv.8–13 and 14–16 is usually attributed to J (Noth, *Exodus*, 141 ff; de Vaux, *EHI* I, 422). But v. 14 is considered as a Deuteronomic expansion (Childs, *Exodus*, 313).

[65] Noth, *Exodus*, 142; Childs, *Exodus*, 315.

with the edge of the sword," "הרג לפי חרב" (Gen 34:26), or החרים לפי חרב (I Sam 15:8) which expresses utter destruction.[66]

However, YHWH is not mentioned at all in the whole section of vv. 8–13, not even as having given Moses the instructions for his action. The plan of Moses and his instructions to Joshua are not described as stemming from the direct oracle of God.[67] Nevertheless, Childs and others understand this battle as the dirct intervention of God himself.[68] For in v. 14 YHWH commands Moses to record in a book his purpose to wipe out the name of Amalek. In vv. 15 ff Moses commemorates the victory with an altar which he named "YHWH is my banner." The point of the naming is to bear witness to YHWH's role in battle; and YHWH is the standard beneath which Israel rallies. The poetic fragment in v. 16 (מלחמה ליהוה) clearly refers to the war against Amalek as YHWH war.[69]

But the contents of vv. 14b and 16 derive from a time and a sphere of activity in which the Amalekites appeared as particularly evil and dangerous opponents of the people of YHWH.[70] In the local traditions in the book of the Judges the serious conflict between Israel and Amalek is not mentioned at all. The inimical relation on both sides begins after the period of the Judges. The battle between the Israelites, and the Amalekites and the Canaanites in Num 14:39–45 is considered as an event after an Israelite settlement in the region of the southern edge of the Judean hill country due to the numerous factual details, such as the mention of the "heights of the hill country," of the place-name Hormah as well as "the Amalekites and the Canaanites who dwelt in the hill country."[71] The first battle between Israel and Amalek was Saul's battle in I Sam 15. Accordingly Ex 17:14 and 16 speak of a special enmity between YHWH and the Amalekites as an exegesis to the previous passages (vv. 8–13) in the light of YHWH war. In this consideration the idea of מלחמה ליהוה in v. 16 is a production of YHWH war. It corresponds with the fact that the Amalekites were the enemy of YHWH (איבי יהוה) in I Sam 30:26. J. H. Grønbaek rightly points out that vv. 14b and 16 depend upon the traditions in Dt 25 and I Sam 15 which reflect the actual experiences of the tribal confederation in Southern Palestine after the immigration.[72] However,

---

[66] Keel, *Siegeszeichen*, 77–79.

[67] Childs, *Exodus*, 314.

[68] *Ibid.*, 315; de Vaux, *EHI* I, 384; J. H. Grønbaek, "Juda und Amalek: Überlieferungsgeschichtliche Erwägungen zu Exodus 17:8–16," *ST* 18 (1964), 43–44.

[69] D. L. Christensen, *Transformation of the War Oracles in the Old Testament Prophecy*, HDR 3 (Missoula, Mont. 1975), 49 (– *War Oracles*).

[70] Noth, *Exodus*, 143.

[71] Noth, *Numbers*, OTL, ET by J. D. Martin (London 1968), 111.

[72] *ST* 18, 40–41; yet E. Jacob (*La Tradition historique en Israël*, 1946, 159) thinks that Dt 25:17 ff depends upon Ex 17:8 ff (*ibid.*, n. 31). Cassuto believes that both Dt 25:17 ff and Ex 17:8 ff come from a common source on the basis of the word-play, הנחשלים in Dt 25:18 and ויחלש in Ex 17:13 (*Exodus*, 206).

Smend thinks that it cannot with necessary certainty be claimed as positive testimony for a YHWH war independent of the tribes of Rachel.[73]

Recently O. Keel has pointed out that the motif of the uplifting of the hands of Moses in vv. 11 ff was influenced by the Egyptian iconographic motif of uplifting of the hand of the gods.[74] Originally in the Egyptian context the gesture of uplifting the hands had double meaning: positive and negative – praise, bless, protect, and attack or destroy. Amun promises the victory to Thutmose III: "The arms of my majesty are raised to crush the wicked, I give you protection, my beloved son, Horus (*ʿwj ḥm.i ḥr ḥrt sḥri ḏw.t di.i ḥwt.k s3.i mrr Ḥr*)."[75] Keel concludes that our text was composed of the four complex traditions in the period of Saul and David: the memory of the battle of Israel and Amalek, the Egyptian composition of the uplifting hands and of destruction, and the transformation of the stone as a throne.[76] It shows that Ex 17:8–16 was combined on the basis of the historical reality of Israel and Amalek in the idea of YHWH war in the period of monarchy. Thus the above evidence suggests that there was no intervention by YHWH in the historical battle of Israel and Amalek in the period of the wilderness. It is a *post-battle* interpretation which emphasizes the role of Moses alone in the battle.

3. THE CONQUEST WARS IN TRANSJORDAN

In the Exodus event YHWH alone fought for Israel, and the Exodus peoples only had to keep quiet and observe the great act which YHWH performed against the Egyptians (Ex 14). But in the narratives of the conquest, according to YHWH's command, the Israelites were involved in aggressive warfare led by Moses or Joshua. According to Num 21:21–35, there were three conquest war events during the period of the conquest in Transjordan. The first war event was Israel's battle against the Amorite king, Sihon. Israel took possession of his land "from the Arnon to the Jabbok, as far as to the Ammonites (vv. 21–26)." The second war event was the simple report of the conquest of Jazer by Moses (v. 32). The last war event was the battle between Israel and Og, the king of Bashan (vv. 33–35). Y. Aharoni assumes that these conquests were not carried out in one campaign or at one time, but rather continued in several waves which were blended together in tradition to form a single campaign

[73] Smend, *Yahweh War*, 103.

[74] *Siegeszeichen*, 95–108.

[75] *Ibid.*, 100, n. 1.

[76] *Ibid.*, 107–8.

of conquest.[77] Here we will deal with two narratives of the conquest wars to examine the motifs of YHWH in the historical reality, omitting Jazer's war due to the brevity of the account.

1) Conquest War against Sihon

1

The literary stratum of the account of the battle against Sihon in vv. 21–26 is still disputed. According to various scholars, it is attributed to J, E, P or post-Dtr.[78] The source must remain an open question for the time being. V. 32 contains a pre-Dtr addition which is unaware of the Deuteronomic picture of the conquest. It must be intended as preparation for 32:1.[79] The victory narrative over Og in vv. 33–35 almost agrees with Dt 3:1–3 and many scholars believe that it comes from Dtr.[80] In the first war event – the Sihon battle, Moses does not appear at all. The initiative is not taken by Moses but by Israel as in the story of Jephthah (Judg 11:19–26). Yet in the parallel passages with the Sihon battle in Dt 2:26 and Josh 12:6 Moses plays the main role. Moreover, in the account of the Sihon battle nothing is said of any divine intervention but it is later introduced as a theological interpretation by the Deuteronomist in Dt 2:30 ff and Num 11:19–26. In v. 21 there is no allusion to YHWH war, this stands in direct contradiction to the parallel in Dt 2:30,33. If we compare the parallel passages in Num 21:23–24, Judg 11:20–21 and Dt 2:30–33, we can see the contrast.

במ" כא:כג־כד	שופ" יא:כ־כא	דב" ב:ל־לג
פסי 23 ולא־נתן סיחן את־ ישראל עבר בגבלו	פסי 20 ולא־האמין סיחון את־ ישראל עבר בגבלו	פסי 30 ולא אבה סיחן מלך חשבון העברנו בו כי־ הקשה יהוה אלהיך את־ רוחו ואמץ את־לבבו

---

77 Y. Aharoni, *The Land of the Bible*: A Historical Geography, ET by A. F. Rainey (Philadelphia 1979), 206.

78 O. Eissfeldt (*The Old Testament*: An Introduction, ET by P. R. Ackroyd, 1965, 195 ff) and M. Haran (*Ages and Institutions in the Bible*, 70) assign it to J, while Noth (*Exodus*, 162) attributes it to E, on the basis of the use of the term "Amorite". Yet de Vaux (*EHI* II, 565) and J. van Seters ("The Conquest of Sihon's Kingdom," *JBL* 91, 1972, 182) do not agree with Noth, because the word "Amorite" instead of "Canaanite" has little meaning beyond the Jordan which defined the boundary of Canaan. M. Ottosson consideres it P – pre-Deuteronomic. But van Seters believes that the source is derived from Deuteronomists (*op. cit.*, 182 ff).

79 Noth, *Numbers*, 166.

80 de Vaux, *EHI* II, 565.

למען תתו בידך כיום הזה		
31 ויאמר יהוה אלי ראה החלתי תת לפניך את־סיחן ואת־ארצו החל רש לרשת את־ארצו		
	ויאסף סיחון את־כל־עמו	ויאסף סיחן את־כל־עמו
32 ודצא סיחן לקראתנו		ויצא לקראת ישראל המדברה
הוא וכל־עמו למלחמה יהצה	ויחנו ביהצה וילחם עם־ישראל	ויבא יהצה וילחם בישראל
33 ויתנהו יהוה אלהינו לפנינו ונך אתו ואת־בנו ואת־כל־עמו	21 ויתן יהוה אלהי־ישראל את־סיחון ואת־כל־עמו ביד ישראל ויכום ויירש ישרעל את כל־ארץ האמרי יושב הארץ ההיא	24 ויכהו ישראל לפי־חרב ויירש את־ארצו מארנן עד־יבק עד־בני עמון כי עז גבול בני עמון

Num 21:23, except v. 23aβ which corresponds with Dt 2:32a, parallels, word by word, Judg 11:20. Here the passage does not contain YHWH's oracle or promise. Yet the parallel passages in Dt 2:30b–31 show strongly YHWH's intervention through an oracle: "For YHWH your (Moses') God hardened his (Sihon) spirit, and made his heart obstinate, that he might deliver him into your hand, as is apparent this day. And YHWH said to me, behold, I have begun to give Sihon and his land before you; begin to take possession that you may inherit his land." The following verses (Dt 2:33 ff) describe the fulfilment of the divine promise in synergism: "And *YHWH* our God delivered him (**ויתנהו יי**) before us; and we smote him, and his sons, and all his people." Judg 11:21 also expresses the same idea of the YHWH intervention. Num 21:24a mentions Israel's victory without the help of YHWH: "Israel smote him (Sihon) with the edge of the sword." The idea of divine intervention by which YHWH destroyed Heshbon, the main city of the Amorite kingdom with other cities (Num 32:3), may be considered as a work of Dtr revision, though the whole chapter of Num 32 belongs to the old Pentateuchal sources.[81] But J. van Seters claims that the reason that the Numbers account of the Sihon battle does not contain the motif of divine intervention corresponds with the later Babylonian chronicle which is entirely lacking in the idea

[81] Noth, *Numbers*, 235.

of divine intervention.[82] As seen in the previous chapters, even annalistic literature does not include the idea of divine intervention until a state had become a powerful kingdom, the rising period to power.

2

However, the idea of the YHWH intervention in war is not a Deuteronomic invention, but rather an earlier thought. A characteristic formula of the YHWH intervention reused by Dtr is נתן יי ביד which is a very common literary and iconographic phrase in the ancient Near Eastern context, as mentioned previously. This *Übereignungsformel* mainly occurs in the Deuteronomic literature as a literary character of YHWH war.[83] Recently W. Richter has pointed out that most (121 of 134 times) of the formulas belong to DtrG (87 times) and its influence (34 times).[84] Yet it indicates that the formula was not invented by the Deuteronomic and the Deuteronomistic school, but by their widespread usage. For this formula was already used in the early context of inquiring of the YHWH oracle and was used by Saul who failed to get it (I Sam 14:37a) and by David who succeeded in getting it (I Sam 23:4,11 ff; II Sam 5:19). The texts:

שמ" א יד:לז	וישאל שאול באלהים הארד אחרי פלשתים התתנם ביד ישראל ולא ענהו ביום ההוא.
שמ" א כג:ד[ב]	ויאמר קום רד קעילה כי אני (יי) נתן את פלשתים בידך.
// יד[ב]:	ויבקשהו שאול כל הימים ולא נתנו אלהים בידו.
שמ" ב ה:יט	וישאל דיד ביהוה לאמר האעלה אל פלשתים התתנם בידי ויאמר יהוה אל דוד עלה כי נתן אתן את הפלשתים כידך.
שמ" א כג:יא[א]	היסגרני בעלי קעילה בידו...[85]
// יב:	ויאמר דוד היסגרו בעלי קעילה אתי ואת אנשי ביד שאול ויאמר יהוה יסגירו.
// כ:	תעתה לכל אות נפשך המלך לרדת רד ולנו הסגירו ביד המלך.

[82] *JBL* 91, 188–89. On the basis of the parallel elements, W. A. Summer ("Israel's Encounters, with Edom, Moab, Ammon, Sihon and Og, According to the Deuteronomist," *VT* 18, 1968, 226) assumes that both Numbers and Deuteronomy are dependent upon earlier traditions.

[83] von Rad, *Krieg*, 7–9.

[84] *Traditionsgeschichtliche Untersuchungen zum Richterbuch*, BBB 18 (Bonn 1963), 22 (— *Untersuchungen*).

[85] The emendation מכר is improbable (*BDB*, 649). It may be emended as סגר. For all the versions are identified with the meaning of סגר. The LXX has πεπρακεν θεο-εξεδωκεν, Sam (ה)ישלמ, Targ בבד and the Vulg tradidit.

// ז:ב — ויאמר שאול נכר אתו אלהים בידי כי נסגר לבוא בעיר דלתים ובריח.

תה" לא:ט — ולא הסגרתני ביד אויב העמדת במרחב רגלי.

The above passages show that the ביד formula appears in both the inquiring of the YHWH oracle and his promise of victory. In the case of Saul there was no promise of YHWH for victory, and so, no answer. On the other hand, in the case of David there was YHWH's assurance of victory. So YHWH said, "I will give the Philistine into your hand." In most of these formulas YHWH gives his speech directly in the first person. Richter considers that the *Sitz im Leben* of the נתן ביד formula was the institution of the inquiry of the divine oracle.[86] For to know the divine will before the beginning of the battle or of the attack would be a decisive factor for victory. Another formula of the Übereignungsformel is the סגר ביד formula. This formula is also used in the context of inquiring of the will of YHWH. Yet YHWH directly does not speak in the first person. This formula is mainly used in the dialogue between man and man, such as Saul to David (I Sam 24:18), David to Goliath (I Sam 17:46).[87] It seems that this originally was the formula of the profane war descriptions which were meant to defeat the enemy. This usage does not appear in the war descriptions of the pre-Monarchy. Yet this formula does not parallel with the oriental usage of the similar meaning such as the נתן ביד formula. In I Sam 23:7 the form נכר ביד seems to be a form mistaken for סגר ביד in the textual transmission. Other versions are identified with the meaning of סגר ביד.[88] On the basis of the parallel of the Übereignungsformel in Mari texts and the נתן ביד formula in the Old Testament, J. G. Heintz has suggested some connection with both formulas.[89] He considers as the point of contact the Samson story in which the Philistines praised their god Dagon who gave his enemy (Samson) into their hand (Judg 16:23–24). Yet it is difficult to accept this idea of direct influence on the Old Testament, because there is at least a time distance of about 700 years between Mari and Israel, though Israel grew up with a common background of Mesopotamian culture in the late period. Recently Keel has considered the Egyptian influence of the Übereignungsformel which was dominantly used in the second half of the second millennium – the period of Ramses – as a possible point of contact.[90] Moreover, the Exodus peoples came out of Egypt during the Ramses period. Yet Egyptian power

[86] *Untersuchungen*, 23.

[87] I Sam 30:15 (An Egyptian to David), I Sam 26:8 (Abisai to David), II Sam 18:28 (Ahimaz to the king).

[88] See no. 85.

[89] "Oracles Prophétiques et 'Guerre Sainte' selon des Archives Royales de Mari et l'Ancien Testament," *VTS* 17 (1969), 112–38.

[90] *Siegeszeichen*, 47–49.

after the Ramses period decreased and never extended to control of the whole Palestine area after that time except for the invasions of Shishak and his successors (935–874 BC). But we can suggest the possibility that when David fled to Gath (I Sam 27) for a year and four months, he learned this formula of divine war through the Philistines who had known the idea of divine war as Egyptian mercenaries during the second half of the second millennium. This idea is supported by the early sources. In Josh 24:11b–12 (E) the Amoritees were a people who were given into Israel's hand by YHWH: "But I gave them (the inhabitants in Canaan) into your hand. And I sent הצרעה (typical terror of divine intervention) before you ..."[91] Noth, von Rad, and Soggin believe that the traditions which are recorded here are both ancient and authentic, Deuteronomistic.[92] But the Amorite kings in this context indicate those of the west Jordan, not Transjordan.[93]

Moreover, Num 21:29b suggests that משלים who cites the Sihon's victory song over Moab for Israel's victory at least knew the idea of divine war when Chemosh gave up his people to the king of the Amorite, Sihon, as divine punishment. For in this context it is possible that the subject of the verb נתן in MT is Chemosh, the god of Moab: "He (Chemosh) has made his sons fugitives, and his daughters prisoners of the Amorites."[94] Such a viewpoint is parallel with the motif of divine war in v. 28: "Behold, a fire shall go forth from Heshbon, a flame from the city of Sihon, it will consume Ar of Moab, the lands of the heights of Arnon." The fire which goes forth and consumes is a very common divine weapon in the ancient Near East and in the Old Testament. These quotations in Jer 48:45–46 were recognized as words of YHWH: "In the shadow of Heshbon the fugitives stood without strength; for a fire has gone out of Heshbon and a flame from the midst of Sihon, and has devoured the corner of Moab and the crown of the head of the roaring people. Woe to these, O Moab, the people of Chemosh is perishing. For your sons are taken into captivity, and your daughters into thraldom." In the end the fragments of the Amorite victory song became the word of YHWH for YHWH's intervention in Jeremiah.[95] It is supported by the translation of the Targum in Num 21:28: "Behold, a strong east wind goes out like a fire from Hesh-

---

91 Cooke, *Joshua*, 217.

92 Soggin, *Joshua*, OTL, ET by R. A. Wilson (London 1972), 228.

93 *Ibid.*, 235.

94 In contrast to MT, Peshita reads: The people of Chemosh have given their sons as hostages and their daughters as prisoners of Sihon, the king of the Amorites. The LXX: Their sons were abandoned for their rescue and their daughters (became) prisoners of the king of the Amorites, Sihon.

95 M. Diman (Haran), "An Archaic Remnant in the Prophetic Literature," *Yedioth=BJPES* 13 (1949), 14–15 (Hebrew).

bon."[96] The east wind is part of YHWH's arsenal – an ancient mythological motif – in His fight against the enemies of Israel, as seen in the previous section. The Targum interpretation would suggest that the fire is really the fire of YHWH.

On the basis of the song of Heshbon (Num 21:27b–30), J. R. Bartlet doubts the historical reality of the Sihon battle with Israel. First of all, the wave of destruction travelling from North to South does not refer to the conflicts with the Israelite tribes who came from the South.[97] The taunt song of the Amorite composition is certainly the report of an Amorite attack on Moabite Heshbon rather than an Exodus Israelite attack.[98] Secondly, it is not certain that Heshbon, Medeba, and Dibon were in Moabite territory in the thirteenth century BC. Bartlet sees the first possibility when Moab took possession of his territory up to the land north of the Arnon as the time of the invasion of Moab described in the story of Ehud (Judg 3).[99] Finally, Heshbon as a city of Sihon does not necessarily mean that Sihon was still its king at the time of the destruction described in the song. Later ages could refer to Heshbon as the city of Sihon just as they could refer to Jerusalem as the city of David.[100] M. H. Segal has suggested that the song of the Moshelim upholds the claim of Jephthah in his passage to the king of Ammon that Israel did not take his territory in Transjordan from Moab, but from Sihon in the age of Jephthah (Judg 11:15).[101]

3

The archeological evidence shows that the southern part of the land east of Jordan, and northwards as far as the region of the Jabbok, only began to be occupied with permanent settlements in the course of the 13th century BC.[102] Thus Noth sees that there was no occasion for warlike conflicts with the people here coming into being, closely related to the Israelite tribes in character and each having its own area.[103] Moreover, he holds that the phrase "from Arnon to Jabbok," first occurs in secondary

---

[96] M. Ottosson, *Gilead*: Tradition and History, CB 3 (Lund 1969), 64; A. Sperber, *The Bible in Aramaic* I (1959), 260.

[97] "The Historical Reference of Numbers 21:27–30," *PEQ* 101 (1969), 94 ff.

[98] N. K. Gottwald, *The Tribes of Yahweh*: A Sociology of the Religion of Liberated Israel, 1250–1050 BCE (NY 1979), 215.

[99] *PEQ* 101, 94, n. 1.

[100] *Ibid.*

[101] *The Pentateuch*: Its composition and Its Authorship, and Other Biblical Studies (Jerusalem 1967), 68.

[102] de Vaux, *EHI* II, 565. Heshbon has no occupation layer from LB IIB (M. Weippert, *IDBS*, 128).

[103] *The History of Israel* (NY/Evanston 1960), 154 (– *HI*).

additions to the Deuteronomic tradition in the 6th century BC, when this territory formed a political unity as the Persian province of Ammon. Thus the phrase cannot be used as evidence for an existence of the thirteenth century BC Ammonite kingdon covering that territory.[104] Such a viewpoint of the Deuteronomist is also based on the theory of the possession of the land. The Dtr evidently believes that Israel has no claim to the land of Edom, Moab and Ammon, because YHWH has already apportioned these lands to their owners (Dt 2:5). But with Sihon and Og, no such kinship or tradition of them receiving possession as a gift from YHWH is mentioned, and so no difficulty is felt in taking their land.[105] From the historical outcome it may be deduced that the land of the Amorites, in contrast to Edom, was a part of the territory that Israel was trying to conquer. Moreover, in Num 21:24 the reason that Israel did not go up to attack Ammon is that the boundary of the sons of Ammon was strong. Num 20:15 presents Israel as a plaintive weakling at the border of Edom, and vv. 20 ff show that Edom refused their passage and met them with a strong army to repel them. But Numbers gives us no explanation for why Israel did attack Sihon. Thus both Numbers' view of Israel's inferiority and Deuteronomy's view of superiority are in contrast, yet Numbers' view is closer to historical reality.

However, it can hardly be doubted that the Sihon tradition preserves the memory of an actual warlike clash, perhaps of a more or less local conflict between the tribe of Israel and the population which they found in the area.[106] It is seen that the early writer included the song of the Amorite composition in his narrative as a sort of document of proof for historical fact.[107] Then who was really the victor? Because in this account Moses is not mentioned, the conclusion has been drawn that it was only the group of Reuben-Gad who were involved or simply the group of Gad.[108] According to Num 32:34–38 and Josh 3:15–28 both Reuben and Gad had settled in a part of Transjordan. On the Moabite Stone, Mesha, the king of Moab, says that the men of Gad always dwelt in the land of Ataroth (line 10). Thus it may be concluded that the Sihon battle with Israel was the historical reality of the occupation war by immediate settlement, but not that of destruction and extermination such as in Joshua's war.[109] There is no motif of YHWH's intervention in the battle. Later this profane war was adopted as a YHWH war by the Deuterono-

[104] J. R. Bartlet, "Sihon and Og," *VT* 20 (1970), 260.

[105] Summer, *VT* 18, 219.

[106] Bartlet, *VT* 20, 272, n. 1.

[107] P. D. Hanson, "The Song of Heshoon and David's NĪR," *HTR* 61 (1968), 297–99.

[108] de Vaux, *EHI* II, 566, ns. 43 and 44.

[109] Y. Kaufmann, *The Biblical Account of the Conquest of Palestine*, ET by M. Dagut (Jerusalem 1953), 86.

mist.[110] In Num 21:32 the Jazer battle is similar to the Sihon battle in which YHWH intervention does not appear, though Moses played the main role in the battle.

2) Conquest War against Og

Most scholars are of the opinion that the account of the battle with Israel and Og (Num 21:33–35) agrees almost entirely with that in Dt 3:1–3 and duplicates the story of the victory gained over Sihon.[111] But M. Ottosson does not believe that the Deuteromonic influence is to be found in Num 21:33–35 and it is highly probable that the Deuteronomist took his information from the Tetrateuch or that both the P-traditionist and the Deuteronomist depend on the same conquest materials.[112] Yet it must be that YHWH's promise in Num 21:34 is most characteristic of the Deuteronomic theology (Dt 3:2). V. 35 is also a formal expression of the idea of the divine war of Dtr: The war of total destruction and extermination. The Übereignungsformel which includes the enemy's people and land as well as the enemy as the objects to be destroyed is Deuteronomistic in character. According to Noth, the Deuteronomist was the first to introduce the story of king Og of Bashan in the story of conquest and all later references to king Og depend on his account.[113] This story is found only in the Deuteronomic literature.[114]

However, it is no longer clear how much historical reality it contains. Some scholars suggest that Og is not a historical person, neither is the name even a personal name nor the name of a king, but that of a geographical region in the second millenium BC.[115] R. de Vaux assumes that the clear intention of this story is to justify the claims made by the half-tribe of Manasseh to a district which the Israelites never in fact possessed.[116] Noth also believes that the Israelites encountered king Og of Bashan merely in stories emanating from the city-state territory of Bashan but not directly as a historical figure; and so the victory of the Israelites over Og at Edrei can scarcely be called a historical event, but merely an indirect expression of the fact that Israel claimed possession of the city-state territory in the Northern land east of Jordan without ever really having possessed it. It is highly probable that no warlike conflicts

[110] Stolz, *Kriege*, 74.
[111] de Vaux, *EHI* II, 567; Noth, *Numbers*, 166.
[112] *Gilead*, 70.
[113] *Ibid.*, 69.
[114] Noth, *Numbers*, 166.
[115] de Vaux, *EHI* II, 567; van Seters, *JBL* 91, 195, n. 31; C. Rabin, *Eretz Israel* 8 (1967), 251–54.
[116] *Ibid.*

with the city-states took place at all in the early period, but that a state of peaceful coexistence developed such as was customary in the other parts of Palestine.[117]

But Bartlet says that it seems hard to deny all historical facts of the very concrete reference to a battle at Edrei.[118] Based on the fact that Og, king of Bashan, remained of the remnant of the Rephaim (Dt 3:11) which is identified with the Anakim of Judah as a giant, Bartlet hints that the men of Judah most likely heard of the figure of Og through their contacts, such as Joab's contact with the Transjordan in David's time. He goes on to argue that the tradition of the defeat of Og derives from clans or tribes who attempted to settle in the region of the Jabbok, – Machir, Jair or Nobah (Num 32:39 ff). It is most likely that Israel knew of Og through them. The battle at Edrei is not necessarily a worthless invention. It is the Jairites who are most often linked with the region of Bashan, and it may well be that traditions about Og's battle with the Israelites stem ultimately from the Jairites,[119] who are the same as Yauri, an Aramaean group referred to by Assyrian kings. This tradition met with the Sihon tradition at the Gilgal sanctuary and the two traditions were preserved in an oral cultic tradition and were adopted by the Deuteronomist. After that Og became an Amorite. However, N. K. Gottwald believes that the victory over Og credited in the Bible to Israel was actually achieved by the Ammonites, some of whom later were defeated by Israel and brought the memory of Og's defeat with them.[120] Thus the above evidence shows that the Og battle also had historical reality, but the motif of divine war was absent as in the Sihon battle until it finally reached the Deuteronomist. It seems better to say that the conquest in Transjordan actually reflected the situation of the settlement in Transjordan at the end of the period of the Judges.[121]

4. THE CONQUEST WARS IN CISJORDAN

Joshua 12 shows us that the conquest wars in Transjordan which we have discussed above, were carried out by Moses (vv. 1–6), whereas the conquest wars in Cisjordan were carried out by Joshua (vv. 7–24). The biblical tradition mentions that the conquest of Canaan was attributed to the leadership of Joshua appearing in Joshua cc. 1–11, the Book of the

---

[117] *HI*, 160.

[118] *VT* 20 (1970), 267.

[119] *Ibid.*, 271.

[120] *The Tribes of Yahweh*, 215.

[121] Y. Aharoni, "The Settlement of Canaan," *WHJP* III, 121.

Conquest.[122] In these chapters there are four war stories which took place in three zones: the battles of Jericho and Ai (cc. 2,6 and 7–8) in the central west; that of the Gibeonites against the confederation of the five kings (c. 10) in the south; and that against the alliance of the kings in the north (c. 11). The single idea of these battle legends is that the conquest of the land of Canaan was brought about by the power of YHWH through his miraculous intervention, which used to be called holy war, not by the force of the Israelites. It is explained as a two-fold miraculous sign: in the realm of the spirit and in that of matter. God strengthened the heart of Isreal while He melted the heart of the Canaanites. Again, He increased the power of Israel, cleaved a way before them, and smote the Canaanites.[123] One wonders whether or not the motifs of YHWH war appeared in the battles of Joshua in the time of the conquest of Canaan.

1

The first common issue in Josh 1–11 is the historical realities of the battles of Joshua. The present literary records which were composed by the Deuteronomist at the end of the 7th century BC[124] present some problems in finding the initial historical reality, because of two obstacles: the later theological reflection in which a historiosophy is subordinated to a theological doctrine and telescoping which is the compression of a string of events into a unified narrative of a relatively brief time-span.[125] The extra-biblical sources do not mention the conquest of Canaan. This deficiency can probably be ascribed to the fact that the Israelite conquest made no ruffle in the international scene. This subjectivity and the adherent suspicion of idealization and aggrandizement, are subservient to political and religious ideologies. Further, the historical truth-worthiness of biblical traditions receded with the lapse of time between events and their literary recording.[126] Thus this official or canonical tradition of the conquest which emerged as the culminating level of biblical consciousness presents a more or less organic and continuous chain of events in a straight-forward

[122] A. C. Tunyogi, "The Book of the Conquest," *JBL* 84 (1965), 374–80. The author believes that the primitive form of Deuteronomy and Joshua 1–11 are originally one work, that it was written shortly after, or perhaps toward the end of the age of the Omrides and that its purpose was to inaugurate a program in which the still surviving Canaanites must be exterminated...(374).

[123] Kaufmann, *The Biblical Account of the Conquest of Palestine*, 75.

[124] *Ibid.*, 2.

[125] A. Malamat, "Conquest of Canaan: Israelite Conduct of War According to Biblical Tradition," *Revue Internationale d'Historie Militarie* 42 (1979), 26–27; *id.*, *Israel in Biblical Times*: Historical Essays (Jerusalem 1983), 49 ff (Hebrew).

[126] *Ibid.*, "Conquest of Canaan," 25.

narrative: the entire territory of Canaan was occupied in a swift military operation under Joshua who is depicted as a supreme military commander with full divine collaboration. All twelve Israelite tribes participated in the Canaan conquest. This conquest was a national war, although the concept of the kingdom does not appear in this period.

However, these elements are in contrast to those in Judg 1 which are attributed to pre-Dtr.[127] In Judg 1 the war was a local war, not national. The military operation was carried out by the individual tribes and their leaders, not the unified Israelites troop and Joshua. In the earliest narratives the individual tribes during the Canaan conquest period established themselves precariously in Canaan in the midst of the native people, either by ruse or by military encounters. On this level Joshua was one of the individual tribal leaders such as Caleb or Gideon. His original name was Hoshea until Moses changed his name to Joshua (Num 13:8,16 and Dt 32:44). From quite an early time Joshua was regarded as an Ephraimite military leader in armed conflicts between the Ephraimite and the neighbouring Canaanite city-states.[128] Yet he does not have any warrior's titles like king David who was called a warrior. Joshua is described only as the servant of Moses (Ex 21:13), of God (Judg 2:8), or a leader of Israel for the occupation. In the program of Josianic national renovation which is understood as the resurrection of the Davidic Empire, Joshua was highly exalted as a supreme military commander like David. Moreover, the emphasis on Joshua himself is most naturally to be understood as reflecting the Deuteronomic ideal of Josiah. Thus the idea of Joshua's exaltation was an implicit message to the contemporaries of the Deuteronomistic redactor: they are to fear and obey Josiah as their ancestors had Joshua, indeed, as they had obeyed Moses.[129] For the Deuteronomic history may be described as a propaganda work of the Josianic reformation and imperial program, as that in the national or imperial renaissance in the ancient Near East.[130]

Regarding the subject of the geographical unities, Soggin points out that the unitary conquest of the country under the sole command of Joshua was a fictional construction which was perhaps already to be found, even before the Deuteronomic preaching, in the pre-exilic cult.[131] a) The southern conquest in Josh 10:28–43 is not connected with the military act of Joshua. With the exception of the Deuteronomist the Judeans were not

[127] B. L. Goff, "The Lost Jahwistic Account of the Conquest of Canaan," *JBL* 53 (1934), 248; M. Weinfeld, "The Period of the Conquest and of the Judges as seen by the Earlier and the Later Sources," *VT* 17 (1967), 93 ff.

[128] Noth, *Pentateuchal Traditions*, 175, n. 491.

[129] Mann, *Divine Presence*, 206.

[130] Cross, *CMHE*, 284.

[131] Soggin, *Joshua*, 18. Cf., de Vaux, *EHI* II, 595.

concerned with Joshua, the Ephraimite. This is confirmed by the fact that up to the time of David Judah had only marginal contact with the twelve tribes, having only very infrequent relations with them.[132] b) Moreover, Josh 1:1—10:15 describes the conquest of the territory of Benjamin. c) Josh 11:1—14 refers to two episodes in the conquest of the north, the battle of Merom and the destruction of Hazor, which seem to be independent of the narrative of the unitary conquest, and Joshua the Ephraimite does not seem to have played any part in its origin.

2

The second common issue in Josh 1—11 is YHWH consultation and oracle. In Josh 1—11 the motif of YHWH consultation does not appear. Divine consultation is the initial stage of divine war. This divination is a widespread phenomenon of divine war in the ancient Near East as we have discussed previously. Before any decisive action was undertaken, such as a declaration of war, a *bārû* priest was summoned to sacrifice a sheep and inspect its liver to determine whether the gods were favorably or unfavorably disposed toward the matter in question. Num 27:12—23 shows us that Eliazar the priest shall ask counsel for Joshua after the judgment of the Urim before YHWH: "At the priest's word, Joshua and his people will go out or come in." This inquiry of an oracle never took place in the context of conquest war by Joshua. The oracular diviner of Joshua like Eliazar did not appear in his war context. But in the period of Judges there is the reminiscence of an instance of divination before the battle. In Judg 6:36—40 Gideon had attempted with the fleece of wool to get divine assurance for this military commission against the Midianiates. Yet this section is isolated from the whole text of Gideon's story.[133] As far as the bibilical materials allow, the practise of divine consultation did not occur in the battle context until the time of Saul and David. In the course of time the techniques of battle oracles were displaced by the authoritative word of the prophet as YHWH's divinely appointed spokesman, the official herald of YHWH's imperium.[134] In all probability, Samuel was a bridge, an oracular diviner (ראה), between the various types of oracular divination by the priest in the premonarchic era and the emergence of war oracles by the classical prophets, though we do not have such war oracles in the received traditions until the ninth century YHWH war tradition in the northern kingdom in which the war oracle had already become a judgment speech.[135]

---

[132] Soggin, *Joshua*, 16, n. 3.

[133] J. A. Soggin, *Judges*, OTL, ET by J. Bowden (London 1981), 132.

[134] Christensen, *War Oracles*, 22.

[135] *Ibid.*, 38.

Of course, only the portions of the story theologized of the conquest of Cisjordan in Jugd 1, which is as close to historical reality as the pre-Dtr level, reflect a trace of consultation, but these are related to Joshua because these are reported as events after the death of Joshua. In fact, it is a piece of reportage rather than a religious interpretation.[136] These portions also do not relate to the story of conquest by the tribe of Judah in the south, but these only mention the conflict narrative of Adonibezek which took place in between Shechem and Beth Shean.[137] The traditions picture the occupation as solely the result of human action. No appeal is made to divine intervention, and no explanation of failure because of Israel's sin is introduced. The phrase (v. 2), "I (God) gave the land into his (Judah's) hand," does not fit in the battle context. For the object of the delivery formula is not an enemy, but the land which already had been promised by God to the patriarchs.[138] The promise oracle belongs to a salvation message, rather than a war oracle which is given from God by divine consultation. It is seen that it is a salvation oracle transformed from a war oracle as the Dtr reaction to YHWH war against Israel. Recently M. Rose has suggested that the demilitarization against war by the YHWHist formed this salvatiion formula as seen in Gen 12:7; 13:14–17; 15:7,18; 24:7; 26:3 ff; 28:13–15.[139] Here the objects of Übergabeformel to the patriarchs are the land, not the enemy. For YHWH war is not a simple guarantee of protection, but a dialectic: "die Gefahr des Kriegs Jahwes gegen Israel wird akut."[140] It corresponds to a theological attempt of the prophets like I Isaiah who tried to overcome the political crisis faced. Moreover, the national idealistic renovation of Josiah stimulated this thought stream and was later accomplished in the movement of the Deuteronomistic school. But in the patriarch narratives the idealistic expansion of the land was given without war like the Isaiahnic dialect, but in the Deuteronomic school it was possessed by the ideal destruction of the enemy.[141] In Josh 1–11 we find the same formulas (6 times) in which the object of Übergabeformel is the land, the city, or the city with the enemy, except the two coalitions of the northern and southern enemy in the plural (10:8,19; 11:6,8) and the three old sources (21:44; 24:8,11) in which the object of the Übergabeformel is the enemy. They are:

---

[136] Gottwald, *The Tribes of Yahweh*, 172.

[137] H. N. Rösel. "Judges I and the Settlement of the Leah Tribes," *Proceedings of the Eighth World Congress of Jewish Studies*, Division A (Jerusalem 1982), 17 (Hebrew).

[138] *Ibid.*, 19. V. 4 – "Yahweh gave the Canaanites and Perizzites into their (the Leah tribes') hand," is a later addition, because v. 4 is duplicated in v. 5 (*ibid.*).

[139] M. Rose, "Entmilitarisierung des Kriegs," *BZ* 20 (1976), 202.

[140] *Ibid.*, 210.

[141] *Ibid.*, 211.

ב:ט[ב]		כי		נתן	יי		לכם	את־הארץ
כד[א]:		כי		נתן	יי		בידנו	את־כל־הארץ
ו:ב	יי			נתתי			בידך	את־יריחו
טז[ב a]:		כי		נתן	יי		לכם	את־העיר
ח:א[ב]	יי			נתתי			בידך	את־עירו ואת־ארצו
יח[א b]:	יי	כי					בידך	אתננה (העי)
י:ח[א b]	יי	כי					בידך	נתתים (המלכים)
יב[א]:				תת	יי			את־האמרי לפני בני ישראל
יט[ב b]:		כי		נתנם	יי	אלהיכם	בידכם	(המלכים)
ל[א a]:				יתן	יי	גם־אותה	ביד ישראל	(לבנה)
לב[א a]:				יתן	יי	את־לכיש	ביד ישראל	
יא:ו[א]	יי	כי	אנכי	יתן				את כלם חללים לפני ישראל
ח[א a]:				ויתנם	יי		ביד ישראל	(אויבים)
כא:מד[ב b]			את־כל־אביכם	נתן	יי		בידם	
כד:ח[ב a]	יי			ואתן		אותם	בידכם	(אויבים)
יא[ב]:	יי			ואתן		אותם	בידכם	(אויבים)

The common element of the object of the above formulas is the land. The land belongs neither to Joshua nor to the people, but to YHWH who will apportion it justly for ths use of his people. So it is suggested that this formula was not used in the battle context as a divine oracle, but in the cultic context as a divine salvation oracle. For the first object on the battlefield to ensure victory is to destroy the enemy; the land is the secondary element of victory. In Israel's worship the land is a promised land. The conquest is a fulfillment of promise. Epic tradition and the Mosaic convenant theology of Dtr emphasize the same theme. The land was not won by Israel. It was a gift of God. There is one hero and only one. It is God himself and to him Israel must give all praise and credit.[142]. Thus this formula suggests that as Moses left Egypt without fighting, so Joshua entered Canaan without dramatic fighting.[143] Further, the content of the formula is in contrast to the character of Joshua's in which he never took the land. The wars of Joshua are those of destruction and extermination, not of occupation by immediate settlement. Joshua does not leave garrisons in the cities which he has captured, but he returns with all his people to the camp at Gilgal.[144].

With the parallel of the delivery formula the **אל תירא** formula occurs in Josh 8:1; 10:8,25. These also seem to belong to the category of the same salvation oracle. As seen in the previous chapters, the "fear not" formula is a common phraseology which was used in both religious and secular contexts in the ancient Near East.[145] At first, this "fear not" formula

---

142 R. G. Boling and G. E. Wright, *The Book of Joshua*, AB 6 (NY 1982), 12.

143 Cf., Lind, *Yahweh is a Warrior*, 78.

144 Kaufmann, *The Biblical Account of the Conquest of Palestine*, 86.

145 J. C. Greenfield, "The Zakir Inscription and the Danklied," *Proceedings of the Fifth World Congress of Jewish Studies* (Jerusalem 1969), 181 ff; Weippert, *ZAW* 84, 472–73; H. W. F. Saggs, "Assyrian Warfare in the Sargonic Period," *Iraq* 25 (1963), 150.

was characterized as *Offenbarungsrede* with Babylonian influence by H. Gressmann and L. Köhler and then as priestly *Heilsorakel* in the ancient cultic institution in Israel by J. Begrich.[146] But recently J. Becker has described this formula as *Beruhigungsformel* of the holy war which had its origin in a Heilsorakel.[147] It is probable that this was given as a divine orcale for victory in the battle. Then, most of these formulas are restricted to Deuteronomy and the Dtr school.[148] In this connection holy war is no longer a reality but a *Theologumenon.*[149] But the origin of the idea of "fear not" is derived from an earlier time, not from Deuteronomy. We find an example in Is 7:4 that the prophet Isaiah gave the oracle of YHWH to king Ahaz who was faced with a national crisis: "fear not (aαb)." In Ex 14:13 (J) Moses gave this oracle to his people who had faced terror from the threat of the Egyptian army: fear not. Thus P. E. Dion has suggested that the formulaic character finally acquired, perhaps around 900 BC, was mainly due to an internal development, a growing emphasis being put on the requirement of fearlessness included in the ideal of absolute faith which the elect people had inherited from the ancient wars of YHWH.[150]

3

The third common issue in Josh 1—11 is utter destruction, so-called חרם, which appears in the utter destruction of the cities of Jericho and Ai (6:21; 8:24,26), of the cities mentioned in 10:28—41,[151] of Hazor (11:20), of the cities of the northern confederacy (1:11—12), and of the Anakim and their cities (11:21). The category of goods which are mentioned under the חרם varies. In the case of Jericho it included both men and women, young and old, oxen, sheep and asses. In that of Ai it was all the people of Ai. In that of the southern coalition against Israel, Joshua smote the city and its king and destroyed utterly the city and every person in it; he left none remaining. In that of Hazor it was all the people.

146 H. Gressmann, "Die literarische Analyse Deuterojesajas," *ZAW* 34 (1914), 254—97, espe. 287—89; L. Köhler, "Die Offenbarungsformel 'Fürchte dich nicht' im Alten Testament," *Schweizerische Theologische Zeitschrift* 36 (1919), 33—39; J. Begrich, "Das priesterliche Heilsorakel," *ZAW* 52 (1934), 81—82. Greenfield, against Gressmann's assessment of the Babylonian influence, suggests parallels with the biblical examples in Genesis and the Zakir inscription which precedes the Assyrian inscriptions (*op. cit.*, 190).

147 *Gottesfurcht im Alten Testment* (Rome 1965), 54.

148 Num 21:34; Dt 1:21,29; 3:2; 7:21; 20:1,3; 31:6,8; Josh 1:9; 8:1; 10:8,25; 11:6.

149 Becker, *op. cit.*, 54.

150 "The 'fear not' Formula and Holy War," *CBQ* 32 (1970), 570.

151 In the battle of Gibeon (Josh 10:1—15) the idea of Ḥerem does not appear. M. Haran, "The Gibeonites: Their Place in the Conquest War of the Land and in the History of Israel," *Issues in the Book of Joshua* (Jerusalem 1971), 126 (Hebrew).

It is hard to believe that in the time of Joshua utter destruction took place in the Canaanite cities. No doubt there was bloodshed and violence. But as far as we know, there was no mass "genocide" committed by the Israelites. We know that the Canaanites were never totally destroyed but most of them were gradually absorbed, and the process did not come to an end even after the exile. Neither can we discern utter destruction in Judah, either before or after David and Solomon. The Canaanite and the other non-Judean groups like the Kenites, Calebites etc., appear peacefully coexisting with Judah (Num 10:29; 24:21; Josh 14:6ff; Judg 4:11; I Sam 14:16), and David was on good terms even with the Jebusites (II Sam 24:18).

Our text is a theological description of Dtr theologians, and these verses from Joshua should not be taken as a battle report from a war correspondent. For the Dtr theologians were more interested in the theological meaning of חרם than in its actual practice. For them this utter destruction symbolizes a radical break or discontinuity in the old Canaanite society and the new covenant society of Israel. The seven nations (Dt 7:2) must be destroyed because "they would turn our sons away from following me (Dt 7:4)," and "teach you to do according to their abominable practices which they have done in the service of their gods, and so to sin against the Lord your God (Dt 20:18)." It is considered that the idea of חרם as a thorough cleansing of YHWH faith against the neighbouring religious practices was a ground core of the religious revival movement of Josiah. The idea of utter destruction in war does not occur in the context of the ancient Near East except in the Hittite kingdom in the second millennium BC. The חרם had its origin in the offensive war,[152] but it cannot be ascribed to the battles of Joshua.

All the above evidence of the common elements of Josh 1—11 tells us that these elements were not related with the historical realities of the conquest of Cisjordan by Joshua. Let us examine the battles of Joshua respectively, to see whether or not the motifs of YHWH war in historical battles is found.

1) The Battle of Jericho (cc. 2—6)

1

There come some questions about the real battle: Did the walls really collapse as reported in Josh 6? If so, would not Rahab's house have been destroyed? Did the people experience the aid of YHWH in the battle? It is observed that we cannot look at Josh 6 as a simple factual account of

[152] Miller, *Divine Warrior*, 157, n. 281; C. H. W. Brekelmans, *De Ḥerem in het Oude Testament* (Nijmegen 1959), 188.

things as they actually happened in the month of March or April in a particular year in the late 13th or early 12[2th] century BC. What we find is rather history remembered through liturgy. The narrative as we have reflects the annual Gilgal festival, in which a ceremonial procession of people taking the part of warriors, priests, ark-bearers, and rear guard circled the ruins of ancient Jericho over a period of seven days, climaxing in the ritualized destruction of "the city". This procession happened only once a day, but seven times on the seventh day. The people remained silent while the horns were blown during week days, but on the seventh day, during the march the walls did fall down flat (6:20).

In Mari and Ugaritic texts we find the ritual activity which was required to be performed for three (ARMT III 30:9–13) or six days (ARMT V 65:19) for a military expedition.[153] In his epic, Keret performs a ritual activity of seven consecutive days as a part of war preparation before battle. In this ritual activity an action is repeated for six consecutive days and completed on the seventh day as the climax of seven days. Keret stays quiet for six consecutive days, but on the seventh day he attempts to attack the king Pabil (*CTA* 14:218–23):[154]

218. d[m] ym wṯn	He did stay quiet a day and a second,
219. ṯlṯ[ ]rbʿ ym	a third a fourth day,
220. ḫmš ṯdṯ ym	a fifth, a sixth day,
221. mk[ ]špšm bšbʿ	then with the sun on the seventh [day]
222 wl yšn[ ]pbl	king Pabil could not sleep.
223. mlk	

The litarary scheme of the climax of seven days already appeared in the Gilgamesh epic XI, II 141–46.[155] In this scheme the six days are divided into three groups of two days each. The first description of the action precedes the mentioning of the days and is repeated verbatim after each one of the three groups of two days. In the temple liturgy in Gen 1 we find the same literary scheme of seven days, during the six consecutive days the creation of the world and all things, and on the seventh – Sabbath day – divine rest. At the same time, the purpose of the ritual activity serves to recall and actualize the original event and its meaning.

Recently M. Gichon has suggested that this pattern of thought of the seven consecutive days was an ancient military stratagem which could take Jericho by an indirect approach and which appears in the collection of

---

153 Glock, *Warfare*, 130

154 Gibson, *CML*, 88.

155 S. E. Loewenstamm, "The Seven Day-Unit in Ugaritic Epic Literature," *IEJ* 15 (1965), 121–33; *ANETS*, 94. In this case the setting is not a war contest: One day, a second day, mount Nisir hald the ship fast, allowing no motion,... (two times repeat up to a sixth day), when the seventh day arrived, I (Gilgamesh) sent forth and set free a dove.

stratagems published by Sextus Julius Frontinus before the first century AD.[156] The function of this strategy is to neutralize and to lull the enemy into a false sense of security by gradually accustoming him to the manoeuvres that will later be used in opening and developing an attack. This shows a possibility of an actual military strategy for a frontal attack. But it is hard to believe that his strategy was used for the taking of Jericho. For this strategy appears in only the official-canonical traditions of the Bible — the late biblical traditions theologized, not the earlier traditions.

Moreover, the literary scheme of the description of city destruction by the conduct of war in Josh 6 is a fixed form which appears commonly in the Hittite texts. S. Gevirtz examined the seven descriptions of city destruction by wars as follows:[157]

1 ḫunusa	2 Ḫattuša	3 Hittite 2	4 Timmu- ḫala	5 Jericho	6 Crisa	7 Carthage
burned	destroyed	destroyed	burned	burned	razed	razed
Strewn with ṣipa	Sown with cress					
		purified				
			conse- crated	conse- crated	conse- crated	conse- crated (?)
Re- occupation prohibited	Future settler cursed	Future settler cursed	Re- occupation prohibited	Future settler cursed	Future settler cursed	Future settler cursed

All the cities have in common both their destruction and a prohibition against their resettlement. Texts 4—7 have in common the element of the consecration of the site, but texts 1—3 have no statement of the Ḥerem of the city.

Archeological evidence shows us that when the Israelites arrived in the late 13th century BC, Jericho was not inhabited as a ruin-mound standing as it now appears.[158] If we follow Kenyon's conclusion, the connection of a destruction of Jericho with an entry of the Israelites into Canaan at the end of the 13th century BC is not possible, unless more evidence is given. Most recently Y. Yadin has suggested a possibility of reusing the MB city wall by the LB settlers and thus the first Israelite

[156] C. Herzog and M. Gichon, *Battles of the Bible* (London 1978), 29.

[157] S. Gevirtz, "Jericho and Shechem: A Religio-Literary Aspect of City Destruction," *VT 13 (1963), 60.*

[158] de Vaux, *EHI* II, 610; K. M. Kenyon, *Digging up Jericho* (London 1957), 256—65.

attack against Jericho may have occurred at the 14th or 13th century.[159] This solution then creates more problems. Because of lack of provable evidence, those who follow the Alt-Noth theory that Jericho was occupied peacefully and that the conquest narrative is a pure aetiology, are most likely to be accurate in the light of present evidence.[160]

2

However, within this completely ritual context there is a little room for some kind of military action in the original event. There are some clues. Josh 2 indicates that when the Israelites arrived in Canaan, the clan of Rahab's house must have been settled in Jericho. In this chapter the activity of spies was the initial stage of war conducted in the ancient Near East and in the Bible. The word חפר (v. 2), which is used to report the spies' activity to the king of Jericho and to Rahab (pre-Dtr), was part of the original story of the spies and Rahab which was incorporated into the history work, not composed for it.[161] It is seen by the contrast between the direction to look at (ראה) the land and the city in v. 2, an introduction added to the story, and the actual use of חפר immediately after in the story itself.

We find in Josh 21:11 that "the men of Jericho fought against you," suggesting an armed clash between Jericho's "mighty men of valor" (6:2) and Joshua's "men of war" or "armed men" (vv. 3,7,9,13). Again, the scarlet cord hanging from Rahab's window (2:18) seems to hint at a secret mode of access by infiltrators into Jericho. Soggin has suggested that the contents in 5:13–15 which mention the encounter of Joshua with the commander of the army of YHWH lead to an obvious conclusion: that the Lord's armies, led by their commander, would assist those of Israel, not so much in performing a procession as in fighting the enemy. Here the conquest appears neither wholly miraculous nor wholly due to Israel's military engagement, but is a combination of both.[162] The idea of the commander of YHWH's army is not designated as the angel of YHWH.[163] The expression of YHWH's army in Ex 12:41 indicates the children of Israel who went out from Egypt as a late priestly creation. It does not fit in the

---

[159] Y. Yadin, "Is the Biblical Account of the Israelite Conquest of Canaan Historically Reliable?" *BAR* 8/2 (1982), 22.

[160] M. Weippert, *The Settlement of the Israelite Tribes in Palestine*, SBT 21, tr. by J. D. Martin (London 1971), 26 ff (— *Settlement*); *id.*, "Conquest of Canaan and Settlement," *IDBS*, 125–29.

[161] D. J. McCarthy, "Some Holy War Vocabulary in Joshua 2," *CBQ* 33 (1971), 228–29.

[162] J. A. Soggin, "The Conquest of Jericho through Battle," *Eretz Israel* 16 (1982), 216.

[163] Miller, *Divine Warrior*, 131; Keel, *Siegeszeichen*, 84. The expression of the drawn sword is a sacramental symbol to scatter the enemy (88).

context of the original campaign of Joshua. Soggin again suggests that the evidence of Josh 2:18 in the LXX as a variant reading. "ἰδου ἡμεις εἰσπορεὑομαθα εἰς μέρος τῆς πόλεος "(הנה אנחנו באים בחלק/בחדרי העיר) is another indicator to describe the real battle of Jericho. For "εἰς μέρος τῆς πόλεος" is a better reading than בארץ in the MT as a precise topographical point. In this consideration the aetiological theory of Alt and Noth is not suitable to the case of the Jericho conquest. De Vaux believes that the conquest narrative of Jericho is not a simple and pure aetiology, but a story based on a historical memory of the taking of Jericho.[164]

In Josh 24:11b we find a Übergabeformel in the first singular perfect: ואתן אותם בידכם. The delivery formula is to confirm and proclaim Israel's faith in God's promise which has already been fulfilled. Victory is already assured even before the fighting begins. At the same time, the story presupposes that the capture of Jericho was accepted as a fact by those who told the story and by those who heard it. The story was theologized on the memory that Jericho was really captured through the battle with the Israelites.[165] Throughout the history of the religion of Israel the living spirit of the Jericho battle by the miraculous intervention of YHWH through ritual activity has been transmitted even in the Book of II Maccabees: "the Jericho story inspired Judas to attack an impregnable fortress with inferior forces and slaughter the inhabitants (12:15–16)."

2) The Battle of Ai (cc. 7–8)

The story of the battle of Ai is presented in a way which is quite different from that of the battle of Jericho. There are five different interpretations of the battle of Ai: military, archeological, literary, aetiological and sacramental phenomenon.

The first interpretation is the military aspect. Recently Gichon and Malamat have suggested that the historicity of the taking of Ai can be understood from the aspect of the military stratagems: intelligence, ambush, enticement of city defenders, surprise attack and night operation.[166] According to the official-canonical tradition Joshua first sent a troop of 3000 soldiers to occupy Ai on the basis of the optimistic report of the scouts but failed (Josh 7:2–5a). Then he had recourse to a military stratagem (Josh 8). He placed a troop of picked men in a concealed position to the west of the town, between Ai and Bethel, and camped with the rest of his men in full view of the enemy. The king of Ai set out with his

[164] de Vaux, *EHI* II, 612.

[165] *Ibid.*

[166] Herzog and Gichon, *Battles of the Bible*, 29–34; Malamat, *RIHM* 42 (1979), 25–52; *id.*, "How Inferior Israelite Forces Conquered Fortified Canaanite Cities," *BAR* 8/2 (1982), 24–35; *id.*, *Israel in Biblical Times* (1983), 58–80 (Hebrew).

men to do battle and Joshua and the Israelites retreated, allowing the enemy to pursue them a long way from the town. The men in ambush entered the town and lit a fire there as a signal to the main force. These turned back and attacked the men of Ai, massacring them. But one doubts whether these stratagems were used for the taking of Ai in the earlier tradition, before the story was organized and theologized as it now stands in the Bible. Otherwise it is clearly an account of a profane war.[167]

The next interpretation is the archaeological point of view. Until now archaeolgical evidence has given us a negative answer — that the Israelites under Joshua did not conquer a Canaanite city on the site of Khirbet et-Tell (Ai), which is the only viable location, for the simple reason that this city did not exist at the end of the thirteenth century BC.[168] There are some solutions: first of all, the location of Ai was not situated at et-Tell. There is no site in the region to the east of Bethel, in contrast to the mention of a city east of Bethel in Josh 7:2.[169] The second solution is that the ruins of Ai were used as a fortified camp by the people of Bethel on the basis of the men of Ai and Bethel in Josh 8:17. Yet the words "and Bethel" are absent in the LXX and in the Syro-Hexaplar.[170] The third solution, mainly by the Albright school, is the identification of the taking of Ai (ruin) with the taking of Bethel by others on the basis of the nearness of Ai and Bethel and the similarity with the story of the taking of Bethel in Judg 1:22—26.[171] But the story of the taking of Bethel does not appear in the Book of Joshua. In Judg 1:22—26 the town of Bethel was captured by the house of Joseph, and there is no mention of its destruction by the Israelites. The archaeological evidence shows us that the town of Bethel was destroyed at the end of the LB Age.[172] The last solution, by J. A. Callaway, is that the capture of Ai could have occurred c. 1125 BC on the basis of the Iron Age I village remains.[173] That the Hivites who settled at et-Tell in the end of LB Age were destroyed by the Israelites during the conquest period under Joshua cannot be proved as a historical reality. For there is no evidence that there were other immigrants into this part of Canaan at this period apart from the Sea People and the Israelites.[174] At

---

167 de Vaux, *EHI* II, 613.

168 *Ibid.*, 617.

169 *Ibid.*, 614, n. 63; J. Simons, *The Geographical and Topographical Texts of the Old Testament* (Leiden 1959), 270.

170 de Vaux, *EHI* II, 615.

171 W. F. Albright, "The Kyle Memorial Bulletin of Excavation of Bethel," *BASOR* 56 (1934), 11; G. E. Wright. *Biblical Archaeology* (Philadelphia 1957), 80; J. Bright, *A History of Israel* (London 1966), 119.

172 de Vaux, *EHI* II, 617, n. 72. De Vaux rejects the date (1240—1235 BC) of J. K. Kelso (*The Excavation of Bethel 1934—1960*, *AASOR* 39, 1968).

173 *IDBS*, 16.

174 de Vaux, *EHI* II, 617.

the same time, if Joshua died at the age of 110 (Josh 24:29), the above data of the conquest of Ai cannot be applied to him who was the only single living Exodus member at that time. All the archaeological evidence of the taking of Ai and its solutions, as de Vaux suggests, are not enough to prove the historical reality of the capture of Ai in Josh 7–8.

The third interpretation beyond the archaeolgical debate is the aetiological point of view of this story suggested by the Alt-Noth school.[175] An explanation was sought for the existence of the ruins of a large town, the name of which was not known and which was called העי (the ruin). Josh 8:28 tells us: "Joshua burned Ai, and made it for ever a heap of ruins, as it is to this day." At the entrance to the gate of the ruined town, there was a great cairn and it was under this heap of stones which stands there to this day, that the corpse of the king of Ai had been placed after he had been taken down from the tree on which he had been hanged. Even Yadin supports the aetiological idea: We must interpret the biblical account of Ai as aetiological.[176]

The fourth interpretation, by de Vaux and W. M. W Roth[177] is that the story of the capture of Ai was originally derived from that of the battle of Gibeah by all the tribes of united Israel against Benjamin as a punishment for the crime committed against the concubine of the Levite of Ephraim in Judg 20, which is part of an appendix to the Book of Judges consisting of early traditions which had been left out by the Deuteronomic editor of the book and were included in the editorial revision which took place after the exile. In both texts, Josh 8 and Judg 20, there are several common elements of the wars. The first attack made by the Israelites was repelled by the enemy in Judg 20:19–21 (the Benjaminites) and Josh 7:4–5 (the people of Ai). The second attack, which also resulted in defeat (Judg 20:22–25) has no parallel in Joshua. In Judg 20 YHWH's reply was: "The first will be Judah (v. 18), march against them (the Benjaminites)" in v. 23, and "go up against them: tomorrow I will give them into your hands (v. 27)." In Josh 8:1 YHWH's reply: "I have given into your hand the king of Ai, and his people, his city and his land." So the Israelites prepared an ambush to the west of Gibeah (Judg 20:29,33) and behind Ai (Josh 8:3,9). The Benjaminites and the people of Ai were drawn a long way from the city (Judg 20:31–32,39; Josh 8:6,16). The Israelites who were in ambush meanwhile entered the city and lit a fire there (Judg 20:37–38; Josh 8:19) and the Benjaminites and the people of Ai saw the city burning (Judg 20:40; Josh 8:20). Thereupon the Israelites turned round and massacred the Benjaminites and the people of Ai who

175 Weippert, *Settlement*, 27–29.

176 *BAR* 8/2, 23.

177 de Vaux, *EHI* II, 619; W. M. W. Roth, "Hinterhalt und Scheinflucht," *ZAW* 75 (1963), 30 ff.

were caught between them and the men who had been in ambush (Judg 20:40 Josh 8:20–22). De Vaux believes that the story of the taking of Gibeah is a tradition of the sanctuary at Mizpah and that of the taking of Ai is a Bethel tradition, the latter being inspired by the former.[178]

Moreover, the story of the taking of Gibeah in Judg 20 is not a single event but is unified and organized as a single battle event. According to Soggin, Gibeah's story consists of three different battle events.[179] The first two battle stories are in Judg 20:18–28. The third battle consists of two different versions: the first versions – vv. 29,36b,37a,38–42a,45,46; the second – vv. 30–36a,37b,42b,47. In the first two battle events the Benjaminites had the victories, but YHWH did not play an explicit part at all. YHWH's consultation, in the form שאל...ביהוה (vv. 23,27), seems identical with that of Judg 1:1 ff which is relatively late in the Deuteronomistic edition.[180] In the first version of the third battle event there is no mention of YHWH intervention at all, but in the second version of that there is one notice the YHWH's positive intervention in v. 35: and YHWH smote the Benjaminites before Israel, and the Israelites routed in that day twenty five contingents (one hundred men) who were swordsmen. This expression of v. 35 is a turning of the boast of v. 32 inside out, in an inclusio, using exactly the same wording.[181] Therefore the motif of YHWH war in the story of the taking of AI is not derived from that of the taking of Gibeah, but from something else, the Deuteronomistic propaganda for the Josianic national revival movement.

The last fresh interpretation by Keel is that the story of the taking of Ai is a sacramental symbol for the victory given by YHWH.[182] In Josh 8:18 and 26, the כידון which Joshua stretched out toward Ai and did not withdraw until he had utterly destroyed all the inhabitants of Ai, was used as a sacramental symbol for the divine victory. The sickle-sword originally was an actual weapon (Gebrauchswaffe) before the end of the second millennium BC in Mesopotamia and Egypt. In this period the sicklesword was recognized as a divine attribute for warfare in Mesopotamia, and then in Egypt it was used as a symbol of divine authorization for royal warfare. But after the end of the second millennium BC it was used only as an ideogram for the sacramental symbol of the divine victory which appeared in the Phoenician's iconographies (pict. 31–32)[183] and in the Old Testament context. Joshua's outstretched sicklesword is the old and enduring ideogram, not obsolete Gebrauchswaffe. Thus, in the ancient Near Eastern

---

178 de Vaux, *EHI* II, 619.

179 *Judges*, 292–96.

180 *Ibid.*, 293. In Judg 20:18 the people ask for god, not YHWH.

181 R. G. Boling, *Judges*, AB 6A (NY 1975), 287.

182 *Siegeszeichen*, 77–82.

183 *Ibid.*, 177.

context those who stretched out the sicklesword in their hands are gods, not men. Yet in our text Joshua like Moses in Ex 17:8–13 was replaced by the divine position to symbolize YHWH's victory. Therefore, all the above evidence does not support the claim that the battle of Ai by Joshua had a historical reality by YHWH's intervention.

3) The Battle of Gibeon (c. 10:1–15)

1

According to the biblical tradition, the Gibeonites were attacked by a coalition of five Canaanite kings who had been threatened by them for having made peace with the Israelites (Josh 9). The men of Gibeon asked Joshua to help them. Then Joshua came up from Gilgal, travelling all night, and defeated the forces of the coalition. In the course of the military action YHWH threw them into a panic before Israel and slew them and chased them by the way of Beth-horon as far as Makkedah. Moreover, when the enemies fled from Israel, YHWH threw down great stones from heaven upon them and they died; there were more who died because of the hailstones than the men of Israel killed with the sword. And Joshua returned to Gilgal (v. 15).

In contrast to the two offensive battles of Jericho and Ai mentioned above, the battle of Gibeon was a classic example of defensive war.[184] From the viewpoint of defensive war it can be understood that the idea of total destruction which was predominant in the case of the battles of Jericho and Ai does not appear in the Gibeon battle as it does in the battle of Samuel and the Philistine in I Sam 7.[185] Many scholars believe that it seems closer to the historical reality of the battle.[186] According to Alt,[187] it was only Gibeon's military action in the whole Book of Joshua that could be ascribed to Joshua himself as a historical person. The battle itself took place at Gibeon, in Benjaminite territory, but it continued along the descent of Beth-horon in Ephraimite territory which is identified with Bit Ninurta in the Amarna letters (*EA* 290).[188] In fact, it was a victorious battle of the group of Ephraim and Benjamin under the leadership of Joshua.[189] Noth believes that the victory achieved at Gibeon by the group of Benjamin and Ephraim against the Amorite kings was historically

184 Boling and Wright, *Joshua*, 284.

185 P. Weimar, "Jahwekrieg", 70.

186 S. Yeivin, *The Israelite Conquest of Canaan* (Istambul 1971), 80.

187 de Vaux, *EHI* II, 631; *Kleine Schriften zur Geschichte des Volkes Israel* I (München 1959), 187–88 (– *KS*).

188 Boling and Wright, *Joshua*, 281.

189 K. D. Schunck, *Benjamin*, BZAW 86 (Berlin 1963), 28 ff; de Vaux, *EHI* II, 628.

authentic. Yet, in the present text Joshua was secondary and later was incorporated with the story of the battle at Gibeon.[190]

In Josh 10:1–15 the enemy of the Gibeonites and Israelites was a coalition of five Canaanite kings which was led by the king of Jerusalem, Adonizedek, not Adonibezek (Judg 1:4–7). According to Josh 10:16–27 the five kings of the southern coalition, after Joshua and his men returned to Gilgal camp following the victory, were killed and hung on the trees and their corpora were thrown into the cave and the great stones against the mouth of the cave were set. This story used to be interpreted by the Alt school as an aetiology which explains the existence of the five trees (v. 26) and of the large stones which are still there today (v. 27).[191] Thus the enemy of the Gibeonites and the Israelites with Joshua, as Noth thinks,[192] was not the same southen coalition of kings who were killed at the cave of Makkedah. If not, Joshua's return to Gilgal between the battle of Gibeon and the affair of the five kings at Makkedah seems highly unlikely. Against the theory of Noth, only G. E. Wright has claimed that on the grounds of the omission of v. 15, Joshua's return to Gilgal in LXX^{BA}, the battle of Gibeon and the Makkedah story are a unit of the same event.[193] On this point, de Vaux has suggested that v. 15 in the LXX must exist, but with v. 43 it was suppressed because of the difficulty that it causes.[194] In other versions – Syrian, Targum, Vulgate and some MSS of LXX–v. 15 is found.[195] As far as the textual evidence is concerned, either v. 15 or 43 might be authentic.[196] Both verses are an indicator of DtrG.[197] Moreover, the connection between Joshua and the southern coalition is far removed from the conquest of the southern region which was taken by Judah and Caleb in Judg 1.

It is possible that the enemies of the Israelites in vv. 1–15 were the Amorite kings in v. 6 (Noth) or the minor kings who had come up from the lowlands, but precisely who they were we cannot say.[198] The word, האמורי which is absent in LXX^{BA}, and the five kings of the Amorites in v. 5 is a feature of Dtr redactors who tried to identify the five kings of Makkedah with the Amorite kings in v. 6. In this possibility the descrip-

---

190 *Das Buch Josua*, HAT 7 (Tübingen 1953), 61.

191 Weimar ("Jahwekrieg", 55–56, n. 50) does not accept the aetiological intepretation. For v. 27bβ as a ground source is an additional explanation which occurs in the story of the Ai conquest (Josh 8:29).

192 "Die fünf Könige in der Höhle von Makkeda," *PJ* 33 (1937), 22–36.

193 "The Literary and Historical Problem of Joshua 10 and Judge 1," *JNES* 5 (1946), 112.

194 *EHI* II, 627.

195 M. J. Gruenthaner, "Two Sun Miracles of the Old Testament," *CBQ* 10 (1948), 276.

196 *Ibid.*

197 Weimar, "Jahwekrieg", 51.

198 de Vaux, *EHI* II, 632.

tions about the other five kings of the southern hill country in 10:1–15 are productions of the Dtr redactors when the battle of Gibeon and the story of Makkedah are joined in Josh 10 with the summary of the southern conquest under the leadership of Joshua. P. Weimar has suggested that the first redactional works can be ascribed to vv. laα,b; 3; 4; 5a; 6abαβ; 7; 8b; 9b, which are organized from the original battle story of Gibeon (vv. laα,bβ; 2aα; 8a; 9a; 10abα) so that the operation of the Israelites against the Gibeonites became that of the Israelite help to Gibeon who was threatened by the coalition of the five Amorite kings.[199] It is supported by similar actions that the king of Jerusalem, Adonizedek requested the help of the four neighbouring kings (vv. 3–4) and that the men of Gibeon were supported by Joshua (v. 6). But what really happened was an encounter between the Canaanites and the Isrealites with Joshua at the head of the tribe of Joseph or perhaps of Ephraim alone.

However, the battle sites mentioned in the passages in vv. 12b–13a which are cited from the Book of Yashar were Gibeon and Aijalon, while in the prose narrative it was Beth-horon. V. 10 states clearly that מכה גדולה took place at Gibeon, not Beth-horon.[200] It may be considered that the war episodes of Gibeon are related to the other war stories which took place in the same region. Incidentally, Gibeon is not mentioned in the early history of Israel from the time of Joshua to Saul, but, only during the reign of David.[201] Nevertheless, the victory of Samuel against the Philistines in I Sam 7:1–12 took place at Mizpah, near Gibeon. Blenkinsopp identifies el-Jib with Mizpah as the place of Samuel's victory.[202] The retreat had passed through Beth-car (v. 11) which is emended as Beth-horon, valley of Aijalon. The account of Jonathan's surprise attack of the Philistines in I Sam 14 also took place near Michmash and Geba, that is about five miles from Gibeon. The retreat is down the valley Aijalon (v. 13) which must have taken the Philistines past Gibeon especially if we read Beth-horon in v. 23.[203] The second of two victories of David over the Philistines in II Sam 5:17–25 is also described as taking place near Gibeon on the basis of the original reading מגבע in v. 25. All three battle descriptions above contain the similar holy war elements: divine oracle, panic and the miraculous intervention of YHWH, etc. Thus it is considered that the battle of Gibeon was composed as a reflection of the battle descriptions above, especially that of David, if Josh 9 reflects the policy of David on Gibeon.[204]

---

199 "Jahwekrieg", 55.

200 J. Blenkinsopp, *Gibeon and Israel*: The Role of Gibeon and the Gibeonites in the Political and Religious History of Early Israel (Cambridge 1972), 43.

201 J. B. Pritchard, *Gibeon*: Where the Sun Stood Still (NJ 1962), 35.

202 *Gibeon and Israel*, 51, n. 58.

203 *Ibid.*, 51.

204 Weimar, "Jahwekrieg", 61–62.

Furthermore, I. Eph'al suggests that the night march of Joshua (v. 9) was a formalistic expression which appeared in the campaign of Gibeon as "the beginning of the middle watch" (Judg 7:19) or in the battle of Saul and the Ammonites as the "morning watch" (I Sam 11:11).[205] In the Near Eastern context the campaigns mainly took place in spring—summer, as in II Sam. 11:1, and because of the hot and dry weather, night marching was better than day. In the Megiddo campaign of Thutmose III the army had marched to Gaza around 200 Km in 10 days (an average daily march of 20 Km).[206]

2

However, how was it possible for the Israelites to carry on pursuing their enemies while such hailstones were falling, or how was it that only the Amorites were killed by the hailstones? In vv. 10—14 the three elements of holy war appear: divine confusion, hailstones from heaven and the standing of the sun and moon. In v. 10aαa YHWH made the enemies panic before Israel. The qal form of המם/הם occurs ten times with YHWH as its subject in the holy war contexts (Ex 14:24; Judg 4:15; I Sam 7:10) and in generalizing predictions of victory (Ex 23:27; Dt 7:23).[207] In these cases the subject is YHWH, while the objects are the enemies of YHWH and Israel, especially the enemy camp (Ex 14:24; Judg 5:15; Sir 48:21).

The motif of divine panic originally was understood as a reaction of theophany in the Near Eastern and the Old Testament contexts. The religious significance of the idea המם is not biblical in the notion of military intervention on the part of the deity nor in the motif of an ensuing panic. The *mysterium tremendum* of power sublimated in the deity everywhere evinces its destructive nature in battle, at the same time inspiring those fighting on the side of the deity with demonic frenzy. In the Egyptian context especially Seth, the war god, was called the god of confusion. In the Mesopotamian context the motif of *ragāmu* was a common idea that when the deities appear in the battlefield, the divine appearance was depicted as making the maintains tremble (Gudea A 18:14) or as causing the four corners of the world to tremble (Tukulti-Ninurta epic and Assyrian annals, etc.).

In the pre-monarchical period the idea of המם appears to have been associated with the appearance of the ark of YHWH on the battlefield

---

205 "The Battle of Gibeon and the Problem of Joshua's Southern Campaign," *Military History of the Land of Israel in Biblical Times*, ed. by J. Liver (1973), 88 (Hebrew).

206 R. O. Faulkner, "The Battle of Megiddo," *JEA* 18 (1942), 2.

207 H. P. Müller, "המם", *TDOT* II, ed. by G. J. Botterweck and H. Ringgren, ET by D. E. Greene et al (Michigan 1978), 419. II Ch 15:16 in the outside military context describes the course of history as God's continual terrorizing of the nations.

(I Sam 4:5): תהם הארץ. In the story of Samuel in I Sam 7:7–12, which actually reflects the victory over the Philistines, YHWH threw the Philistines into panic before Israel with thunder (v. 10). In the prose narrative of the campaign of Deborah and Barak (Judg 4:5), YHWH threw Sisera into panic (v. 15). It resulted from the vanguard motif of YHWH who went out before the army. In Ex 14 YHWH also threw the Egyptian army into panic (v. 24 – J). The idea of המם is due mainly to a theoretical schematization of military ideology of Dtr 1 and 2 (Dt 2:15; 7:23; 28:20; Ex 23:27).[208] But originally this idea does not belong to the Deuteronomic school. Some scholars believe that the idea of המם/הם comes from a pre-Dtr idiom.[209] In the battles between David and the Philistines the idea of divine panic does not appear, but the vanguard motif of YHWH (יצא יהוה לפניך) in II Sam 5:17–25 contains the idea of divine panic which was the cause of the Philistines' defeat.[210] For in Judg 4:14, after the vanguard motif (יצא לפניך יהוה), the motif of YHWH panic appears in v. 15: "ויהם יהוה את סיסרא...לפני ברק." At least it can be said that the idea of YHWH panic in battle appeared after the period of David.

The next element of holy war is the great stones from heaven (v. 11). Recently Weinfeld reviewed the phenomenon of throwing stones from heaven in the Near East and in the Bible.[211] It is seen in the hymn of Ishkur (Adad in Akkad). Enlil commands his son Ishkur to take small and large stones and to throw them on the rebellious land (lines 22 ff):[212]

> Take small stones, who is like you when approaching it;
> Take large stones, who is like you when approaching it.
> Rain down on it your small stones, your large stones,
> Destroy the rebellious land to your right,
> Subdue it to your left.

We read that in the third campaign of Sargon, king of Aššur, the divine warrior Adad gave his voice to the enemy in the floating cloud and heavenly stone (aban šamē). We also find in another place Adad who throws fire stones (aban išāti) and burning stones (aban anqullu/aqqull).[213]

In v. 11 the big stones thrown down by YHWH are interpreted as אבן ברד. Hailstones are a natural phenomenon in Israel. The coastal plain has an average 5–8 days of hail per year, mostly in midwinter.[214] A similar phrase is found in Is 30:30: "and (the Lord) shall show the descending

208 *Ibid.*, 421.

209 Weimar, "Jahwekrieg", 50; Stolz, *Kriege*, 20, 191.

210 Weimar, *op. cit.*, 50.

211 "Divine War in Ancient Israel and in the Ancient Near East," 175–76.

212 *ANETS*³, 578.

213 Weinfeld, "Divine War in Ancient Israel and in the Ancient Near East," 176–77. Cf., Ezek 28:14.

214 E. Orni and E. Efrat, *Geography of Israel* (Jerusalem 1971), 115.

blow of his arm,... with cloudburst, and tempest, and **אבן ברד**." Isaiah knew the tradition and used it for eschatological illustration: "He (the Lord) will be angry as in the valley of Gibeon, to do his deed, ... (Is 28:21)." In Ex 9:23–24 we read that "the Lord sent thunder and **ברד**, and the fire ran down on the ground and the Lord threw **ברד** upon the Egyptian land." Hailstones as a divine weapon in the war context also appear in Ezek 38:22 and Job 38:22–23. Thus it is considered that the tradition of hailstone as a divine weapon belongs to pre-Dtr.[215]

On the structural function of the hailstone passage, de Vaux has suggested that the relationship between vv. 10 and 1 is that between the prose account of the battle of the waters Kishon (**המם** in Judg 4:15) and the poetic song of Deborah (Judg 5:20), according to which the stars fought from high in heaven against Israel's enemy.[216] But it may be seen that the prose account of vv. 10–11 is compared with the poetic account of vv. 12–13.

The last element of holy war in the battle of Gibeon is the standing of the sun and moon in heaven which is cited from the Book of Yashar.[217] Vv. 12b–13a originally to back to another event and were later attached to the present narrative, because of the geographical situation which it shared. Because of the natural phenomenon of stopping the sun and moon, some scholars tried to prove that the miracle of Gibeon and Aijalon was a historical fact and that it had given the victory to Joshua in his conquest period of West Jordan.[218] J. Phythian-Adams proposed the fall of a metereorite phenomenon of the 14th century BC for the event of Gibeon.[219] But it does not fit with the conquest period of Joshua. J. F. A. Sawyer has suggested that on the basis of astronomical phenomenon the historical fact of the miracle of the battle of Gibeon is identified with the eclipse of the sun on Septemter 30, 1131 BC which covered the land with darkness from Hazor to Beer Sheba.[220]

---

[215] Stolz, *Kriege*, 88–89.

[216] *EHI* II, 632.

[217] This book is mentioned in II Sam 1:18 and I K 8:13. It is considered as a collection of pieces of poetry attributed to Israel's heroes such as Joshua, David and Solomon. I. L. Seeligmann believes that his book is the result of an abbreviation of the Book of the Glory of Israel (ספר הישר: ספר הדר ישראל), "Menschliches Heldentum und göttliche Hilfe," *TZ* 19 (1963), 396, n. 23. But Soggin rejects the suggestion, because there are no grounds for this view (*Joshua*, 122, n. 2).

[218] Among them, W. J. Pythian-Adams, "A Meterorite of the Fourteenth Century," *PEQ* 78 (1946), 116–24; R. B. Y. Scott, "Metereological Phenomena and Terminology in the Old Testament," *ZAW* 64 (1952), 11–25; J. F. A. Sawyer, "Joshua 10:12–14 and the Solar Eclipse of 30 September 1131 B.C.," *PEQ* 104 (1972), 139–46; F. R. Stephenson, "Astronomical Verification and Dating of Old Testament Passages Referring to Solar Eclipses," *PEQ* 107 (1975), 119.

[219] See no. 218 above.

[220] See no. 218, espe. 144.

3

However, the intention of the Dtr redactors was that the battle of Gibeon was not a simple battle of men determined by natural phenomena, but a battle which had been won by YHWH's intervention. If the sun not setting is the direct cause of the victory, the mention of the moon makes no sense, unless a parallelism in which the two major heavenly bodies are involved is a favorable omen such as the Assyrian omen which was reviewed by J. S. Holladay.[221] The divine intervention in the quotation which is introduced by an editorial particle, אז,[222] then, is different from the prose narrative in vv. 10–11 which explained why the Canaanites were in a state of panic – YHWH had caused it with his hailstones. In this example of poetry the Israelites ask for and obtain a miracle simply in order that they should have time to win their victory.

None of these explanations have proved satisfactory. Hiller and others have suggested that the sun and the moon were not the planets, but two deities of the sky, as the solar worship at Aijalon.[223] Joshua tells the sun to be silent in Gibeon and the moon to be quiet in the valley of Aijalon in order to prevent them from giving a favorable oracle. Hiller believes that there was a sanctuary of the sun at Gibeon and of the moon at Aijalon. Opposing this idea, de Vaux has asserted that there is no evidence for the presence of the sun and moon cults at Gibeon and Aijalon.[224] Miller and Boling say that the sun and moon have already been absorbed into YHWH's assembly as a part of the vast host gathered around him (Ps 148:3). The sun and moon are in YHWH's entourage. It is as his subordinates that they are addressed.[225] But the point of view which has been suggested by Holladay is accepted as a better interpretation by some scholars.[226] According to the Assyrian astronomical forecasts at the time of the full-moon, the fourteenth, fifteenth or sixteeenth days of the month, if the sun and the moon appear at the proper time and place to be visible together, everything would be favorable, but if the moon was late in appearing or disappeared too soon, everything would go badly. The focus of our text, as de Vaux has pointed out,[227] is the fact that the sun and the moon remained visible together at the required time until the revenge of

[221] Soggin, *Joshua*, 122; J. S. Holladay, "The Days the Moon Stood Still," *JBL* 87 (1968), 166–78.

[222] Boling and Wright, *Joshua*, 282.

[223] J. Hiller, "Der Name Eva," *ArOr* 26 (1958), 653–55; J. Dus, "Gibeon – eine Kultstätte des šmš und die Stadt des benjamitischen Schicksals," *VT* 10 (1960), 353–74; J. Blenkinsopp, *Gibeon and Israel*, 50.

[224] *EHI* II, 634.

[225] Boling and Wright, *Joshua*, 278; Miller, *Divine Warrior*, 123–28.

[226] de Vaux, *EHI* II, 634.

[227] *Ibid.*, 635.

the Israelites had been taken on the enemy. A similar description appears in the Greek context. In the Iliad II 412–415 Agamemnon prays to Zeus not to let the sun go down before the Achaeans have won the victory.[228] Thus in our context the intention of Dtr 2 was to show a great miracle by bringing the victory through the sun and the moon under the control of YHWH.

De Vaux has proposed an understanding of the literary structure of the text.[229] Vv. 12b–13a is a poetic expression of YHWH's help that Israel received, in contrast to the prosaic expression of that in vv. 10–11. This parallel structure appears as a literary structure in the Near East and in the Bible. The double accounts of prose and poetic style are characteristic of the literary structure of Thutmose III (the battle of Megiddo) and of Ramses II (the battle of Kadesh). The prose account of the Exodus in Ex 14 can be compared with the song of Moses in Ex 15. In the relationship of the prose account of the battle against Sisera in Judg 4 with the song of Deborah in Judg 5 which tells how "from high in heaven the stars fought, from their orbits they fought against Sisera" (v. 20), the editor of vv. 13b–14 took this poetic expression literally in his desire to exalt YHWH who was fighting for Israel (v. 14b) and in his wish to exalt his hero, Joshua. Therefore de Vaux has concluded that the miracle of the sun is without historical foundation.[230] The only historical fact is the peace treaty between the Gibeonites and the Israelites.[231]

Thus it is more reasonable to say that the battle of Gibeon and the Israelites' victory by Joshua have historical reality, but the present descriptions were composed by those who knew the tradition of YHWH war such as David's war in the late period.

4) Southern Conquest Wars (c. 10:28–43)

Josh 10:28–39 preserved the memory of an ancient tradition about the conquest of the south by Joshua. In contrast to it, Judg 1:1–20, which preserves the tradition of the individual conquest to the south, tells us that the southern conquest was accomplished by the tribes of Judah and Simeon, and of Calebite and Kenite, not by Joshua. In Josh 10:36–37 Hebron was conquered by Joshua and all the Israelites, but in Judg 1:20 and Josh 15:13–19 it was attributed to Caleb. In all these verses there is no mention about YHWH war in the battles.

---

228 Weinfeld, "Divine War in Ancient Israel and in the Ancient Near East," 180–81; Soggin, *Joshua*, 122.

229 *EHI* II, 634–35.

230 *Ibid.*, 635.

231 Haran, "The Gibeonites," 104.

Yet, regarding those biblical passages the Albright school insists that the archaeological evidence shows an identification with the destruction of the southern cities and the biblical passages in Josh 10:28–39. Most of the excavated mounds in this region, identified as particular ancient cities with a high degree of probability, show evidence of having been extensively or totally destroyed during the end of 13th and early 12th century BC.[232] They are Lachish (Tell ed-Duweir), Eglon (Tell 'Aitun or Tell el-Ḥesi), Hebron (el-Khalil), and Debir (Tell Beit Mirsim or Khirbet Rabud). Wright questions: "If Joshua once conquered the territory of Judah, why did not it have to be reconquered by the various tribes who settled there?"[233] Soggin answers this: "One wonders how many operations, and of what nature, were carried out in this region in the space of only a few decades." To take into account only the archaeological findings without comparing them with these factors is too one-sided.[234]

Regarding the topographical and geographical situation of the region, some see that behind vv. 28–39 lies a traditional itinerary which seems to have been followed by Sennacherib in 701 BC, according to II K 18:13, and in 587 BC by Nebuchadnezzar, according to Jer 34:7, in order to lay siege to Jerusalem, after having reduced to submission the system of fortified cities surrounding it.[235] But Wright's view is the opposite.[236] The adaptation of the military strategy by Sennacherib is unconvincing. Eph'al has suggested that with the descriptions of the conquest in vv. 28–39, it actually was not possible to continue conquering all the six cities listed on that day, nor to be continued even for one day or two.[237] The Bible does not mention the continuing siege campaigns until the time of David.

Only the three cities, Libnah, Lachish and Eglon (Adulam-LXX) in vv. 30, 32 and 35 (LXX) of the list, consisting of a brief memory of the conquest of the six cities, include the conventional YHWH intervention words stating that YHWH gave the city (not enemy) into Israel's hand. Libnah is not mentioned in the battle of Gibeon/Beth-horon. Even the identification of Libnah (Tell Bornât) ca. 10 Km NW of Lachish, is not certain. Here the YHWH intervention formula is the work of Dtr redac-

---

232 Gottwald, *The Tribes of Yahweh*, 194, n. 124; Aharoni, *The Land of the Bible*, 371–85.

233 *JNES* 5, 112.

234 *Joshua*, 132; *id.*, "Ancient Biblical Tradition and Recent Archaeological Discoveries," *BA* 23 (1960), 95–100. The debate of the archaeological interpretation can be found in contrast in the two delegates of two schools. For the Albright school, J. Bright, *Early Israel in Recent History Writing*, SBT 19 (London 1956), 79 ff; For the Alt school, M. Noth, "Der Beitrag der Archäologie zur Geschichte Israels," *VTS* 7 (1960), 262–82, espe. 277 ff (– "Beitrag der Archäologie").

235 Soggin, *Joshua*, 130.

236 *JNES* 5, 109.

237 "The Battle of Gibeon," 88.

tors. In LXX the subject of the Übereignungsformel in v. 30aαβ is not YHWH but the men — "ἔλαβον (וילכדוה)" which is lacking in MT as haplography. LXX has: "καὶ ἔλαβον αὐτην καὶ τὸν βασίλέα αὐτης (They captured it and its king)." In the southern conquest stories this phrase is repeated in v. 32, 35, 37, after the YHWH oraculous formula, except in v. 39.[238] The addition of its king as an object to the city being conquered is seen as a balancing structure called a palistrophe (double stanza).[239]

Lachish with Tell Beit Mirsim suffered a total destruction at about the end of the Bronze age. It remained unoccupied after its destruction, whereas Tell Beit Mirsim was immediately resettled. Archaeology to date has nothing to say on the question of whether the destroyers of the cities were Canaanite insiders or invading outsiders.[240] The king of Lachish is not mentioned in the destruction. The objects of Ḥerem are limited only to living things, not including other materials. The phrase ביום ההוא in vv. 28, 35 (2 times) indicates the day of action, the day of the great battle long remembered in story and song, which was later connected with the origins of the prophetic and eschatological day of YHWH.[241] The above evidence is not positive that in the historical reality of the conquest of Libnah and Lachish by Joshua the experience of YHWH war is included.

5) Northern Conquest Wars (c. 11:1—15)

The northern conquest wars by Joshua are found in Josh 11:1—15, which has an intentional parallelism with Josh 10, a fact which is emphasized by the use of the same formula in both chapters.[242] The northern

---

[238] Soggin (*Joshua*, 120) sees the verb as singular while Boling (*Joshua*, 290) considers it a plural verb, but the sudden appearance of the plural form in the sentence creates confusion as to who the subject is. Both forms appear in vv. 28, 35 and 37 (plural), and vv. 32 and 39 (singular).

[239] Boling and Wright, *Joshua*, 294.

[240] Aharoni, *The Land of the Bible*, 219.

[241] Blenkinsopp, *Gibeon and Israel*, 51; *id.*, "Jonathan's Sacrilege," *CBQ* 26 (1964), 429. P. A. Much (*Bajjôm Hāhū*, Oslo 1936, 6 ff) sees that the phrase is not an eschatological term but a temporal adverb. Opposing him, L. Černý (*The Day of Yahweh and some Relevant Problems*, 1948, 99 ff) asserts that the concept of the day of Yahweh is a pre-exilic idea of Hebrew eschatology and is peculiar to Israel. Von Rad ("The Origin of the Concept of the Day of Yahweh," *JSS* 4, 1959, 97—108; *id.*, *Old Testament Theology* II, 119—28) assumes that the *Sitz im Leben* of the concept of the day of YHWH derived from the holy war tradition. But recently M. Weiss ("The Origin of the Day of the Lord — Reconsidered," *HUCA* 37, 1966, 29—60) has argued against this that the origin of the day of YHWH was an independent concept and became the origin of the later eschatological version after Zephaniah. Most recently, Y. Hoffmann, "The Day of Lord as Concept and a Term in the Prophetic Literature," *ZAW* 93 (1981), 37—50.

[242] de Vaux, *EHI* II, 655.

coalition is the counterpart of the coalition of the southern five kings. The parallel chapters provide us with a picture of the conquest of the whole of the north and of the south of Canaan seen as two military expeditions conducted by Joshua as the leader of the whole of Israel. The composition is the work of the pre-Dtr collecter.[243]

What historical reality does the narrative of the northern conquest war contain? There are various editorial elements of Dtr 2 to be added to the original fact memorized: the list of the early inhabitants of Canaan (v. 3), in which the Jebusites of Jerusalem play no part here; the extension to the whole of Israel (vv. 8, 13–14), the figure of Joshua (vv. 6, 10, 12, 15) and the theme of the holy war carried to the extreme (vv. 6–9).[244] The battle of the waters of Merom is considered to be related to that of the waters of Megiddo (Judg 4–5). For in both, the main enemy of the Israelite is Jabin, king of Hazor. In Josh 11 Jabin personally takes part in the action, whereas in Judg 4 he sends Sisera, the general in command of his army. But the battle in Josh 11 belongs to the time of Joshua, whereas that in Judg 4 belongs to the time of the Judge Barak and the prophetess Deborah. If Hazor had already been destroyed in Josh 11, how could Hazor again have played a primary and decisive role in a Canaanite league several generations later? Moreover, the archaeological finds indicate that the huge lower city at Hazor was permanently laid waste, and the upper city was not rebuilt until the time of Solomon.

Several solutions have been suggested to account for the two contradictory traditions. O. Eissfeldt has pointed out that both narratives in Josh 11 and Judg 4–5 are the same event, that the victory of Barak is the only historically authentic event, and that the memory of the victory of Barak was divided into two to show the northern conquest by Joshua as an accomplished fact.[245] However, this solution is contrasted to the geographical factor. The geographical setting, as de Vaux points out,[246] is different in each case – the battle of Judg 4 is described as taking place on the plain of Jezreel, whereas the battle of Joshua was fought in upper Galilee.

The next solution is that both battles in Josh 11 and in Judg 4–5 as two different historicial events have a reverse chronological order. B. Mazar and Aharoni have suggested that the battle of the waters of Merom took place after Barak's victory and therefore dates back to the

---

[243] *Ibid.*, 244.

[244] Soggin, *Joshua*, 136.

[245] "Die Eroberung Palästinas durch Altisrael," *WO* 2 (1955), 168 ff; *id.*, *CAH* II 34 (1965), 9–10 (De Vaux, *EHI* II, 658, n. 5).

[246] *EHI* II, 658.

time of the Judges.[247] According to this solution, the two wars do not belong to the first stage of penetration but to a later period. The battle itself is not mentioned and it only says (v. 7b): "They fell upon them (Canaanites)." The victory of Barak, which was achieved by the Israelites and resulted in the defeat of Sisera and his allies, was not accompanied by a conquest of Canaanite towns, but it certainly destroyed the power of the Canaanites in the north of Palestine. This victory was followed by another battle in upper Galilee, the battle of the waters of Merom, which took place during the reign of Jabin. The battle of Merom was eventually associated with Joshua and all of Israel. This assumption is supported by the results of the Galilee survey which show a stage of occupation that preceded the conquest of the Canaanite districts. Aharoni has concluded that the Canaanite city Hazor had been destoryed by the Israelites at the end of 12th century BC as the *terminus ad quem*, that is, a generation or so after the date of the Israelite settlement.[248] The second victory enabled the Israelites to control the whole region. Hazor was unable to hold its own and was consequently destroyed. The Alt school asserts that the mention of Jabin, king of Hazor in Judg 4 would place the event described in Josh 11 in a fairly late period.[249] So the destruction of Hazor in Joshua occurred quite late in the Israelite settlement process, permitting Jabin, who is not mentioned in Judg 5, to be still on the scene in the period of the Judges.

If we accept the reverse chronological order of the two battles above, the date of the battle of Barak and Deborah must be considered as an integral part of the conquest cycle and should be dated as early as the second half of the 13th century which is identified with the destruction of Hazor on the basis of the archaeological finds.[250] On this idea Malamat thinks that the early dating of the battle of Barak and Deborah is an improbability.[251] For the battle of Barak and Deborah includes a new element: the appearance of the Sea-people who came up into Palestine during the days of Ramses III (1184–1153 BC). Furthermore, the mention of the tribe of Dan between Gilead and Asher (Judg 5:17) and the reference

---

[247] B. Mazar, "Beth She'arim, Gaba and Harosheth of the Peoples," *HUCA* 24 (1952–53), 83–84; Aharoni, *The Land of the Bible*, 223 ff; *id.*, "The Battle of the Waters of Merom and the Battle with Sisera," *Military History*, 91–109, espe. 108 (Hebrew); *id.*, "The Settlement of Canaan," *WHJP* III (1971), 117–18.

[248] *Military History*, 104–7; *id.*, *The Land of the Bible*, 229; Yadin, *BAR*, 8/2, 20.

[249] Weippert, *Settlement*, 34.

[250] Yadin and others, *Hazor* I–II (1958–60); Yadin, "Hazor", *Archaeology and Old Testament Study*, ed. by D. W. Thomas (Oxford 1967), 258–59; F. Maass, "Hazor und das Problem der Landnahme," *Von Ugarit nach Qumran*, Festschrift des O. Eissfeldt, BZAW 77 (1958), 105–17; J. Gray, "Hazor", *VT* 16 (1966), 26–52.

[251] "The Period of Judges," *WHJP* III, 136; de Vaux, *EHI* II, 791.

to Shamgar son of Anath (v. 6) who defeated a band of 600 Philistines (Judg 3:31) fits well with a late dating. Consequently the battle of Barak and Deborah must be dated later than these elements.[252]

The last solution is that the two battles were independent events and the battles of Barak and Deborah are not related to the taking of Hazor. De Vaux explained the discrepancy between the destruction of Hazor by Joshua and the battle of Jabin of Hazor and Deborah in Judges by concluding that the battle of Deborah had been fought in the late 12th century but it had nothing to do with Hazor.[253] Jabin did not originally belong to the Deborah story but only Sisera from Horosheth-ha-goim. The reference to Jabin king of Hazor in Judg 4 is an additional gloss (Judg 4:17b) or the editorial framework (Judg 4:1–3,23–24).[254] The name of Jabin is not the name of a person but a Hazor dynastic name, as known from an unpublished Mari text, which yields the name of the patron deity, when it mentions Ibni-Adad, king of Hazor.[255] Yadin has suggested that the fact that Hazor was destroyed with fire by Joshua during the battle of Joshua with Jabin king of Hazor, the head of the northern Canaanite coalition, as described in Josh 11:1–15, and is identified with the archaeological evidence of the Hazor excavation where a large Canaanite city was suddenly destroyed and set on fire in the 13th century BC (the end of LB age), no later than about 1230 BC.[256] The main archaeological evidence for this period is Mycenaean III B type pottery (stratum XIII) which was not used after about 1230 BC. There is no mention about the miraculous story of the capture of Hazor. Noth stresses the fact that the battle of Merom under Joshua was an heroic war narrative in which the historical content, which can no longer be properly recognized, was presupposed, but which comes from the period of the settlement or of the extension of Israelite occupation in the arable land.[257] But later Noth conceded the point that the destruction of Hazor at the end of the 13th century BC does admit to a link with the capture of it by Israelites and with the event which stands behind Josh 11:1–15.[258] It may be true that Hazor was destroyed during the period of Joshua and settled by the Israelites. In Judg 1:27–33 Hazor is not included among the Canaanite towns in the north of Canaan listed as not conquered. De Vaux believes that the story of the battle of the waters of Merom is an episode in the settlement of the northern tribes. Its victory was gained not by Joshua

---

252 *Ibid.*, 137.

253 *EHI* II, 791 ff.

254 *Ibid.*; Yadin, *BAR* 8/2, 23.

255 Boling and Wright, *Joshua*, 3–4.

256 See no. 250 above; *BAR* 8/2, 20.

257 *Josua*, 67; Weippert, *Settlement*, 34.

258 "Beitrag der Archäologie," 273; Weippert, *ibid.*, 36–37.

but by the tribes of Naphtali and Zebulun.[259] It is supposed that Barak was a man of Naphtali (Judg 4:6) and he summoned Zebulun and Naphtali (vv. 6, 10). Naphtali had already settle before the battle of the waters of Merom. This victory then broke the Canaanite hegemony in northern Canaan and enabled the Israelite tribes to settle independently. It also made possible the victory of Barak and Deborah, in which Naphtali played a leading part.[260]

How could the inferior Israelite forces gain the victory over the northern Canaanite coalition with the horses and chariots at the waters of Merom? Most recently Malamat has again emphasized that the Israelite conquest was carried out by military stratagems.[261] In v. 6 the divine encouragement, "fear not formula," is a characteristic of the Deuteronomistic corpus and in v. 8 the Übereignungsformel is the fulfilment of the oracle in v. 6. In v. 6 the two operations: "You hamstring their horses, and you shall burn their chariots," presumably refer to the beginning and end of the action respectively. That is, by crippling the horses, the warriors were forced to flee on foot, leaving their unattended chariots to be subsequently consigned to flames. It was a plan that surely deserves to be called inspired.[262] Josh 11:7 probably suggests a surprise attack: "Joshua with all his people of war came suddenly upon them from the mountain (LXX),[263] by the waters of Merom, and fell upon them." Even though we can say that the victory of the battle at the waters of Merom was gained by military strategy – surprise attack, the motif of YHWH war in the battle context does not appear.

Thus the above evidences show that the war descriptions in the Exodus-Conquest traditions are cases of theoretical holy war which grew in the light of the traditions of YHWH war.

---

[259] *EHI* II, 666–67; Gottwald, *The Tribes of Yahweh*, 154.

[260] de Vaux, *ibid.*; Gottwald, *ibid.*, 730, n. 110.

[261] *BAR* 8/2 (1982), 24–35.

[262] Boling and Wright, *Joshua*, 307.

[263] Soggin, *Joshua*, 134.

Chapter VI
Wars in the Traditions of the Judges and Saul

1. CHARACTERISTICS OF THE JUDGES' WAR

1

From the period of the Judges, which is considered to have begun after the death of Joshua, to the establishment of the united monarchy, that is, less than two centuries from the beginning of 12th century until approximately 1000 BC, there were many regional wars of struggle for existence which took place between the Israelite tribes and their neighbours: the Moabites (Ehud), Aramaeans (Othniel), Midianites (Gideon), Ammonites (Jephthah), Canaanites (Deborah and Barak), and Philistines (Saul). This period was marked by the decline of the major powers in the ancient Near East which facilitated the rise of small nations in Syro-Palestine.[1] The Egyptian power that had continually controlled Syro-Palestine since the middle of the second millennium began to decline from the end of 19th Dyn., because of internal and external affairs. Especially after the death of Ramses III, the Egyptians could not control Syro-Palestine again until the 21st Dyn. (945 BC). The powerful Hittite kingdom, in contrast to the Egyptian NK, had also disappeared from the political scene with the death of the last king, Šuppilulimus II (ca. 1200 BC). In the Mesopotamian context the Assyrian power was declining during this period, except for the rise of the brief period of Tiglathpileser I (1115–1077 BC), who restored Assyrian power, extending its borders on all flanks even to the Phoenician coast and anticipating the rise of the mighty Assyrian empire in the 9th century BC. These environmental factors of power aided the political consolidation and settlement of the nations in Transjordan, of the Aramaeans in Syria, of the Philistines in the coastal plain of the Mediterranean, and of the Israelite tribes in the hill country of Palestine. This interim vacuum of power between the wane of the Egyptian rule and prior to the rise of Assyria as an effective political power in Syro-Palestine brought about many local contests to take political hegemony in this area. In this political struggle for existence the Israelite role was decisive, overcoming the authochtonous Canaanite population,

---

[1] A. Malamat, "The Egyptian Decline in Canaan and the Sea-Peoples," *WHJP* III, ed. by B. Mazar (TA 1971), 23 ff, 38; Yadin, *Warefare* II, 247.

stemming the Transjordanian nations and nomadic raids on the east, and entering into a fierce and bitter conflict with the Philistines, who saw themselves as heirs to Egyptian rule in the land.[2]

The biblical traditions call those who had responded to these mlitary contests to save their people from a time of crisis "savior-judges", whose character was defined as charismatic leadership by M. Weber,[3] whether they are the major judges (Othniel, Ehud, Gideon, Deborah and Barak, Jephthah and Samson) or the minor (Tola, Jair, Ibzan, Elon and Abdon).[4] Their leadership is characteristically spontaneous and personal, the authority being neither hereditary nor dependent upon their social status within the tribes, and it was certainly not supported by any kind of bureaucratic apparatus: A sporadic leadership.[5] In this sense Saul also was a spontaneous military commander for the Ammonite war (I Sam 11:1–15), even though he was called *nāgīd*. In contrast, Jephthah was chosen by the tribal elders (Judg 11:9).

It is also supposed that even the minor judges (Judg 10:1–5; 12:8–15) were engaged as tribal war leaders in actual battle. The minor judge Tola had been called מושיע (Judg 10:1). The phrase, "Tola arose to save (להושיע) Israel," is not necessarily a late editorial interpolation. It might even be the original heading of the entire list of the minor judges.[6] But there are no war accounts about the minor judges.[7] Even though Gideon was engaged in the war with the Midianiates, he was called neither savior nor judge, whereas Abimelek was called a savior, even though he was not connected with any war. It is not clear that the distinction between major judge and minor has been made on the basis of the criterion מושיע. It seems that the minor judges, as the judge-officers in the province, resembled the *dayyānū* (DI.KUD.MEŠ) judges in Mari, who were in charge of judgment in the small courts.[8] The Book of Judges shows us that the motivation for the rise of the savior-judges was to save their people from the oppression of the neighbouring enemy. In the descriptions of the initial stage of the military conflict between the Israelite tribes and their enemy, the Israelites were always oppressed by and subject to their enemy.

---

[2] Malamat, *ibid.*, 38.

[3] *Ancient Judaism*, ET by H. H. Gerth and D. Martindale (Gelencoe, Ill. 1952), 98 ff; Malamat, *WHJP* III, 130, n. 4.

[4] Y. Kaufmann, *The Book of Judges* (1962, Jerusalem 1978^5), 46–48 (Hebrew); Malamat, *ibid.*, 131; T. Ishida, "The Leaders of the Tribal Leagues Israel in the Premonarchic Period," *RB* 80 (1973), 514 ff.

[5] Malamat, *ibid.*, 130. The function of the judge as a military authority in the time of emergency contrasts to that of nāši as an administrative authority in the time of peace (E. A. Speiser, *CBQ* 25, 1963, 111–17; M. Weinfeld, "Chieftain", *EJ* V. 5, cols 420–21.

[6] Malamat, *ibid.*, 131.

[7] Kaufmann, *The Book of Judges*, 46–48; Malamat, *ibid.*

[8] M. Weinfeld, "Judge and Officer in Ancient Israel," *Israel Oriental Studies* 7 (1977), 88.

In the late Dtr framework this situation was described as the result of the religious sin of the Israelites against their God, YHWH, in a pattern in which the people of Israel did what YHWH thought to be evil: they forgot YHWH their God and worshipped the Baals and all the Asherim. Then the anger of YHWH was kindled against Israel and he gave them into the hands of Cushan-rishathaim, king of Aram Naharaim, and the Israelites were in subjection to him for eight years (Judg 3:7–8). This pattern in which the Israelites were given into the hand of X and in subjection to X for Y years, because of the forgetting of YHWH by the Israelites and the anger of YHWH towards them, is repeated in the beginning part of the savior-judges' stories: 3:12–14 (Ehud), 4:1–3 (Deborah and Barak), 6:1 (Gideon), 10:6–8 (Jephthah) and 13:11 (Samson). However, the substance of this pattern is much earlier. The idea "to forget YHWH" already occurs in Hosea and Isaiah and was influenced by the Dtn/Dtr and Jeremiah.[9] For this thought is a historical-theological discourse (eine geschichtstheologische Abhandlung) for the purpose of teaching present generations and perhaps future ones, too.[10]

2

Regarding historical reality, this description might reflect the fact that the Israelites in the initial stage of the savior-judges, even in a different time and place, were inferior to their neighbours. Even in the time of the war of Deborah and Barak against the Canaanites, which is considered as the late period of the judges, the Israelite forces were very inferior to the Canaanite forces. The Israelite forces were composed only of light infantry, whereas the Canaanite forces were well trained armies who possessed superior technology, including formidable chariots. Judg 4:13 mentions that Sisera, the commander of the Canaanite army, had nine hundred iron chariots, even exaggerated in number, and all the men on foot. Even in the time of the battle of Michmash by Saul and Jonathan neither sword nor spear was available to any of the soldiers who were with Saul and Jonathan – only Saul and his son Jonathan had them (I Sam 13:22).

In confrontation with the superiority of the neighbouring enemies, it was natural that the Israelite tribes were confederated into a unit of two, three, or more tribes with the military strategy to overcome their enemies. Even among the enemies, the five lords of the Philistine cities (Ashdod, Gath, Ashkelon, Ekron and Gaza) confederating to bring the rising king Saul to their knees (I Sam 28–31) is a good example of a confederation. They were independent, but cooperated in the event of a common danger

---

9 W. Richter, *Die Bearbeitungen des Retterbuches in der Deuteronomischen Epoche*, BBB 21 (Bonn 1964), 56, n. 159 (– *Bearbeitungen*).

10 *Ibid.*, 88.

from outside for the protection and support of each other.[11] It has been suggested that at the end of the third millennium BC the city-states of Sumer and Akkad cooperated for protection and support around the common sanctuary of Nippur for twelve months of the year.[12]

Weber (1923) described the Israelite confederacy itself as a war confederation under and with YHWH as the war god of the union; Israel was not a tribal name but the name of an association, and cult league.[13] His concern lies in the military function of the confederacy. In this connection Noth (1930) has presented Israel as a twelve-tribe confederacy around a central sanctuary where the ark was first at Shechem and finally at Shiloh, as in the amphictyonies of Greece and Italy.[14] On the basis of the hypothesis of the Israelite amphictyony of Noth, von Rad has constructed the idea of holy war as the reaction of the tribal confederacy, even though all the twelve tribes did not take part in battle. For him the motif of mustering the soldiers in a time of crisis was a criterion to determine holy war.[15] Accordingly, YHWH was not a tribal God, but the God of Israel, the tribal confederacy.

Recently the Israelite amphictyony theory in the period of the Judges by Noth, however, has been severely criticized by many scholars.[16] Their principal objection to this theory is its purely speculative character. Nowhere in the Book of Judges and of Samuel is there a reference to such an organization.[17] The figure 12 which is used elsewhere in the Bible with the same symbolic value as in Greece and Italy was not only an essential issue, but also there were no wars during the period of the judges in which either the whole of the twelve tribes or even their majority took part. In the song of Deborah, which reflects the maximal unity achieved by the Israelites, we find ten tribes, but among them four tribes (Simeon, Levi, Judah and Gad) are missing. So only six tribes took part in the actual battle of Kishion, yet the prose account of the same battle (Judg 4) mentions only two tribes: Zebulun and Napthali. J. Weingreen has claimed that the whole unity of the twelve tribes was never actualized, except in the united monarchy of David and Solomon, throughout the history of Israel.[18]

---

[11] B. D. Rahtjen, "Philistine and Hebrew Amphictyonies," *JNES* 24 (1965), 100 ff.

[12] W. W. Hallo, "A Sumerian Amphictyony," *JCS* 14 (1960), 88–96. Cf., G. Fohrer (*History of Israelite Religion*, ET by D. E. Greene, London 1973, 91, n. 10) disagrees with him.

[13] *Ancient Judaism*, 81.

[14] Noth, *Das System der zwölf Stämme Israels*, 39 ff; *id.*, *HI*, 89–109.

[15] *Krieg.*, 6 ff.

[16] See n. 3 of Introduction; de Vaux, *EHI* II, 695–716; J. Weingreen, "The Theory of the Amphictyony in Premonarchial Israel," Festschrift of T. H. Gaster, *The Journal of the Ancient Near Eastern Society of Columbia University* V (1973), 426–33.

[17] M. C. Astour, "Amphictyony", *IDBS*, 24.

[18] *Op. cit.*, 426 ff.

In fact, the premonarchic tribal political system was a dual monarchy, consisting of two independent groups of tribes, each group being under the leadership of a leading tribe such as Joseph (Ephraim) in the north and Judah in the south.[19] Even the period of the reign of David and Solomon was envisaged not as a united monarchy, one homogenous state, but as a dual monarchy.[20] In this sense Smend rejects the connection with YHWH war and tribal confederation. Tribal confederation is nothing more than a hypothesis, in which there is no coinciding between YHWH war and tribal confederation, even if it seems probable.[21] He has claimed that the unity of all Israel in the time prior to the formation of the state did not appear *per se* in the war.[22] So the idea of the unity of Israel before the formation of the state is abandoned. For only single alliances participated in the holy wars of the time of the Judges, and not Israel as a whole. Even in the song of Deborah the unity of the tribal league is not called Israel.[23] He sees the tribal league in the song of Deborah as a postulate of Israel, but its reality is with Saul.[24] The holy war as the whole unity of the twelve tribes should be a cultic event without historical reality as seen in the victory of king Jehoshaphat over Moab and Ammon (II Ch 20).

However, because YHWH is not a tribal God but the God of Israel, his war is surely in principle a war of Israel.[25] It is considered that YHWH, as the God of Israel, was involved in the wars of Israel.[26] It is possible that in the premonarchic time the name of Israel simultaneously was applied to the whole as well as a part of the tribal community,[27] for the name of Israel as the tribal league is not limited to only the whole unity of the twelve tribal league. The two or four tribal confederacy as a warlike league is recognized as Israel-El fights. In the context of the two (Zebulun and Napthali) or six (Ephraim, Benjamin, Machir, Issachar and two above) tribal confederacy (Judg 4—5), it is clear that his tribal community was called Israel, because its common God YHWH was called the God of Israel (4:6; 5:3,5).[28] In the case of Gideon's confederacy, which consisted of the four tribes (Manasseh, Asher, Zebulun and Napthali with Abiezer), Israel is described by the term "liberation of Israel": "with what shall I save Israel (6:14,15)?" The camp of Gideon was also called "the camp of

[19] *Ibid.*, 429.
[20] *Ibid.*, 430.
[21] *Yahweh War*, 27.
[22] *Ibid.*, 30—32.
[23] *Ibid.*, 40.
[24] *Ibid.*
[25] *Ibid.*
[26] *Krieg*, 26; Smend, *Yahweh War*, 40.
[27] Ishida, *RB* 80, 530.
[28] *Ibid.*, 523.

Israel" (7:15). In the story of Jephthah his tribal community was called Israel (10:17; 11:4,5,26,27,33). Their God, YHWH was assumed to be the God of Israel.

3

The real issue, however, is whether or not YHWH intervened to help Israel in the actual military activity of the tribal league, not in the cultic context. Though the materials we have are limited, it is not at all impossible to find the historical reality of the military activity of the savior-judges beyond the Dtr theological framework. In other parts of the Bible the historical memories known from the savior-judges are preserved as historical realities about them.[29] Samuel, in his farewell speech (I Sam 12:9–11), which is formulated as the pragmatic framework of the Judges, lists Israel's oppressors on the one hand and its saviors on the other, in the major events of the Judges. Unlike the order in Judges, however, the sequence of oppressors is given: Sisera, the Philistines and Moab; while the saviors are Jerubaal, Barak (LXX), Jephthah and Samuel himself. Moreover, in Ps 83, which is composed probably in the time of the Judges or somewhat later,[30] we find a list of Israel's oppressors: "Edom and the Ishmaelites, Moab and the Hagarites, Gebal (Byblos), Ammon and Amalek, Philistia with the inhabitants of Tyre, Assyria, Midian, Sisera, and Jabin at the river Kishon (vv. 7–10)." The theophanic description of YHWH in Judg 5:4–5 is paralleled with Ps 68:8–9 in which יהוה is replaced as אלוהים: "God, when you go out before your people, when you march through the desert, the earth trembles and the heavens drop at the presence of God, the one of Sinai, at the presence of the God of Israel (vv. 8–9)." Israel's defeat of the Midianiates in the days of Gideon is echoed in Is 9:3 – "The day of Midian", and in 10:26 as "in the slaughter of Midian at the Rock of Oreb."

In addition to the lack of extra-biblical sources, the difficulty is that the historical reality of the savior-judges was suppressed by the historiographical and pragmatic framework which was schematized as follows:[31]

a) Subjugation by an enemy
b) The saviors receive the spirit of YHWH (charismatic leader)
c) The saviors sent a call up throughout all the land of Israel (tribal league by muster)
d) The saviors went out to war
e) YHWH gave the enemies into the hand of the saviors – the victory

---

[29] Malamat, *WHJP* III, 133.

[30] *Ibid.*, 134, n. 17.

[31] Richter (*Untersuchungen*, 179–81) analyzed this scheme as the first type of the holy war formula with the element of total destruction.

The first element, the savior-judges as the challengers to the war crisis imposed upon the Israelites by their neighbours, always appeared after the oppression by an alien people which lasted for some years: for eight years by Aram before Othniel (3:8), eighteen by Moab before Ehud (3:14), twenty by Canaan before Deborah (4:3), seven by Midian before Gideon (6:1), eighteen by Ammon before Jephthah (10:8), and forty by Philistine before Samson (13:1). Although the numbers such as twenty or forty are considered as the stereotyped figures of DtrG,[32] it is possible that these descriptions may reflect the socio-political reality of the Israelite tribes in weakness before they were liberated from the enemy's oppression locally: the historical reality of the tribes in the pre-monarchic period. The order of oppressions by the enemies in the Book of Judges may not be in chronological order, because if we posit the tribal territorial principle as a guideline in the present structure of the Book of Judges, the chronological credibility of the actual sequence of historical events, as presented in the Book is naturally impaired.

4

The second element is to understand the spirit of YHWH. The saviors with the spirit of YHWH are recognized as charismatic leaders. The authority of the charismatic leader was dialectic leadership, challenging the traditional legal authority such as the elders of tribes.[33] Deborah, as a woman, had no standing in the agnatic-patriarchal order, it was she, however, who roused the people to fight for their freedom, who stirred Barak to action and, in short, who was the driving force behind the battle.[34] But the most indicative example of the incompetency of the traditional leadership and the rise of a fringe personality is the episode of Jephthah, who stood outside the normal social framework. The elders of Gilead sought in their hour of peril a leader from their midst, but in vain. Hard-pressed, they turned to Jephthah the outcast, "the son of a harlot," who had been ousted by his brothers from his patrimony.[35] For Jephthah, his saviorship was not dependent on social class or status, or sex. Deborah as a woman was a judge and prophetess. Also, none of the saviors belonged to the noble lineage except Ehud, the son of Gera (Gen 46:21) and Othniel, the son of Kenaz, Caleb's younger brother (3:9). The function of the saviors who possessed this charismatic leadership was in fact limited to each Judge's own tribal territory or somewhat more. Even Deborah did

---

[32] Richter, *Bearbeitungen*, 135–39.

[33] A. Malamat, "Charismatic Leadership in the Book of Judges," *Magnalia Dei*: The Mighty Acts of God, ed. by F. M. Cross et al (NY 1976), 154.

[34] *Ibid.*, 160.

[35] *Ibid.*

not reach the national area, for there is no indication of a pan-Israelite status in this period.[36] At the same time their post was non-hereditary or non-transferable. Thus their function contrasts with that of a king in the monarchy.[37] In this connection Saul had a transitional function between a charismatic savior and a king. Non-hereditary authority and function of the savior-judges show a trace of the socio-political reality in the premonarchic period.[38]

The idea of the spirit of YHWH often occurs in the thoughts of the northern prophets who influenced the formation of the thought of the Deuteronomists. This thought can be traced back to the period of the monarchy. For Saul and David were recognized as the par excellence saviors who had the charismatic spirit of YHWH in I Sam 10:6,10; 11:6; 16:14,23; 18:10; 19:9 (Saul): I Sam 16:13; 19:23 (David). Even though the materials appear in the Dtn/Dtr literary corpus, Stolz ascribes the passages in which YHWH's spirit came upon Gideon (6:34) and Jephthah (11:29) to the pre-Dtr usage.[39]

However, Deborah was a savior-judge who did not have the charismatic sign — YHWH's spirit. In this sense it seems that in fact the saviors actually had no religious relationship. This is supported by the fact that the rise and authority of the saviors was not necessarily linked to important religious centers.[40] In this respect it is noteworthy that not even one of the Israelite saviors arose in a place of special status in Israel's history, and certainly not at any site of cultic significance such as Shechem, Bethel, or Shiloh. Gideon's residence, Ophrah, became an Israelite cultic seat only after the act of deliverance; Jephthah only after his appointment moved to Mizphah and made it his permanent abode (11:16,34). Soggin believes that the savior-judges in the period of the Judges were purely secular war leaders and by a later author they were interpreted as religious saviors in the course of transforming the wars fought by the saviors into wars of YHWH.[41] So Boling has suggested that the wars in this period are not primarily YHWH war.[42]

There is no doubt about the historical reality of the third (the tribal league by muster) and the fourth (the saviors participated in wars) elements.

---

[36] B. Lindars, "The Israelite Tribes in Judges," *VTS* 30 (1979), 99.

[37] Malamat, *Magnalia Dei*, 162; Ishida, *RB* 80, 572.

[38] Ishida, *The Royal Dynasties in Ancient Israel*: A Study on the Formation and Development of Royal Dynastic Ideology, BZAW 142 (Berlin/NY 1977), 185. Abimelek's inheritance of Gideon's authority is a case of usurpation and the real successor of Saul was David rather than Saul's son, Ischbaal.

[39] *Kriege*, 123, 127.

[40] Malamat, *Magnalia Dei*, 162 ff.

[41] *Judges*, 6.

[42] Boling, *Judges*, 29.

The last element — Gottesübereignungsformel — we have already examined in the previous section.

Our next task is, therefore, if we see the historical reality of the wars in the period of the Judges, to determine whether or not the motifs of YHWH war in their respective historical battles are found. We shall limit our examination to the wars in the *Retterbuch* (cc. 3—8) with which Richter has dealt.[43] For the rest of the war descriptions in the Book of Judges are less historical than the old stories in the Book of Saviors. Samson's episode (cc. 13—16) is not connected with an actual battle confrontation. Shamgar ben-Anath was a savior (3:31) who saved Israel, but how he was related to the God of Israel, YHWH, is not mentioned in our text. He was a simple Canaanite warrior who helped the Israelites to be liberated. The narrative of the civil war against Benjamin (cc. 19—21) also has less historical reality as a late theological reflection at the time of the Judges. Here we will examine the war descriptions of Othniel, Ehud, Gideon, Deborah and Barak, and of Saul.

2. THE WARS OF THE JUDGES

1) Othniel's war against Aram (c. 3:7—11)

In 3:8 (MT) the king of the enemy of Israel is called Cushan-Rishathaim, "King of Aram-Naharaim," which refers to northern Mesopotamia and eastern Syria. But the period of the Judges was not one in which threats to Israel came from so far afield. For it is difficult to assume that a ruler from Aram Naharaim should undertake such a large scale campaign in southern Canaan for the mere subjugation of a single tribe or even several tribes.[44] Scholars often emend Aram by reading "Edom" (ד instead of ר).[45] On the presupposition of the southern origin of Othniel's war, Malamat has proposed that the war of Othniel was a confrontation with the Egyptian invader to Canaan, Setnakht, the founder of the 20th Dyn (the end of the 13th century BC).[46] But Soggin rejects this solution as highly speculative.[47]

Richter, following Noth, has argued that this episode is a "Beispielstück" by $^{R}Dtr_2$ under the influence of Deutreronomy before the final redaction of the Deuteronomistic history.[48] In the same line, this episode

[43] *Untersuchungen*, 319—43.

[44] Malamat, *WHJP* III, 26.

[45] Boling, *Judges*, 81.

[46] *WHJP* III, 27.

[47] *Judges*, 47.

[48] *Bearbeitungen*, 23—26, 52—61, 90—91, 114—15.

has no narrative or descriptive element, no form of action. Moreover, because of the schematic formulation of the episode, the detailed materials of the actual war are lacking. Soggin has suggested that we may clearly presuppose the insertion of this passage in the redaction of Judges, the last, latest phase of Dtr.[49] A. D. H. Mayes points out that the expression that it was all Israel which was oppressed and all Israel which was delivered, shows that the quite local tribal tradition limited to very small groups had later been taken into the history of Israel as a whole, Israel in the editorial framework. Because none of the saviors came from Judah, the intention behind 3:7–11 was to provide a charismatic savior for Judah.[50] But T. Ishida rejects a pure Deuteronomistic composition of this episode by the Noth school.[51] In any case, the given evidence does not allow us to determine whether the motifs of YHWH war in the actual war event occurred.

2) Ehud's War against Moab (c. 3:12–30)

Ehud's war narrative is possibly close to historical realities without the Dtr framework. Actually this tradition was a dispute, in which the tribe of Ephraim was later involved, between the tribes of Benjamin and the Moabites. But it is not possible to clarify all the background of this event. Soggin has suggested that before being taken over by Dtr, this story seems to have been an eminently secular narrative. There is even an eschatological theme which contributes to a ridiculous tension (v. 24b).[52] Moreover, Ehud was also a savior who did not have the spirit of YHWH — a purely secular leader. Only the message of God serves as a stratagem for Ehud. Soggin has concluded that only the war which he organized as a holy war comes from the Dtr redaction.[53] The evidence above shows that the Ehud war was not a YHWH war — it was a simple war.

3) Gideon's War against Midian (cc. 6:1–8:32)

There is no doubt that the war of Gideon and the Midianites has a historical reality which took place in the conflict betwen Gideon's own clan, Abiezer of Manasseh (Josh 17:2), and later with the joining of all the members of Manasseh, Asher, Naphtali and Zebulun, Ephraim, and the Midianites and the Amalekites with the children of the East as a struggle for survival in the period of the Judges. It seems that because of

---

[49] *Judges*, 47.

[50] *Israel in the Period of the Judges*, SBT 29 (London 1974), 76.

[51] *RB* 80, 526, n. 63.

[52] *Judges*, 53.

[53] *Ibid.*, 56.

the identification of the tradition of the three hundred chosen warriors and the vintage of the Abiezerites in 8:2 in which Gideon replied to the complainer of the Ephraimites, the only participants in the first step of this battle, in fact, were the members of Gideon's own clan, Abiezer of Manasseh. Nevertheless, in this stage Gideon won the victory by his perfect stratagem.[54] This victory was already remembered in the Book of Isaiah as "the day of Midian" (Is 9:3). Moreover, in Ps 83 more concrete realities with the event of Deborah and Barak were preserved:[55] "Treat them (enemies) like Sisera, like Jabin at the river Kishon, destroy them (like Midianites) at the En-dor, let them be dung for the ground (κόπρος τῄ γῄ). Make their nobles like Orteb and Zeeb, all their heads like Zebah and Zalmunna (vv. 10–12)." In this Psalm there are two historical realities of the battle of Gideon: a list of Israel's oppressors and the special ties between the Phoenician coast and Philistia, and Assyria. In vv. 7–8, among the oppressors of Israel, Amalek was one of the nomadic tribes who joined at that time in the incursions of the Midianites. In v. 9 there is mention of the connection between the Phoenician coast and Philistia. Malamat has pointed out that "Assyria is joined with them" alluding to the campaigns of Tiglath-pileser I to Lebanon and Phoenicia, and to the initial Assyrian appearance on the horizon of Israel.[56] The reality of the battle is also supported by the geographical background of the battlefield of the Gideon camp at Mt. Gilboa (instead of Gilead) near En-harod, and the place near Mt. Tabor where the brothers of Gideon were killed by the Midianites, and the Midianite camp at En-dor near the Hill of Moreh, which were placed within or near the territory of the Israelite tribal alliance of Manasseh, Naphtali, Asher, Zebulun and Ephraim.[57]

Next, historical reality in the battle is seen by the careful stratagem of Gideon. Regarding the miltary approach, Malamat has suggested ten aspects of Gideon's military strategems which brought him victory:[58] a) an exact and accurate plan of operations, b) the use of a limited number of soldiers, c) choice of soldiers from a qualitative point of view to compensate, d) concentration of command in strong hands, e) the suiting of the plan of operations to physical conditions, f) knowledge of the area and familiarity with the terrain, g) a personal reconnaisssance, h) timing of the military schedule: the night attack, i) simplicity of method in carrying out the plan, and j) the continuing pursuit after the attack. These military

---

[54] Soggin, *Judges*, 148; Aharoni, *The Land of the Bible*, 263.

[55] M. Dahood, *Psalm* II, AB 17 (NY 1981^3), 273.

[56] *WHJP* III, 134.

[57] A. Malamat, "The War of Gideon and Midian," *The Military History*, 111–12 (Hebrew); M. Naor, "The Geographical Background of Interpretation of Gideon," *Issues in the Book of Judges* (Jerusalem (1971), 255 (Hebrew).

[58] *Ibid.*, 112–16; *id.*, *PEQ* 85 (1953), 62–64.

and tactical factors which gave the victory to Gideon and the Israelites can be seeen as the historical realities of the battle of Gideon and the Midianites. In the light of these realities, Malamat dates the battle of Gideon and the Midianiates with the allied desert tribes toward the end of the 12th century BC.[59]

Another historical reality is seen in the taunt of the princes of Succot (8:6). The princes of Succot asked Gideon: "Do you have the hands of Zebah and Zalmunna, the kings of Midian?" This story (8:4–9) belongs to the Book of Saviors. It was a common war custom in the ancient Near East at the end of the second millennium BC to bring back hands of the enemies as an evidence of their slaughter. In 7:9–15 a divination which was interpreted by the dream of the enemy soldier is considered as a possible reality: a loaf of barley bread rolled into the camp of Midian; when it came to the tent, it struck it and made it fall and turned it upside down. Then it lay there, flattened, which could only mean the sword of Gideon, son of Joash, the Israelite. Soggin sees that it is probably a part of the earliest stratum of the story, except vv. 12 and 14.[60]

Then with these historical realities can we find the motifs of YHWH war in the battle of Gideon? The relationship of Gideon and YHWH is first found in the calling stories for the warrior mission which appear three times: 6:11b–17,25–32,33–35.[61] Vv. 11b–17 describe Gideon as a warrior with charismatic elements. Here the element he has is: "This is your strength (v. 14a b) to be a mighty warrior (גבור חיל)." The communication between Gideon and the angel of YHWH would indicate the late level of the literary stratum (E).[62] In the second section (vv. 25–32) Gideon received another call and mission directly from YHWH to destroy the altar of Baal. Vv. 25–27a and 32a belong to a pre-Dtr redaction of the Book of Saviors. Here the focus of the story is the success of Gideon, not that of YHWH. In reality there is no aetiological and cultic interest. In the former section Gideon is called on to fight against an external enemy; there the real fight is with those within. It is a symmetry which presupposes the religious situation of the 8th and 7th centuries.[63] The last section, vv. 33–35, the revised version of 7:2 ff,23 ff, also does not belong to the earliest phase of the traditions which sees only a confrontation between the Abiezerites and Midianites. This tradition of Gideon's calling and mission belongs to the late tradition.[64]

---

[59] *WHJP* III, 142.

[60] *Judges*, 140; Richter (*Untersuchungen*, 239) ascribes to vv. 11b, 13–21 as original.

[61] C. F. Whitley, "The Sources of the Gideon Stories," *VT* 7 (1957), 158 ff.

[62] *Ibid.*, 161.

[63] Soggin, *Judges*, 128.

[64] W. Beyerlin, "Geschichte und heilsgeschichtliche Traditionsbildung im Alten Testament," *VT* 13 (1963), 1–25.

Even in the original description of the actual battle (7:16–21), which belongs to the Book of Saviors, the motif of YHWH intervention does not appear. The passage in 7:22, in which YHWH directed each man's sword within the camp against his companion, is a late interpretation of the actual battle story of Gideon. For Soggin has suggested that v. 22 seeks in some degree to correct v. 21: The victory of the three hundred is not caused by a stratagem, but by YHWH's intervention. The verse is, in fact, an interpolation intended at a stylistic level: V. 21 ends with **ויניסו** and v. 22b begins again with **וינס המחנה**... with the only difference the third personal plural of v. 21 and the third person singular of v. 22.[65] Here we assume probably that the main function of the preservation for the battle tradition was cultic. In our text the cultic element is not completely absent, although it is not as evident as in the Chronicles passages (II Ch 20:1–30) in which the Amorites and Edomites, allied against Judah, were destroyed in the ritual act. Although to break the jars with the torches alight inside them and to hold horns is quite a difficult operation, in the cult it is not improbable to stimulate the reality and its feeling. The sounding of the horns cannot in fact be understood as a secular act, seeing that here we have the **שופר**, the ram's horn, which is still sounded in acts of solemn worship even today.[66]

But in the Book of Isaiah the event of Gideon was already interpreted as an event of YHWH war: "And the Lord of hosts shall stir up a whip for him (Assyria) like the slaughter of Midian at the rock of Oreb (10:26a)." Thus the transformation of the battle of Gideon into a war of YHWH is considered to be not later than the 8th century BC by the prophet Isaiah. It is probably paralleled by the idea of a pre-Dtr redactor in which the enemies of Gideon were thrown into confusion by God[67] and they fled, and in which Gideon did not fight. Only YHWH won, and this is strictly analogous to the one at the Reed Sea (Ex 14–15) which accords only YHWH as the protagonist.[68]

4) The War of Deborah and Barak against a Canaanite Coalition (cc. 4–5)

1

There is no doubt about the historical reality of the battle of Deborah and Barak against a Canaanite coalition, because this battle is reported in two literary forms: prose (Judg 4) and poetry (Judg 5) which are found

[65] *Judges*, 145.
[66] *Ibid.*
[67] *Ibid.*, 146.
[68] Boling, *Judges*, 148.

in the ancient Near East, as well as elsewhere in the Bible such as Ex 14 and 15. First of all, who were the enemies? In Judg 4 the enemy was Jabin, king of Canaan, and his army commander, Sisera, who had nine hundred chariots of iron (vv. 2–3,23–24 only Jabin). Yet Jabin does not occur in Judg 5. He appears only in the Dtr layer of the above passages. Yadin believes that Jabin was a king of Hazor in the time of Joshua (c. 11) and here "Jabin, king of Canaan" is a late editorial gloss, added to an authentic historic text by a later editor.[69] So in this battle the real protagonist is Sisera, not Jabin king of Canaan who reigned in Hazor.[70] Soggin has proposed that if in Judg 3:31 there possibly was a coalition between the Israelites and the Canaanites against the Philistines, in this case there is a coalition between the Philistines and the Canaanites against the Israelites. Since Sisera is a Luvian name, it could be connected with a Sea people, the Philistines, even though these are not mentioned in the texts.[71] But in 5:19 the kings came and fought, then the kings of Canaan fought at Taanach, near the waters of Megiddo. In 4:13 Sisera called out all his mounted forces: nine hundred chariots of iron, and all the men on foot, from Harosheth to the river Kishon. Thus the enemies are considered to be the Canaanites: kings, general and soldiers.

In Judg 4 the ten contingents of soldiers were mustered from only two tribes: Naphtali and Zebulun, while in Judg 5 the forty contingents of soldiers from the six tribes actually had participated in this battle: Ephraim, Benjamin, Machir (Manasseh), Zebulun, Issachar and Naphtali. The southern tribes such as Judah and Simeon are not mentioned in this battle. In this connection, G. W. Alström has concluded that the song of Deborah was composed at a time when Judah was not a part of Israel or had not yet come into closer contact with the peoples of central and northern Canaan.[72] This means that the victory song in c. 5 cannot be seen as having accompanied the actual victory celebration, or that it cannot have been composed by an eye-witness, but is rather a poem a century or so removed from the actual events.[73] C. Rabin has supported the idea that the song of Deborah was composed to encourage the Israelites who had felt a lack of tribal unity and military weapons in a troubled period facing the threat of the Philistines, probably in the time of Saul and later.[74] More

---

69 *BAR* 8/2, 23.

70 Soggin, *Joshua*, 63.

71 *Ibid.*, 68; Malamat, *WHJP* III, 137.

72 "Judges 5:20 ff and History," *JNES* 36 (1977), 288.

73 *Ibid.*, 288, n. 15; P. R. Ackroyd, "The Composition of the Song of Deborah," *VT* 2 (1952), 162; C. Rabin, "The Song of Deborah as a Cultural Document," *Issues in the Book of Judges* (Jerusalem 1971), 116–17 (Hebrew).

74 *Ibid.*, 117–18; *id.*, "Judges 5:2 and the Ideology of Deborah's War," *JJS* 6 (1955), 125–34.

recently, Soggin, following G. Garbin, has pointed out that the language of the song of Deborah is older than the classical Hebrew of the 8th century BC, but later than that of the agricultural calendar of Gezar, from the end of the 10th century BC, not to mention Ugaritic and ancient Phoenician.[75]

2

On the basis of the archaeological evidence and of the litarary style and archaic language of the Deborah song, Albright, J. Bright, and others have proposed that the battle of Deborah and Barak against Sisera took place in the 12th century BC.[76] Recently, on the name basis of the use of the YHWH in the song, D. N. Freedman has suggested the theory of the 12th century as in Ex 15 and Ps 29.[77] Like the Albright school, de Vaux, on the ground of "before Machir's migration into Transjordan," keeps the same date — the middle of the 12th century.[78] Like Albright and Bright, Malamat dates the battle of this song as the last quarter of the 12th century (1125 BC), on the basis of Dan's tribal migration to its northern habitat and of the reference to Shamgar son of Anath (v. 6) who defeated a band of 600 Philistine warriors (3:31) who had appeared in Canaan only in the days of Ramses III.[79] On the basis of the parallelism between the Deborah song and the epic of Tukulti-Ninurta, P. C. Craigie has also pointed to the early dating of the Deborah Song.[80]

Recently, Mayes has argued that the victory of the Israelite tribes against Sisera should be dated shortly before Israel's defeat by the Philistines at Aphek, sometime in the course of the second half of the 11th century BC.[81] This victory was the first stage in the course of transition

---

[75] *Judges*, 80—81; *id.*, "Bemerkungen zum Deboralied, Richter Kap. 5, Versuch einer neuen Übersetzung und eines Vorstosses in the älteste Geschichte Israels," *TLZ* 106 (1981), 625—39. He points out even the second century BC elements of the song (634).

[76] *Yahweh and the Gods of Canaan* (London 1968), 11; J. Bright, *A History of Israel* (London 1960), 157; A. Globe, "The Literary Structure and Unity of the Song of Deborah," *JBL* 93 (1973), 493—512. Robertson (*Linguistic Evidence*, 154—55) describes Judg 5 as the end of the 12th century, but there is a time span which begins from the 13th century to the 8th century. Not can we establish even a relative chronology. Still there is controversy over the early date of Judg 5.

[77] *Magnalia Dei*, 61—63.

[78] *EHI* II, 795.

[79] *WHJP* III, 136—37.

[80] "The Song of Deborah and the Epic of Tukulti-Ninurta," *JBL* 88 (1969), 253—65. Albright already has suggested the possible connection between both the song and the epic (*BASOR* 62, 1936, 26—27).

[81] "The Historical Context of the Battle against Sisera," *VT* 19 (1969), 359; *id.*, *Israel in the Period of the Judges*, 96. De Vaux rejects this late day as "out of the question", but does not give any valid reason (*EHI* II, 759), while Soggin accepts the late date of Mayes (*Judges*, 93, 97 ff).

by which the Israelite tribes progressed from acting as independent units to employing their combined strength in a time of battle. This stage marks the end of the power of the city-states to obstruct common action by the northern and mid-Palestine tribes. This stage should be preceded by the stage of the expulsion of the Philistines from the mountains in the time of Saul, which opened the way for communication between Judah and its northern neighbours.[82] We suppose that, although the Philistines came to Canaan in the 12th century, they needed a certain amount of time to occupy the place of the Canaanites: more than a century. Thus it is possible that the victory of Deborah and Barak took place at a late time — the beginning of the 11th century, and the composition of the victory song was not long after the event, but before the monarchy. For it does not reflect the idea of the institution of the monarchy.[83] Actually the period of the rising power of the Philistines was close to the time of Samuel and Saul. The military situation of the Israelites in 5:8aβ: "then there was the battle in the gates, yet there was neither shield nor spears (מגן אם־יראה ורמח) in the forty contingents of Israel" was similar to that of the Israelites in the time of Saul (I Sam 13:22a): "in the day of battle there was neither sword nor spear (חרב וחנית) to be found in the hands of all the people that were with Saul and Jonathan."

The battle descriptions of Deborah and Barak against Sisera appear in cc. 4 (prose) and 5 (poem) in which the song of Deborah is considered to be much older than the prose narrative, even though the prose narrative also does not exclude the earlier tradition. But in two descriptions there are certain discrepancies: The numbers of the tribal confederacy and the scene of the actual battle. In c. 4 only two tribes (Naphtali and Zebulun) participated in the battle against Sisera, while in c. 5 four more tribes (Ephraim, Benjamin, Issachar, and Manasseh = Machir) took part. In c. 4 the battle took place between the river Kishon and Mt. Tabor, more towards the north side of the valley of Jezreel, while in c. 5 it took place more towards the south or south-east side of the plain, at Taanack by the waters of Megiddo (5:19). Nevertheless, two areas are united by the river Kishon.[84] C. 5 does not mention the actual fighting of those tribes called up, except for the movement of the enemy: the kings of Canaan came and fought and were destroyed (vv. 19—21). Kaufmann considers that the battle of Deborah and Barak in both chapters was not a single battle but two separate ones. Yet the battle in c. 5 was another battle which was not related to Sisera.[85]

---

[82] *Id.*, "Israel in the Pre-Monarchy Period," *VT* 23 (1973), 170.

[83] Soggin, *Joshua*, 80.

[84] Aharoni, *The Land of the Bible*, 224.

[85] *Judges*, 118.

However, Malamat thinks that the battles described differently are rather two different stages of one and the same battle.[86] The actual cause of the battle: Barak summoned ten contingents (אלפים) of men from Naphtali and Zebulun to Khirbet-Kedesh in the territory of Issachar,[87] and then he led them to Mt. Tabor, the operational base. This base gave the Israelite command the advantage in timing the attack to suit their deeds — certainly a major factor in their operational plan.[88] But they could not continue to control the valley of Jezreel. Then the two tribes needed the help of the neighbouring tribes to keep control of the valley as in the case of Gideon's war, in which first two tribes, the Naphtalites and the Zebulunites, and later the Ephraimites, joined them in the defeat of the enemy who had already been put to flight. Thus this cooperation among the Israelites in the pre-monarchic time was encouraged as a struggle for existence to overcome the Canaanites and the Philistines. In this sense c. 5 reflects an idea of a מלחמה חובה.[89] On the basis of the descriptions of the rains in 5:4—5, and 21 it was pointed out that the Israelites seemed to have delayed their attack as a stratagem till the rainy season, which often turns the low lying valleys into quagmires, such as the rain swollen Kishon river (v. 21).[90] But in c. 4 there is no mention of the rains and flood of the Kishon river. If there were rains at that time, Kaufmann asks why only the enemies and their chariots, and not the Israelites, were bogged down?[91] Rather, Barak pursued together the chariots and enemies who fled to the Haroshet-haroim, even though only Sisera came down from his chariot and fled to the tent of Yael. otherwise, it is supposed that the Israelites gained the victory by a military strategy of using a side attack from the mountains of Galilee or a rear attack from the mountains of Zebulun.[92] It is considered that because of the confusion which resulted from the unexpected attack, Sisera fled and was killed by Yael. As a result, the Israelites brought an end to the Canaanite hegemony in the valley of Jezreel, despite the fact that all the main Canaanite centers in this area do not seem to have been conquered at that time (4:23). The tribes of Manasseh, Zebulun and Naphtali were able to expand their territory and later could easily respond to the demand of Gideon's war. This victory, as mentioned above, secured for the first time the territorial connection between the northern tribes and the central.

---

86 *WHJP* III, 137.

87 Kaufmann, *Judges*, 117; Aharoni, *The Land of the Bible*, 224; M. Haran, *Temple and Temple-Service in Ancient Israel* (Oxford 1978), 33—34, n. 35.

88 Malamat, *WHJP* III, 139.

89 Rabin, *JJS* 6, 133.

90 Malamat, *WHJP* III, 139; Aharoni, *The Land of the Bible*, 224.

91 *Judges*, 118.

92 *Ibid.*

3

Here our task is whether or not the motif of YHWH war appeared in the reality of the course of battle. In 4:6b–7 Deborah as a diviner delivered the divine oracle to Barak: "It is certain that YHWH, God of Israel, has commanded you; go, deploy the troops at mount Tabor, ... I (YHWH) will deploy Sisera, Jabin's army commander, against you at the brook Kishon, with his chariots and troops; I will give him into your hand." This exercise of divination before battle was well known as an initial step of divine war in the ancient Near East. In I K 22 this practise of divination before a battle was carried out by the king Jehoshaphat and the four hundred prophets. Here the initiator of the event was the king, and the subordinates were the prophet-diviners. But in our context the initiator was the diviner, Deborah, not Barak, the field commander, while Barak was subordinated to Deborah and his function was secondary. Here the relationship between Deborah and Barak was similar to that of Samuel and Saul who was subordinated to Samuel. The combined leadership of military and religious leaders was a characteristic of divine war conduct. This leadership contrasts with that of the single leadership of religious and military men like Joshua. It is a symptom of the preparatory stage of the formation of states. But after the formation of the monarchy the order of the leadership of religious and military was reversed; for example, David and his priests Abiathar and Zadok who were appointed by the king. The functional relationship between king and diviner was a living social reality in the monarchial period.[93] If Barak, as Soggin suggests,[94] was the original protagonist on the Hebrew side and the participation of Deborah was a creation of the earliest redactors at the pre-Dtr stage to give a pan-Israelite character to the battle, Barak primaily was not related to any divine mission from YHWH. If so, that his participation depended only upon Deborah as a prophetic diviner which appears in the secondary additions, means that his action was a normal act of war without a religious description.

4:15 shows that YHWH confounded Sisera, all the chariotry and fighting force before Barak. According to this statement, Barak did not fight, but only chased the chariotry and fighting force. Deborah gave a divine confidence to Barak: "This is the day in which YHWH gave Sisera in to your hand. Does not YHWH advance before You (4:14a)?" In 4:14aβ the motif of YHWH's vanguard (יהוה יצא לפניך), which is not found in c. 5, is strikingly similar to that of YHWH vanguard in II Sam 5:24 = I Ch 14:15. We have already discussed that the motif of a divine vanguard was very popular in the ancient Near East. In 4:15 then the confusion

[93] Boling, *Judges*, 99.

[94] *Judges*, 72.

motif of holy war is exactly similar to that of Ex 14:24, Josh 10:10, I Sam 7:10, and in others as follows:[95]

שמ″ יד:כדב	ויהם את מחנה מצרים
יהו″ י:י	ויהמם יהוה לפני ישראל... מאשר הרגו בני ישראל בחרב.
שופ″ ד:וט־רו	ויהם יהוה את סיסרא ואת כל הרכב ואת כל המחנה לפי חרב לפני ברף ... וברק רדף אחרי הרכב...
שמ″ א ז:יb־יא	ויהמם וינגפו לפני ישראל ויצאו אנשי ישראל מן המצפה וירדפו את פלשתים...
דב″ ב:וט	וגם יד יהוה היתה בם להמם מקרב המחנה עד תמם.
דב″ ז″כג	ונתנם יהוה אלהיך לפניך והמם מהומה גדלה עד השמדם
שמ″ כג:כזאb	והמתי את כל העם אשר תבא בהם...

Here, as seen previously, the subject of the verb **המם** is YHWH. Its object is the enemies of Israel or their camps. Yet, the case of a human as the subject occurs in late usage (Esth 9:24 — Haman, Jer 51:34 — Nebuchadnezzar). It has been recognized that except in Ex 14:24 (J), all the occurrences of the idea of confusion are Dtn or Dtr (Ex 23:27; Dt 2:15; 7:23).[96] In the Dtn ideology of holy war, the confusion idea of YHWH was used to express "Soli Deo gloria".[97] It is clear that in Dt 2:15 the idea of confusion used as the negative intervention of YHWH against Israel is a Dtr usage. However, our text presents the positive intervention of YHWH against the enemy of Israel, not Israel herself. On the other hand, except in Ex 14:24, the victory accounts over the enemies include the idea of synergism. After the description of confusion caused by YHWH, human action is followed by the verbs **רדף** or **הכה**. It seems that the idea of the cooperation of man and God in battle is older than that of the fighting of God only which originated from the prophetic conviction (**בטח**) of Isaiah (7:4—14). If it is correct, the idea of divine confusion in I Sam 7:10, Judg 14:15, Josh 10:10 should not be later than that in Ex 14:24. The idea of confusion that the thunder as a divine voice makes in our passages is exactly paralleled with II Sam 22:14—15 (= Ps 18:14—15) which is considered to have been written down in its present form not later than the ninth—eighth centuries BC.[98] Weimar has concluded that

[95] See ns. 207—209 of chapter V.

[96] Stolz, *Kriege*, 20.

[97] Stolz, "**המם**", *THAT* 1 (1977), 504.

[98] Cross and Freedman, *Ancient Yahwistic Poetry*, 128.

the original tradition of Deborah's war was composed in the south in the light of the idea of YHWH war which began from David's victory over the Philistines,[99] but later it was touched by the area of the northern state.

4

In the Song of Deborah the motif of holy war is dramatically depicted in vv. 4–5 and 20–21. Here the protagonist in the battle was neither Deborah nor Barak, but only YHWH who was the Lord of nature and history. The one who saved the Israelites was not Barak and his army but YHWH, the God of Israel. The decisive role for the victory was not the fighting of the Israelites, but the intervention of YHWH in the battle. This idea is already expressed in the descriptions of the theophany of YHWH in vv. 4–5: "Lord, when you go forth from Seir, when you advance from the territory of Edom, th earth trembles, the heaven leaps, the clouds turn into water. The mountains leap before Lord, the Lord of Sinai, before the Lord, the God of Israel." Because of the comparatively early date of Judg 5, it is tempting to see vv. 4–5 as the original of the motif of divine appearance rather than as a late composition gloss. But this attempt does not give a good answer to the question of the place of vv. 4–5 in the entire poem. The explanation that these verses come here because of the primary importance of YHWH's theophany for victory in holy war does not effectively answer the question of why they were not used at the turning point of the story, vv. 20–21, where cosmic and natural elements are paramount.[100] Some view vv. 4–5 as a traditional *incipit* from which the song begins,[101] rather than a late YHWHistic addition to an earlier epic account (vv. 12–30).[102] We have already seen in the previous chapters that the motif of divine appearance in battle in the ancient Near East was a very popular theme. In this connection many scholars have supposed that this motif as a conventional literary stock could have influence on the formation of the idea of YHWH's theophany.

---

[99] Weimar, "Jahwekrieg", 50. Stolz (*Kriege*, 104 ff) sees that the original tradition of Deborah's war was composed in the north such as Jael's story without religious colour, and later was theologized as YHWH war by the royal theologian in the Jerusalem court.

[100] Mann, *Divine Presence*, 183.

[101] U. Cassuto, *Biblical and Oriental Studies* I, ET by I. Abrahams (Jerusalem 1973), 258–59; W. F. Albright, "A Catalogue of Early Hebrew Lyric Poems (Ps 68)," *HUCA* 23 (1950–51), 20; Richter, *Untersuchungen*, 69 ff; E. Lipiński, "Judges 5:4–5 et Psaume 68:1–11," *Bibl* 48 (1967), 186 ff; A. Globe, "The Text and Literary Structure of Judges 5:4–5," *Bibl* 55 (1974), 168–78. Vv. 4–5 parallels exactly with Ps 68:8, a theophanic passage which has been reviewed by them; Mann, *Ibid.*

[102] H. P. Müller, "Der Aufbau des Deboraliedes," *VT* 16 (1966), 446–59; Richter, *Untersuchungen*, 69 ff (5:4c,5a only).

If so, we have to seek a possible point of contact: Why, when and for what purpose did Israel adopt the idea?

First of all, it seems, as Soggin, following E. Lipiński, suggests,[103] that YHWH did not, in fact, come from the south solely join in the battle in the north and that the text is a confession of faith to the God of Israel who fights alongside his people whenever it seems necessary. Here YHWH is the God of Sinai. Since this idea is found in a common store of ancient literature which appears in Habakkuk 3, Dt 33 and Ps 68, as well as in the ancient Near East sources,[104] it is not necessary for vv. 4–5 to be confined to the original composition related to the battle event (vv.20–21). Here we see the conjunction of YHWH's theophany and the military encounter (vv. 4–5,19 ff), out of which the victor emerged as a newly established political power. Mann has suggested that the reality of the tribal confederacy, even if not national, was correlated with an affirmation of the supremacy of YHWH.[105] But it is considered that the real supremacy of YHWH was correlated with the political reality of the Davidic monarchy which had proclaimed YHWH as a national tutelary God. It resembles the exaltation of YHWH in the period of the united monarchy. Soggin argues that vv. 4–5 presuppose a theological systematization which suggests a later stage of transmission, when the ancient epic was inserted into a theological and cultic context intended to provide an interpretative key: the hymn is no longer about the mighty men of Israel, but the glorious deeds of YHWH.[106] Thus it is more reasonable that the idea of YHWH's theophany in our text was probably formulated in the royal theology of Jerusalem in the court of David.

Moreover, vv. 20–21 show that YHWH fights against the enemy of the Israelites through his creatures in heaven and on earth. From the heaven fought the stars; from their course they fought against Sisera. The Kishon river swept them away, with the river overwhelming them. The motif of stars fighting from heaven was a common idea in the ancient Near East in the second millennium BC, but in the Bible the star is not identified with YHWH the God, only with his agent or messenger.[107] The intervention of celestial powers is directly decisive for the YWHW war, but it is a poetic hyperbole which has no power proof.[108] It is a cosmic element. The motif of the river which swept the enemy away, as we have seen in the previous Exodus event, is a mythological motif of divine war, such as the idea of the crossing of the Jordan river in Josh 3–4. The

[103] Soggin, *Judges*, 85.
[104] Mann, *Divine Presence*, 176–89.
[105] *Ibid.*, 188.
[106] Soggin, *Judges*, 95.
[107] Weinfeld, "They Fought from Heaven," 27.
[108] Smend, *Yahweh War*, 82, n. 30.

subject of the song of the Sea is exclusively the victory of YHWH by his miracle, while the subject of the song of Deborah includes human participation in the victory.[109] But both songs ascribe the victory to YHWH. From the viewpoint of the *Werbelied*, Soggin suggests that:[110]

> Israelite faith felt it necessary to provide this originally secular song with a liturgical and theological framework; it may have been for what we might call a catechetical reason, or because it was placed in the context of Israelite worship. A song which celebrated the tribes who came to the battle along with their leaders has now become a song which is essentially a celebration of the God of Israel and his glorious achievements: Yahweh who comes from his southern desert sanctuary is the same god who inspires the judges, the saviours of the people, and the prophets who shed light on him through their words; he is the one who fights the peoples' battles, thus fulfilling his ancient promises. The original scope of the song is twisted by this new interpretation, but it is to that conversion that we owe the fact that a considerable part of the song has been preserved.

Thus we are forced to conclude that the two motifs in vv. 20—21: shooting star and river, were not actually connected with the reality of the war of Deborah and Barak. It is an idea which was adopted under the influence of YHWH war in the time of the Davidic monarchy. The original scope of the song was twisted by this new idea.

3. SAUL'S WARS (I SAM 10:27b—11:15; 13—14; 15; 31)

1

Primarily Saul was a mighty warrior who had grown up in the house of a warrior (גבור חיל) in Gibea (I Sam 9:1). He is the first man who fought for the liberation of all the tribes of Israel against the enemies, the surrounding neighbours: the Ammonites in the east, the Amalekites in the south, the Philistines in the hill country and west, and others (I Sam 14:47—48).[111] I Sam 10:27b (4QSam[a])[112]—11:15 shows Saul's first victory[113] over the Ammonites in the land east of Jordan. Now it is generally

---

[109] Lind, *Yahweh is a Warrior*, 74.

[110] Soggin, *Judges*, 99. Kaufmann (*The Conquest of Canaan*, 66) sees the war descriptions in Judg 5 as YHWH war in the national scope.

[111] Z. Kallai, "The Wars of Saul," *The Military History of the Land of Israel in Biblical Times* (1971), 144 ff (Hebrew); S. Abramsky, *Kingdom of Saul and Kingdom of David* (Jerusalem 1977), 34 ff (Hebrew).

[112] P. K. McCarter Jr. (*I Samuel*, AB 8, NY 1980, 198—99) reconstructs a long passage of 10:27b which occurs in only 4QSam[a] and in the Greek text used by Josephus (see Ant VI 68—71).

[113] In fact, it is seen that the battle of Michmash was Saul's first decisive action against the Philistine (Abramski, *Kingdom of Saul and Kingdom of David*, 37 ff; C. E. Hauer Jr., "The Shape of Saulide Strategy," *CBQ* 31, 1969, 153).

agreed that the victory narrative has a reliable historical reality although embellished by the tendency of the author to interpret the victory as achieved by one inspired with divine charisma.[114] The historical reality is supported by references elsewhere to the close relationship between Jabesh-Gilead and the tribes of Benjamin and Saul in particular. Judg 19–21 records the fact that Jabesh-Gilead did not participate in the punishment of Benjamin.[115] After the defeat of Saul at the Gilboa battle (I Sam 31:11 ff and II Sam 2:4b ff) it is the men of Jabesh-Gilead who brought Saul's body from the Philistines and gave it an honorable burial.

In the present text the picture drawn of Saul is that of a charismatic warrior, **נגיד** (9:16)[116] who received the spirit of God (**רוח אלהים**), not the spirit of YHWH,[117] and who mustered the soldiers which appear only here outside the Book of Judges, and who did not leave one of two together. Moreover, like Gideon (Judg 7:16), Saul divided his men into three companies (11:11) and attacked the enemy during the morning watch smiliar to Ex 14:24. In this sense Saul is supposed to be the last judge and at the same time, the first king, chosen by the people and Samuel (vv.

---

[114] McCarter, *I Samuel*, 207, n. 7; B. C. Birch, *The Rise of the Israelite Monarchy*: The Growth and Development of I Samuel 7–15, SBL 27 (Missoula, Montana 1976), 58 (– *The Israelite Monarchy*). In v. 8b the notice of the mustering of the men of Judah is a secondary addition, because it is unlikely that such a separation of Judah from Israel would date before division of the kingdom when Israel and Judah became distinct entities (Birch, *ibid.*, 55; von Rad, *Krieg*, 20 ff).

[115] M. Buber, *Kingship of God*, ET by R. Scheimann (1956, London 1967), 9; Birch, *The Israelite Monarchy*, 58.

[116] Alt (*EOTHR*), 254 ff) explains the status of Saul before becoming king designated as nāgīd, a charismatic leader chosen by YHWH, much similar to the judge who had possessed the spirit of YHWH. Yet the function of Nāgīd by Saul is distinguished from his charismatic role as king (W. Beyerlin, "Das Königscharisma bei Saul," *ZAW* 73, 1961, 186–201; J. A. Soggin, "Charisma und Institution im Königtum Sauls," *ZAW* 75, 1963, 54–65). But in the original setting the function of nāgīd by Saul was that of Savior for Israel from the enemies before the Davidic age (W. Richter, "Die Nāgīd-Formel," *BZ* NF 9, 1965, 83). L. Schmidt (*Menschlicher Erfolg und Jahwe Initiative*, WMANT 38, Neukirchen/Vluyn 1970, 141–44, 191 ff) points out that, although the title nāgīd was applied to king, priest, treasure superintendent, leader of house and tribes after the monarchy, the original function of nāgīd before the monarchy was that of military leader. Cross (*CMHE*, 220, n. 5) cites two extra Biblical sources of the 9th–8th century BC, to support the military aspect of nāgīd – military commander: Sefireh III:10 and the Nora stone, line 7. The divine designation before being king is proved by the warriorship (B. Halpern, "The Uneasy Compromise," *Traditions and Transmission*: Turning Points in Biblical Faith, Festschrift of F. M. Cross, ed. by B. Halpern and J. D. Levenson, Eisenbraun 1981, 72); Abramsky, *Kingdom of Saul and Kingdom of David*, 159–64.

[117] Stolz, *Kriege*, 130, n. 7. Ths usage of the spirit of God is older than that of the spirit of YHWH.

12–14) as a result of the victory over the Ammonites.[118] Von Rad has pointed out that I Sam 11 shows the holy war idea on the basis of the scheme of the amphictyony.[119] Richter, following him, has argued that the story of Saul's victory over the Ammonites gives a good example of the first type of holy war scheme which appears in Judg 3 and 6.[120] Its structural elements are: information of the situations and the enemy, possession of divine spirit, mustering of the tribal levy, victory, and total destruction. Our text includes all these elements except the last element.[121] However, the elements which are related with deity occur in v. 6a (the possession of divine spirit), in v. 7bα (the dread of god upon the people in the course of mustering), and in v. 13b (YHWH's salvation in Israel). The possession of God's spirit is described in terms of great anger,[122] and the dread of YHWH (פחד יהוה) upon the people is not the same thing as YHWH making fearful (המם) the enemy.[123] V. 13b is a direct allusion to v. 9 in Dtr usage. In the viewpoint of the hypothesis of amphictyony the idea of the holy war ended with Saul.[124] Furthermore, our text does not include the decisive factor, the motif of YHWH's intervention in the battle. So it is supposed that Saul's war against the Ammonites was a normal war reflecting the rising power of Saul. If the anointing story of Saul as king in I Sam 9:1–10:16 reflects his qualification as king, and the story of his selection as king in 10:17–25 implies a method of choosing Saul as king, this text may explain the motivation of the people and Samuel to make him king, in the wake of the decisive victory over the Ammonites. All these imply that Saul, who was already king *de jure*, has now become king *de facto*.[125] What, after victory, the victor used to become a king is similar to the case of the beginning of the ancient Near East states.

---

[118] M. Tsevat, "The Emergence of the Israelite Monarchy: Eli, Samuel, Saul," *WHJP* IV/1 (1979), 75. S. Talmon ("Kingship and Ideology of the State," *WHJP* V, ed. by A. Malamat, 1979, 9, 13) explains the reasons that Saul's rise to power was not different from that of the judges, and the king's role is not confined to calling up the army in time of emergency as it had been under the judges.

[119] *Krieg*, 20 ff. G. Wallis (*ZAW* 64, 1952, 57–61) argues a parallelism of the biblical method of levy in I Sam 11:7 ff and Judg 19:29 ff with the Mari sources.

[120] *Untersuchungen*, 177–79; Birch, *The Israelite Monarchy*, 56–58.

[121] Stolz (*Kriege*, 129, n. 3) contends that v. 11bβ does not reflect the idea of total destruction, but only the scattering of the enemies.

[122] P. R. Ackroyd, *The First Book of Samuel* (Cambridge 1971), 91 (– *I Samuel*). H. W. Hertzberg (*I and II Samuel*, OTL, ET by J. S. Bowden, 1960, London 1976, 93) shows that Saul's anger is clearly different from being possessed by the spirit of God (– *Samuel*).

[123] Stolz, *Kriege*, 131, n. 12. See n. 130 above. Besides our text this word in Ex 15:16; Dt 2:25; 11:25 is used for the conquest of Canaan by the Dtn/Dtr and that in Is 2:10,19,21 is related with the day of Yahweh as eschatological fear. Cf., Miller, *Divine Warrior*, 116.

[124] Stolz, *Kriege*, 201–22.

[125] McCarter, *I Samuel*, 205.

2

In the battle of Michmash against the Philistines in I Sam 13:16–14:23a, an idea of divine intervention is found. The Philistine camp at the Michmash pass and the Israelite camp at Geba were separated by a deep ravine, a mile or two apart in the rugged hill country south of Bethel. Jonathan and his weapon-bearer suddenly attacked the front post of the Philistines, on the conviction that YHWH would give them victory, for nothing could prevent YHWH from going on to victory, whether many or few (14:6b). This conviction is well compared with that of David fighting the Philistine giant Goliath in 17:45 ff. Our text shows that only two, Jonathan and his weapon-bearer, smote about twenty men of the enemy (14:14). It was not easy for two to smite so many men. So this picture reflects supernatural power. In 14:15 the enemy camp is depicted: There was a convulsion (חרדה) in the camp and in the field; all the soldiers of the garrison and the raiding parties were terrified; the earth quaked; and it became a divine convulsion (חרדת אלהים).[126] Here the decisive factor is neither the heroism of Jonathan and his weapon-bearer not even the timely arrival of Saul and his army (14:20a), but the confusion of the Philistines turning against each other in a very great panic (14:20b). This confusion was the practical confusion which was caused by the Philistines themselves on the battlefield, while the confusion which appeared in the holy war context which we mentioned just before, is a theological confusion which YHWH as subject made. The essence of the story is that God himself went into the attack and so the enemy was panic-stricken. The Philistines fell as they suddenly recognized a supernatural power before them. It expresses a theological statement by describing events in terms of the intervention of God.[127]

We can suppose a possibility that the Hebrews as mercenaries under the Philistines revolted against their lords (14:21): "the Hebrews[128] (the slaves – LXX) who sided previously with the Philistines went up into the camp, and they too turned to be with Israel under Saul and Jonathan." We can say that the distrust by the commanders of the Philistines toward David and his men may probably have caused the revolt of the Hebrews at the battle of Michmash (27:1–28:2). This is also supported by the fact that in 13:3 as soon as Jonathan attacked the garrison of the Philistines (the Philistine governor) in Geba, the news spread among the Philistines that the Hebrews were in revolt (LXX).[129] The LXX reading δουλοί

---

[126] LXX may reflect the convulsion of YHWH (ἔκστασις παρα κουριου).

[127] Ackroyd, *I Samuel*, 111–12; Blenkinsopp, *CBQ* 26, 429 ff.

[128] LXX reads *hoi douloi.*

[129] LXX reads ἠθετηκασιν οἵ δουλοι (פשעו העבדים), while Targum, Peshta and Vulgate follow MT. Many scholars prefer the LXX (Wellhausen, *Der Text der Bücher Samuelis*, 1871,

(עבדים) instead of Hebrews (עברים), can support the idea that the new event seems no more than a slave revolt to the Philistines.[130] It is seen that Jonathan's assassination of the Philistine governor (13:3a) is an act of rebellion and initiated the long war between the Philistines and Israel that continued throughout Saul's lifetime.[131]

However, at this stage there is still doubt as to whether or not this battle was recognized as a YHWH war, because of the failure to consult YHWH before the battle (see below). In v. 45 Jonathan succeeded with God on this day. It was understood that YHWH was not connected with this battle. But later the narrator concludes that YHWH saved Israel on that day (v. 23). In the prophetic description of accusation in I Sam 10:19 the savior was God, not YHWH.

3

The motif of the divine consultation is an initial aspect of divine war. Here we find only certain practises of the divine consultation in which Saul failed to receive the oracle of YHWH. In v. 3 for this purpose the priest of YHWH took part in the battle with Saul and the soldiers: Ahijah, the priest of YHWH in Shiloh carried out the ephod (LXX). Just before Saul and his army went into Jonathan's surprise attack, Saul ordered Ahijah to bring the ephod (the ark — MT) in v. 18,[132] in order to seek the will of YHWH for the attack. But he could not seek the oracle (v. 19):

80—81; S. R. Driver, *Notes on the Hebrew Text of the Book of Samuel*, 1890, Oxford 1913, 99; H. P. Smith, *A Critical Exegetical Commentary on the Books of Samuel*, ICC, 1899, Edinburgh 1969, 93, — *Samuel*; K. Budde, *Die Bücher Samuel*, KHC 8, 1902, 84, — *Samuel*; Hertzberg, *Samuel*, 164; M. H. Segal, *The Books of Samuel*, Jerusalem 1976, 94—96, Hebrew; Ackroyd, *Samuel*, 104; McCarter, *I Samuel*, 226; J. Weingreen, "Saul and the Ḫabirū," *Fourth World Congress of Jewish Studies* I, 1967, 63—66). But some scholars still prefer the MT: H. J. Stoebe, *Das erste Buch Samuelis*, KAT 8/1 (Gütersloh 1973), 241—43; Gottwald, *The Tribes of Yahweh*, 420—25. The MT reading is contrasted to: a) the name "Hebrews" which they used to be called by the foreigner, by the Egyptians (Ex 1:15) or by the Philistines (I Sam 4:6; 14:11 etc.) as contrasted to all Israel in v. 4aα. Saul would never call Israel Hebrews. b) the verb שמע (cf., 13:7; 14:21) in v. 4aα is not necessary to be repeated. This revolt is not a religious conversion that happened after the second temple period (cf., J. Milgrom, "Religious Conversion and the Revolt Model for the Formation of Israel," *JBL* 101/2, 1982, 169—76.

130 Hertzberg, *Samuel*, 104.

131 McCarter, *I Samuel*, 227.

132 P. R. Davis, ("Ark or Ephod in I Sam 14:8," *JTS* 26, 1976, 82—87) and A. Bartal ("For the Ark of God was on that day with the children of Israel," *Beth Mikra* 26, 1981, 305—8) support the MT reading, because of the confusion of the narrator of the events from that time with those during the period of David such as Uzzah and Eleasar being the same person as Ahi and Ahijah.

"Saul said to the priest, withdraw your hand." Of course, Jonathan and his armour-bearer went up to the outpost of the Philistines without any consultation of YHWH and Saul too went into the battle without the approval of YHWH. Nevertheless, the narrator shows us that at this moment there was certain supernatural help beyond the control of Saul and Jonathan in the camp of the Philistines in vv. 20b–21: "Every man's sword was against his fellows, and there was great confusion." Now the Hebrews who had been with the Philistines before that time and who had gone up with them into the camp, even they also turned to be with the Israelites who were with Saul and Jonathan: a divine intervention as a revolt inside the Philistine camp.[133] In vv. 37–44 the purpose of the oracle was not for battle, but for determining whether the people or the king's house could break the ban on eating forbidden: Saul's methods of warfare are similar to those of some of the Judges.[134] The above evidence shows that at least there was a practice of divine consultation in battle and for that reason a priest accompanied the commander of the army, as seen in other battles in the ancient Near East.

In I Sam 15:1–9 we find the southern campaign of Saul against the Amalekites. It is generally agreed that c. 15 was composed in a late period by the prophetic writer or the pre-Dtr, on the basis of the late elements such as Ḥerem or the speech form.[135] But the fact of the campaign of Saul against the Amalekites is not denied on the basis of the passage in 14:48. In addition, the tradition in which Samuel kills Agag, the Amalekite king, before YHWH in Gilgal in v. 33 is an old divine war custom which was well known in the ancient Canaan and Egyptian contexts in the second millennium BC. We find Ramses III who smite his enemies before his god who lifted up a *kidon.*[136] In v. 12 Saul set up a monument (יד) for himself in Carmel in southern Judah as a mark of his victory.[137] It cannot be supposed that Saul's victory pillar contained some description of YHWH's help, because of the ascription of the glory of the victory to Saul himself. This would certainly still have been pointed out for a long time as Saul's victory stela until the story was composed by a prophetic writer.

Finally with the death of Saul and Jonathan in the battle of Gilboa with the Philistines, the kingdom of Saul actually ended as an abortive kingdom which could not conquer the political entity of the Philistines,

---

[133] Stolz (*Kriege*, 135) sees the proto-type of YHWH intervention in the battle of Jonathan who was not a charismatic warrior type like Saul.

[134] Yadin, *Warfare* II, 263.

[135] Stolz, *Kriege*, 136–38; Birch, *The Israelite Monarchy*, 94–108; McCarter, *I Samuel*, 269–70; Hertzberg, *Samuel*, 123 ff; Stoebe, *Das erste Buch Samuelis*, 178 ff; A. Weiser, "Samuel 15," *ZAW* 54 (1936), 1–28; Cross, *CMHE*, 220, n. 4.

[136] Keel, *Siegeszeichen*, 80, n. 1 (*ANEPS*, no. 817). *MH* II pls 85, 101–102, 105, 120–22.

[137] Hertzberg, *Samuel*, 126.

even though his son Ishbaal succeeded to his throne (II Sam 2:10). Although the kingdom of Saul advanced in military power and activity more than that of Abimelek, both as abortive kingdoms have striking similarities. Saul (I Sam 13:1; 15:1,17,35) and Abimelek (Judg 9:6) became kings over Israel. Saul was appointed with the possession of the spirit of YHWH by Samuel while Abimelek was guaranteed by the assembly of Shechem. They ruled three years (Abimelek – Judg 9:22) or two (Saul – I Sam 13:1) over Israel.[138] They selected warriors as mercenaries or a standing army. In Judg 9:4 Abimelek hired mercenaries from the treasury of the sanctuary of Baalberith. In I Sam 14:52b, whenever Saul saw any young warriors he attached them to himself. So he chose three thousand men of Israel, two thousand were with him in Michmash and the hill country of Bethel, and a thousand were with Jonathan in Geba of Benjamin (I Sam 13:2). Abimelek killed 70 of his brothers for his political power, but the youngest brother, Jotham was saved and fled to Beer (Judg 9:16–21). Saul killed 85 priests for his political power, but Abiathar was saved and fled after David (I Sam 22:6–23). Abimelek and Saul put their soldiers into three companies (Judg 9:43; I Sam 11:11).[139] Both received an evil spirit (Judg 9:23; I Sam 16:14b). The last scene of the death of the two men is depicted in the same structure: Abimelek/Saul said to weapon-bearer, "draw your sword, and thrust me with it, lest these uncircumcised men (a woman for Abimelek) kill me." But his weapon-bearer would not pierce him (pierced Abimelek) and Abimelek/Saul died (Judg 9:54; I Sam 31:4).

These similarities above suggest that both kingdoms ended with a similar political destiny, even though both were different in size and area in their political exercise and function. We cannot see the exaltation of YHWH as a supreme God and the idea of YHWH's help in the political power of the kingdom of Saul. For the holy war traditions of I Sam 7–15 more closely reflect the period of the divided monarchy.[140] In fact, here one has to admit that the end of the period of the Judges and the time of Saul were an initial and preparatory stage of YHWH war which flowered in the time of the Davidic kingdom. Most recently Weinfeld, following Kaufmann, has asserted that the government of Gideon boasted certain features of monarchy[141] which could construct some elements of YHWH war.

---

[138] In Judg 9:22 the verb שר (hold sway over) instead of מלך (rule) suggests that the biblical author avoids calling Abimelek king or judge (Malamat, *Magnalia Dei*, 164; Boling, *Judges*, 175). Ackroyd (*I Samuel*, 101–4) and W. McKane (*I and II Samuel*), London 1963, 89), following S. R. Driver, see that the length of Saul's reign was a customary emendation, the 22 years in I Sam 13:1. According to a late tradition, it was 40 years (Acts 13:21; Josephus Ant VI, 14:9).

[139] In his first battle against Gaal Abimelek put his army into four companies (Judg 9:34).

[140] Birch, *The Israelite Monarchy*, 157, n. 4.

[141] M. Weinfeld, "Literary Creativity," *WHJP* V, 41.

Chapter VII
YHWH War of David

Throughout the whole history of Israel David's kindgom was not only the first, but also the greatest state to arise on the soil of Palestine, except the Hyksos.[1] First David defeated the Philistines, and they were reduced to their pentapolis and then the coastal area (II Sam 5:17–25). Next he turned his attention to Moab and Aramaean; both became vassals to Israel (II Sam 8:7–10). Next he attacked the Ammonites and Ammon became part of the Davidic territory (II Sam 12:26–31). After that, David conquered Edom (II Sam 8:13–14; II K 11:15–17). Thus David became king of Judah and Israel. Ammon and the Canaanite city-states were incorporated into Judah and Israel. In Aram, Edom and Moab he ruled through his provincial governors or vassal chiefs. He made a treaty with Tyre and Hamat. So David became an undisputed overlord as the most powerful political leader among his contemporary neighbouring states from Egypt to the Euphrates.

Because Palestine was free from external pressures during his time, David could establish his kingdom by successfully exploiting the unique international power vacuum prevailing in the ancient Near East. In Egypt and Mesopotamia there was at that time no great power which might have encroached on Palestine and Syria and enforced a claim to rule over it. The Egypt of Dyn 21 was weak, disunited and restricted by the theocratic rule of the priests of Thebes.[2] It has also been suggested that the marriage of Solomon with a daughter of pharaoh is to be seen as the inferior Egyptian status in a political power vis-à-vis Israel at that time.[3] In Mesopotamia Babylon had long since lost its importance as a political power as a result of the foreign rule of the mountain people, the Kassites, which had now lasted for centuries. After the golden age of the Middle Assyrian empire, Assyria, the rising power of the time, declined again around the turn of the millennium. In Asia Minor there had been no power of any significance since the fall of the mighty empire of the

---

[1] Noth (*HI*, 197, n. 3) sees that the Hyksos kingdom had at one time formed a great Palestine-Syrian state before they conquered Egypt.

[2] *Ibid.*

[3] A. Malamat, "Aspects of the Foreign Polices of David and Solomon," *JNES* 22 (1963), 10 ff.

Hittites.[4] There environmental factors beyond the control of David might have been considered as divine support making his kingdom to rise. The achievement of David in his battles began to give a legitimation of divine mission. Thus his kingdom had proved that he could defeat his neighbouring enemies with the help of YHWH and could make his kingdom strong under the protection and guidance of YHWH. In this consideration one must examine the whole aspect of YHWH war which was begun in the time of David: 1) The Concept of YHWH War, 2) YHWH the Divine Warrior, 3) YHWH's Intervention in Battle, 4) The Ark in Battle, 5) The Salvation of David, and 6) War Conduct.

1. THE CONCEPT OF YHWH WAR

In the descriptions of the Davidic wars the concept of war is understood as matters under the jurisdiction of the lawsuit of YHWH. This idea is found in Saul's battle against David. After David had cut off the skirt of Saul's robe in the cave of Engedi and left the cave, David said to Saul (I Sam 24:13—16):

ישפט יהוה ביני ובינך[5] ... והיה יהוה לדין ושפט ביני ובינך
וירא וירב את־ריבי וישפטני מידך.

Here David appealed to YHWH the judge and cast his case before YHWH with the confidence that YHWH could deliver him from the hand of Saul, because the victory depended only upon the decision of YHWH. The appeal of David to YHWH parallels that of Ḫattušiliš III to Ishtar, of Tukulti-Ninurta I to Šamaš, the lord of judgment. As we have seen previously, the motif of appeal to the divine warrior in the ordeal of war is a common idea in the Mesopotamian war descriptions in the second millennium BC as well as in the Bible. In this sense, war is an ultimate remedy for wrong, for war is a divine judgment for the violator of a treaty.[6] But as far as we know, the concept of war as a lawsuit in the Egyptian context appears only in the mythological description of Horus and Seth.

So the victory results from the judgment of YHWH. This result appears in the reports of the battle against Absalom's revolt by the messengers of Joab (II Sam 18:19b,31bβ).

שפטו יהוה מיד איביו. שפטך יהוה היום מיד כל הקמים עליך.

---

[4] Noth, *HI*, 197.

[5] Cf., Gen 16:5 (Abraham and Sarah); 31:53 (Laban and Jacob).

[6] Glock, *CTM* 41, 598.

The above wars of David were domestic, and so it is supposed that the judgment of YHWH as a lawsuit was an apologetic or legitimacy for David. But it is interesting that in the case of the Ammonite war (II Sam 10:12b = I Ch 19:13b) the word שפט or דין does not occur. Yet Joab had encouraged Abishai, his brother: "Be of good courage, and let us be strong for our people and for our God,[7] and may YHWH do that which seems good in his eyes." Here in the war of David against the foreign enemy, YHWH does not appear as a judge, but it is implied that the war was within the matters of YHWH's decision. It depended upon the free decision of YHWH. For whether it was good or not is judged from the side of YHWH. Yet in the war story of Jephthah and the Ammonites (Judg 11:27), YHWH is depicted as a judge. In Psalms the judgeship of YHWH is clearly depicted (7:9; 9:9; 75:8; 94:2; 96:10,13).

The concept of war as a lawsuit is depicted by another legal term: ריב. This term is found in the action of Absalom instead of king David (II Sam 15:2,4). In the war story of Jephthah against the Ammonite king the term occurs (Judg 11:25b ff). Jephthah says to the messenger of the Ammonite king: "Did he (Moab) ever make a complaint against Israel?" Jephthah goes on to claim: "I have not therefore committed any wrong against you but you do an evil deed in making war on me. YHWH the judge will judge this day between the Israelites and Ammonites." In the words of David to Saul (I Sam 24:15) and to Abigail (*id.*, 25:39), the term ריב appears as a legal procedure in which YHWH as the judge controls the destiny of the enemies of David. Yet the difference between the above two examples of Jephthah and David is that in the case of Jephthah the object of YHWH's salvation is the Israelites including Jephthah — the people; whereas, in the case of David it was David, the individual person who was saved by YHWH. In our contexts no conditions such as the breaking of a treaty by the decision of YHWH, are given. The judgment of YHWH depends only on his decision. In this consideration one presupposes the special bond between David and YHWH: The covenant of grant.[8] In his last words, David says: "He (YHWH) made me an everlasting covenant, ... for all my salvation is in Him, and He causes to prosper all my desire (II Sam 23:5)." Moreover, the relationship of David and YHWH is described as a son and his father (II Sam 7:14).[9] David is called the son of YHWH (Ps 2:7), and YHWH is his father (Ps

---

[7] BH proposes ארון instead of עדי, because of dittography.

[8] M. Weinfeld, "The Covenant of Grant in the Old Testament and in the Ancient Near East," *JAOS* 90 (1970), 184—203. The covenant of grant contrasts to that of treaty as obligation (184 ff). In this light Judg 5:23, which reflects the tribal obligation to come to the aid of YHWH, can be understood as the curse of one who breaks the right of a vassal.

[9] G. Cooke, "The Israelite King as Son of God," *ZAW* 73 (1961), 202—25.

89:27–28). On the basis of the covenantal structure, the enemy of Israel was also the enemy of YHWH; in addition, the war of Israel was the war of YHWH (I Sam 17:47; 18:17, 25:28). David was the vassal of YHWH, and YHWH was the suzerain of David.[10] In this connection warfare is an extension of YHWH's supreme rule through Israel by means of the covenant of grant.

Comparing the OT and the ancient Near East materials regarding ריב, J. Harvey and J. Limburg have suggested that the term ריב was used in connection with international legal activity.[11] Especially, the phrase "וירב את ריב" in I Sam 24:15 as a case of law parallels the Hittite *ḫanneššar hannanzi* as the court procedure of a law case.[12] In the song of David (Ps 35:23–26) the concept of war is depicted as a lawsuit. The idea of ריב as lawsuit is not late, and it is in contrast to the usage of the prophetic lawsuit speeches. In the prophetic speeches YHWH is the prosecutor as well as the judge against his people.[13] The ריב is always YHWH's ריב, because of the sin of the Israelites.[14] It is seen that the lawsuit *Gattung* of the prophets is an adaptation of the declaration of war by a suzerain against a disloyal vassal.[15] Later in this period war was interpreted as the command of YHWH, carrying out the divine will and plan, like the Egyptian concept of war. Especially, this idea of war as YHWH's command was emphasized by the Deuteronomists. Therefore, one may say that the concept of war as a lawsuit in the Davidic period was close to that of the Mesopotamian war, but the cumulative idea of war developed in the late period was much nearer to that of the Egyptian war as the positive divine command.

---

[10] R. de Vaux, *The Bible and the Ancient Near East*, ET by D. McHugh (London 1972), 152–66. The suzerainship of YHWH to David appears in Pss 3:4; 59:12; 74;10; 115:9–10; 114:2 (Dahood, *Psalms* II, AB 17, 283).

[11] J. Harvey, "Le RIB-Pattern, réquisitoire prophétique sur la rupture de l'alliance," *Bibl* 43 (1962), 172–96; J. Limburg, "The Root ריב and the Prophetic Lawsuit Speeches," *JBL* 88 (1969), 291–304.

[12] Wolf, *the Apology of Ḫattušiliš*, 141.

[13] K. Nielsen, *Yahweh as Prosecutor and Judge* (Sheffield 1980), 74–83; G. E. Wright, "The Lawsuit of God, a Form Critical Study of Deuteronomy 32," *Israel Prophetic Heritage*: Essays in Honor of J. Muilenberg, ed. by B. W. Anderson and W. Harrelson (NY 1962), 26–67; Cross, *CMHE*, 188–90.

[14] Limburg, *op. cit.*, 301. Is 3:13–15; Mic 7:9; Hos 4:1–3,4–6; Jer 50:34; 51:36; Dt 32:7–14 and passim (see *A New Concordance of the Bible* III, ed. by A. Even-Shoshan, Jerusalem 1980, 1073–74, – *NCB*).

[15] Glock, *CTM* 41, 597.

2. YHWH AS A DIVINE WARRIOR

1

The word גבור is a warrior title for YHWH. Only later El is called "אל גבור" (Is 9:5; 10:21), yet it is not related to the war contexts, rather it is just a part of the name. The title occurs three times more with El as an adjective: האל הגדול הגבור (Dt 10:17; Jer 32:18; Neh 9:32). YHWH is called not only the judge but also the warrior. In Ps 24:8 which belongs to the time of David,[16] YHWH is praised as follows:

מי זה מלך הכבוד
יהוה עזוז וגבור
יהוה גבור מלחמה

In this liturgy fragment it is clear that YHWH as the king of glory was recognized as the divine warrior. Actually the term, גבור/גבור חיל was an honourable title for a hero or victor which is found mainly from the time of Judges to that of David.[17] In fact, it was a warrior title which was given to David (I Sam 16:18; II Sam 17:8) and his heroes (II Sam 10:7; 17:10; 20:7; 23:8,9,16,22), even though Gideon (Judg 6:12), Jephthah (Judg 11:1) and Joshua's warriors also have this title.[18] It is an implication that YHWH, the tutelary God of David, was understood as the divine warrior of David.

In connection with גבור, the עזר which is found in Ps 118:7 which probably belongs to the time of David, is given to YHWH as a warrior title: "YHWH is, for me, my great warrior."[19] This term is cognate with Ugarit, *ilǵẓr* (El is the warrior), but mainly appears in the late biblical sources.[20] In this passage the warrior epithet parallels the epithet king.

---

[16] Smend, *Yahweh War*, 83; Cross, *CMHE*, 91 (A tenth century BC); A. Weiser, *The Psalms*: A Commentary, OTL, ET by H. Hartwell (London 1965), 236 (the time of Solomon); H. J. Kraus, *Psalmen* I, BK 15 (Neukirchen—Vluyn 1960), 193—206. P.-R. Berger ("Zu Ps 24, 7 and 9," *UF* 2, 1970, 335—36) points out the early Mesopotamian parallels of vv. 7 and 9 (*ARMT* X 9, 12, Amarna no. 264, 18). Yet it is not necessary to see it as the Hashimonian date as M. Treves does ("The Date of Psalm 24," *VT* 10, 1960, 434).

[17] H. Fredricksson, *Jahwe als Krieger*: Studien zum alttestamentlichen Gottesbild (Lund 1945), 59—60. In the pre-exilic prophetic literature this term indicates the elites of the army of Israel who were powerless in contrast to YHWH God, while in the post-exilic sources it is used to indicate the foreign soldiers (60).

[18] Josh 1:14; 8:3; 10:7.

[19] Dahood, *Psalms* III, AB 17A (NY 1970, 1981), 154, 157. V. 10 (All nations surrounded me, but in YHWH's name I cut off their foreskins) is an indicator reflecting the time of David.

[20] *Id.*, *Psalms* I, AB 16 (NY 1968, 1979), 210; F. M. Cross, "YHWH and the God of Patriarchs," *HTR* 55 (1962), 240; P. D. Miller, "El the Warrior," *HTR* 60 (1967), 412 ff. Ezek 12:14; Job 6:13; I Ch 12:1.

Like the function of an earthly king who goes out before the people and fights their battles (I Sam 8:20), the warlike function of YHWH as king can be understood in the same way in that YHWH goes out before the soldiers and fights for them. In Part One it was mentioned that one of the epithets of divine warriors in the ancient Near East was "king," as Marduk in Babylonia and Aššur in Assyria have the epithet *šar/šar ilāni* or as Amun in Egypt had the title *nswt nṯrw*. In the Egyptian Middle kingdom the designation of god as king was already an epithet to the supreme god. YHWH the warrior became the suzerain of the earth; likewise, David the warrior became suzerain of the earth in his days. In a fragment of the exaltation hymn to YHWH (Ps 47:3–4) he is depicted as king and Elyon who subdued the enemies.[21]

For YHWH is awesome Elyon,
The great king over all the earth.
He subjugated peoples beneath us,
nations underneath our feet.

This cultic celebration of YHWH's imperial accession is based on the relatively recent victories of David's age which raised Israel from provincial obscurity to an empire of the first rank. Consequently the foreign princes present at the ceremony would be the princes of the subject nations who had come to Jerusalem to pay homage to the Israelite king and his divine suzerain. In the days of the Davidic-Solomonic empire it was a periodic reality, not just idle talk or a vague hope for the future. Tribute had to be paid, presumable yearly (II Sam 8:2,6,10–12); new accessions in the subject countries probably had to be approved in Jerusalem; a new accession in Jerusalem probably required a trip by the subject rulers to pledge their allegiance to the new Davidic king.[22] So the recognition of YHWH as king is not, as Rosenberg asserts,[23] from the time of second Isaiah.

2

The second epithet of YHWH as the divine warrior is **צבאות**. In Ps 24:10 the epithet of YHWH as warrior-king occurs:

מי הוא זה מלך הכבוד
יהוה צבאות
הוא מלך הכבוד

---

[21] J. J. M. Roberts, "The Religio-Political Setting of Psalm 47," *BASOR* 221 (1976), 132; I. L. Seeligmann, "Psalm 47," *Tarbiz* 50 (1980–81), 28 ff.

[22] Roberts, *ibid.*

[23] R. A. Rosenberg, "Yahweh becomes King," *JBL* 85 (1966), 297–307.

This special term has been translated into various forms:[24] "YHWH the mighty one", "YHWH hosts of the celestial army", "YHWH militant", "YHWH, (God) of armies (Israel's)", "YHWH Ẓebaoth", "He who brings armies into existence", "He who sustains armies", "He who overthrows armies (of Israel's enemy)", or "Creator of the heavenly armies".

Most recently J. A. Emerton points out that YHWH Ẓebaoth (YẒ) can be read as YHWH of Ẓebaoth. For in the inscription of Kuntillet ʿAjrud "YHWH šmrn and YHWH tmn" can be interpreted as YHWH of Samaria and YHWH of Teman.[25] Yet Ẓebaoth is not the name of a place like Samaria and Teman. It is an explanation of a function of YHWH such as armies. It seems to be meant as an appellative in apposition to YHWH as a nominal sentence rather than a verbal sentence, "He brings armies into existence", or the construct state, "YHWH of hosts".[26]

The epithet YẒ is the name of the God of the armies of Israel, the all-powerful god.[27] For it has some military sense like the Akkadian ṣâbu or Ugaritic ṣbu. It is supported by the fact that in I Sam 17:45 YẒ is in apposition to the God of the battle of Israel (אלהי מערכות ישראל). When David became the king over all Israel in Jerusalem, YHWH, using the long form, who was with David, was the God of armies (II Sam 5:10).[28]

First of all, the epithet, as J. P. Ross and others point out,[29] originally does not indicate the heavenly powers, because of: a) its late and Dtr usage, b) its singular form, c) the prophetic objection to the worship of the heavenly hosts, and d) its mythological contexts. The designation does not appear until the time of the Judges.[30] This situation perhaps reflects the lack of YHWH warriorship in the historical context up to that time.

---

[24] W. R. Arnold, *Ephod and Ark*, HTR 3 (Cambridge/London 1917), 147–48; O. Eissfeldt, "Jahwe Zebaoth," *KS* 3, ed. by R. Sellheim and F. Maass (1950, Tübingen 1966), 103 ff; J. P. Ross, "Jahweh ṢᵉḆĀʼÔṮ in Samuel and Psalm," *VT* 17 (1967), 76 ff.

[25] "New Light on Israelite Religion: The Implications of the Inscriptions from Kuntillet ʿAjrud," *ZAW* 94 (1982), 2–20.

[26] Albright and his students see YẒ as a verbal sentence (A Review Article: *L'épithéte divine Jahvé Ṣᵉbaʼôt*: Étude philologique, historique et exégétique, by B. N. Wambacq, O. Praem. Bruges 1947, *JBL* 67, 1948, 377–81; D. N. Freedman, "The Name of the God of Moses," *JBL* 79, 1960, 152 ff; Cross, *HTR* 55, 252; *id.*, "The Divine Warrior in Israel's Early Cult," *Biblical Motifs*: Origins and Transformations, ed. by A. Altmann, Cambridge, Mass. 1966, 28; Miller, *Divine Warrior*, 151–55). Yet its understanding as construct state is the general tendency, while Arnold (*Ephod and Ark*, 142) sees Ẓᵉbaʼôt as indeterminate and adjectival genetive.

[27] E. Kautzsch, "Die ursprüngliche Bedeutung des Namens jhwh ṣᵉbaʼôt," *ZAW* 6 (1886), 20; Wambacq, *L'épithéte divine Jahvé Ṣᵉbaʼôt*, 4–16.

[28] This expression occurs mainly in the late prophetic sources: I K 19:10,14; Jer 5:14; 15:16; 35:17; 38:17; 44:7; Hos 12:6; Am 3:13; 4:13; 5:14,15,16,27; 6:8,14; Ps 89:9.

[29] *BDB*, 839; *VT* 17, 77.

[30] Josh 6:17 only in the LXX.

After that time, it is seen that the epithet Ẓebaoth was a military designation of YHWH as a god of war.[31]

Among 285 occurrences in the Hebrew Bible, only 6 times are these related with David. Some scholars still have doubts about its clear connection with David and his time, becuase the epithet as a two-word name predominantly appears in the prophetic literature (251 times). Ross sees the epithet YẒ in I Sam 17:45 as a later addition.[32] S. R. Driver and others believe that the epithet YẒ is not earlier than the three word epithet, YHWH, the divine warrior (יהוה אלהי צבאות = YEẒ).[33] According to Driver, the earliest form is YEẒ with an article (יהוה אלהי הצבאות) which occurs in Am 3:13, 6:14; 9:5.[34] But in the story of David against Goliath the warlike image of YHWH without YẒ has not changed. Without YẒ YHWH is called "the God of the battle of Israel" in v. 45b which may well have read originally: "I came to you in the name of the God of the battle of Israel, whom you defied."[35]

Moreover, in the story of David and Goliath there are some contradictions such as Elhanan's victory over Goliath (II Sam 21:19)[36] or David's appearance before Saul (I Sam 16:14–23; 17:12–31,55–18:5). Yet the purpose of this story was the legitimatization of David as a warrior who described his superiority to Saul. This motive was possibly contemporary with the program of legitimatization of the Davidic kingdom by the royal scribes. The structure of the fighting between two warriors was dual combat which was a popular fighting style used to save soldiers and weapons in Israel and the ancient Near East.[37] The theological description which victory attributes to the name of YHWH without weapons seems to be a very ancient idea which has roots in Ps 20:8 where the answer is announced by a priest to the prayer of the congregation for the king setting out for battle.[38] This idea was very popular in the war descriptions of the ancient Near East in the second millennium BC.[39] M. H. Segal has suggested that I Sam 17:42–47 was originally a historical report of the

---

[31] M. Tsevat, "Studies in the Book of Samuel, YAHWEH ṢEḆA'OṮ," *HUCA* 36 (1965), 57–58; W. Eichrodt, *Theology of the Old Testament*, ET by J. A. Baker (London 1969), 192–94.

[32] *VT* 17, 83, n. 2.

[33] *BDB*, 839; von Rad, *Old Testament Theology* I, 18.

[34] *Ibid.*

[35] Ross, *VT* 17, 81, n. 2.

[36] L. Martin, "'Elhanan – der frühere Name Davids," *ZAW* 68 (1956), 257–59; Stoebe, *Das erste Buch Samuelis*, 315.

[37] J. J. Glück, "Reviling and Monomachy as Battle-Preludes in Ancient Warfare," *Acta Classica* 7 (1964), 25–31.

[38] Weiser (*The Psalms*, 206) sees it as the time of David against Duhm (Hashimonian), while Kraus dates it before the 7th century BC in Jerusalem (*Psalmen* I, 165 ff).

[39] Abramsky, *Kingdom of Saul and Kingdom of David*, 130–31.

conversation between two warriors before battle such as that of the Homeric heroes.[40] In particular, cultic elements such as the *kidon* of Goliath (v. 45) and the term קהל (v. 47) show that this story was remembered by the assembly through the celebration of David's victory that all the assembly may know that YHWH saves not with sword and spear, for the war was a YHWH war. Thus it is considered that the theological implication of YHWH's victory without weapons was contemporary with David. If so, there is no ground to see YẒ as a late addition.

Secondly, the epithet YẒ is clearly seen in relation with the ark. This was the epithet of YHWH given to the ark, the palladium of YHWH war. In the story of the returning of the ark from Baalah-Judah to Jerusalem YẒ who sits enthroned on the cherubim occurs. The connection of YẒ and the ark, before this event, appears on the ark of the covenant in Shiloh (I Sam 4:4) as the title of YHWH. Here the ark and the name had military associations and first occur together. Some scholars consider that YẒ originally was the cultic name of God in the Shiloh sanctuary.[41] Both events above show the connection of the epithet YẒ with the ark from Shiloh to Jerusalem. As it was under David's patronage that the ark was made the focus of the national cult in new national capital, it is not surprising to find him a special protégé of the God of the ark.[42] The removal of the ark to Jerusalem was not only an act reflecting the political and military achievement of David's new empire, but was also an appropriation of the ancient cultic symbol of YHWH's presence. Contrary to the idea of a historification of myth or of a cultic legend of the return of the ark to Jerusalem, it is the historical and cultic actions that are perfectly understandable within the context of the momentous historical event in question.[43] One of David's intentions in transporting the ark to Jerusalem was to establish himself as king of Israel, like the kings of the other nations: A king with a capital and national cult under royal patronage. In this connection YẒ was a most appropriate title for the God who was to establish a new dynasty. It is natural that Nathan pronounced the divine promises to the house of David under the name of YẒ (II Sam 7:8,26,27).

Thirdly, in the early Psalms which belong to the Davidic or post-Davidic period (24; 59),[44] the warrior epithet of YHWH YẒ and YEẒ

---

40 "The Composition of the Books of Samuel," *JQR* 55 (1965), 329; *id.*, *The Books of Samuel*, 145–46; Hertzberg, *Samuel*, 152; Stoebe (*Das erste Buch Samuelis*, 339) sees it primarily as a kerygmatic report. Von Rad (*Krieg*, 42 ff) recognizes it as Novelistik in the post-Solomonic period.

41 Eissfeldt, *KS* 3, 113 ff; Ross, *VT* 17, 79; Kraus, *Psalmen* I, 99, 324.

42 Ross, *VT* 17, 82.

43 Mann, *Divine Presence*, 217.

44 Dahood, *Psalms* II, 67, 311.

are found.[45] In Ps 24:7–10, as mentioned above, Ẓebaoth clearly parallels another warrior title of YHWH – גבור or גבור מלחמה. In this context Ẓebaoth certainly reflects the same meaning of the warrior designation above. In Ps 59:6 YHWH, the divine warrior, God of Israel is portrayed as the God who punishes all the nations and does not show mercy to wicked traitors. In vv. 10–11 "my God is a fortress, truly am I protected; God himself is my bulwark, a rampart is my God. God will go before me, will let me gloat over my defamers." In Ps 48 YẒ has a special association with YHWH's kingship in the Jerusalem cult. So this epithet was a sign of YHWH as the war God of Israel.[46]

Some scholars have argued that the title YẒ reflects the influence from the name of the god of the Canaanite shrine, that is, Baal Ẓebaoth rather than El Ẓebaoth.[47] The epithet of YHWH רכב בערבות is Ps 68:5 must have been affected by the epithet *rkb ʿrpt* of Baal. Yet the warlike image of Baal appears mainly in the Ugaritic mythical descriptions. In the Pentateuch YẒ is absent, Elyon often appears. In the prophets YẒ is frequent, and Elyon scarcely to be found.[48] The term *ršp ṣbi* (UT 2004:15 = PRU V 4:15), Reshep of host, implies that it was an epithet of the Canaanite divine warrior Reshep. The term *abi ṣābi* or *rabi ṣābi* was a special term to indicate an official in charge of a team or a troop.[49] In this light one can suppose that YẒ as a proper name[50] was a special epithet given to YHWH the divine warrior in the Davidic period.

3

The third epithet of YHWH as the divine warrior is איש מלחמה which appears in the early composition poetry (Ex 15:3).[51] The title, אנשי מלחמה does not apply to god, only man,[52] but איש מלחמה can be

---

[45] In Psalms YẒ occurs 9 times (24:10; 46:8,12; 48:9; 69:7; 84:2,4,13; 90:17), YEẒ one time (89:9). The third compound (Ps 59:6; 80:5,8,15,20; 84:9) adds an enclitic -m to אלהי (Tsevat, *HUCA* 36, 50, n. 11; Dahood, *Psalms* II, 68–69). Here the ratio of YẒ/YEẒ is similar to that of 10:1 of YẒ/YEẒ in Samuel. It is considered that the chronology of YẒ to YEẒ is more reasonable (Tsevat, *ibid.*, 51) than the reverse (von Rad, *Old Testament Theology* I, 18). For God of hosts is an additional interpretation such as God of fathers, God of Jacob, or God of Israel to YHWH. Moreover, YẒ in th cultic context of the late period was the name of YHWH confessed as creator-judge (J. L. Crenshaw, "YHWH Ṣᵉbaʾôt Šᵉᵉmô: A Form-Critical Analysis," *ZAW* 81, 1969, 156–75).

[46] Wambacq, *op. cit.*, 175.

[47] R. E. Clements (*God and Temple*, 34, n. 4) following Eissfeldt and de Vaux, suggests El Ṣᵉbaʾôt, but Ross strongly rejects this idea (*VT* 17, 90, n. 1).

[48] *Ibid.*

[49] *CAD* Ṣ, 46 ff.

[50] J. Obermann, "YHWH in Recent Discoveries," *JBL* 68 (1949), 304–6.

[51] Robertson, *Linguistic Evidence*, 153 ff.

applied to man and god.[53] Among the four early occurrences of איש מלחמה, twice it is given to David (I Sam 16:18; II Sam 17:8), once to Goliath (I Sam 17:38) and once to Machir (Josh 17:1). Yet the three late occurrences do not apply to an individual person.[54] Wolf has suggested that this warrior title of David was given to him after his victory over Goliath and his military promotion is paralleled to Ḫattušiliš's appointment as a general, *EN KARAŠ*.[55] Thus it can be considered that this epithet of YHWH was also given to Him after David's warriorship.

The above three warlike epithets of YHWH, גבור/גבור מלחמה, צבאות and איש מלחמה, unmistakably suggest that YHWH was recognized as the divine warrior of the Davidic kingdom. This warlike idea is identified with the descriptions of his thanksgiving song to YHWH when David was saved from the grasp of all his enemies by YHWH (Ps 18 = II Sam 22). David said as follows (vv. 14–15,18–19,35–36):

> YHWH thundered from the heavens,
> and the Most High gave forth his voice.
> He forged his arrows and scattered them,
> he multiplied his shafts and dispersed them.
>
> He rescued me from my powerful foes,
> and from my enemy though stronger than I.
> He went before me on the day of my disaster,
> and YHWH became my staff.
>
> He trained my hands for battle,
> lowered the miraculous bow into my arms.
> And you gave me your shield of victory,
> with your right hand you sustained me,
> and by our triumph you made me great.

This idea of YHWH's warriorship is strengthened by the fact that YHWH the divine warrior parallels the divine warriors who appeared in the rising time of each empire of the ancient Near East. In the Mesopotamian context, as we have discussed in Part One, Inanna/Ishtar became the war goddess under the Sargonic empire of Akkad, Marduk the war god under the first Babylonian Dynasty, and Aššur the divine warrior under the Neo-Assyrian empire. In the same way, Teshub was recognized as the divine warrior in the Hittite New kingdom. Amun-Re became a powerful divine warrior under the Egyptian New kingdom. In the light of the examples above it is not surprising to find YHWH as the divine

[52] Num 31:49 (Moses' soldiers); Josh 5:4,6; 6:3; 10:24 (Joshua' soldiers); Joel 2:7; 4:9 (the soldiers of Judah); I Ch 12:38 (the men of Reuben, God, and Manasseh); II Ch 8:9 (the Israelites).

[53] See *NCB* II, 662.

[54] Judg 20:17 (soldiers); Is 3:2 (warriors); Ezek 39:20 (warriors).

[55] *The Apology of Ḫattušiliš*, 136.

warrior under the Davidic empire. Most scholars believe that the image of YHWH as the divine warrior was influenced by that of Baal in the Canaanite pantheon. Yet Baal the war god (the Akkadian Adad) in the sources as far as we know is a mythical divine warrior. YHWH originally was the divine warrior in the historical battles of David, but the mythical divine warrior of YHWH mainly appears in the exilic and post exilic period. In Is 42:13 we find the continuation of YHWH's warriorship:[56] YHWH shall go forth as a גבור, he shall stir up ardour like איש מלחמה; he shall cry, indeed roar, he shall show himself mighty against his foes. In Joel 4:9–19 YHWH is depicted as the warrior: "Proclaim this among the nations; prepare war, stir up the mighty men, let all the men of war draw near, let them come up. Beat your ploughshares into swords, and your pruning hooks into spears; let the weak say, 'I am a warrior'." In Zeph 3:17 YHWH is also described as follows: "The Lord, your God, is in your midst, a warrior who gives victory;" ... Here the image of YHWH as a warrior is the same but the reality of the context is quite different: history and myth. In Ps 46:7–12 YHWH is well portrayed as the cosmic and mythic divine warrior and savior of the peoples in troubled times. In Ps 89 (vv. 6–19) the warlike image of YHWH, who crushed the mythical monster Rahab as a corpse, reflects the late eschatological and apocalyptic aspects which tried to give hope in faith without historical reality. From the 8th century the prophetic interpretation of the judgment idea of YHWH who fights against his peoples in battle was the other aspect of the warlike image of YHWH in battle: negative intervention of YHWH.

Therefore the above evidence shows that the warrior image of YHWH was primarily a conventional idea in the time of the Davidic kingdom like that found in the other empires of the ancient Near East, even though it had been partly influenced by them. In fact, it is seen that the people had first experienced the function of YHWH as the divine warrior in history, that is, the Lord of history, and then as the Lord of nature who controls heaven and earth, and finally as the cosmic and mythical Lord beyond history in the post exilic period.[57]

3. YHWH'S INTERVENTION IN BATTLE

It is natural that YHWH as the divine warrior participated in battle to help his servant David and his men. For the first time, one finds the motif of YHWH's intervention in two very significant battle events, just

---

[56] Stolz, *Kriege*, 48.

[57] J. P. Hyatt ("Was Yahweh Originally a Creator Deity?" *JBL* 86, 1967, 337) believes that the warlike aspect of YHWH was added to the creator aspect of YHWH in the late period.

after David became the king of Israel and Judah. The first battle of the two is the battle of David over the Philistines in the valley of Rephaim (II Sam 5:17–21; 23:13–17). In the military strategy this event was important and was the initial stage in conquering Jerusalem, the capital of the whole of Israel, and in connecting the south and the central part. In this consideration this event was a divine triumph which was accomplished by YHWH's intervention on the battlefield. In v. 20 David came to Baal-perazim and defeated the Philistines there on the conviction of YHWH's oracle; "go up, for I will certainly give the Philistines into your hand." In addition, David confessed that "YHWH has broken through my enemies before me, like a bursting flood" (v. 20aβ). So this battle place was called Baal-perazim, that is, "Lord of breaking through." Here the name as Lord of the break must certainly first have arisen as a result of the event described; according to this, David must have "broken through the enemy lines." It is significant that the concept of YHWH as the Lord of breaker (פרץ) is related to that of the three mighty warriors of David who brought the water for him to drink from the enemy camp in Bethlehem which they had broken through (בקע). When the three warriors brought the water to David, YHWH brought the victory to David by breaking through the enemy lines.

Moreover, here we find the visible participation of the god of the enemy. In v. 21, there were the divine emblems (עצבים) as the visible symbols of the enemy god which the Philistines abandoned. In the LXX the emblems were replaced with gods. These objects clearly show that the Philistines used to bring their divine emblems on the battlefield as one of the objects of divine warfare. Here David and his men carried them away, while in I Ch 14:2 David had the gods burnt. In I Sam 31:9 there was a house for this emblem — like a temple. After Saul was killed on Mt. Gilboa by the Philistines, his head and weapons were sent around the land of the Philistines to display them in the house of the divine statue and among the people. This fact reflects the idea that the Philistines had conducted the divine war by the carrying of the divine emblems as the visible sign of the divine warrior on the battlefield. But in this battle the ark as the visible symbol of YHWH did not appear, because the ark still had not reached the hand of David.

The idea of YHWH's intervention is expressed by the vanguard motif. In the second battle (II Sam 5:22–25) YHWH also appears to be a vanguard to lead David and his army in the front line of the battlefield. YHWH said to David in the third person singular: "then YHWH has gone out before you to smite the army of the Philistines." In fact, David did as YHWH commanded him and smote the Philistines from Gob to Gezer.[58] This battle was also a decisive event for connecting the power

---

[58] Segal (*The Books of Samuel*, 265) prefers to read Gob, instead of Gibea.

of David in a northernly direction to the territory of the Philistines as far as the Mediterranean Sea. Hertzberg sees that David attacked the Philistines from Jerusalem.[59] This time David is to plan not a breakthrough, but a flanking movement. The steps of YHWH, the sign for the attack, will be seen in distinct, waving movements on the top of the trees, the whole idea corresponding with that of tree oracles.[60]

The motif of a vanguard in v. 25 is a particularly popular idea, as discussed in Part One. If we compare it with the ancient Near East formulas, it is easily understood that it is a conventional formula for the description of divine war:

Israel	(דוד) יצא יהוה לפנך
Hittite	God piran huwaiš king
Egypt	God r-ḥ3t king
Mesopotamia	God alāk ina maḫri/pani king

Ḫattušiliš III claimed that Ishtar of Samuḫa, his patron divine warrior marched before him in the battle (II:24,38; IV:10). Amun-Re, the divine warrior, proclaimed to Thutmose III in the battle of Megiddo: "Behold, I am in front of you, my son" (*RI* V 10:1). In many places the Mesopotamian divine warriors go before their kings. Even in the Greek context this form appears: God προμάχοί king (Iliad 4.505).[61] In all the cases the subject is "divine warrior," whereas the object of the preposition is "king." The idea that a deity goes out before the king in battle is of similar logic to the idea that a king goes out at the head of his soldiers as in I Sam 8:20. The life-setting of the vanguard motif is considered as the royal context. At this point our text differs from two other occurrences (Judg 4:14; Ps 68:8). In Judg 4:14 the subject is YHWH but the object of the preposition is the general, Barak, whereas in Ps 68:8 the subject is God, but the object is the Exodus people, not the king. So it is seen that these two examples are the formulas transformed from the original setting of the descriptions of the Davidic battle. The differnet usage is also shown by the idiomatic phrases. The phrase ... יי יצא לפני has more military connotation and comes very close to the idea of march/go out to the battle, while the phrase ... יי הלך לפני which parallels the vanguard formula of Mesopotamia is used when describing the guidance of the Israelites from Egypt to Canaan (Ex 13:21; 14:19; Num 14:14; Dt 1:30; 31:8, cf., I Sam 12:2).[62] Therefore, it seems that because the vanguard motif of a divine warrior in battle is conventional, that of YHWH in II Sam 5:24bβ (I Ch 14:15) is the creation of the biblical writers in the time of the Davidic

---

59 *Samuel*, 275.
60 *Ibid.*, 274.
61 Wolf, *The Apology of Ḫattušiliš*, 224.
62 *Ibid.*, 129–30; *BDB*, 424.

kingdom. The above two battles were the offensive wars which were decided by the oracle of YHWH. "YHWH said to David, go up, for I will certainly give the Philistines into your hand" (v. 19b): or "you shall not go up (against them), go around to their rear, and come upon them opposite the balsam trees" (v. 23). Though these were offensive wars, there is no idea of Ḥerem.

The result of YHWH's intervention is directly to lead the enemy to disability. In the story of the conflict of Saul and David, David said, "YHWH will strike him (Saul) down" (I Sam 26:10a): יהוה יגפנו. It is difficult to determine whether the idea was contemporary with David or later, because of the late usage of the word נגף:[63] In I Sam 25:38 Nabal was already stricken by YHWH. This punishment is regarded as intervention sent directly from YHWH.[64] In the story of Saul and David another word for YHWH's intervention is "תרדמת" (I Sam 26:12).[65] It means "had fallen on the soldiers."[66] Budde compares תרדמת יהוה with חרדת אלהים in I Sam 14:15. The former is YHWH's action, the latter is not a divine action.[67]

Moreover, the motif of YHWH's intervention in battle was continually preserved in the divided monarchy. In the battle of Ahab, the king of Israel (869–850) and Ben-hadad, YHWH said to Ahab through the man of God, "I will give all this great multitude into your hand, and you shall know that I am YHWH" (I K 20:28). But the prophets began to interpret this motif in the opposite direction: YHWH's intervention was against Israel. Amos warned Israel: "Therefore thus says YHWH God, an adversary there shall be and shall surround the land, and he shall bring down your power from you, and your palaces shall be spoiled" (Am 3:11). So they historically experienced this disaster in the defeat of Samaria by Sargon II in 721 BC (II K 17:1–6). The day of YHWH's negative intervention was understood as the day of judgment, that is, the day of YHWH.[68] The real picture of the day of YHWH as judgment is found in the prophetic literature. Amos proclaims to his people (5:18):

---

[63] *BDB*, 172.

[64] Driver, *Samuel*, 206.

[65] The same word is used in unmilitary contexts as the direct intervention of God. Gen 2:21 (Adam); 15:12 (Abram); Judg 4:21 (Sisera).

[66] Stoebe, *Das erste Buch Samuelis*, 643, 647,

[67] Budde, *Samuel*, 170; Stoebe, *ibid.*, 647; Ackroyd, *I Samuel*, 203.

[68] See n. 241 of chapter V; A. J. Everson, "The Days of Yahweh," *JBL* 93 (1974), 329–37; J. Gray, "The Day of Yahweh in Cultic Experience and Eschatological Prospect," *Svensk Exegetisk Ärsbok* 39 (1974), 5–37. Both agree that the concept of the day of YHWH as the intervention of YHWH include both the idea of judgment and salvation in history, but the day of YHWH as hope predominantly appears in the exilic and post exilic cultic context.

> Woe to you who desire the day of the Lord!
> Why would you have the day of the Lord?
> It is darkness, and not light;

Later this idea of the divine judgment together with that of the salvation of YHWH became the tenets of the Deuteronomistic theology. Therefore we see that the motif of YHWH's intervention developed in two directions: salvation and judgment through the history of Israel's religion. The interpretation of defeat as the result of religious sin, as seen in Part One, is in common with the ancient Near Eastern context from the third millennium BC as in *the curse of Akkad*. However, the positive motif of YHWH's intervention in the time of the monarchy is contrasted with that of YHWH's negative intervention in the period of the exile — post exile in which YHWH smites the cosmic mythical enemies such as the dragon or Rahab (Is 51:9b—10):

> Was it not thou that didst cut Rahab in pieces,
> that didst pierce the dragon?
> Was it not thou that didst dry up the sea,
> the waters of the great deep;

Keeping in mind the invisible symbol of YHWH's intervention, the following section will review the visible symbol of YHWH's intervention and presence in the battles of David: the ark in battle.

4. THE ARK IN BATTLE

1

In connection with the motif of YHWH's intervention in battle, it is considered that the ark as a visible symbol of YHWH's intervention participated in the battles of David. Of course, the participation of the ark is not the absolute factor of YHWH war.[69] Yet the function of the ark[70] as the war palladium is to encourage the fighting spirit of soldiers in which their divine warrior fights against their enemy. In Part One we have dealt with the divine emblem (šu-nir) as the visible sign of divine participation on the battlefield, as well as in cultic processions. Like various forms of the divine symbol in the ancient Near East,[71] the ark is depicted in several different forms, even though we do not exactly know the form.[72] The combination of ark and cherubim (I Sam 4:4; II Sam 6:2) is an

[69] W. Caspari, "Was stand in Buche der Kriege Jahwes?" *ZWT* 54, NF 19 (1912), 145—46.

[70] Arnold (*Ephod and Ark*, 95 ff) defends the oracle function of the ark.

[71] Mann, *Divine Presence*, 265—68.

[72] M. Haran, "The Ark and the Cherubim," *IEJ* 9 (1959), 30—38, 89—94; H. Davies, "The Ark of Covenant," *ASTI* 5 (1966), 43 ff.

expression of reflection of the ark which was placed in the Solomonic temple. Until the premonarchic period the ark with the combined form did not appear in the battle context. But Stolz has argued that since the Davidic-Solomonic kingdom, the ark played the main role as a military sanctuary in the Jerusalem cult, as seen in Pss 24, 47, 68, 78, 132 and the song of the ark (Num 10:35–36).[73] Then do these materials reflect the historical reality of the participation of the ark in the battles of David?

Our discussion is inclined to assume that the use of the ark in battle was limited to the period of David. In the story of the Jericho battle (Josh 3–6) we see the participation of the ark which was carried by the priests into the battlefield of Jericho. Yet some scholars believe that the legend of the Jericho battle is a cultic document of the spring festival by Dtn/Dtr, on the basis of the content such as the Exodus tradition, the literary viewpoint or the terminologies like תרועה.[74] But here the ark appears only in appendixes.[75] In Judg 20:27 the ark is used for inquiring of the YHWH oracle before battle. But this corpus also belongs to a late production, on the basis of the literary style and the reality of the battle.[76] In the battle story of Ebenezer (I Sam 4:1–22), after the first defeat, the soldiers brought the ark from the Shiloh sanctuary on to the battlefield as a sign of the guarantee of the victory over the Philistines. Yet it seems that the transportation of the ark is a last resort and it was not normal practice at that period for the ark to accompany the armies of Israel.[77] It is generally agreed that this story as the initial stage of the whole ark narrative is not a historical but a theological narrative which indicates the defeat of Israel as the end of an era.[78]

However, this theological description was formed in response to those who asked the question: Why did YHWH defeat us today before the Philistines? This question reflects the historical situations before the time of David's rise to power: under the oppression of the Philistines. Miller and Roberts have pointed out that this narrative was formulated in the period of religious crisis between the disastrous defeat at Ebenezer

---

73 *Kriege*, 29 ff.

74 *Ibid.*, 60–62.

75 Smend, *Yahweh War*, 76.

76 Arnold (*Ephod and Ark*, 117 ff) argues that this passage belongs to the original and authentic narrative of the war against the Benjaminites.

77 W. McKane, "The Earlier History of the Ark," *Glasgow* 21 (1965–66), 70.

78 Smend, *Yahweh War*, 76; F. Schickleberger, *Die Ladeerzählungen des ersten Samuel-Buches*, FB 7 (Würzburg 1973), 175 ff; Miller, *Divine Warrior*, 145 ff; A. F. Campbell, *The Ark Narrative*: A Form Critical and Traditio-Historical Study, SBL 16 (Missoula, Mont. 1975), 152–53, 189–200; *id.*, "Yahweh and the Ark," *JBL* 98 (1979), 32.

and much later victorious David, in order to remove the theological problem that created the need for it.[79] This was the answer of YHWH's superiority over Dagon in history. In these descriptions one finds the idea that the ark as the visible symbol of YHWH's presence and power appears on the battlefield, while the hand of YHWH as the invisible manifestation of that same presence and power is compared with the ark. The ark and the hand of God are the principal thematic elements and vehicles for the divine agency.[80] In v. 8 the response of the Philistines is "the hand of the mighty god (יד אלהים אדרים)." Stolz has pointed out that this expression belongs to the Dtn/Dtr usage,[81] but Roberts attests that this expression is of conventional lexical stock in Israel and in the ancient Near East.[82] In their study of the ark narrative, Miller and Roberts again claim that the hand of YHWH is the invisible symbol of YHWH's power and presence.[83] They believe that this theological description was composed before David's victory removed the above theological problems.[84]

2

Some scholars hold that the ark participated in the battle of Saul on the basis of I Sam 14:18 (MT).[85] But the LXX reads: "Saul told Ahijah, bring the ephod here, for he wore the ephod on that day before Israel." Most scholars prefer the LXX reading. For the ephod was elsewhere the means of giving the oracle (I Sam 23:9; 30:7), whiel the ark was not used in consulting the oracle.[86] In addition, the ark returned from the Philistine territory, remained at Kiryat-jearim (I Sam 7:1) until David removed it thence to his newly occupied capital of Jerusalem (II Sam 6). There is not enough evidence to support the idea that the ark was in the battle of Saul.

---

79 P. D. Miller and J. J. M. Roberts, *The Hand of the Lord*: A Reassessment of the Ark Narrative (Baltimore/London 1977), 74–75.

80 *Ibid.*, 67.

81 *Kriege*, 51, n. 5.

82 "The Hand of Yahweh," *VT* 21 (1971), 249.

83 *The Hand of the Lord*, 67.

84 *Ibid.*, 75.

85 Arnold, *Ephod and Ark*, 13 ff; Stoebe (*Das erste Buch Samuelis*, 264) sees that the ark of God can be a correct reading in the whole framework (vv. 15, 23a). Segal (*The Books of Samuel*, 106–7) puts forth a possibility that the ephod was in the ark. P. R. Davies, "Ark or Ephod in I Sam 14:18?" *JTS* 26 (1975), 82–87; A. Bartal, "For the Ark of God was on That Day with the People of Israel" (I Sam 14:18), *Beth Mikra* 26 (1981), 305–8 (Hebrew).

86 Smith, *Samuel*, 112; Hertzberg, *Samuel*, 113 –14; Budde, *Samuel*, 62; Driver, *Samuel*, 110; Ackroyd, *I Samuel*, 114; McCarter, *I Samuel*, 237.

However, in the story of Uriah and David (II Sam 11:11) Uriah told David: "the ark, and Israel and Judah dwell in Succoth (not in booths),[87] and my lord Joab and the servants of my lord are camping in the open field...." Only here we see the strong evidence that the ark participated with the people of Israel. Here the professional army of Joab and his servants were at the front line and the ark and the mustering soldiers were in Succoth near the enemy camp. J. Maier sees this evidence as a late description without historical reality.[88] Yet it is not necessary to see it as a purely theological description. In the story of Absalom's revolt the ark is brought back to Jerusalem by the priests (II Sam 15:25): "carry the ark of God back into the city." This passage suggests that the ark actually had to participate in battle, but not due to duty necessarily.

The next source is Num 10:35–36. This ark song is an ancient liturgical fragment. When the ark was set forward and rested, Moses said:

קומה יהוה ויפצו איביך וינסו משנאיך מפניך.
שובה יהוה רבבות אלפי ישראל.

This fragment does not prove the existence of the ark in the desert period.[89] G. B. Gray thinks it is a liturgical fragment of the Shilonite period.[90] However, Maier supposes that this source is an insertion of some interpolators in the post exilic period.[91] Especially, because of the inverted NUNs at Num 10:35–36, some thought that this source was borrowed from an apocryphal or pseudepigraphical book of Eldad and Medad. But S. Z. Leiman has pointed out that this misunderstanding comes from the medieval sources which no longer understood the earlier midrashic materials.[92] But these above assertions are due to the absence of the warlike function of the ark. The ark, as reviewed above, had participated on the battlefield since the days of David. In this connection it is considered that the ark song was used as the liturgical fragments since the days of David and Solomon.[93] The initial phrase, קומה יהוה in v. 35 is a term which appears in Pss 3:8; 7:7; 9:20; 10:12; 17:3; 132:8, and II Ch 6:41,[94] while the phrase שובה (שבה) יהוה in v. 36 is also a term which occurs in Pss 6:5; 90;13, and 126:4. A *terminus ad quem* is provided by the inclusion in the

---

87 Yadin, *Warfare* II, 275; *id.*, "Some Aspects of the Strategy of Ahab and David," *Bibl* 36 (1955), 341 ff.

88 *Das altisraelitische Ladeheiligtum*, BZAW 93 (Berlin 1965), 62–63 (— *Ladeheiligtum*).

89 Davies, *ASTI* 5, 33–34.

90 *Numbers*, ICC (1903, Edinburgh 1956³), 164 ff; Maier, *Ladeheiligtum*, 4, n. 17.

91 *Ladeheiligtum*, 11, n. 62.

92 "The inverted Nuns at Numbers 10:35–36 and the Book of Eldad and Medad," *JBL* 93 (1974), 354–55.

93 E. Nielsen, "Some Reflections on the History of the Ark," *VTS* 7 (1959), 65; Cross, *CMHE*, 100; McKane (*Glasgow* 21, 69) recognizes this source as ancient sayings.

94 Noth, *Numbers*, 80.

YHWHistic work.[95] These passages reflect that the ark as the visible symbol of YHWH's participation in battle functions to defeat the enemy and after battle it returns to the community of Israel for rest in the cultic context.

Finally, II Sam 5:21 shows us that when David defeated the Philistines, he might have discovered the fact that the Philistines used their divine emblems in the battle. Thus from all this evidence the conclusion is drawn that the ark as the visible symbol of YHWH's intervention participated in the battles of David or later in the ritual warfare in the Davidic-Solomonic kingdom.

5. THE SALVATION OF DAVID

In the battles of David in which YHWH participated as the invisible and the visible symbol of YHWH's intervention, David was always saved by his divine warrior YHWH. In the royal annalistic reports we find this evidence: "YHWH gave victory to David wherever he went (II Sam 8:6b,14b)." Some scholars considered v. 14b as a Dtr passage.[96] Yet it is a conclusion of the war accounts of David.[97] For evidently his contemporaries and their successors regarded these deeds as a miracle.[98] In this connection the passages in the list of David's three mighty warriors (II Sam 23:8–12) are seen as having the same conclusion: "YHWH wrought the great victory (v.12b) on that day (v. 10aβ)." Here we see two great acts of salvation by YHWH for Eleazar and Shammah respectively. These warriors were regarded as the warriors whose deeds are particularly valued in a YHWH war. So we can suppose that such instances were recorded as the conclusion of the heroic list which was composed in the time comtemporary with David's rule.[99]

The salvation formula of YHWH for David is contrasted with that of Saul. The formula in the case of Saul does not include a single person as an object. In the battles of Saul against his enemies we read: "For today

---

[95] *Ibid.*; in Pss 74:22; 82:8 God instead of YHWH occurs.

[96] Budde (*Samuel*, 240–42) assumes v. 6b as borrowing from v. 14b; M. Noth, *Überlieferungsgeschichtliche Studien* (Halle 1943), 65.

[97] Smith, *Samuel*, 308; Segal, *The Books of Samuel*, 283.

[98] Hertzberg, *Samuel*, 289.

[99] Hertzberg, (*ibid.*, 405) sees that the heroic deeds of the three warriors were written down in the "Book of the Wars of Yahweh," but it is hard to see its existence as a Book in the Bible (N. H. Tur-Sinai, "Was there a Book of the Wars of YHWH in the Bible," *BIES* 24, 1959–60, 146–48, Hebrew; S. M. Paul, "Book of the Wars of the Lord," *EJ* 4, col 1218). B. Mazar ("The Military Elite of King David," *VT* 13, 1962, 318) sees that the list of David's warriors was composed in the period of David's rule in Hebron.

YHWH has wrought salvation in Israel" (I Sam 11:13), or "YHWH saved Israel that day" (I Sam 14:23,39, cf., Judg 6:36). In the war of Michmash Jonathan told his armour bearer, "YHWH will work for us, for nothing hinders YHWH from saving by many or by few" (I Sam 14:6,9bβ). Here the object of the salvation of YHWH is Jonathan and his army rather than king Saul, even though Saul is implied in his army. Furthermore, the epithet, "the servant of YHWH" is given only to David among the Israelite kings.[100] This epithet is never applied to Saul.[101] In the tenth century Psalm (144:10) we find: "(YHWH) who gave victory to his king, who rescued David his servant," and in the Psalm of the same period (132:10) we find again: "For the sake of David your servant, turn not away the face of your annointed." The salvation of David, the servant of YHWH, in the battles can imply the limitation of the lifetime of David. So this idea of David's salvation as the servant of YHWH is peculiar to David's time.

In the cases of the judges the object of YHWH's salvation was always the children of Israel, a group of the tribes, not a single person. YHWH raised up saviors (3:9) or judges (2:16,18) in order to save Israel. In Judg 2:18aβb YHWH was with the judges and saved them (the children of Israel) from their enemies. Gideon asked for the angel, "If God save Israel through my hand" (6:36b). The above evidence shows us, as Abramsky supposes,[102] that the idea of the salvation of king David as a single person by YHWH began to appear in the time of the Davidic kingdom. It is supported by the fact that the salvation of David by YHWH was regarded as an ideal model and source for future salvation through the late history of Israel which is found in Psalms (20:7; 28:8; 60:20–22 etc.) and in the prophetic words (Hos 13:4; Is 37:35 = II K 19:34; 43:11; 45:21; Jer 14:8; Ezek 37:23; Zech 12:7 etc.).[103] Thus the idea that YHWH saved David in wars forms the backbone of the history of salvation in Israel as the theological-historical statement which has been a dogma for the messianic kingdom in the future.

In the lifetime of David there was a certain anti-Davidic tendency such as the incident of Shimei or Sheba's revolt. There was a certain royal

---

[100] Exceptionally, the title for Hezekiah in II Ch 32:16 is used in contrast to the servants of Sennacherib. For David the epithet is used in the prophecies of YHWH, II Sam 3:18; 7:5,8; I K 11:13,32,34,36,38; 14:8; II K 19:34; 20:6, by David himself when he addresses God, I Sam 23:10–11; 25:39; II Sam 7:19–29 (ten times), and by Solomon when speaking about his father, I K 3:6; 8:24–26. There is an echo of this usage in the Psalms, Pss 78:70; 89:4,21; 132:10; 144:10, and in the messianic prophecies of Jer 33:21,22,26; Ezek 34:23–24; 37:24 (de Vaux, *The Bible and Ancient Near East*, 154.)

[101] *Ibid.*

[102] *Kingdom of Saul and Kingdom of David*, 117–25.

[103] *Ibid.*, 122–25.

reaction to the revolt in which the history of David's rise to power, as an apology of David, was to show David's accession to the throne of all Israel, north as well as south, to have been entirely lawful, and, moreover, that his kingship was established by the divine warrior YHWH's plan. Here the leitmotif must be the legitimation of David and his kingship. A. Weiser has examined some elements of the legitimation of king David who was supported by YHWH:[104] YHWH was with David (I Sam 16:18; 17:37: 18:12,14,28; 20:13; II Sam 5:10; 7:3,9), the spirit of YHWH came upon David (I Sam 16:13; II Sam 23:2), while it departed from Saul (I Sam 16:14a); David gained the oracles of YHWH (I Sam 23:2,4,9 ff; 30:7 ff; II Sam 2:1; 5:19,23), while Saul failed to get them (I Sam 14:37; 28:6,16); David's own testimony (II Sam 6:21): And David said to Michal, "Praised be the Lord, who chose me above your father, and above all his house, to appoint me as prince over Israel, the people of the Lord;" or the third person's testimony (I Sam 25:28–30): "Pray forgive the trespass of your handmaid (Abigail); for the Lord will certainly make my lord (David) a sure house, because my lord is fighting the battles of the Lord; and evil shall not be found in you so long as you live. ...;" (II Sam 3:9–10,18 – Abner); or the ark narrative (II Sam 6). Even the foreigners had recognized David as their overlord (II Sam 5:11) and so David perceived that YHWH had established him king over Israel (*id.*, v. 12a). These supporting elements of YHWH meant to bring some of the YHWH authority upon David, and the people obeyed him in sociopolitical matters because his power derived from YHWH's sovereignty.[105]

Recently some scholars have attempted to identify the story of David with the apology of Ḫattušiliš, the Hittite king.[106] H. Wolf has defined the story of David as an apologetic document when compared with that of Ḫattušiliš III and has found more than twenty five common elements.[107] These are the theological leitmotifs of the apology of David. The decisive influence of YHWH's special favor for David runs throughout the narrative, the end of which is marked.[108] Thus it is seen that the apology of David in its original formulation was of Davidic date.[109] These above evidences show us that the concept of salvation of king David belongs to his own time.

---

[104] "Die Legitimation des Königs David," *VT* 16 (1966), 325–54.

[105] Talmon, *WHJP* V/1, 7–8.

[106] H. A. Hoffner, "A Hittite Analogue to the David and Goliath Contest of Champions," *CBQ* 30 (1968), 220–24; *id.*, "Propaganda and Political Justification in Hittite Historiography," *Unity and Diversity*, ed. by H. Goedicke and J. J. M. Roberts (Baltimore 1975), 49–62; P. K. McCarter, "The Apology of David," *JBL* 99 (1980), 489–503.

[107] *The Apology of Ḫattušiliš*, Appendix, 176–78.

[108] McCarter, *JBL* 99, 503.

[109] *Ibid.*, 502.

6. WAR CONDUCT

How did David conduct YHWH war? The war is divided into three stages: before battle, battle, and after battle. The time of the campaign usually was spring—summer (II Sam 11:1). Let us analyze the conduct of war of YHWH by David in this order.

1) Before the Battle

1

What and how did David prepare before his battles? The first task before the battle was to find the will of YHWH in relation to the war. In Part One we have discussed how inquiring of the divine will before battle or in battle was a conventional phenomenon which was carried out by the priests or the diviners through oracle, dream, sacred lot, natural phenomena such as bird or waters, or extispicy performed on animals. The first example of divine consultation in battle is Saul's consultation of YHWH in I Sam 14:18 (the ark — MT, the ephod — LXX), 36—37; and 28:6.[110] But YHWH did not answer him, whether by dreams or by urims or by prophets (28:6b).

However, actually the real activity of the YHWH consultation was exercised in the battles of David. For the divine consultation the priests participated in the battles as in Mari.[111] One finds the literary character of the Davidic consultation of YHWH in comparing other formulas of divine consultation. The four different formulas of the divine consultation appear as follows:

1	שופ"	א	אב	וישאלו	בני	ישראל	ביהוה ...	(נתן ביד)
2	שמ"א	יד	לז	וישאל	שאל		באלהים צ̇	
3	שמ"ב	ה	יט	וישאל	דוד		ביהוה צ̇	(נתן ביד)
4	מל"א	כב	חב	לדרשת			את יהוה צ̇	(נתן ביד)

In the first formula, **שאל ביהוה**, the subject is the children of Israel — a group (cf. Judg 20:23,27).[112] Judg 20:23 is not connected with the delivery

---

[110] The divine consultation by the priest Eleazar for Joshua (Num 27:12—23), and that by the levite priest for the Dannite leaders (Judg 18:5—14 — ephod, theraphim, a graven image and a molten image) are not related to the battle contexts. The divine consultation of Gideon (Judg 6:36—40 — oracle, 7:9—10 — dream), that for the civil wars between the Benjaminites and other Israelites (Judg 20:27—28), or that of Judah tribe (Judg 1:1—2) are related with the battles, but they are far from the real realities of the battles. And the consultation of Saul by the Urim and Thummim in I Sam 14:41—42 is not for the war conduct.

[111] Glock, *Warfare*, 130.

[112] Cf., I Sam 10:22.

formula, while the object in Judg 1:1b is the land of Canaan, not an enemy. It seems that this formula is a later transformation of the original form. But it is not later than the prophetic formula in the 9th century BC.[113] In Judg 20:18 the subject as a group inquired of God, not YHWH. The second formula is שאל באלהים. This formula is not connected with the delivery formula (Judg 18:15; 20:18; I Sam 14:37; 22:13,15). The subject of this formula is a priest or Saul, except the children of Israel (Judg 20:18). Because of the absence of the divine delivery formula, it is not clear that this formula originally was related with the battle context, except in the case of Saul (I Sam 14:37). The third formula שאל ביהוה, is a characteristic type of the Davidic divine consultation (I Sam 23:2,4; 30:8; II Sam 2:1; 5:19,23).[114] The subject of this formula is always David himself.[115] Although the priests such as Ahimelek or Abiathar used to inquire of God for David, their function in the battles was secondary. The object of the consultation is always YHWH, not God.[116] In this case the delivery formula follows as the YHWH promise oracle. This oracle was directly given to David by YHWH himself. YHWH himself participated on the battlefields (II Sam 5:19,23). Richter has recognized this formula as the oldest type which was exercised by the priestly house of Eli.[117] Moreover, this formula is distinguished from that of the prophetic consultation. The last formula, דרש את יהוה, which starts from the 9th century BC,[118] is the literary character of the prophetic consultation. This formula mainly occurs in the prophetic literature (58 times).[119] The message of the YHWH oracle is delivered to the king through the prophets. In this sense the divine messages of Samuel (I Sam 28:19) or Deborah (Judg 4:7,14) functionally belong to this category.[120] In this connection, R. Bach has concluded that the traditions of the holy war were taken up into prophecy already at the time of the establishment of the state or immediately thereafter.[121]

Through what did David inqurie of YHWH? First David used the ephod. When Saul planned to attack David at Keilah, David told Abiathar the priest to bring the ephod and David inquired of YHWH as follows (I Sam 23:11–12):

---

[113] B. O. Long, "The Effect of Divination upon Israelite Literature," *JBL* 92 (1973), 491.

[114] I Sam 23:2,4; 30:8; II Sam 2:1; 5:19,23.

[115] In I Sam 22:10 the priest Ahimelek inquired of YHWH for David, but it is not a war context.

[116] שאל באל (I Ch 14:10,14) is a later variation.

[117] *Untersuchungen*, 183–85.

[118] *Op. cit.*, 490 ff.

[119] *NCB* I, 276

[120] Richter, *Untersuchungen*, 23. n. 17.

[121] *Die Aufforderungen zur Flucht und zum Kampf im alttestamentlichen Prophetenspruch* (Neukirchen–Vluyn 1962), 112.

> Will the men of Keilah deliver me up into his hand?
> Will Saul come down, as thy servant has heard?
> O Lord God of Israel, I beseech thee, tell thy
> sevant. And the Lord said, He will come down.
> Then said David, will the men of Keilah deliver
> me and my men into the hand of Saul? And the Lord
> said, they will deliver thee up.

In determining the campaign of Ziklag, David again told Abiathar to bring the ephod and inquired of YHWH as follows (I Sam 30:8):

> And David inquired of the Lord, saying, shall I
> pursue after this troop? Shall I overtake them?
> And he answered him, pursue: for thou shalt surely
> overtake them, and without fail recover all.

The use of the ark for YHWH consultation is not clear,[122] even if in I Sam 14:18 Saul told Ahijah to bring the ark (MT), because in the LXX it is the ephod, instead of the ark of God. In the same chapter v. 3 the same priest, Ahijah, had already carried the ephod. In this context, if the object which Saul asked for must be something for consultation, in the light of the above descriptions, the ephod is better fit for the context. In the battle of David over the Philistines in the valley of Rephaim he obtained the oracle of YHWH through the sounds of the bakha tree (II Sam 5:24). There is no YHWH consultation in the revolt of Absalom. Yet Absalom consulted with Ahithobel, a professional royal counseler.[123] Therefore, the above evidence implies that divine consultation for the battle was exercised by king David and his priests.[124] These salvation oracles of YHWH have been preserved in the oracles against foreign nations as the judgment oracle of YHWH by the prophets.[125]

2

The next task is the mustering of soldiers for a war crisis. In the period of the Judges it was a normal activity in the time of emergency. In the battle of Saul against the Ammonites he mustered the soldiers of

---

[122] In Judg 20:27 the ark of the covenant is a late addition. According to Arnold (*Ephod and Ark*, 114 ff), the covenant is a Dtr usage but the ark is the original instrument for the divine consultation. But we do not have clear information as to how the ephod as the priestly garment was used to inquire of God (cf., M. Haran, "The Form of the Ephod according to Biblical Sources," *Tarbiẓ* 24, 1956, 380–91, Hebrew). F. C. Foote ("The Ephod," *JBL* 21, 1902, 21) assumes that the ephod looks like an apron from which the lots were cast or a pouch into which the priest put his hands and drew the lots.

[123] Lind, *Yahweh is a Warrior*, 120.

[124] C. H. Gordon, *Ancient Near East* (NY 1965), 162.

[125] J. Hayes, "The Usage of Oracles against the Nations in Ancient Israel," *JBL* 87 (1968), 81–92; Christensen, *War Oracle*, 17 ff; Y. Hoffmann, *The Prophecies against Foreign Nations in the Bible* (TA 1977), 267 ff (Hebrew).

three hundred and thirty contingents in Bezek (I Sam 11:8). But from the time of Saul there was a standing army of three thousand soldiers which could respond immediately to an emergency (I Sam 13:2) without the militia. Like Saul, David had two separate formations of the army: The regular army and the militia.[126] The regular force was a standing army of professional career men. This regular army was made up of two distinct ethnic groups, the Israelites and the foreign mercenaries. The number of this Israelite regular army was about four hundred men (I Sam 22:2: 25:13) or in later times about six hundred men (*id.*, 23:13; 27:2). The regiment was divided into three units: Two fighting units and one unit to guard the weapons (I Sam 25:13; 30:9–10,21–25). The thirty among them (II Sam 23:8–39) were the special warriors who served as the commanders of the militia. The three among them were the commanding officers of the three units of the army. Mazar has pointed out that the organization of the army was influenced by the Philistines.[127] Another group of the regular army was the foreign mercenary units, drawn mostly from the Sea people, including the Philistines.[128] They were from among the people whom David met in his time of escape from Saul, the Cherethites, Pelethites and the Gittites from Gath. They served as the members of the king's bodyguard and were used mainly in internal clashes, particularly to quell domestic rebellion such as Absalom's revolt. Thus, except in the time of emergency there was no militia by mustering.

However, in a time of emergency people were called up for action only during that time, and this was the militia. In the time of Absalom's revolt, besides the standing army, the militia was called up for action. It is not clear through what method and manner the peoples were called up. In the periods of the Judges and Saul the trumpet was often used for the call-up.[129] But the use of a trumpet for call up is absent in the time of David. When Sheba rebelled against David, only Sheba summoned the people to follow him by blowing the trumpet. Yet the trumpet was used to signal a decisive message like victory on the battlefield. In the story of the rebellion of Sheba we can guess the duration of the call-up. In the case of Sheba, David commanded Amasa (II Sam 20:4–5): "Assemble me the men of Judah within three days, and be you here present. So Amasa went to assemble the men of Judah, but he tarried longer than the set time which he had appointed him." Because of this delay, the brunt of the fighting to crush the rebellion fell upon the veterans and mercenaries of

---

[126] Yadin, *Warfare* II, 275.

[127] *VT* 13, 314.

[128] Yadin, *Warfare* II, 277.

[129] In Judg 3:27 (Ehud) and 6:34 (Gideon) the trumpet is used for calling up, and in II Sam 2:28; 18:6; 20:22 it is used to halt the fighting, not for a call-up. In I Sam 13:3 its usage is to signal a victory and in Josh 6 and 7 the trumpet's function is cultic.

the regular army. The picture of David's militia eventually being developed into a highly efficient and brilliantly organized fighting force is well documented in I Ch 27:1—15 as the organization of the time of David.[130] According to the report of Joab (II Sam 24:2—9), in the time of David there were valiant men who drew the sword in thirteen hundred contingents for the militia through all the land. Thus the militia was not the formative factor for YHWH war, in contrast to von Rad's *Aufgebot.*[131] For the decisive battles of David which were understood as YHWH war were carried out by his regular army under Joab rather than the militia force which was assembled in the time of emergency.

2) The Battle

According to the favorable oracle of YHWH the battles of David were conducted. The army must march toward the enemies and attack them. Here the priest must accompany the army. As the priest Ahijah went with Saul (I Sam 13:4), the priest Abiathar went with David to Keilah (I Sam 23:6). In other battles the priests were not mentioned. Yet, because the ark was on the battlefield of Joab against the Ammonites, it is supposed that the priest would be there, too. In the time of Absalom's revolt, the priests Zadok and Abiathar were with the ark in Jerusalem. We have no information regarding the order of the march of the soldiers with the ark. If we were to hypothesize the procession of the ark and the soldiers in the attack of Jericho in Josh 6, the order of march could have been the armed soldiers, the ark and then the general soldiers. This is a possible suggestion concerning the order of march in the campaign or in the cult.

How did David do battle against the enemy? There were three types of battles by David: a) David fought alone against the Philistine Goliath (I Sam 17:12—58). The dual combat was a customary battle style used to save unnecessary bloodshed.[132] In this single battle David had the conviction that YHWH helped him fight against the Philistine. b) The regular army and David alone fought against the neighbouring enemies around them. The battle of David against the Philistines in the valley of Rephaim is an example of this case.[133] This decisive battle was understood as YHWH's breaking through the battle and giving the victory to David (II Sam 5:17—21). The other battles in II Sam 5:6; 10:17; 15:13—15 are examples of the same case. Moreover, the regular force was used for attack against the principal enemy of David, and in particular for engagements

---

[130] Yadin, *Warfare* II, 280—84.

[131] *Krieg*, 6, 37—38.

[132] Glück,. *Acta Classica* 7, 25.

[133] Alt, *EOTHR*, 271—72.

which demanded great mobility and speed in action. c) The united force of the regular army and the militia fought against the enemies. The battle of David over the Ammonites (II Sam 10:15–11:1) was this type. In the campaign of the Ammonites (II Sam 11:11) Joab and his regular army were in the front line of the battlefield and the militia men with the ark abode in Succoth, the advanced strategic base for the Transjordan campaign.[134] Most of the battles of David were conducted by the regular army rather than the militia.[135]

Whenever David attacked the enemies, he exercised some sort of mobilization of army and strategy. Like the army division of Abimelek or Saul, David divided the army into three divisions. These three divisions were engaged in his battle against Absalom as follows (II Sam 18:2): "and David sent forth one third of the people under the hand of Joab, and another third under the hand of Abishai the son of Zeruiah, Joab's brother, and the final third under the hand of Ittai." Yet in the decisive battle of Joab over the Ammonites, the army as the strategy to break the siege between the Aramaean army and the Ammonite force was divided into two parts, and one under Abishai went forth against the Ammonites in front of Joab, and the other under Joab led against the Aramaeans at the rear of Joab.[136] As soon as Joab and his soldiers drew near to battle against Aramaeans, the Aramaeans fled, even though the text does not give the reason for their flight. It was considered that YHWH intervened for Israel, as Joab said that YHWH would do what seemed good to him (II Sam 10:12). When David attacked Jerusalem, he used a method of encouragement to the soldiers (II Sam 5:8): David said on that day, "whoever reaches up the gutter (צנור)[137] and smites the Jebusites (first), ..., he shall be chief and captain." Joab the son of Zeruiah went up first, and was made chief.[138]

As a result the victory was given to David, and was announced through the sound of the trumpet (II Sam 18:16–17; 20:22). In connection with the sound of the trumpet in battle some asserted that the תרועה is a character of holy war.[139] But this term is not found in the battles of David,[140] except in the procession of the ark by David (II Sam 6:15). This term occurs in the late war descriptions as תרועה מלחמה (Jer 4:19; 49:2).

---

[134] Yadin, *Warfare* II, 270–71.

[135] On this point von Rad asserts that the concept of holy war as the voluntary reaction of the people disappeared from the beginning of the kingdom, because of the mechanical operation of the organized troops (see n. 131 above).

[136] Yadin, *Warfare* II, 274.

[137] E. L. Sukenik, "The Account of David's Capture of Jerusalem," *JPOS* 8 (1928), 12 ff.

[138] Yadin, *Warfare* II, 268.

[139] Caspari, *ZWT* 54 NF 19, 146; von Rad, *Krieg*, 11.

[140] Cf., I Sam 17:20,52.

It is supposed that this term was a cultic usage developed in the Jerusalem cultic tradition.[141] In the battles of David the weapons used are a simple sword, spear, sling, stone and so on. The war chariot and horse are not found in his battles. The chariot and horse were first used by Absalom (II Sam 15:21) and Adoniah (I K 1:5), but they were not used in the battle context. It seems that the situation of the weapons was similar to that of the battles of Saul. For in the descriptions of YHWH war we are told that the weapons are not important for carrying out YHWH war, as David says: "YHWH saves not with sword and spear, for the battle is YHWH's" (I Sam 17:47).

3) Post-Battle

The last conduct of war is to treat the spoils and to celebrate the victory after the battles. In the ancient Near Eastern context it is customary that the spoils were dedicated to the divine warriors who gave the victory. This custom is found in the annal of David (II Sam 8:11–12):

> These (spoils/gifts) also King David dedicated to
> the Lord, together with the silver and gold which
> he had dedicated from all the nations he subdued,
> from Aram, Moab, the Ammonite, the Philistines,
> Amalek, and from the spoil of Hadadezer the son of
> Rehob, king of Zobah.

It is a similar custom that the weapons captured were also dedicated to the temple. This is found in the story of the battle of David and the Philistine Goliath (I Sam, 17:54): "David took the head of the Philistine and brought it to Jerusalem, but he put his armour in the tent of YHWH." At that time in Jerusalem David had no tent.[142] Yet it is supposed that it was taken someplace near the YHWh sanctuary like Mizpah, where David later took the sword of Goliath back again (*id.*, 21:8–9). It is compared with the action after the death of Saul on Mt. Gilboa, as we mentioned previously, when the head of Saul and his armour bearer were sent to the territory of the Philistines to carry the good news to the house of their divine emblems and to the people, and his armour was put in the temple of Ashtaroth (I Sam 31:9–10). The devotion of the weapon which was taken by victory to his divine warrior is found in the apology of Ḫattušiliš II:46–47: "The weapon which I wielded then I (afterward) dedicated and placed it before the goddess my lady (= in her sanctuary)."[143]

With the dedication of spoils to YHWH some of them were distributed to the soldiers or the elders of the Judean towns. The equal distri-

---

[141] Stolz, *Kriege*, 46–48.

[142] Hertzberg, *Samuel*, 154.

[143] Hoffner, *CBQ* 30, 224–26.

bution of the spoil by David to the soldiers who had and had not participated in the campaign of the Amalekites in I Sam 30 was a statute and an ordinance for Israel to this day (I Sam 30:25). In the time of David there was no idea of total destruction of the spoils of the enemies in the descriptions of the battles (Ḥerem). The war custom which brings the hand or the foreskin of the enemy as spoil was an ancient style in Egypt. It is found in David's action (I Sam 18:27): "David arose and went, along with his men, and killed two hundred of the Philistines, and David brought their foreskins and he laid them in full number before the king (Saul) that he might become the king's son-in-law."

Finally, the highest action is to celebrate the victory, especially for YHWH the divine warrior. In the course of this celebration of victory YHWH is exalted as the supreme God and king-warrior. In Ps 24:7–10 we again see the praise and exaltation of YHWH as the divine warrior in the procession of the ark to the sancturary by Davidic rulers.[144] There is no mention about the steles or the monuments erected by the Davidic kingdom to praise YHWH who gave the victory, except the Jerusalem temple.

[144] Cross, *CMHE*, 91–92; A. Cooper, "Ps 24:7–10: Mythology and Exegesis," *JBL* 102 (1983), 37–60.

Conclusion

In Part Two our examination has led to the conclusion that in the official/canonical traditions of the Exodus-Conquest (Chapter V) and even in those of the Judges and Saul (Chapter VI), the motifs of YHWH war are not found in the historical realities of battles, and for the first time in the rising period of the Davidic kingdom, the motifs of YHWH war began to appear in the historical battles of David. The following factors are the results of our examination:

1. In the canonical traditions of the Reed Sea event (Ex 14 and 15) in Chapter V the only protagonist was God, not men, while in those of the war of the Israelites against the Amalekites (Ex 17:8–16) the protagonist Moses was depicted as a divine man. In both traditions the human soldiers played no role. This is contrasted with the idea of synergism in which YHWH helped his people fight against their enemy. Thus these traditions reflect the later theological understanding of the saving act of YHWH.

2. In most of the canonical traditions of the Conquest and the Judges, however, God and soldiers fought together in the battle contexts. Here we recognize that from this time the war descriptions reflect the traditions which were formulated on the basis of the historical realities of battles. But these traditions do not reflect the religious dimensions of battles. The present traditions of battles in the Book of Joshua and of the Judges are seen as the reflections of a later theological understanding composed in the light of YHWH war. These war traditions that were schematized by the Deuteronomistic theology are termed "holy war" by modern scholars. The idea of Ḥerem is an example of the holy war traditions.

3. The war traditions in the period of the Judges are much closer to the historical realities of battles as the struggle for existence in the given environmental conditions. But von Rad's idea of holy war as the reaction of the twelve tribal confederation is no longer supported. For even at the end of the period of the Judges all the twelve tribes did not take part in battles. In the song of Deborah (Judg 5), which reflects the maximal unity achieved by the Israelites, there are only six tribes, and the prose account of the same battle (Judg 4) mentions only two tribes: Zebulun and Naphthali.

4. The traditions of Saul's battles show that his battles were described in religious dimensions close to the historical reality. In his war conduct Saul tried to find the YHWH oracles, but failed to get them. The priests

also accompanied him in the battles, but they could not obtain the YHWH oracles. Further, the kingdom of Saul actually ended as an abortive kingdom which was absorbed into the kingdom of David. Thus it was the understanding that the help of YHWH was not attested to in the political realities of the kingdom of Saul.

5. In Chapter VII the traditions and the historical and annalistic records of the Davidic battles show that the idea of YHWH's help and intervention in the battles began to appear in the rising period of the Davidic kingdom. It is the same phenomenon that the motifs of divine war began to attest to in the rising period of each empire or kingdom in the ancient Near East.

6. The wars of David were recognized as the lawsuit of YHWH and His intervention in the battles, and later were understood as the command of YHWH. This interpretation also exactly parallels the ancient Near Eastern concept of divine war.

7. YHWH was understood as the divine warrior. It is seen by His warlike epithets such as גבור, צבאות and איש מלחמה. In the ancient Near East there were many divine warriors, but in the Bible only YHWH was recognized as the divine warrior, and El was not attested to in war contexts as a warrior.

8. YHWH intervened not only to help the army on the battlefield but He also marched in front of the king and soldiers. But the motif of YHWH's intervention in the divided monarchy was recognized as negative toward his people by the prophets.

9. In the battles of David, the ark, the visible divine symbol, took part with the priests. The participation of the ark parallels that of the divine emblems or standards of war in the ancient Near East.

10. The victory after the battles was given to YHWH, and the spoils obtained were dedicated to YHWH and His treasures. At the same time YHWH was exalted as the supreme God just as other divine warriors were in the ancient Near East. Ps 24 is a good sample description of YHWH warriorship. Therefore, we may conclude that the motifs of YHWH war were formulated in the Davidic kingdom in the light of those of divine war in the ancient Near East.

Selected Bibliography

Abramsky, S., *Kingdom of Saul and Kingdom of David.* Jerusalem 1977 (Hebrew).

Ackroyd, P. R., "The Composition of the Song of Deborah." *VT* 2 (1952) 160–62.

–, *The First Book of Samuel.* Cambridge 1971.

Aharoni, Y. "The Settlement of Canaan." *WHJP* III (1971) 94–128.

–, "The Battle of the Waters of Merom and the Battle with Sisera." *Military History of the Land of Israel in Biblical Times.* Ed. by J. Liver (1973) 91–109 (Hebrew).

–, *The Land of the Bible*: A Historical Geography. Tr. by A. F. Rainey. Philadelphia 1979.

Albrektson, B., *History and the Gods*: An Essay on the Idea of Historical Events as Divine Manifestations in the Ancient Near East and in Israel. CB 1. Lund 1967.

Albright, W. F., "The Kyle Memorial Bulletin of Excavation of Bethel." *BASOR* 56 (1934) 2–14.

–, A Review Article: "L'épithéte divine Jahvé Ṣᵉba'ôt by B. N. Wambacq, O. Praem. Bruges 1947." *JBL* 67 (1948) 377–81.

–, "A Catalogue of Early Hebrew Lyric Poems (Ps 68)." *HUCA* 23 (1950–51) 1–40.

–, *From the Stone Age to Christianity.* NY 1957.

–, *Yahweh and the Gods of Canaan.* London 1968.

Alt, A., *Kleine Schriften zur Geschichte des Volkes Israel* I. München 1959.

–, "The Formation of the Israelite State in Palestine." *Essays on Old Testament History and Religion.* Tr. by R. A. Wilson (Oxford 1966) 223–310.

Armerding, C. E., *The Heroic Ages of Greece and Israel*: A Literary and Historical Comparison. University Microfilms, Ann Arbor, Michigan 1968.

Arnold, W. R., *Ephod and Ark.* HTR 3. Cambridge/London 1917.

Avishur, Y., *Pairs of Words in Biblical Literature and Their Parallels in Semitic Literature of the Ancient Near East.* Unpublished Ph. D. Diss. of the Hebrew University 1974 (Hebrew).

Bach, R., *Die Aufforderungen zur Flucht und zum Kampf im alttestamentlichen Prophetenspruch.* Neukirchen–Vluyn 1962.

Bächli, O., *Amphiktyonie im Alten Testament*: Forschungsgeschichtliche Studie zur Hypothese von M. Noth. STZ 6, Basel 1977.

Bartal, A., "For the Ark of God was on That Day with the Children of Israel." *Beth Mikra* 26 (1981) 305–8.

Bartlet, J. R., "The Historical Reference of Numbers 21:27–30." *PEQ* 101 (1969) 94–100.

–, "Sihon and Og, the Kings of the Amorites." *VT* 20 (1970) 257–77.

Batto, B. F., "The Reed Sea: Requiescat in Pace." *JBL* 102 (1983) 27–36.

Becker, J., *Gottesfurcht im Alten Testament.* Rome 1965.

Berger, P.-R. "Zu Ps 24, 7 und 9." *UF* 2 (1970) 335–36.

Beyerlin, W., "Das Königscharisma bei Saul." *ZAW* 73 (1961) 186–201.

–, "Geschichte und heilsgeschichtliche Traditionsbildung im Alten Testament." *VT* 13 (1963) 1–25.

–, Ed. *Near Eastern Religious Texts Relating to the Old Testament.* Tr. by J. Bowden. Philadelphia 1978.

Birch, B. C., *The Rise of the Israelite Monarchy*: The Growth and Development of I Samuel 7–15. SBL 27. Missoula, Mont. 1976.

Blenkinsopp, J., "Jonathan's Sacrilege." *CBQ* 26 (1964) 423–49.
–, *Gibeon and Israel*: The Role of Gibeon and the Gibeonites in the Political and Religious History of Early Israel. Cambridge 1972.
Boling, R. G., *Judges*. AB 6A. NY 1975.
Bolling, R. G. and Wright, G. E., *The Book of Joshua*. AB 6. NY 1982.
Borger, R., "Gott Marduk und Gott-König Sulgi als Propheten: Zwei Prophetische Texte." *BiOr 28 (1971) 3–24.*
–, *Assyrisch-Babylonische Zeichenliste*. AOAT 33. Neukirchen 1978.
Breasted, J. H. *Ancient Records of Egypt* II-III. Chicago 1906–7.
Brekelmans, C. H. W., *De Ḥerem in het Oude Testament*. Nijmegen 1959.
Bright, J., *Early Israel in Recent History Writing*. SBT 19. London 1956.
–, *A History of Israel*. London 1966.
Buber, M., *Kingship of God*. ET by R. Scheimann. 1956, London 1967.
Burrows, E., *Ur Excavations Text* II: Archaic Texts. London 1935.
Carter, C. W., *Hittite Cult-Inventories*. Unpublished Ph. D. Diss., the University of Chicago 1962.
Campbell, A. F., *The Ark Narrative*: A Form Critical and Traditio-Historical Study. SBL 16. Missoula, Mont. 1975.
–, "Yahweh and the Ark." *JBL* 98 (1979) 31–43.
Caspari, W., "Was stand im Buche der Kriege Jahwes?" *ZWT* 54 NF 19 (1912) 110–158.
Cassuto, U., *A Commentary on the Book of Exodus*. ET by I. Abrahams. Jerusalem 1967.
–, *The Godedess Anath*. ET by I. Abrahams. Jerusalem 1971.
–, *Biblical and Oriental Studies* I. ET by I. Abrahams. Jerusalem 1973.
Černý, J., "Stela of Ramesses II from Beisan." *Eretz Israel* 5 (1958) 75–82.
Childs, B. S., *Memory and Tradition in Israel*. SBT 57. London 1962.
–, "Deuteronomic Formulae of the Exodus Tradition." *W. Baumgartner Festschrift* (1967) 30–39.
–, *The Book of Exodus*: A Critical, Theological Commentary. OTL. Philadelphia 1974.
Christensen, D. L., *Transformation of the War Oracles in the Old Testament Prophecy. HDR 3. Missoula, Mont. 1975.*
Civil, M., "Šu-Sin's Historical Inscriptions: Collection B." JCS 21 (1967) 24–38.
von Clausewitz, C., *On War*. 1832, 1968.
Clay, A. T., *Babylonian Texts*: Miscellaneous Inscriptions in Yale Babylonian Collection I. New Haven 1925.
Coats, G. W., "The Traditional Character of the Reed Sea Motif." *VT* 17 (1967) 253–65.
–, "The Song of the Sea." *CBQ* 31 (1969) 1–17.
–, "History and Theology in the Sea Tradition." *ST* 29 (1975) 53–62.
–, "Conquest Traditions in the Wilderness Theme." *JBL* 95 (1976) 177–90.
Cohen, S., *Enmerkar and the Lord of Aratta*. University Microfilms, Ann Arbor, Michigan 1973.
Conray, C., "Hebrew Epic: Historical Note and Critical Reflections." *Bibl* 61 (1980) 1–30.
Cooke, G., "The Israelite King as Son of God." *ZAW* 73 (1961) 202–25.
Cooper, A., "Ps 24:7–10: Mythology and Exegesis." *JBL* 102 (1983) 37–60.
Cooper, J. C., *The Return of Ninurta to Nippur*: An-gim dím-ma. AnOr 52. Rome 1978.
Craigie, P. C., "The Song of Deborah and the Epic of Tukulti-Ninurta." *JBL* 88 (1969) 253–65.
–, *The Problem of War in the Old Testament*. Michigan 1981.

Cross, F. M., "YHWH and the God of Patriarchs." *HTR* 55 (1962) 225–59.
–, "The Divine Warrior in Israel's Early Cult." *Biblical Motifs*: Origins and Transformations. Ed. by A. Altmann (Cambridge, Massa. 1966) 11–30.
–, *Canaanite Myth and Hebrew Epic*. Cambridge, Massa. 1973.
Cross, F. M. and Freedman, D. N., *Studies in Ancient Yahwistic Poetry*. *SBL* 21. Missoula, Mont. 1975.
Curto, S., *The Military Art of the Ancient Egyptians*. ET by A. Coath. Turin 1971.
Dahood, M., *Psalms* I–III. AB 16–17a. NY 1965–70.
Davies, G. I., *The Way of Wilderness*. London 1979.
–, A Review Article: "*Er Spaltete das Meer* by S. I. L. Norin." *VT* 31 (1981) 110–17.
Davies, H., "The Ark of the Covenant." *ASTI* 5 (1966) 30–47.
Davis, P. R., "Ark or Ephod in I Sam 14:8." *JTS* 26 (1976) 82–87.
Dion, P. E., "The 'fear not' Formula and Holy War." *CBQ* 32 (1970) 565–70.
Dossin, G. "Une Révelation du Dieu Dagan à Terqa." *RA* 42 (1948) 125–34.
Driver, S. R. *Notes on the Hebrew Text of the Books of Samuel*. 1890, Oxford 1913.
Edgerton, W. F. and Wilson, J. A. *Historical Records of Ramses III*. Chicago 1936.
Eichrodt, W. *Theology of the Old Testament* I. ET by J. A. Baker. London 1969.
Eissfeldt, O. "Jahwe Zebaoth." *KS* 3. Ed by R. Sellheim and F. Maass (1950, Tübingen 1966) 103–23.
–, "Die Eroberung Palästinas durch Altisrael" *WO* 2 (1955) 158–171; *KS* 3, 367–83.
–, *The Old Testament*: An Introduction. ET by P. R. Ackroyd. Oxford 1965.
Emerton, J. A., "New Light on Israelite Religion: The Implications of the Inscriptions from Kuntillet ʿAjrud." *ZAW* 94 (1982) 2–20.
Eph'al, I., "The Battle of Gibeon and the Problem of Joshua's Southern Campaign." *The Military History of the Land of Israel in Biblical Times*. Ed. by J. Liver (1973) 97–90 (Hebrew).
Even-Shoshan, A., Ed., *A New Concordance of the Bible* I–III. Jerusalem 1977–80.
Falkenstein, A. *Sumerische und Akkaische Hymnen und Gebete*. Zürich/Stuttgart 1953.
–, *Sumerische Götterlieder* I. Heidelberg 1959.
Farber-Flügge, G., *Der Mythos Inanna und Enki unter besonderer Berücksichtigung*. Studia Pohl 10. Rome 1973.
Faulkner, R. O. "Egyptian Military Organization." *JEA* 39 (1939) 32–47.
–, *A Concise Dictionary of Middle Egyptian*. Oxford 1976.
Fohrer, G. *Überlieferung und Geschichte des Exodus*: Eine Analyse von Ex 1–15. BZAW 91. Berlin 1964.
Frankfort, H. *Cylinder Seals*. London 1939, 1965.
–, *Kingship and the Gods*. Chicago/London 1948, 1978.
Fredriksson, H. *Jahwe als Krieger*: Studien zum alttestamentlichen Gottesbild. Lund 1945.
Freedman, D. N., "The Name of the God of Moses." *JBL* 79 (1960) 151–56.
–, "Divine Names and Titles in Early Hebrew Poetry." *Magnalia Dei*: The Mighty Acts of God, G. E. Wright Festschrift. Ed. by F. M. Cross et al (Garden City, NY 1976) 55–107.
Fulco, W. J. *The Canaanite God Rešep*. AO 8. New Haven 1976.
Gardiner, A. H., "The Carnarvon Tablet I." *JEA* 3 (1916) 95–110.
–, *Egypt of the Pharaoh*. London 1961, 1980.
Gevirtz, S., "Jericho and Shechem: A Religio-Literary Aspect of City Destruction." *VT* 13 (1963) 52–62.
Gibson, J. C. L. *Textbook of Syrian Semitic Inscriptions* I. Oxford 1971.
–, *Canaanite Myths and Legends* by G. R. Driver. Old Testament Studies 3. Edinburgh 1978.

Globe, A. "The Literary Structure and Unity of the Song of Deborah." *JBL* 93 (1973) 493–512.

–, "The Text and Literary Structure of Judges 5:4–5." *Bibl* (1974) 168–78.

Glock, A. E. *Warfare in Mari and Early Israel.* Unpublished Ph. D. Diss. of University of Michigan 1968.

–, "Early Israel as the Kingdom of Yahweh." *Concordia Theological Monthly* 41 (1970) 558–605.

Glück, J. J. "Reviling and Monomachy as Battle-Preludes in Ancient Warfare." *Acta Classica* 7 (1964) 25–31.

Görg. M., *Gott-König-Reden in Israel und Ägypten.* BWANT 5. Stuttgart 1975.

Goetze, A. *Ḫattušiliš.* MVÄG 29. 1925, Darmstadt 1967.

–, "Zur Schlacht von Qades." *OLZ* 11 (1929) 834–37.

–, "Die Pestgebete des Muršiliš." *KF* 1/2 (1929) 161–75.

–, *Die Annalen des Muršiliš.* MVÄG 38. 1933, Darmstadt 1967.

–, *Kleinasien.* München 1957.

–, "Critical Reviews of *Keilschrifttexte aus Boghazköi* X (1960) by H. G. Güterbock and H. Otten." *JCS* 16 (1962) 24–30.

–, "Warfare in Asia Minor." *Iraq* 25 (1963) 124–30.

Goldin, J., *The Song at the Sea.* New Haven/London 1971.

Gordon, C. H. *The Ugaritic Textbook.* AnOr 38. Rome 1965.

Gottlieb, H., "Myth in the Psalms." *Myths in the Old Testament.* Ed. by B. Otzen, H. Gottlieb and K. Jappesen (London 1980) 62–93.

Gottwald, N. K. "Holy War in Deuteronomy: Analysis and Critique." *Review and Expositor* 61 (1964) 296–310.

–, *The Tribes of Yahweh*: A Sociology of the Religion of Literated Israel, 1250–1050 BCE. NY 1979.

Grayson, A. K. *Assyrian Royal Inscriptions* I. Wiesbaden 1972.

–, *Assyrian and Babylonian Chronicles.* NY 1975.

Greenfield, J. C., "The Zakir Inscription and the Danklied." *Proceedings of the Fifth World Congress of Jewish Studies* (Jerusalem 1969) 179–91.

Grønback, J. H., "Juda und Amalek: Überlieferungsgeschichtliche Erwägungen zu Exodus 17:8–16." *ST* 18 (1964) 26–45.

Güterbock, H. G., "Keilschrifttexte nach Kopien von T. G. Pinches: 'Bruchstück eines altbabylonischen Naram-Sin Epos.'" *AfO* 13 (1939–41) 46–50.

–, "The Deeds of Šuppiluliuma as Told by His Son, Muršiliš II." *JCS* 10 (1956) 41–68, 75–98, 107–119.

Gurney, O. R., *The Hittites.* 1952, 1962.

Habachi, L., *The Second Stela of Kamose and His Struggle against the Hyksos Ruler and His Capital.* ADAIK 8. Glückstadt 1972.

Hallo, W. W., *Early Mesopotamian Royal Titles*: A Philological and Historical Analysis. 1957.

–, "A Sumerian Amphictyony." *JCS* 14 (1960) 88–96.

Hallo, W. W. and van Dijk, J. J. A., *The Exaltation of Inanna.* YNER 3. New Haven/London 1968.

Hallo, W. W. and Simpson, W. K., *The Ancient Near East*: A History. NY 1971.

Halpern, B. "The Uneasy Compromise." *Traditions and Transmission*: Turning Points in Biblical Faith, Festschrift of F. M. Cross. Ed. by B. Halpern and J. D. Levenson (Eisenbraun 1981) 59–96.

Haran (Diman), M., "An Archaic Remnant in the Prophetic Literature." *Yedioth* 13 (1949) 14–17.

–, "The Form of the Ephod according to Biblical Sources." *Tarbiz* 24 (1956) 380–91.
–, "The Ark and the Cherubim." *IEJ* 9 (1959) 30–38, 89–94.
–, "The Gibeonites: Their Place in the Conquest War of the Land and in the History of Israel." *Issues in the Book of Joshua* (Jerusalem 1971) 101–26 (Hebrew).
–, *Ages and Institutions in the Bible.* TA 1972 (Hebrew).
–, *Temple and Temple-Service in Ancient Israel.* Oxford 1978.
Harvey, J. "Le RIB-Pattern, réquisitoire prophétique sur la rupture de l'alliance." *Bibl* 43 (1962) 172–96.
Hay, L. S. "What Really Happened at the Sea of Reeds?" *JBL* 83 (1964) 397–403.
Hayes, J., "The Usage of Oracles against the Nation in Ancient Israel." *JBL* 87 (1968) 81–92.
Heimpel, W., "Held". *Reallexikon der Assyriologie* 4. Ed. by D. O. Edzard (1972–75) 287–93.
Heintz, J. G., "Oracles Prophétiques et 'Guerre Sainte' selon les Archives Royales de Mari et l'Ancien Testament." Congress Volume. *VTS* 17 (1969) 112–38.
Helck, W., *Urkunden der 18 Dynastie* 17. Berlin 1955.
–, *The Ritualszenen auf der Umfassungmauer Ramses II. in Karnak.* Wiesbaden 1968.
–, "Kriegsgott". *Lexikon der Ägyptologie* III/5. Ed. by W. Helck and W. Westendorf (Wiesbaden 1979) 788–89.
Herrmann, S., *Israel in Egypt.* SBT 27. ET by M. Kohl. London 1973.
Hertzberg, H. W., *I and II Samuel.* OTL. ET by J. S. Bowden. London 1976.
Herzog, C. and Gichon, M. *Battles of the Bible.* London 1978.
Hirsch, H., "Die Inshriften der Könige von Agade." *AfO* 20 (1963) 1–82.
Hoffner, H. A. "A Hittite Analogue to the David and Goliath Contest of Champions." *CBQ* 30 (1968) 220–24.
–, "Propaganda and Political Justification in Hittite Historiography." *Unity and Diversity*: Essays in the History, Literature, and Religions of the Ancient Near East. Ed. by H. Goedicke and J. J. M. Roberts (Baltimore 1975) 49–62.
Holladay, J. S., "The Days the Moon Stood Still." *JBL* 87 (1968) 166–78.
Hornung, E., "Zur geschichtlichen Rolle des Königs in der 18 Dynastie." *MDIK* 15 (1957) 120–33.
–, *Geschichte als Fest*: Zwei Vorträge zum Geschichtsbild der Frühen Menschheit. Darmstadt 1966.
Hyatt, J. P., *Commentary on Exodus.* London 1971.
–, "Was Yahweh Originally a Creator Deity?" *JBL* 86 (1967) 369–77.
Imparati, F. and Saporetti, C., "L'autobiografia Ḫattušiliš I." *Studi Classici e Orientali* 14 (1965) 40–85.
Ishida, T., "The Leaders of the Tribal Leagues Israel in the Premonarchic Period." *RB* 80 (1973) 514–30.
Jacobsen, T., *Toward the Image of Tammuz and Other Essays on* Mesopotamian History and Culture. HSS 21. Ed. by W. L. Moran. Cambridge, Massa. 1970.
–, "Religious Drama in Ancient Mesopotamia." *Unity and Diversity*: Essays in History, Literature, and Religions of the Ancient Near East. Ed. by H. Goedicke and J. J. M. Roberts (Baltimore 1975) 65–97.
–, *The Treasures of Darkness*: A History of Mesopotamian Religion. New Haven/London 1976.
–, "The Stele of the Vultures Col I–X." *AOAT* 25. ET by K. Bergerhaf et al (Neukirchen-Vluyn 1976) 247–59.
Jones, G. H., "Holy War or YHWH War?" *VT* 25 (1975) 642–58.

Kaiser, O., *Die Mythische Bedeutung des Meeres in Ägypten, Ugarit und Israel*, BZAW 78. Berlin 1959.

Kallai, Z., "The Wars of Saul." *The Military History of the Land of Israel in Biblical Times*. Ed. by J. Liver (1973) 132–48 (Hebrew).

Kammenhuber, A. *Orakelpraxis, Träume und Vorzeichenschau bei den Hethitern*. Heidelberg 1976.

Kaufmann, Y., *The Biblical Account of the Conquest of Palestine*. ET by M. Dagut. Jerusalem 1953.

–, *The Book of Judges*. Jerusalem 1978 (Hebrew).

Keel, O., *Wirkmächtige Siegeszeichen im Alten Testament*. OBO 5. Göttingen 1974.

Kenyon, K. M., *Digging up Jericho*. London 1957.

King, L. W., *Babylonian Boundary-Stones and Memorial Tablets in British Museum*. London 1912.

Kitchen, K. A., *Ramesside Inscriptions*: Historical and Biographical II-V. Oxford 1968.

Korošec, V., "The Warfare of Hittite from the Legal Point of View." *Iraq* 25 (1963) 159–66.

Kraus, H. J., *Psalmen* I. BK 15. Neukirchen–Vluyn 1960.

Kuentz, M. C., "La Stele du Marriage de Ramses II." *ASAE* 25 (1925) 181–238.

Lambert, W. G. "The Reign of Nebuchadnezzar I: A Turning Point in the History of Ancient Mesopotamian Religion." *The Seed of Wisdom*: Essays in Honor of T. J. Meek. Ed. by W. S. McCullough (Toronto 1964) 3–13.

–, "Enmeduranki and Related Matters." *JCS* 21 (1969) 126–31.

–, A Review Article: "History and the Gods by B. Albrektson." *Orientalia* 39 (1970) 170–77.

–, "Destiny and Divine Intervention in Babylon and Israel." *The Witness of Tradition*. OTS 17 (Leiden 1972) 65–72.

–, "Studies in Nergal." *BiOr* 30 (1973) 355–63.

–, "The Historical Development of the Mesopotamian Pantheon: A Study in Sophisticated Polytheism." *Unity and Diversity*: Essays in the History, Literature, and Religion of the Ancient Near East. Ed. by H. Goedicke and J. J. M. Roberts (Baltimore/London 1975) 191–99.

Landsberger, B. and Tadmor, H., "Fragments of Clay Liver Models from Hazor." *IEJ* 14 (1964) 201–18.

Legrain, L., *Royal Inscriptions and Fragments from Nippur and Babylon*. PBS 15. Philadelphia 1926.

Leiman, S. Z., "The Inverted Nuns at Numbers 10:35–36 and the Book of Eldad and Medad." *JBL* 93 (1974) 348–55.

Lichtheim, M., *Ancient Egyptian Literature* I–II. Berkeley 1973.

Limburg, J., "The Root ריב and the Prophetic Lawsuit Speeches." *JBL* 88 (1969) 291–304.

Lind, M. C., "Paradigm of Holy War in the Old Testament." *Biblical Research* 16 (1971) 16–31.

–, *Yahweh is a Warrior*: The Theology of Warfare in Ancient Israel. Pennsylvania/Ontario 1980.

Lindars, B. "The Israelite Tribes in Judges." *VTS* 30 (1979) 95–112.

Liver, J., "The War of Mesha, King of Moab." *PEQ* 99 (1967) 14–31.

Loewenstamm, S. E., "The Seven-Day Unit in Ugaritic Epic Literature." *IEJ* 15 (1965) 121–33.

–, *The Tradition of the Exodus in its Development*. Jerusalem 1972 (Hebrew).

Long, B. O., "The Effect of Divination upon Israelite Literature." *JBL* 92 (1973) 489–97.

Loretz, O., "Ugarit-texte und Israelitische Religionsgeschichte: The Song of the Sea." *UF* 6 (1974) 245–47.

Luckenbill, D. D., *Ancient Records of Assyria and Babylonia* I. NY 1926, 1968.
Machinist, P., *The Epic of Tukulti-Ninurta I*: A Study in Middle Assyrian Literature. Unpublished Ph. D. Diss. of Yale University 1978.
Martin, L., "'Elḥanan – der frühere Name Davids." *ZAW* 68 (1956) 257–59.
Maier, J., *Das altisraelitische Ladeheiligtum*. BZAW 93. Berlin 1965.
Malamat, A., "Aspects of the Foreign Policies of David and Solomon." *JNES* 22 (1963) 1–17.
–, "The Ban in Mari and in the Bible." *Biblical Essays* 1966 – Proceedings of the 9th Meeting of OuTWP, 40–49.
–, "The Egyptian Decline in Canaan and the Sea-Peoples." *WHJP* III, 23–38.
–, "The Period of the Judges." *WHJP* III, 129–63.
–, "The War of Gideon and Midian." *The Military History of the Land of Israel in Biblical Times*. Ed. by J. Liver (1973) 110–23.
–, "Charismatic Leadership in the Book of Judges." *Magnalia Dei*: The Mighty Acts of God. Ed. by F. M. Cross et al (NY 1976) 152–69.
–, "Conquest of Canaan: Israelite Conduct of War According to Biblical Tradition." *Revue Internationale d'Historie Militarie* 42 (1979) 25–52.
–, "How Inferior Israelite Forces Conquered Fortified Canaanite Cities." *BAR* 8/2 (1982) 24–35.
–, *Israel in Biblical Times*: Historical Essays. Jerusalem 1983 (Hebrew).
Mann, T. W., *Divine Presence and Guidance in Israelite Traditions*: The Typology of Exaltation. Baltimore/ London 1977.
Mayes, A. D. H. "The Historical Context of the Battle against Sisera." *VT* 19 (1969) 353–60.
–, "Israel in the Pre-Monarchy Period." *VT* 23 (1973) 151–70.
–, *Israel in the Period of the Judges*. SBT 29. London 1974.
Mazar, B. "Beth She'arim, Gaba and Harosheth of the Peoples." *HUCA* 24 (1952–53) 75–84.
–. "The Military Elite of King David." *VT* 13 (1963) 311–20.
McKane, W., "The Earlier History of the Ark." *Glasgow* 21 (1965–66) 68–77.
McCarter, P. K., Jr., *I Samuel*. AB 8. NY 1980.
–, "The Apology of David." *JBL* 99 (1980) 489–503.
McCarthy, D. J., "Some Holy War Vocabulary in Joshua 2." *CBQ* 33 (1971) 228–30.
Melchert, H. C. "The Acts of Ḫattušiliš I." *JNES* 37 (1978) 1–22.
Mercer,. S. A. B. Ed., *The Tell El-Amarna Tablets* I. Toronto 1939.
Miller, P. D., "El the Warrior." *HTR* 60 (1967) 411–31.
–, *The Divine Warrior in Early Israel*. HSM 5. Cambridge, Massa. 1973.
Miller, P. D. and Roberts, J. J. M., *The Hand of the Lord*: A Reassessment of the Ark Narrative. Baltimore/London 1977.
Morenz, S., *Egyptian Religion*. ET by A. E. Keep. London 1973.
Müller, H. P., "Der Aufbau des Deboraliedes." *VT* 16 (1966) 446–59.
–, "המם". *TDOT* III. Ed. by G. J. Botterweek and H. Ringgren. ET by D. E. Green (Michigan 1978) 419–422.
Naor, M., "The Geographical Background of Interpretation of Gideon." *Issues in the Book of Judges* (Jerusalem 1971) 253–75 (Hebrew).
Neu, E., Der *Anitta-Text*. StBoT 18. Wiesbaden 1974.
Nielsen, E., "Some Reflections on the History of the Ark." *VTS* 7 (1959) 61–74.
Nielsen, K., *Yahweh as Prosecutor and Judge*. Sheffield 1980.
Norin, S. I. L., *Er Spaltete das Meer*: Die Auszugsüberlieferung in Psalmen und Kult des alten Israel. CB 9. Lund 1977.

Noth, M., *Das System der zwölf Stämme Israels*. BWANT 4/1 Stuttgart 1930, Darmstadt 1966.
—, *Überlieferungsgeschichtliche Studien*. Halle 1943.
—, *A History of Pentateuchal Traditions*. 1948. ET by B. W. Anderson. NJ 1972.
—, *Das Buch Josua*. HAT 7. Tübingen 1953.
—, *Exodus*. 1959. ET by J. S. Bowden. Philadelphia 1962.
—, *The History of Israel*. NY/Evanston 1960.
—, "Der Beitrag der Archäologie zur Geschichte Israels." *VTS* 7 (1960) 262—82.
—, *Numbers*. 1966. OTL. ET by J. D. Martin. London 1968.
Obermann, J., "YHWH in Recent Discoveries." *JBL* 68 (1948) 301—23.
Oettinger, N., *The Militarischen Eide*. StBoT 22. Wiesbaden 1976.
Ohler, A., *Mythologische Elemente im Alten Testament*. Düsseldorf 1969.
Oldenburg, U., *The Conflict between El and Baal in Canaanite Religion*. Leiden 1969
Oppenheim, A. L., *Ancient Mesopotamia*. 1964, 1977.
Otten, H., "Keilschrifttext, Hattusilis I's Annal." *MDOG* 91 (1958) 73—84.
—. *Die Apologie Hattušiliš III*. Wiesbaden 1981.
Ottosson, J. *Gilead*: Tradition and History. CB 3. Lund 1969.
Paul, S. M., "Book of the Wars of the Lord." *EJ* 4 (Jerusalem 1971) col 1218—19.
Pettinato, G., *Die Ölwahrsagung bei den Babyloniern* I. Studi Semitici 21. Rome 1966.
Pritchard, J. B., *Gibeon*: Where the Sun Stood Still. NJ 1962.
—, Ed. *Ancient Near Eastern Texts Relating to the Old Testament*. 3rd ed. with Supplement. Princeton 1969.
—, Ed. *The Ancient Near East in Pictures Relating to the Old Testament*. 3rd ed. with Supplement. Princeton 1969.
de Pury, A., "La Guerre Sainte Israélite: Réalité Historique ou Fiction Litéraire?" *ETR* 56 (1981) 5—38.
von Rad, G., *Der heilige Krieg im alten Israel*. Zürich 1951.
—, *Old Testament Theology* I—II. ET by D. M. G. Stalker. NY/Evanston 1962, 1965.
Rabin, C., "Judges 5:2 and the Ideology of Deborah's War. *JJS* 6 (1955) 125—34.
—, "The Song of Deborah as a Cultural Document." *Issues in the Book of Judges* (Jerusalem 1973) 108—30 (Hebrew).
Redford, D. B., "The Hyksos Invasion in History and Tradition." *Orientalia* 39 (1970) 1—51.
Richter, W., *Traditionsgeschichtliche Untersuchungen zum Richterbuch*. BBB 18. Bonn 1963.
—, *Die Bearbeitungen des Retterbuches in der Deuteronomischen Epoche*. BBB 21. Bonn 1964.
—, "Die Nāgīd-Formel." *BZ* NF 9 (1965) 71—84.
Roberts, J. J. M., *The Earliest Semitic Pantheon*: A Study of the Semitic Deities Attested in Mesopotamia before Ur III. Baltimore/London 1972.
—, "Nebuchadnezzar I's Elamite Crisis in Theological Perspective." *Essays on the Ancient Near East in Memory of J. J. Finkelstein*. Ed. by M. de J. Ellis (Hamden 1972) 183—86.
—, "Origin of the Zion Tradition." *JBL* 92 (1973) 329—44.
—, "Myth versus History." *CBQ* 38 (1976) 1—13.
—, "The Religio-Political Setting of Psalm 47." *BASOR* 221 (1976) 229—32.
Robertson, D. A., *Linguistic Evidence in Dating Early Hebrew Poetry*. Missoula, Mont. 1972.
Rösel, H. N., "Judges 1 and the Settlement of the Leah Tribes." *Proceedings of th Eighth World Congress of Jewish Studies*, Division A (Jerusalem 1982) 17—20 (Hebrew).
Rose, M., "Entmilitarisierung des Kriegs." *BZ* 20 (1976) 197—211.
Rosenberg, R. A. "Yahweh becomes King." *JBL* 85 (1966) 297—307.
Ross, J. P., "Jahweh Ṣ^eB̄Ā'ÔṮ in Samuel and Psalms." *VT* 17 (1967) 76—92.
Roth, W. M. W., "Hinterhalt und Scheinflucht." *ZAW* 75 (1963) 296—303.

Saggs, H. W. F. "Assyrian Warfare in the Sargonic Period." *Iraq* 25 (1963) 145–54.
Sawyer, J. F. A., "Joshua 10:12–14 and the Solar Eclipse of 30 September 1131 B. C." *PEQ* 104 (1972) 139–46.
Schmidt, L., *Menschlicher Erfolg und Jahwe Initiative*. WMANT 38. Neukirchen–Vluyn 1970.
von Schuler, E., *Die Kaškäer*. UAVA NF 3. Berlin 1965.
Schunck, K. D., *Benjamin*. BZAW 86. Berlin 1963.
Schwally, F., *Semitische Kriegsaltertümer* I: Der heilige Krieg im alten Israel. Leipzig 1901.
Seebass, H., "Erwägungen zum altisraelitischen System der zwölf Stämme." *ZAW* 90 (1978) 196–219.
Seeligmann, I. L., "Menschliches Heldentum und göttliche Hilfe." *TZ* 19 (1963) 385–411.
Segal, M. H., "The Composition of the Books of Samuel." *JQR* 55 (1965) 318–39.
–, *The Pentateuch*: Its Composition and Its Authorship, and other Biblical Studies. Jerusalem 1967.
–, *The Books of Samuel*. Jerusalem 1976 (Hebrew).
van Seters, J., 'The Conquest of Sihon's Kingdom." *JBL* 91 (1972) 182–97.
Sethe, K. *Urkunden der 18 Dynastie*. Berlin 1927, 1961.
–, *Amun und die acht Urgötter von Hermopolis*. Berlin 1929.
Sjöberg, A. W., "Ein Selostpreis des Königs Hammurabi von Babylon." *ZA* NF 20 (1961) 151–70.
–, "Hymns to Ninurta with Prayers for Šūsîn of Ur and Būrsîn of Isin." *AOAT* 25 (1976) 411–26.
Snaith, N. H. *The Distinctive Ideas of the Old Testament*. London 1957.
–, "ים סוף": The Sea of Reeds: The Red Sea." *VT* 15 (1965) 395–98.
Soggin, J. A., *Joshua*. OTL. ET by R. A. Wilson. London 1972.
–, *Judges*. OTL. ET by J. Bowden. London 1981.
–, "Bemerkungen zum Deboralied, Richter Kap. 5, Versuch einer neuen Übersetzung und eines Vorstosses in die älteste Geschichte Israels." *TLZ* 106 (1981) 625–39.
–, "The Conquest of Jericho through Battle." *Eretz Israel* 19 (1982) 215–17.
Sollberger, E., *Corpus des inscriptions royales presargoniques de Lagaš*. Geneva 1956.
Sollberger, E. and Kupper, J. R., *Inscriptions Royales Sumeriennes et Akkadiennes*. Paris 1971.
Smend, R., *Yahweh War and Tribal Confederation*: Reflections upon Israel's Earliest History. Tr. by M. G. Rogers. Nashville/NY 1970.
Smith, H. P. *A Critical Exegetical Commentary on the Books of Samuel*. ICC. 1899, Edinburgh 1969.
Stadelmann, R., *Syrisch-Palestinensische Gottheiten in Ägypten*. Leiden 1967.
Starr, I., "Omen Texts Concerning Holes in the Liver." *AfO* 26 (1978–79) 45–55.
Steindorff, G. and Seele, K. C., *When Egypt Ruled the East*. Chicago 1942, 1957.
Stephenson, F. R., "Astronomical Verification and Dating of Old Testament Passages Referring to Solar Eclipses." *PEQ* 107 (1975) 107–20.
Stoebe, H. J., *Das erste Buch Samuelis*. KAT 8/1. Gütersloh 1973.
Stolz, F., *Jahwes und Israels Kriege*. ATANT 60. Zürich 1972.
–, "המם". *THAT* 1 (1977) 502–4.
Sturtevant, E. H. and Bechtel, G., *A Hittite Chrestomathy*. 1935, Philadelphia 1952.
Summer, W. A., "Israel's Encounters, with Edom, Moab, Ammon, Sihon and Og, According to the Deuteronomist." *VT* 18 (1968) 216–28.
Tallqvist, K., *Der Assyrische Gott*. StOr 4/3. Helsinki 1932.
–, *Akkadische Götterepitheta*. StOr 7. Helsinki 1938.
Talmon, S., "YHWH War." *Encyclopedia Biblica* 4 (Jerusalem 1963) 1064–65 (Hebrew).
–, "Kingship and the Ideology of the State." *WHJP* V, 3–26.

Thureau-Dangin, F., "ASAKKU". *RA* 38 (1941) 41–43.
Treves, M., "The Date of Psalm 24." *VT* 10 (1960) 428–34.
Tsevat, M., "Studies in the Book of Samauel, YAHWEH ṢEḆA'OṮ." *HUCA* 36 (1965) 49–58.
–, "The Emergence of the Israelite Monarchy: Eli, Samuel, Saul." *WHJP* V, 61–75.
Tungogi, A. C., "The Book of the Conquest." *JBL* 84 (1965) 374–80.
Tur-Sinai, N. H., "Was there a Book of the Wars of YHWH in the Bible," *BIES* 24 (1959–60) 146–48 (Hebrew).
Ünal, A., "Zum Status der Augures bei den Hethitern." *RHA* 31 (1973) 27–56.
–, *Ein Orakeltext über die Intrigen am hethitischen Hof.* Heidelberg 1978.
de Vaux, R., *Ancient Israel*: Social Institutions I. ET. NY/Toronto 1965.
–, *The Bible and the Ancient Near East.* ET. London 1972.
–, *The Early History of Israel* I–II. ET by D. Smith. London 1978.
Velde, H. T. *Seth, God of Confusion.* Leiden 1977.
Wainwright, G. D., "The Origin of Amūn." *JEA* 49 (1963) 21–23.
Wambacq, B. N., *L'épithéte divine Jahvé Ṣ^{e}ba'ôt.* Brouwer 1947.
Watts, J. D. W., "The Song of the Sea – Ex XV." *VT* 7 (1957) 371–80.
Weber, M., *Ancient Judaism.* Tr. and ed. by H. H. Gerth and D. Martindale. NY 1921, 1952.
Weidner, E. F., *Politische Dokumente aus Kleinasien.* BoSt 8/9. 1923, NY 1970.
–, *Die Inschriften Tukulti-Ninutras I. und seiner Nachfolger.* AfO Beiheft 12. Graz 1959.
von Weiher, E., *Der Babylonische Gott Nergal.* AOAT 11. Neukirchen–Vluyn 1971.
Weimar, P., "Die Jahwekriegserzählungen in Ex 14, Jos 10, Richter 4 und I Sam 7." *Bibl* 57 (1976) 38–73.
Weinfeld, M., "The Conquest of Canaan Land and the Native Ḥerem." *Beth Mikra* 12 (1967) 121–27 (Hebrew).
–, "The Period of the Conquest and of the Judges as seen by the Earlier and the Later Sources." *VT* 17 (1967) 93–113.
–, "The Covenant of Grant in the Old Testament and in the Ancient Near East." *JAOS* 90 (1970) 184–203.
–, *Deuteronomy and the Deuteronomic School.* Oxford 1972.
–, "Judge and Officer in Ancient Israel." *Israel Oriental Studies* 7 (1977) 65–88.
–, "They fought from heaven." *Eretz Israel* 14 (1978) 23–30 (Hebrew).
–, "Divine War in Ancient Israel and in the Ancient Near East." *Researches in the Bible and in the Ancient Near East on Seventieth Birthday of S. E. Loewenstamm.* Ed. by Y. Avishur and J. Blau (Jerusalem 1978) 171–81 (Hebrew).
Weingreen, J., "The Theory of the Amphictyony in Pre-Monarchial Israel." Festschrift of T. H. Gaster. *The Journal of the Ancient Near Eastern Society of Columbia University* V (1973) 426–33.
Weippert, M., *The Settlement of the Israelite Tribes in Palestine.* SBT 21. ET by J. D. Martin. London 1971.
–, "Heiliger Krieg in Israel and Assyrian." *ZAW* 84 (1972) 460–93.
–, "Conquest of Canaan and Settlement." *IDBS* (1976) 125–29.
Weiser, A. *The Psalms*: A Commentary. OTL. ET by E. Hartwell. London 1965.
–, "Die Legitimation des Königs David." *VT* 16 (1966) 325–54.
Wellhausen, J., *Der Text der Bücher Samuelis.* Göttingen 1871.
Westermann, C. *The Praise of God in the Psalms.* ET by K. R. Crim. Richmond, Virginia 1965.
Whitley, C. F., "The Sources of the Gideon Stories." *VT* 7 (1957) 157–64.

Wifall, W., "The Sea of Reeds as Sheol." *ZAW* 92 (1980) 325–32.

Wijngaads, I. "הוציא and העלה." *VT* 15 (1965) 91–102.

Williams, R. J. "Literature as a Medium of Political Propaganda in Ancient Egypt." *The Seed of Wisdom*, T. J. Meek Festschrift. Ed. by W. S. McCullough (Toronto 1964) 14–30.

Wilson, J. A. *The Burden of Egypt*. Chicago 1951.

Wilson, J. A. et al., *Before Philosophy*. Maryland 1946, 1963.

Wolf, H., *The Apology of Ḫattušiliš compared with the Apology of* ... University Microfilms, Ann Arbor, Michigan 1967.

Wright, G. E., "The Literary and Historical Problem of Joshua 10 and Judges 1." *JNES* 5 (1946) 105–14.

–, "The Lawsuit of God, a Form Critical Study of Deuteronomy 32." *Israel Prophetic Heritage*: Essays in Honor of J. Muilenberg. Ed. by B. W. Anderson and W. Harrelson (NY 1962) 26–67.

Wright, Q., *A Study of War* I. Chicago 1942.

Yadin, Y., "Some Aspects of the Strategy of Ahab and David." *Bibl* 36 (1955) 332–51.

–, *The Art of Warfare in Biblical Lands* II. Jerusalem 1963.

–, "Hazor". *Archaeology and Old Testament Study*. Ed. by D. W. Thomas (Oxford 1967) 258–59.

–, "Is the Biblical Account of the Israelite Conquest of Canaan Historically Reliable?" *BAR* 8/2 (1982) 16–23.

van Zijl, P. F., *Baal*: A Study of Texts in Connexion with Baal in the Ugaritic Epic. AOAT 10. Neukirchen-Vluyn 1972.

van Zyl, A. H., *The Moabites*. Pretoria Oriential Series 3. Pretoria 1960.

Index of Biblical References

I Samuel

II Samuel

Second Canonical Books

New Testament

Subject Index